THE MEDIA AND DISASTERS

PAN AM 103

JOAN DEPPA

WITH MARIA RUSSELL, DONA HAYES
AND ELIZABETH LYNNE FLOCKE

David Fulton Publishers
London

David Fulton Publishers Ltd
2 Barbon Close, London WC1N 3JX

First published in Great Britain by
David Fulton Publishers 1993

British Library Cataloguing in Publication Data

A catalogue record for this book is available from the British Library

ISBN 1–85346–225 X

Cover photograph by Alevroyiannis (Rex Features Ltd.)
Designed by Almac Ltd, London
Typeset by ROM-Data Corporation Limited, Falmouth, Cornwall
Printed in Great Britain by Biddles Limited, Guildford

Contents

In memory of
the 270 who perished...

In sympathy for
the thousands who suffered...

Pan Am Flight 103
December 21, 1988

Acknowledgements

Many voices speak in these pages about the profound effect that the bombing of Pan Am 103 and its coverage had on their lives. Others told of experiences equally as moving; their testimony informed the writing of this book even though they may not find themselves quoted directly here. All who participated in the study contributed to our understanding of the complex interaction of survivors, media and institutions in the wake of disaster.

Less obvious is the contribution by a host of others, beginning with students and colleagues in the S.I. Newhouse School of Public Communications at Syracuse University. Many of the questions that impelled this investigation were asked first — with all the earnestness and idealism of youth — by aspiring journalists and public relations practitioners in our classes. They listened intently and critically as we shared our findings, and this classroom dialogue helped focus our conclusions. The study represents one aspect of work undertaken by an informal faculty research group in the months following the disaster. Three members of that group, Nancy Weatherly Sharp, Fiona Chew and Frances Ford Plude helped with the planning and execution of key portions of this research. Other faculty provided support that ranged from helpful advice to indispensable covering of classes so that one or more of us could travel. Three successive deans, Edward Stephens, Larry Myers and finally David Rubin, were instrumental in obtaining funds to finance the research. Dean Rubin also arranged for use of the Lexis/Nexis data base, which proved to be an important research tool. The list of graduate students and secretaries who assisted with logistics of transcription, copying and correspondence is too long to present here, but we would be remiss not to single out Elvis Pearline Charles, our research assistant during the last three years of the project. Richard Phillips, Dean of Hendricks Chapel, and the University's Human Subjects Committee provided invaluable guidance as we prepared for research with grieving relatives and other survivors.

The possibility that communications professionals could have experienced symptoms of post-traumatic stress led us to two experts in the field, Dr. Michael Blumenfield in Vahalla, New York, and Dr. Margaret Mitchell in Glasgow, Scotland, who provided both counsel and hospitality.

Librarians on both sides of the Atlantic played a critical role. Syracuse University's Bird Library and the Dumfries and Galloway Regional Council Library in Dumfries began early to develop special archives on this disaster. Alastair Johnston at the Dumfries Library not only provided a work area for the inspection of media reports, but permitted his printer to be used to make hard copy of notes and manuscripts produced on a computer loaned to the project by Apple U.K.

The effort to make this a research work that is a "good read" is due in no small part to people in Lockerbie. Originally, two books were envisioned—one for a general audience, focusing on Lockerbie, and the other a scholarly tome summarizing the research findings from all the sites. In lively meetings at a Lockerbie pub, members of the Media Awareness Group asked why two books were needed. Why not write the research so clearly that the Lockerbie experience could be understood in the context of the tragedy as a whole? That friendly challenge helped influence both the style and the shape of the writing.

With trials of first-time authors so well documented, addressing a first book to audiences on both sides of the Atlantic should have been intimidating. In fact, it would have been had we not encountered our publisher, David Fulton, so early in the process. His patience and good humor helped to keep us on track, and he secured the services of Yvonne Messenger, our copy editor, who carefully polished the final manuscript. By that time, it had already been read and critiqued by three colleagues at the Newhouse School, Dean David Rubin, William Glavin and Sharon Hollenback.

We must also acknowledge the support and understanding of family and friends. This was not an easy book to research or to write, and it consumed more time than any of us could have envisioned. Their tolerance and patience did much to make it possible.

Finally, we wish we could have learned the lessons in these pages in another way. But like the relatives and friends of the victims, who have campaigned so hard for airline security, and the people of Lockerbie, who discovered their own quiet role in providing a place of solace to the grieving, the murder of these 270 and the suffering of those caught up in the tragedy made it imperative that we find a positive response. Toward the end of our interviews with survivors, they often expressed a wish: "maybe some good can come from this." To that end this book is dedicated.

Joan Deppa
with Maria Russell,
Dona Hayes and
Elizabeth Lynne Flocke
Syracuse, August 1993

Introduction

Years after Pan Am 103 blew apart over Lockerbie, Scotland, the bombing still makes headlines, although the stories tend to be about the geo-politics of the tragedy and its potential as a fuse to trigger other international events. The headlines at the time were more dramatic, riveting in the way they portrayed a disaster that was at once global and profoundly personal. From the cryptic bulletins first aired by broadcasters to the pages of newsprint that attempted to capture the full scope of the tragedy, this story could not be ignored.

Behind the headlines another story unfolded, sometimes terrifying, sometimes troubling, sometimes touching. This story was how the media and the people they encountered in pursuit of the news experienced the journalistic process. It was the story of institutions, some prepared, some unprepared, to satisfy the public's need for information and the survivors' need for privacy. As the days passed, it became the story of how the participants learned from the experience and especially how individuals involved in the disaster became adept at speaking, on their own terms, through the media.

This book represents an attempt to examine the lessons from this tragedy, as well as the unanswered questions raised by the coverage and institutional response. Although all the authors have had experience as professional communicators and now teach public communications at Syracuse University, we have tried to take a critical stance that may satisfy neither those who want a book that bashes the media and institutions involved nor those who would welcome an apology that absolves news and public relations professionals of all misconduct. In many cases, we found those who were most critical of the coverage of this event were professionals themselves, who months and even years after the tragedy are still struggling with issues of ethics and communications practices that it raised.

We came to the study from another, sadder perspective as well. Thirty-five students from the Syracuse University study-abroad program had perished on the plane. So we were personally caught up in the mourning brought on by the tragedy, not only by our own sense of loss but also by the grieving of parents and families of those young victims, and the distress of students who wept for dear friends and, in many cases, confronted the finality of death for the first time. We witnessed first-hand some of the difficulties described here, and we faced tough questions from students, especially aspiring journalists, who had been dismayed by the conduct of some professional journalists who came to campus.

We took our first look at these issues at the suggestion of news people in Syracuse, New York, who were concerned about criticism that followed the initial coverage. The student chapter of the Society of Professional Journalists staged a forum in the spacious campus chapel at which an invited panel of local reporters, photographers, editors and broadcasters discussed their coverage and answered questions and complaints from students. It was a tense evening that made it clear that one of the original goals of the event — to come up with guidelines about media conduct in covering disasters — could not be easily met.

In subsequent discussions with our colleagues, we began to realize just how complex the issues were and how important it was that we address them. This book by no means covers all these issues, nor does it examine all coverage of the event. Instead, it focuses on what we hope are especially instructive incidents and issues. In other words, it represents only a beginning in a relatively uncharted area of communications research: the media and disasters.

Most of the material reported here is based on face-to-face interviews, some in small groups, but many one-to-one. Those for the chapter dealing with survivors' experience in the immediate wake of the tragedy were conducted under a guarantee of confidentiality, so no names are used. The Lockerbie interviews were conducted by the primary author during four visits there between October 1989 and June 1990. Interviews of family members were conducted by all the authors, assisted by three colleagues, Nancy Sharp, Fiona Chew and Frances Ford Plude. The primary author interviewed journalists in New York, London and Scotland for the chapter on newsgatherers. Although those newspeople were given the option of anonymity, only one elected to exercise it and only two approached for interviews declined. Dona Hayes conducted all the interviews of reporters for Syracuse television stations as part of a study that provided a guarantee of confidentiality. Elizabeth Lynne Flocke conducted most of the interviews with journalists at the Syracuse Newspapers and although many indicated a willingness to be quoted by name, it was decided that they should be given the same protection as their local broadcast counterparts. Maria Russell interviewed public relations and information officers on both sides of the Atlantic, all of whom agreed to be quoted by name.

In Part II, the research deals with the public role played by families in the months and years following the tragedy. The leader of one of the American family groups was interviewed by the primary author, as was the leader of the

British group; related material was drawn from published accounts of their activities as advocates. The description of Lockerbie's Media Awareness Group and the problems associated with post-traumatic stress are also based on interviews and research by the primary author.

When disaster hits a small town, the news is shared immediately. Neighbors put down whatever they are doing and turn their attention to those who are suffering. Some hurry to the scene, ready to assist in the rescue or recovery efforts. Others prepare for the casualty victims' immediate needs for warm food, shelter, clothing. Still others seek to express their sympathy, to show they care by a kind word, even if they have nothing tangible to offer.

So it is in the the world-wide community linked by communications. Now that messages can bounce off portable satellites, connecting remote sections of the world, we experience tragedy "live," just as near neighbors have since humans first formed communities. Although the late Marshall McLuhan may not have anticipated the specific technology that would bind us together in a single society, his concept of the world as an interconnected "global village" helps to explain the way people are forging new relationships, especially during tragic events.

The bombing of Pan Am 103 made this clear, partly because it happened over a small market town in the Scottish Borders, where neighbors do rally round, and partly because it represented a murderous attack on civilians that claimed lives from twenty-one different countries. In retrospect, it can be seen as a turning point in the coverage of epic tragedies, marking the first time that advances in technology and transportation permitted "live" coverage of an event of this magnitude. Since then, it has become almost routine to witness terrible occurrences "live." Portable satellite dishes, cellular telephones and laptop computers mean that coverage that once would have been impossible is viewed as the norm. The "live" war in the Gulf followed the "live" tragedy of Lockerbie, the "live" football crowd disaster at Hillsborough, England, and the "live" coverage of the 1989 Lomo Prieta earthquake that shook the San Francisco Bay area. Logistically, instant coverage has become possible from anywhere.

But the news people covering those tragedies have less time to make journalistic decisions, no time to reconsider what they transmit and little opportunity to think through the ethical issues involved. The instantaneous nature of communication places additional burdens on those struggling to deal with a catastrophe — as victims, survivors and rescue workers, governments and institutions — at the same time that it opens channels through which critical resources can be marshalled.

What is happening is that imperceptibly, day by day, the way humankind communicates about events is changing, so that over the span of a few months or a few days, media and individuals gain new abilities to gather and transmit information. The change takes place in two dimensions: time and space. In fact, our ability to accumulate and communicate information has outstripped our capacity to understand the meaning of the messages media transmit and the impact of journalistic methods.

The bombing of Pan Am 103 provides a case in point. Every available technology was brought to bear on this story, from the seismic readings that recorded the plane's impact on Lockerbie to the rapid deployment of reporters, photographers and television crews, cellular telephones and satellite transmitters to the site of the tragedy and to scenes of deep distress where relatives and friends were learning of their losses. The technological links made the journalistic effort global in scope, but the response of the worldwide audience was in many ways neighbor-to-neighbor. The scope that technology gave to caring for one another showed that, in times of tragedy, we now truly live in a global village.

Pan Am 103 marked a turning point in global media coverage, one that cannot be reversed. We will have to learn how to live with the fact that, logistically, live coverage of anything that happens anywhere in the world has become a relatively simple matter, but the ethical dilemmas and decisions this access creates are anything but simple. To date, journalists have tended to operate with little knowledge of the impact of their behavior on the people they seek out in pursuit of the story of a tragedy. Their ethical decisions have tended to be made, in other words, with incomplete information about their consequences.

From a different perspective, those in the helping professions have tended to perceive journalists as enemies from whom survivors must be protected at all costs. In fact, the growing body of research on disasters tends to describe the media role only in negative terms, and yet evidence from a tragedy that the media all but ignored, a rail accident in the north of England,[1] shows that *not covering* a disaster can have a damaging effect on those who survive it.

Another group that both affects media coverage and is affected by it can be categorized as institutions. How do they manage their communication in such a crisis and how are they affected by the changing nature of communications and the behavior of the media? Special attention needs to be given to the way in which institutions heighten or lessen the impact of media attention on survivors of the tragedy.

The ultimate institution is, of course, government. It is expected to help its citizens not only confront but also, whenever possible, prevent disasters. It also provides the context in which the media operate in gathering and transmitting information. It is where, for example, the public's need for information — as met by the media — comes in conflict with the need to provide a fair trial to those accused of a crime. This has been an important issue in this disaster because it was in every sense a mass murder that occurred in Scotland, which has more rigorous requirements for evidence and against prejudicial pre-trial publicity than neighboring England, and certainly greater protection against pre-trial publicity than in the United States.

How open government is to public scrutiny of its own workings is also critical. How reliable are its provisions for airline security, for example? It may make a great deal of difference whether that question is covered by the Official Secrets Act, as is the case in Britain, or the Freedom of Information Act, as it is in the United States. On the other hand, even an FOIA may not guarantee easy access to information from a recalcitrant bureaucracy.

How truthful government is in speaking to the public through the media may also be an issue, especially in times of changing diplomatic conditions. The cause of this particular disaster was international in the ultimate sense of the word: it seemed from the outset to be aimed at an American airliner, probably in retribution for some action by the U.S. government. The official response from that government, which was slow in coming, and disinformation, which flooded into the public arena from a variety of "intelligence" sources, left angry doubts.

A word of warning: while we have used media here as a collective term, this study will show that the news organizations and newspeople encompassed by that term tend to reflect individual differences as well as professional similarities. We believe that understanding of various journalistic practices by other professions and the public at large will permit a more informed response to disaster coverage. We also hope that media professionals will see that they have an individual and a collective responsibility — indeed, a self-interest — in understanding the effects that their methods can have on those caught in these terrible events.

It may help the reader to think of this as a behind-the-scenes look at a tragic drama being played out on a global stage. We have let each group speak the truth about the tragedy and its initial repercussions from its own perspective. Sometimes the "actors" contradict each other. Sometimes they appear to have been so caught up in the event and the emotions that it created that they remember details differently. We signal those conflicts that might cause confusion, and in some cases have been able to offer an explanation. We hope this format helps readers to consider carefully what each group of players — survivors, newsgatherers and institutions — has to say. We have purposefully withheld our evaluation of each group's perspective and our recommendations until the end of its section.

The aftermath of this disaster has been more than an epilogue. Fortunately, in many ways, it is a story that reaffirms what humankind collectively can accomplish in adversity, so some parts of the section dealing with the aftermath have been a joy to research and write. But the reality of disasters is that they are traumatizing, not only for the survivors of this particular tragedy, but for those playing communications roles as well.

In the final chapter, we reflect on coverage of both the disaster and its long-term aftermath. It is clear that the interactions among survivors, the media and institutions are complex; they demonstrate the growing interdependence in our increasingly complicated world, especially our need for information and for access to the means of communication. In fact, those who set into motion the events described in this book must ultimately be seen as engaging in a communications act. Whatever the motive for the bombing, it sent a dreadful message to the world: we are all vulnerable.

Part I: THE TRAGEDY

1 December 21, 1988

Pan American Airways Boeing 747 *Maid of the Seas*, flying in from San Francisco, landed for the last time at London's Heathrow Airport about 10 minutes after noon. According to official inquiry documents,[1] at some time during the next six hours and 15 minutes, Pan Am employees loaded a Samsonite suitcase containing a Toshiba radio-cassette player into a luggage container that was to be placed in the forward cargo hold. The cassette player concealed Semtex plastic explosive.

The suitcase had arrived from Frankfurt aboard Pan American Flight 103A and, investigators found, "probably arrived at Frankfurt on a flight or an airline other than Pan Am." In London, it was subjected to X-ray screening but there was no procedure to make sure that it was accompanying a passenger. Pan Am personnel at Frankfurt Airport probably followed the same procedures, the inquiry documents said.

The risk that unaccompanied baggage might contain an explosive device and that Semtex-type plastic explosives contained in electronic equipment could escape detection was, in the words of the documents, "generally recognized in December 1988." In fact, U.S. Federal Aviation Authority regulations specified that unaccompanied baggage could be carried only if it was physically searched.

Passengers, clutching presents and souvenirs, brief cases and shopping bags, went through the security checks and boarded the plane in a festive mood. Babies cooing in their mothers' arms or crying at the unfamiliar surroundings added to the hubbub as carry-on bags were stowed and seat belts buckled. At 6:25 p.m., the *Maid of the Seas* took off from Heathrow and headed northwest, a route that would take it over Scotland before it turned toward New York.

In Lockerbie, a quiet market town of 3,500 just north of Scotland's border with England, the work of the day was over for most people. At 7 p.m., many settled down to watch an episode of "This is Your Life," while others set off for the weekly bingo game at the local cinema. At the same time, passengers in the Pan American 747 were anticipating an evening meal. Many, including college students, tourists and business people, were heading home for the holidays via New York or Detroit, the scheduled destination of the flight that had originated in Frankfurt, Germany.

Two minutes and 50 seconds later, as the plane neared its cruising altitude of 31,000 feet, an explosion ripped it apart. Alan Topp, a veteran controller at the Scottish air traffic center at Prestwick, saw the small green cross inside a square box that had represented Pan Am 103 on his radar screen disappear and thought the system was malfunctioning.[2] The first call logged by the computer in the regional fire control center in nearby Dumfries was at 7:04 p.m. and described a "huge boiler explosion" at Lockerbie.[3] Other calls came almost simultaneously, including one from the wife of an off-duty fireman reporting a plane crash.

On-duty Lockerbie firemen headed for Rosebank Crescent and Park Place, where a major portion of the fuselage had landed, breaking a gas main on impact. An off-duty official of the regional fire brigade, who had been visiting relatives in Lockerbie, was drawn to the Sherwood Crescent area, where the plane's wings, loaded with fuel, had slammed into houses and broken through another section of gas main.

Residents of both areas helped evacuate neighbors to safer areas. An estimated 350 men, women and children were moved out through the smoke and debris. Seven of the residents of Sherwood Crescent had died when wings and part of the fuselage had landed on their homes. Four others died when they were caught in the path of the rapidly spreading fire, fed by aviation fuel and fanned by high winds.

Flames raged out of control as firemen improvised water relays to quench the flames. As it plunged to earth, one of the plane's four engines had broken a 6-inch (150 mm) water main serving the south end of the town, and firemen initially had to make do with water carried by pumpers and milk tankers from remote fire hydrants. Working in dense smoke and without the benefit of street lights, firemen were aided by units from neighboring towns, but it was not until they managed to divert water from the broken main and send it via a circuitous route to the Sherwood area that they were able to contain the fire within the huge crater gouged out by the impact of the wings and the explosion. By the time firemen could say the fire was under control and reduce the number of men on duty to 20, it was 11:30 p.m, four-and-a-half hours after the impact.

Five area residents had been taken to the hospital in Dumfries, and a number received minor first aid, but most of the ambulances summoned to the scene were never used. The terrible truth was that all 259 of those who had been on board the airliner were dead. Some had come to earth with sections of the fuselage that landed in the village, many others fell on the rolling hills that surrounded the valley. And in the once quiet neighborhood of Sherwood Crescent, eleven local people had perished, their lives ended in the fiery havoc wrought by the falling wings.

2 *Survivors*

Lockerbie shattered

The sound alerted them. To some, the noise built like the earth tremor the town had experienced a decade or so earlier. Others thought immediately of an aircraft; low-flying military planes that train in the area had long been a concern.

A few actually saw the plane as it plunged across the sky. "We didn't know what it was at the time, you understand," one man said. "We heard the crash, and the smoke and flames, and all the rest of it. The engine was shooting towards us; my wife was standing in the street just a few hundred yards from where it landed. The whole place shook; the house shook, everything shook."

Two sisters meeting at the town cross in the center of Lockerbie heard the rumble. "I said it was thunder," one recalled. "And there was a train at the station, and I said, 'Oh, it's that train starting up.' Then it got louder and there was a loud crack and the sky just went bright red."

A man headed for the front door of his home on Park Place in Rosebank Crescent, a group of town houses built by local authorities, slightly up the hill from the main street, reaching it just as there was a terrible explosion down the hill in Sherwood Crescent. That was the wings hitting owner-occupied houses at the edge of the town. "This great ball of fire went up and a lot of debris started to fall round us, so we dived back into the house. Then it stopped."

All the lights went out. As soon as the man thought it was safe, he grabbed a flashlight and ran outside. The house next door was demolished. Another one in the neighborhood was half-demolished.

"I looked in, as much as I could, to see there was nobody in these houses and I cleared the next two houses out," he recalled. "By this time, I'd discovered there was a bad gas leak and I was frightened the whole place could explode at any minute, so I cleared the whole area and got everybody away in the road until the police and fire brigade arrived. They were very quick."

The two sisters at the town cross ran down to where they thought the plane had come down, but someone was already in place to keep people away, especially from the petrol station. "At that point they were still frightened that the garage might go up — because it landed so close," the second sister said. "And it was obvious that there was not a lot that could be done."

So they hurried back, with one sister running up to the housing estate where she lived because on the way, someone had told them that parts of the plane had come down in that area. The other sister went to check on their parents. "And then I came back down to see if there was anything that could be done," she said. "But by this time, the streets were so congested that it was obvious we were going to be more in the way than anything else." So they, and a number of other residents, went to play bingo. One woman remembered seeing a couple sitting at the window of a hotel, eating their dinner, as if nothing had happened. A woman came out of her door with a broom, swept the rubble off her sidewalk and went back inside.

The enormity of the disaster had not sunk in.

Because of the low-flying military jets, many people assumed a plane with one or two flyers had crashed. In Rosebank Crescent, the debris told a different story. The number of plane seats, the food containers for serving airline meals, the scattered clothing, and the carnage made it clear that this was a civilian aircraft. The fuselage had come down in the back gardens of the council houses on Rosebank Crescent and Park Place. Sixty-two bodies were recovered from that area, many of them students from a Syracuse University overseas study program.

No residents died in that section of the town, but in Sherwood Crescent eleven lives were lost and fire spread rapidly to neighboring homes. One of the falling engines landed on a water main, cutting the supply of water available to fight the flames. The raging fire threatened to spread to the nearby petrol station; the fuel from its tanks could engulf the homes and small businesses surrounding it.

People who escaped from their homes found flames everywhere, in their tiny front gardens and on the houses along Sherwood Crescent. Cars on the main north–south highway just to the east appeared to be burning. Where homes had been set in neat rows, a great crater had been blasted out of the ground. In addition to the eleven who perished, several were injured, and many houses were damaged beyond repair.

In nearby Sherwood Park, a resident recalled, "The main thing that you could see round here was fire and rubble, a tremendous amount of rubble. It's hard to understand how much was out there unless you see a picture which some neighbors took. And the flames and everything were as high as (the house). The next thing that sticks in the mind is how quickly the streets were filled with emergency vehicles, fire, ambulance, police. There was a tremendous amount here within 20 minutes. We moved out very quickly." This resident took his family to the home of his wife's sister in another town.

Horror at what had happened mixed with moments of great relief. One woman remembers looking at Sherwood Crescent and thinking she would never see many people who lived there again. By the time she finished calling emergency services, neighbors from further down the street had come up because they thought the area where she lived had actually been hit. "One lady offered to come with me, because my husband's elderly aunt lived in Sherwood Park and I said I was going round to see if I could find her. She said, 'Not on your own. I'm an off-duty nurse,' which I knew although we really hadn't spoken before that night. So the two of us grabbed coats. We got round to Sherwood very quickly and began to meet people from Sherwood Crescent. It was sheer disbelief. A few minutes before you thought these people were dead; they couldn't be otherwise. But you have to remember that we were thinking the whole plane was down there, not just part of it."

One man had a cut on his head. With wry humor, he said it proved how hard a television screen was. The impact had propelled him into the screen. It was a lucky injury; a huge piece of debris fell through the ceiling onto the chair where he had been sitting.

Someone else told the woman where her husband's aunt was and, with some difficulty, the elderly relative was persuaded to leave. "She didn't want to move," the woman recalled. "We only discovered two days later that she didn't know what, in fact, had happened that night. She was actually in the back of the house, so she didn't see what happened. So we persuaded her that she wasn't safe, which she wasn't."

A husband and wife who work with the British Red Cross heard the terrible sounds as a call to service. "We knew something quite drastic had happened, and when we tried to go down into Sherwood Park, it was all blocked up. There were so many people there ahead of us," he said.

The man had seen a car go into the area with a green beacon on top, the way doctors signal that they're responding to an emergency. "We were thinking about an aircraft with one or two people in it at the most, so I thought if there's a doctor down there, I'll go up to the police station and say if they're needing any help, just let us know." They turned up that way but never got there because a policeman spotted the Red Cross worker just as he got out of the car. "Up to Rosebank Crescent, Doctor," he said. "It's bad up there, and we understand there's nobody up there yet." So the couple went up to that part of the town. "Then we discovered this scene of the inflatable dinghy across the road, all the power lines being down, all the lights being out, a body lying just behind the dinghy and then this piece of fuselage down in the garden of, I think, No. 72. So that was the first indication I had that this was not a military jet.

"The police were very keen to get the local inhabitants out of there because they reckoned the gas main was away (likely to explode) as well, and there was no saying how long it would be before there'd be another fire and/or explosion," the man said. So they went down and opened the Red Cross hall in Sidney Place, about a quarter of a mile away, and began taking people in for minor first aid and other forms of basic care.

The news broke rapidly. Some news people who were alerted initially received a tip that a military jet had crashed into a petrol station in Lockerbie and exploded. How they reacted depended on their role. For broadcasters who take their role as an early warning system seriously, the first step is to use the telephone to get enough information to alert the public to a dangerous situation. For the foot soldiers of the news media, the task is to get to the scene as rapidly as possible, work their way to the front and then get word of the calamity out to waiting news directors and editors, who will help them convey it to the anxious public.

The first broadcasts began about a half-hour after the impact. They may have served a useful purpose, warning motorists who were traveling along the A74 between Glasgow and Carlisle that evening to stay away from the danger and make way for emergency vehicles, but those first bulletins also terrified those listeners and viewers who knew the town.

A Lockerbie resident was in Dumfries when someone came up and told the group he was with: "I've just heard on the radio that a jumbo jet has crashed on Lockerbie." "Now, it's not a thing one tends to actually believe," the resident noted, "so peculiarly we didn't actually believe it, but when the gentleman pressed his point, we did try and phone, and then discovered the phone lines were in trouble."

The group jumped in the car and headed for Lockerbie, a drive that normally takes between 20 and 30 minutes, depending on traffic along the winding, two-lane road. "We could see loads of rescue vehicles and flashing lights, and so we detoured a way round about, because we didn't think we'd get into the town directly." Eventually, because they knew the back roads, they did get into Lockerbie. "My main concern at that point was my family, as it always tends to be, and I think most people were exactly the same. We live just in Douglas Terrace, which is 250 yards from Sherwood Crescent. As we were coming back, they put out on the radio that a jumbo jet had crashed in Lockerbie and the first report said that it had crashed on a petrol station in the Sherwood Crescent area of Lockerbie."

The Townfoot petrol station is only 200 yards from the man's back door. "So the silence in the car from then on was, you know...," he said. "When I got back into town, I could see the smoke, rescue people and fire hoses. My end of the street was evacuated. The police were stopping people going any further." Fortunately, he soon encountered someone who had seen his wife and family, and he was able to find them.

An uplands farm about four miles north of the town, surrounded by hills, was shielded to an extent from the initial trauma of the experience. "But we did hear a massive rumble," the farmer recalled, "and we'd had a lot of low flying jets in the area, and we really just put it down to a low flying jet. It was about half an hour later on the TV when I first realized something was seriously wrong."

The farmer tried to reach his father, who lives at the bottom end of the town, and his brother, who lives at the top, but couldn't get through by phone. "So I just jumped in the car, which on hindsight did not seem a very bright thing to do. The way they were reporting it on TV, the bottom end of the town had been completely obliterated. It took me two hours to travel six miles to see if my father was okay." Fortunately, he was unhurt.

Those kinds of reassuring events happened over and over around Lockerbie, as local people tried to find out what was happening to their community. But others heard the reports, reasoned that there was nothing they could do and spent hour after hour in a dreadful state of suspense, watching the television and trying to understand the disaster and its impact on their small town.

The news on BBC television was a mixture of careful reporting and conjecture. Its news people had held back from airing the initial alert until it could verify that a Pan Am aircraft had disappeared from the radar and that disappearance had coincided with a massive explosion on the ground. But its main evening news broadcast at 9 p.m. could be described as chaotic.

At that point the BBC was still relying primarily on the telephone to get its news. Its announcer quoted the Rescue Coordination Centre in Edinburgh, which said that Civil Air Traffic Control authorities reported that there had been an explosion on the ground and this coincided with a Pan Am Boeing 747 disappearing from the radar screens. Rescue Coordination said they understood it had crashed on the town of Lockerbie.

"Details are still sketchy," the BBC announcer said, "but from the scene, we know that the aircraft did hit a filling station, thought to be the Townfoot filling station in Lockerbie. It hit several houses and cars at the scene."[1]

BBC reports from the scene included two telephone interviews with eye witnesses. One was a guest at a hotel a half-mile away. Another, which seemed to confirm the report that the petrol station had been hit, was from a man who had just driven past the station when he heard the explosion. It rained debris down upon him and embedded an aluminum bolt from the plane in his car. He was so shaken that he kept going and did not stop until he reached home. He could tell the interviewer that the accident was in a residential area near the center of town, but not much else.

Bert Houston, a correspondent from BBC Radio Cumbria, was one of the first regional reporters to arrive and came close to an accurate account of what had happened in a report included later in the BBC-TV 9 o'clock newscast.

"The scene is one of horror and bewilderment," he said. "No one seems to know exactly what happened. But certainly at least four houses have disappeared in smoke and flames. At the moment fire and rescue services are trying to take injured and dead to the Town Hall where a refuge center has been set up. A helicopter is circling the scene at the moment, and police, ambulance and firemen are still tackling it in an area of the town called Sherwood Crescent where the houses were demolished. Apparently the aircraft has hit a hill about three miles from Lockerbie and then wreckage has been strewn as it traveled the distance to the town and landed on the houses and some other property."[2]

That statement reflected the fact that the nose cone on the plane had fallen to earth at Tundergarth, a tiny settlement on top of the hills three miles east of Lockerbie. Parts of the plane were strewn on the town itself. Only the way in which the jumbo jet had blown apart in the air was missing from his report, and that fact would take time to establish.

Houston made no mention of the petrol station, and apparently no one from the BBC thought to ask about it, because in several subsequent portions of the newscast the information that the plane had hit the filling station was repeated. By 9:17p.m. a BBC television producer, Wallace Traill, had reached Lockerbie from Glasgow and with considerable difficulty had managed a telephone link with the London newsroom. Their exchange follows:

Traill: The town, to use a cliché, is in chaos at the moment. All the roads in and out of the town are blocked. Telephones are down, and there are a string of burning houses along the south end of the town. I counted them out to be seven. And there is a large crater at the edge of the main dual carriageway, the A74, the Glasgow–Carlisle Road. At the moment police and firemen are unable to give casualty figures. But there are certainly casualties on the ground as well as in the aircraft.

Announcer (Michael Buerk): Is the wreckage still burning? Are the rescue services able to get close to it?

Traill: The rescue services are close to the wreckage, but the wreckage is widely dispersed. The crater itself is still burning, and, as I say, there are at least seven houses which were 10 minutes ago still burning quite fiercely.

Announcer: Are there any indications, apart from the wreckage of the houses that you can see, of casualties on the ground among the townspeople of Lockerbie?

Traill: It seems certain that there are casualties but neither the police nor the fire services are able to produce any statement as to the numbers or to the severity of the casualty list at the moment.

Announcer: So what are the rescue services doing? What's actually happening in front of your eyes there at the moment?

Traill: Well, they are some distance from me. I've had to—because the phones are down, I've had to leave the scene but there are firetenders fighting the fires in the burning houses. It's mostly a question of dousing down the crater because there are just fragments.

Announcer: From what you can see would there have been any chance of any of the passengers on board the airliner surviving the crash?

Traill: From what our sources in Lockerbie are saying, there is almost no chance, I'm afraid.

Announcer: And what about the townspeople in Lockerbie? Have they moved away from the town while all this has happened?

Traill: There has been an evacuation and there is a fair amount of congestion and, I'm afraid, a fair number of sightseers as well. The roads are blocked but the police have put a cordon about a quarter of a mile around the crash site.[3]

Nowhere in the interview did Traill mention the petrol station, and he was not asked about it. The BBC recapped its report late in the broadcast and repeated, "Eyewitnesses said there was a huge fireball when the plane came down on a petrol station near a housing estate in the village of Lockerbie."[4]

To anyone who knew the town that sounded as if a large section must have been destroyed; the petrol station, ringed by homes and small shops, is one street over from Sherwood Crescent. An explosion centered on and fed by the fuel in the station would have leveled many more homes.

The media presence had been almost immediate. Within minutes, journalists from nearby communities, such as Dumfries and Annan, found their way to the flaming portion of the wreckage in Sherwood Crescent. Television crews from Glasgow, Edinburgh and Carlisle arrived in a little over an hour. Chartered planeloads of media flew up from London while rescue workers were still trying to evacuate families who would be in jeopardy if the flames reached the petrol station. Reporters in other countries, alerted by the wire services, hopped the first available flights for Britain.

In the first tumultuous hours, the media, like the people in Lockerbie, were mostly trying to understand the scope of the disaster. They had to correct the early reports that the petrol station had exploded, and they were trying to work out an explanation based on the facts that were emerging: The plane had not crashed whole; it had been torn apart in flight. Like many of the local people who saw the flames rising from Sherwood Crescent, they expected the death toll on the ground to be much higher.

The media were searching for eye-witnesses. Some townspeople talked to them about what they had seen; others decided against it. One man said he decided not to talk right then, even though he knew journalists were looking for him. He recalled standing in a crowd right next to journalists who wanted to talk to him, unrecognized because he was not wearing his professional garb.

Some, caught up in helping their families cope, did not even realize they would have to decide whether to talk to news people. One family had taken refuge at a friend's home until the small hours of the morning, but wanted to get back into their own house, if possible that night. "It may sound a little peculiar, but we'd left the Christmas tree lights on, and the children were pretty upset, and the thought of a night out wasn't going to suit them," the father of the family recalled.

About 2 o'clock in the morning police did let some families back into their homes. "I'd just put the children all back upstairs to bed," the man said. "The children were all in one room because they were a little bit frightened. My wife and I were just downstairs. Then there was a ringing at the door bell. Whereupon three or four reporters from the national press, described as Fleet Street's finest, started to ask me my opinions on what had happened and where I was, and could they use my telephone. I'm afraid at that point I told them to go away in no uncertain fashion."

A woman in an apartment across from the town hall said she finally tried to get some sleep about 3 o'clock in the morning. But fire engines, police cars, and ambulances traveled back and forth in the town square beneath her windows all that night. "I didn't sleep very well. I got up and wandered." She looked out the window and saw a glare of high-power lights. "The torches for the television cameras were all lighting the square."

In Dumfries, in Glasgow and in Lockerbie, people from the Regional Council and Strathclyde police used to dealing with media queries under more normal circumstances answered phone calls from all over the world, hour after hour, repeating what little information they had. Police Superintendent Angus Kennedy of the Strathclyde Police Headquarters in Glasgow, already known to many members of the media as the press officer of Britain's second largest police force, arrived by Chinook helicopter about 7 a.m. to try to bring some sort of order out of the journalistic chaos. The Scottish Information Office, which functions as the British government's communications arm for any disaster that happens in Scotland, had already arrived the night before and commissioned the Masonic Lodge as a media center. That is where, a short time later, Kennedy took Chief Constable John Boyd for the first of many news briefings.

Most local people were unaware of the steps Kennedy and others took to provide the swelling corps of news people with regular doses of information and photo opportunities, even though such efforts undoubtedly lessened the impact of the news corps simply by reducing their need to travel round the town and the surrounding countryside. What the people saw were the camera teams, photographers, reporters with notebooks and satellite dishes in the streets.

The throngs of media surprised one woman when she decided to go to her job in a nearby town the morning after the disaster. She said she opted for work, "because, quite literally, I didn't know what to do. I said I'd go provided I could go down the main road and not a country road, because by then we realized the situation would be debris everywhere. My husband said he wasn't too happy about my driving, which to be honest neither was I, so he would take me. It was only when we got to the police station that I had my first indication of what it was like in the town with the media. We looked up, we looked down, and it was swarming. There wasn't a single local person to be seen, literally. It was so bad, our car was actually on television as we went down Main Street.

"My husband had actually gone to the office first before he was taking me, so he could open up the office, and he was televised crossing the street and his sister saw him in Bristol. And a friend of ours who lives in Lancashire said, 'I know you didn't like the media very much — it got harassing — but that was the first sign of normality to a lot of us because we knew him. We thought, that's someone going to work.' And his sister saw him, so she knew he was all right because we hadn't been able to contact her at all."

A local businessman had a similar experience when he went to open his shop in the town center. "The town was full of media, TV crews and journalists from all over the globe. They were set up in the car park, just down there. I mean, you couldn't come up the street without encountering a camera crew. On the next couple of days we tried to function normally, which was a bit difficult. And then as a normal person on the street, encountering journalists who wanted an interview, you would be stopped and they'd say, 'Would you like to say a few words?' Usually I said no at that point because I couldn't speak about anything."

A resident of Rosebank Crescent remembered the media as being everywhere. "If you went to Peter's shop to buy a paper, the camera was over your shoulder, watching what type of paper you were buying. If you were standing in groups on the street, they'd ask you, 'What do you think about this disaster?' We were confused; we just didn't know the answers — what had happened, who had died, who the local people were in Sherwood Crescent who were dead."

Two people from the Rosebank Crescent neighborhood had bought a house in Sherwood Crescent shortly before the disaster, and their former neighbors had believed they were dead. Until people from Rosebank saw them walking up the street, they were more concerned about the fate of those friends than the questions reporters were asking, the man explained.

A man living higher up the side of the valley was concerned about his brother and sister-in-law who lived at the foot of the town. He had not been able to reach them on Wednesday night, so about lunch-time he and his wife went down to the police station to see if they could get some information about their relatives. "There were reporters right in the yard of the police station — they were on the pavement with big cameras and everything," his wife said. "They wouldn't move to let you pass." "You had to go into the road," her husband added. "It may have been an over-reaction from us, given the circumstances and that, but it was upsetting."

An official arrived at the Incident Control Centre at Lockerbie Academy, having agreed with his superior the previous evening that he would represent their office on Thursday, and immediately was confronted with newspaper reporters. "I went to the local inspector of police and actually they tried to come in — holding my coat-tails — into the police office," he said. "And then when I came out again eventually, pester, pester, pester."

Because he had been asked by the police constable to direct part of the search for bodies at Tundergarth, that turned out to be his first and last encounter with the media. By 3 p.m. he had marked 35 bodies on hillsides where, in happier times, he had hunted for game.

All day Thursday more and more media arrived on the scene. It was becoming clear just how exceptional this disaster was, even though there was no official hint that it was caused by a bomb. News people numbered in the hundreds by the end of the day. Add them to the hundreds of police, Royal Air Force and Army personnel and support services from professional and voluntary organizations, estimated to total 2,300 at the peak of the effort,[5] and it becomes clear why the 3,500 residents of Lockerbie felt overwhelmed.

Stories began to circulate of media conduct that would be clear violations of any code of journalistic ethics. Someone saw photographers lift the covers from bodies to look at the victims beneath. A police officer was said to have spotted the offender and to have removed the film from the man's camera.

One family who were evacuated out of a house that subsequently had to be demolished spent the night in a local hotel. The next morning a journalist from a British tabloid managed to gain entrance to the dining room where the family was having breakfast by telling the hotel staff that he was related to those people.

There were also stories of reporters pretending to be clergy or social workers to try to gain access to people who had suffered loss.

"There was great pressure to get pictures and stories on those that lost their homes or were related to those who were killed," a local businessman recalled.

"The pressure was on anybody who had pictures of the dead children, who had children in the same class, who went to the same ballet class. If you look back at the aftermath of the disaster, very few pictures were actually printed of the deceased, mainly because everybody in Lockerbie got so fed up with some of the prying that went on and so nobody would give them any pictures. It was just intrusive."

The behavior of the media was not all bad. One man commented that they presented Lockerbie in a very good light. "It's a good place, and that came over on the media. It still comes over in spite of bits and pieces of squabbles, the negative things that always crop up. So from that point of view, the press was being good, in presenting Lockerbie as it is."

The people who were stopped on the streets for interviews did well in this man's estimation, although not necessarily by their own. One man who was interviewed recalled that he tended to get very complicated and, in his words, "was talking a lot of rubbish." But what prompted him to stop giving interviews at that time was the pressure for sensational statements. "Gory details they were after. That's what they wanted to know. If you'd tell them something straightforward, they weren't interested. I never spoke to them for weeks after that."

One relief worker, interviewed live on television, learned a different kind of lesson, this one about the power of the media to rally support. A Border Television crew from nearby Carlisle interviewed him live on December 22, shortly after the local district council had decided it could rehouse the people who'd lost their houses. They would put them in "transit houses," temporary accommodations that had recently been used by some council house residents while the council was refurbishing their own homes. Because the council had decided that all these people should be back in their usual houses for Christmas, the transit houses were all empty. "They were able to allocate (transit houses to) everybody who'd lost a house — maybe not a house that they would choose, but still it had a roof, a front door and all the usual things of houses. But that was all. They were empty. And the first things that were needed were blankets."

So when Border Television asked what was needed, "without thinking, I said 'blankets.' Well, here we had blankets to the ceiling. So we were able to deliver bedding and blankets and very rough and ready kind of furniture to get them started."

People who were interviewed by the media tended to omit horrific details, to avoid talking to them about the carnage on their doorsteps. Most media, too, tended to avoid describing in detail the horror of the scene. The search parties removed the bodies and debris from the hills around the town quickly, for fear that it would be blown away or covered by snow. But they left much of the wreckage that fell in Rosebank because the area could be secured.

When authorities began removing bodies from the neighborhood the day after the tragedy, the people in Rosebank were aghast at some of the journalists on the scene. A body had been hanging on the chimney of a house that was half-demolished. "The day they brought the body down, the photographers were running around stupid," a neighborhood resident recalled. "They were running through my garden up on to my step to get as near as they could to get a photo of it being brought down. That was really ghastly and I thought they were pigs at the time."

One British tabloid used a photograph of the recovery on its front page, as did *Time* and *Newsweek*, the American news magazines, and the *Washington Post* newspaper.[6]

The area was then cordoned off, making it harder for news people to bother the residents. But all over the town, local people were finding ways of eluding journalists. A woman living right across from the Town Hall said she kept away from them. "I could see them every day," she said, but explained that her door was not on the main street and she made a pointing of driving whenever she went out. "Once I can remember walking down to the flower shop to get a flower to put down to the Town Hall (serving as a chapel of rest for coffins of the victims), and that's the only time I can remember walking down the street within the first week of the disaster. If I had to go down the street, I'd drive down. I know it sounds lazy, but I avoided where they actually were."

Why was she so keen to avoid the media? "Because I've seen where there's been disasters or something tragic has happened, and I got the impression from some of the reports on television that they tend to intrude on people's grief. And I just didn't want that. Plus the fact I don't think I could have handled it. In fact, I'm sure I couldn't have. I'd have probably said some rubbish."

Local people soon learned some of the key spots to avoid if they did not want to face the media. The British television crews had their satellite set up in the parking lot behind a bank, just outside the entrance to the town's park. The news briefings were held at the Masonic Lodge near the police station, just down the street from the Blue Bell Hotel, adopted by the news corps as its local hangout. Journalists also made regular trips to the Incident Control Centre at the Lockerbie Academy, at the other end of town.

Some sections of the town never saw a reporter, although the community is so small that anyone going to the post office, to the railway station or the grocery store was very conscious of the media presence. Those working in the town center had to face the media just to do their jobs.

People in Lockerbie were also learning that not all reporters are alike. What they had found most disturbing was the tabloid press. "The better quality papers were more considerate and kind and sympathetic, and more accurate," one man said. "If you were doing an interview with them and said, 'I don't want you to print that,' they didn't print it, which was fair. So there was that trust, and trust can be developed into the positive aspect because the media can help people in a situation like this — or it can hinder them."

One of the worst experiences with the media came during Christmas mass at the Holy Trinity Roman Catholic Church. "There was a ban on press for the service in our church, and the following day the *Sun* newspaper published a full report of that service, plus photographs, and a totally inaccurate description." The priest had tears in his eyes during the service, but the *Sun* reported he had collapsed on the altar and been rushed off to hospital. The headlines read "Priest collapses during service. Bishop orders him to rest."

Most media did leave townspeople alone Christmas weekend. They just seemed to fade away, residents said. But one man met a photographer on Christmas Day. Just before the holiday, the man had managed to get his family back into their damaged home. "We got the place reasonably tidied up on the inside, but we were told not to touch anything outside, and that was a bit of a disaster really — with the rubble hanging about," he recalled.

"We'd got our two girls new bicycles for Christmas. Well, they couldn't take them out to the garden. We've got a bit out the back, but they could not go on that because it was two foot high in rubble. And they could not go up the road toward Sherwood Crescent. The only place to give them a go on their bikes was to go up the Carlisle Road, and they couldn't have got very far before we were pounced on. The photographer wanted to know who we were and what was the girls' names. We told them, 'Just leave them alone. We don't want anything to do with you,' and came back down here and came in the house."

His family had several phone calls in the next two weeks and occasionally people turning up at the door. "I must say they do seem to go the rounds," the man said. "We had two or three lots of Americans and that didn't bother me too much. I always refused to give interviews at that time, because it seemed to be intruding on your personal feelings and that. Some people tended to have difficulty refusing them, but I never found it a problem. I just showed them the gate and told them, 'Get lost.' But I found the telephone calls very troublesome. I think most of the people on this street were getting phone calls at certain times; they were very persistent types of phone calls. But I always refused to say anything to them."

The man said he thought the throngs of news people made it especially difficult in face-to-face encounters. "On a one-to-one basis or a small crowd, it's easier to talk. But if you're surrounded, which is what it was like sometimes in the streets in the days after — some of these groups were maybe a dozen or 20 press at once — most people can't handle that."

Another experience with the media stemmed from the fact that the family actually was on a missing list until Saturday after the disaster. "I'd been in and reported that the family was okay, but the guy in the Town Hall that I'd seen had lost the sheet of paper, so we didn't know we were on the missing list until a neighbor came in and saw me Friday night and told me about it. We had a letter from an Australian family with the same name as ours two or three months after and they knew within a day or two days of the disaster that we were missing, and yet nobody round here knew — I didn't even know myself. But these people in Australia were getting better coverage than we were. Plus, they weren't giving names out in this country, but they were abroad."

This complaint may reflect the lack of local media in Lockerbie, which is covered directly only by a weekly newspaper in nearby Annan. In fact, the information vacuum prompted the creation of a newsletter called *Community Update* following the disaster. For many residents, including this family, the regional and national media nevertheless provided an important source of information. "Mostly I watched television news reports and that. And they were fairly good. In this area here we had to watch the television news reports because that was the only place we were getting information really. Information was nil here for the first few weeks. And watching the news everyday was the way we picked it up. Of course, they were shooting in the dark a bit themselves, I think."

The funerals began after Christmas. There was a ban on news coverage again for the first service, which was for 10-year-old Joanne Flannigan. "But you could see them at the back of the church openly writing, which is an intrusion," one witness said.

By the time of the memorial service on January 4, arrangements had been worked out to keep the presence of the press to a minimum. Angus Kennedy worked with the clergy to obtain information that could be given to the media, such as hand-outs on prayers, so they would have something to write. By then, he also had arranged a well established system of pooling for picture opportunities that even took into account the fact that American and European television use different technical systems. "The press were very well controlled at the memorial service," one resident recalled. "They were well warned." "It was very good. I cannot remember seeing a reporter," said his friend. "They were there obviously, but they kept well out of the way."

A man with an official role in the town was interviewed often, mostly over the telephone. "I was never interviewed at all on television because I was never available; I was always working hard — no time to stand in the street. I think I've spoken to every paper in the United Kingdom at varying times. It's not always the same reporter from any one paper. They just seem to come on when they want a story. The only thing I would say about it is, unless you're being sensational or controversial, it's not reported."

As an example, he cited a query he had received about the fact that no member of the Royal Family attended the memorial service. "It was reported quite correctly in the *Daily Mail* what I'd said on Monday, but on the Friday, I think it was the *Sun* that reported me as being furious at no member of the Royal Family being there. All I said was there were a lot of people, as I was speaking for the community, who were kind of disappointed because a rumor had got up that there would be a royal presence at the memorial service. It turned out to be the Royal Household, as opposed to the Royal Family. At that stage I was angry, not at the Royal Family, but at the *Sun* newspaper. I mean, there were two extremes: the first one was correct; the last one was entirely wrong."

Because he could view the issue both as a member of the general public and as someone involved heavily with the arrangements, the official said he could understand that there was enough pressure on the police and security without having to have a member of the Royal Family there. "And, as it happened, when Prince Charles did come, it was a better time."

The tide of humanity that came to help the stricken town threatened to overwhelm it. Early on, regional officials realized that local people wanted and needed to take the lead in the town's recovery. Neil McIntosh, chief executive for the Regional Council of Dumfries and Galloway, called a meeting on December 27 at the Queens Hotel of more than 100 individuals who identified 27 separate issues that required attention; the requests ranged from clarification of the date schools would reopen to a ban on low-flying aircraft in the Lockerbie area. But one of the most telling statements was the feeling at that point that local organizations and representatives had been overlooked in response to the disaster. Also expressed was the view that relatives and friends of the aircraft victims, many of them Americans who had flown to Scotland, at that point were being kept away from the townspeople.[7]

That meeting led to the formation of the Community Liaison Steering Group, made up of residents of the local council and community organizations, a member of the clergy and representatives of newly formed neighborhood groups. It became a means of canvassing local opinion on the many issues that needed to be dealt with rapidly in the following weeks.

In addition, a Community Liaison Office was set up the Library in the High Street, where it was easily accessible, to present a "human face" to the complex emergency response and to encourage self-help efforts. At this "one-stop shop," people could come by and explain their problems and be referred to the appropriate agency or resource. It also coordinated in-kind offers of help, such as outings for children and the elderly to give them some respite from the disaster scene. Notice boards communicated news related to the disaster and the recovery efforts, as did a *Community Update* newsletter published from the office and distributed door-to-door. And, significantly, cards and expressions of sympathy from all over the world were displayed on a large notice board in the foyer.

Lockerbie people who served at the reception desk of the Community Liaison Office, answering questions, putting people in contact with other members of the team or just listening to those who wanted to talk, were also a natural contact point for the media.

"Up to that point, I'd had no contact with media at all," one volunteer recalled. "NBC (one of America's major networks) was the first I spoke to, but the Regional Council representative took over on that, which was fair enough. I mean, I wasn't very sure at that point what the situation was anyway.

"So the next to come in were from TV-am, the ITV breakfast program, and there was no one from Region that night. There was always a quiet time round about 6 o'clock in the evening and we were just sitting, just peacefully chatting, and they walked in and they wanted an interview," she said. Her colleague disappeared. "I suddenly found I was at the table on my own. So, finally, I elected to do it. What they actually did was try to set up a phone call as we would normally get it. You know, 'Community Liaison, can I help you?' And find out who it is and what they need.

"Then they asked what thoughts I had and when did I think Lockerbie would go back to normal. A lot of people have commented since because I made a very strange remark at the time, but I think I was right. I said that Lockerbie would take a long time to get back to normal, if ever. Don't ask me because I can't explain why I said that. I said it with conviction because I felt it. I think now, on reflection, I was correct. Lockerbie will never be the same again. There will be normality, but never the same normality."

She did a number of other interviews in the days that followed with no real problem. BBC2, the second channel offered by BBC Television, ran a special program just so that all the volunteers could be thanked for what they'd done. "But, and to this day, I've never discovered why, they set up an interview on BBC World Service (for the volunteers at the reception desk). And we did this interview, and that was the one time I can remember sitting and thinking, 'Why am I here? I am not doing any good.' I meant with the media. My work on that desk — that would be far more beneficial. And that was my feeling, you know. I just had had enough."

At the end of the World Service broadcast, the volunteer was in tears although she said she has no idea what they were talking about that triggered that reaction. The woman reporter was interested in what she was saying, but her manner was less sympathetic than other journalists the volunteer had encountered. "She was pushing. There were two of them actually doing it, but she was far more pushing. I couldn't relate to them at all."

In the weeks following the disaster, the volunteer said people seemed to be operating on a totally different level. "It was not normal. Probably we were work-weary. (Given) the hours we put in we were probably working on adrenaline. To a certain extent, we coped with the media. It was difficult — if anyone had told me a week before that I'd sit in front of television cameras or be interviewed, I would have said they were mad. I'm the last sort of person to do something like that. And yet, we all just did it. In fairness, we probably weren't harassed quite as much as the people in the street were. It was a definite thing we were in for; they knew we were doing something. It was Community Liaison, and it had to work."

She remembers one confrontation in the library vividly. "A certain local free-lance reporter was going through the Electoral Roll; it's made up of everyone eligible to vote in the town. He was standing at the actual library desk, so I went up and passed the time of day, and I said, 'Can I help you?' 'Yes, you could. Can you tell me where (a family's) relatives live?' 'No. If you want that information, kindly get in touch with the police.' 'I have, and they haven't been forthcoming.' 'Well,' I said, 'I'm afraid you're not going to get anything more from me.' 'Oh, I'll just keep thumbing through this till I find them.' 'I said, 'You won't.' But that was what he was doing. If there was someone with that family's name on the Electoral Roll, they were going to be harassed. There wasn't any relative on the roll and I knew that. I also knew where their relatives were. Sometimes instinct to protect can be very strong."

The media were present in Lockerbie daily for weeks and weekly for months. Like the investigators working from their base at the local school, trying to solve this murder mystery on an epic scale, the strangers seeking story after story were a reminder that the town would never regain its quiet anonymity. During the summer the news people seemed to fade from view. But in Lockerbie everyone knew they would be back.

Kennedy Airport

About 15 minutes on the road from John F. Kennedy Airport, the mother of a Syracuse University student heard a very muffled report on the car radio: "Something about a flight originating from Heathrow Airport to JFK missing over Scotland. I instantly felt all the blood in my body go down to my feet." She opened the car window and her husband asked, "What's the matter?" "And I said, 'Oh nothing, I just need some air.' And it wasn't until we got to the parking lot of the Pan Am Building that I actually told him what I heard."

In the parking lot, they could see another sign of a major news story, parked vans that had carried television crews to the airport. But the journey to the airport from their home had been long and they decided to do the practical thing: visit the restrooms.

An area of the Pan Am Building near the First-Class Lounge had been cordoned off, and dozens of reporters, photographers and television camera crews were behind the ropes. When the mother came out of the restroom, she said she approached a uniformed airline official near the media and asked what all the fuss was about. "He indicated that a plane had gone down, a Pan Am plane. And I said, 'What was the flight number?' And he said, '103.'" That was her daughter's flight. The woman collapsed, screaming, "Not my baby, not my baby."

A freelance television reporter working for the BBC recalled hearing a terrible noise. "I didn't really know what was going on. I didn't realize that this was someone who'd come to the airport, had her daughter on the flight and had just discovered it. It just was very strange. I'd never heard anything like it. I just had an automatic reaction." He told his crew, "Look, just get it."

Then the newsman said he realized what was going on, "that it was a horrible event really, because she lost control, and she fell to the ground, spread eagled in a way, and she was screaming. It took me a while to realize what it was. I didn't know whether she'd been assaulted at first; it was so strange."

While the woman was on the floor, with her husband trying to shield her from the cameras, the newsman estimated that about 10 television cameras were trying to capture the event. "And after it became clear (what was happening), people did back up a bit, but they still wanted to get that shot and there were print cameras, too."

"All I remember is losing control," the mother said. "I remember lights all over. I felt like I was visually being raped by the media. I'm usually a woman who is very much in control. I'll have to say that was one of the few moments in my life where I was out of control. And I felt the media chose to use that moment. I felt violated. I felt exploited. And no one was there to protect me."

Her husband and others helped her to her feet and into the First Class Lounge, where an emergency medical trauma person, a nurse and other people she took to be officials were waiting.

The woman's brother had heard a brief report on the radio and recalled that his niece was supposed to be flying home from London that day. "So we rushed home and I turned on the television. I was watching CNN and the report came on that said they had some pictures that they were going to show that weren't really nice to look at." That's when they showed the woman screaming on the airport terminal floor and he recognized his sister. "That's how I knew," he said.

The woman and her husband did not want their other daughter to learn about the tragedy that way. They reached the daughter's boyfriend, who knew where she was, and he was instructed to take her to her aunt's house. "I didn't want to go," the daughter said. "I wanted to go home." When she arrived there, a reporter was waiting and wanted to interview her, but her boyfriend's sister kept the journalist occupied in front of the house. "I didn't want to talk to anyone because I didn't know anything," the daughter said. So the reporter went to a neighbor's house and questioned the people there.

Inside the Pan Am terminal, other families were learning of their loss. A couple and their son had driven down to the airport in the afternoon, had eaten supper and were waiting for information about the flight's arrival to show up on the board. As time ticked away, they wondered about it. They noticed a lot of news cameras and the husband commented, "There must be a famous basketball team or something coming in." "I found a quiet little place in one of the departure lounges and sat down — I had brought my knitting with me. I thought that would be relaxing," the wife recalled. Her husband paced the hallways and noticed that more and more news people were arriving. "We had no indication at all at this juncture what was going on; we never suspected anything," the mother recalled. "We were simply concerned the flight was not on the arrival board."

Before they had left for the airport at 3 p.m., her son had called the toll free Pan Am number and had been told the plane was in the air. So he asked his dad, "Well, do you want me to call that 800 number?" This time when he asked about Pan Am 103, he was transferred to another person who said, "We have lost contact with that plane." The family speculated that the plane must be over Canada, or even approaching JFK. "I said, 'Go back and try again, and see if you get this same message again,' thinking it might be a joke. The disbelief was starting to set in," the mother recalled. He received the same transfer, but this time the second person said, "The airliner is down. Haven't you seen the TV?"

The son found his father who, in turn, approached an airport security guard who apparently summoned Pan Am agents on a beeper. They asked, "How many are in your party?" and then instructed the father, "Gather everybody together and come with us."

The mother was still knitting, but recalled that she was already beginning to feel panicky. So when she saw her husband and son and the agents approach, she said, "Oh, my God. Something's wrong." She called it the moment of dread. "As they approached me, one of them put his hand on my left shoulder. They said, 'Come with us. We're taking you to a briefing lounge.' There was no handle on what was happening. The shock started to go deeper. I said, 'I don't know what is happening.' There was confusion and frustration with that. And as we were led into the briefing lounge, I went past about four TV monitors on the right hand side. They were on and, of course, I didn't want to hear. I was shutting my mind out one way... and my heart glued to anything I could hear. And I heard 'Pan Am crash' and I turned around at the monitor and there was a picture of a fuselage. I said, 'Oh, my God, she's dead.' And then they took us into the room and they never briefed us. I kept waiting. I was waiting for Pan Am officials to come and address us and that never happened."

She estimated that 25 to 30 family members were in the lounge. "The confusion there was that you didn't know who was an official Pan Am person and you didn't know who were passengers' families. As it turned out, there were a lot of grief counselors there from the American Red Cross and then there were ministers, priests and rabbis." A Pan Am official had approached them and taken down their names and addresses shortly after they arrived in the lounge. The woman recalled that the official said, "Don't give up hope. We're trying to make contact and get our communications straight and then we'll report back to you. And don't listen to the media." "I remember sitting down and someone asking if I wanted a Coke or something. I was just going into shock. I just retreated and, you know, caved in."

What happened next confused the woman. A *Daily News* reporter confirmed that a group of the media did try to get in through a door to one side of the family lounge, but did not succeed. The woman saw that attempt and, recalling the scene, believed she had seen the woman collapse in front of the media, not in the main portion of the terminal, but inside the lounge. In her words: "And I remember turning around and seeing (the woman who collapsed on the floor), and this was my first encounter with what I called the horror of the media, because she had come into the room — she had just gotten in — and that's when she fainted, swooned or collapsed."

Asked if the woman had actually collapsed in the briefing room, she confirmed that was what she recalled. Then she asked, "Am I wrong? I may be wrong." Later she tried again to express what she remembered. "It was a blur somewhat, but this is what I can recall, that I can envision, in terms of what happened. I remember her coming into the room and then the door was absolutely packed full — I mean up to the top — with reporters and cameras and they just followed her in and there is no way that the door could have been closed. I saw her; this woman, you know, screamed and I said, 'Oh my God' because you couldn't help it. And then when I saw the reporters come in and they were going right at her. I remember that — swooping on over — it was like this herd of wild cattle coming. It was just awful. And I said,

'Oh my God, what are they doing? Oh my God, are they going to come for me next?' I was petrified. They were penetrating the room. And that was my biggest fear, you know." She also remembered fearing that they would go after her family, especially her son. She recalled telling him to "just sit over there somewhere" and that she hung on to her husband. In retrospect, she said, she thought it must have been very hard for her son to see all this. "I thought that was very much a violation. I really feared them coming into the room, coming at me like that."

The woman said she began to feel better when she spotted a familiar face, a mother she had met during a summer orientation for parents of students in the study abroad program that Syracuse University had held in New York. They talked and commiserated for a while and then became concerned about another mother in deep distress, who was not responding to the professional counselors. The two women quietly introduced themselves, then one took one of her hands and the other cradled her. "I don't think (the woman) knows. I don't think she remembers that whole experience."

The woman recalled how she had retreated within herself a short time earlier. "That's how I adapted. I was crushed in, retreating within. Another thing I found is you can't predict how you're going to react. So anything that does happen is okay. That is important, too."

About 10 p.m., the airline confirmed that her daughter had, in fact, been a passenger. At that point, Pan Am officials offered to put the family up in a hotel. But her husband felt it was important for them to go home. She was fearful at that point of having to face the media. "It scared me to death that they would come at me and make my grieving and my shock worse." The family was taken out a back door to their car and they drove home.

Another mother learned from a friend, whom she was meeting face-to-face for the first time, that her son had probably died on the downed plane. The friendship had developed from another tragedy the previous year; a staff member of the exchange program supervising her daughter's stay in South America had to call the family and tell them the girl was dying. The staff member and mother had formed a strong bond in the interim. They had planned to meet in a departure lounge at JFK, and the mother had brought pictures of her daughter and planned to introduce the friend to her son, her only surviving child, when he arrived at the airport. "And now she has to tell us this news," the mother said.

The problem then was to get a private place in the Pan Am terminal at Kennedy. This was particularly important to the mother because the previous year she had been delayed in Miami Airport while flying to be with her dying daughter, and Eastern Airlines personnel would not let her use a private phone. So she had had to call the clinic to see if her daughter was still alive from a phone in the public area of the terminal, and that is where she learned of her daughter's death.

To get to the First Class Lounge at Kennedy, the place set aside for families needing privacy, meant going past the media. "The press that night was in a real frenzy, and I was very angry with them because of the lights; the lights they use are so blinding. Here you have a person who is in shock who is now blinded on top of it. They recognized me as a family member because the guard has his hands around my shoulder — and was pushing people back," she recalled. She remembered one reporter in particular. "He said, 'How do you feel?' and I looked at this guy and said, 'That is a stupid question.'

"I was manhandled by the press physically. I had someone hold me in place by standing on my foot — and that left me bruised — so they could talk to me. They also impeded my passage. They held me in place and I was blinded by the lights. This guy said, 'Is there anything you want to say?'" she added, then remembered saying, "Yeah, you're in my way. That's what I wanted to say. Just let me past."

Those experiences, while very different in some respects for different families, represent the face the media presented to the grieving families at Kennedy Airport that night.

The woman who had collapsed on the floor had to contend with the fact that that dramatic image was repeated and repeated. "I recall coming home from Kennedy Airport in the taxi with my husband and, looking forward in the car, I saw a newspaper — I can't remember what the headlines were, but it had to do with Pan Am — and I asked the taxi driver, 'Can I see that newspaper?'" It was the *Daily News*. "And there on the front page was a picture of myself on the floor of the airport, and I was actually appalled. I just couldn't believe it. This was the news of the day."

From the time she returned home, she said, "I was glued to the television. I wanted to know everything there was to know. I wanted information. I've always been a person who wanted facts; don't give me fiction, just tell me what I need to know. I'll make the judgments." As time passed, she came to believe that people grieve the way they live, and she had always lived according to the principle that one should make informed choices. She even recalled talking about it with her daughter before she had set off for London. So she saw her use of the media for information both as part of the grieving process and as a search for information on which to make choices about what she should do.

Surprisingly, perhaps, in view of the treatment she had received at the airport, she did agree to be interviewed after she returned home. Initially, the couple had gone to the woman's sister, where they had a chance to spend time with their other daughter and talk through what had happened. "I think it was the way the media approached me on the phone," she explained. "They were not pushy. They asked permission. They said they did not want to discuss anything that I didn't want to discuss. They knew it was a difficult time and they would accept the fact if I chose not to do it. And I think it was the professional way in which they approached me, with a lot of sensitivity and acknowledgment that it was difficult. And that I indeed had the right to refuse both to meet with them or to discuss certain things.

"Along about that time, too, there was more information forthcoming, but I didn't have original information. Before we departed from the airport, already there was news speculation that it was a bomb. And soon after that there was some information that some people had had a warning about this, that Pan Am had received notification. At that point, if these things were true, I had a sense of anger and I felt that needed to be acknowledged. So I think that was another factor that influenced my decision. I think you tend to want other people wakened to the truth."

Even when she spoke about the airport episode months later, it was clear the hurt had not left her. Although she had come to see the media as a potential ally in dealing with the government and in correcting problems with airline security, thinking of herself at that terrible moment in her life remained extremely painful. And because video clips of dramatic moments tend to be repeated again and again, she had been forced to relive it.

The Geraldo Rivera show on which family members were invited to appear several months after the tragedy opened with a clip of the woman on the floor of Kennedy Airport. Her brother said he called the producer of the show, who told him, "I'm awfully sorry if I offended you." "Well, I just hope my sister didn't see it, because I know I felt the pain. Every time I see it, I get pain," the brother recalled saying. "Well, will it help if I send her flowers?" he quoted the producer as saying. "That's not the point," the brother retorted. "Well, I guarantee you, sir," the producer told him, "we will never show that again. We'll put it in a safe and it will be locked away and we'll never see it again."

Two weeks later, the brother said, the same program did another show and showed the same scene again. "Right after he promised me he wouldn't do it."

The woman who had been manhandled by reporters became convinced that if they had approached her differently the night of the tragedy, perhaps with one reporter who would then "pool" information with other reporters, she would have been able to respond. "But I didn't want to be mobbed. If someone had been permitted to approach me quietly and say, 'Hello, my name is so-and-so. Here is my card. I'm from the AP. We recognize this is a very difficult time for you. Would you care to make a statement to us or would you perhaps like to make a statement to us in half an hour?' And it would be appropriate for them to remind that person that this may be a historic event. The thing you don't realize is that I was very offended that the news of the crash was on television. I took it as a private occurrence at that moment. I did not put it in the context of being a public event. I needed to be told this is a public event; this is an international incident."

She also suggested the media find a technological alternative to the harsh lights of television cameras and flash bulbs. "I think they would get a lot more cooperation and the family members, who are also victims in a tragedy, would not be subject to further physical upset."

This woman defended the action of the media in filming and photographing the mother who had collapsed on the floor, although she conceded she arrived at this position as the story developed, not on the night of the tragedy. "The media should portray the horrors — someone screaming on the floor," she said. "I think that is appropriate because the public has got to know how horrible it is. I think it is very important to report the raw emotions, as distasteful as it is to most people who treasure their privacy. They cease to be private people at that moment, and it's just one of life's hard knocks. No, it's not nice to have someone watching you screaming, yelling and crying. Even if it is me." She said many people who have come to the aid of the families have mentioned how affected they were by the footage of the mother on the floor. "So there comes a point where you have to put down your own ego for the greater good."

In dealing with media in her home town, this mother felt she was in control from the start. Most of the local media knew her as an advertiser. The family had someone meet the media outside the house, find out what they wanted and then a message would be relayed: "All right, at such-and-such an hour. I needed to have the control. That's all. So if (the request) was 10 after 1, I would say, I will speak to her at 1:15."

The mother who had been in the First Class Lounge with her husband and son, and who thought she saw the media come into the lounge, carried that image in her mind for more than a year. It was only when she told her husband what she had been telling the interviewer about seeing the mother collapse *inside* the lounge that she began to realize that part of the experience might have been imagined.

Although she gave interviews and even wrote newspaper stories about her daughter, she had difficulty using the media. "For the first month, I couldn't look at TV at all. I remember sitting in my little family room and saying to (my husband), 'Okay, let's watch the 10 o'clock news every night and that's it.' So I would put the news on and then, of course, there would be Pan Am. And then if I could get up, turn off the set, leave the room, I was good.

Sometimes they would just flash without letting you know in advance. And I remember one time screaming when it came on. It was too much of a stark reality for my mind to comprehend and (at that time) there was just too much I couldn't deal with."

As time went on, however, she collected clippings and played a very active role in dealing with the media on behalf of the family group trying to focus attention on issues arising from the tragedy. As a journalist and a former journalism teacher, she felt she had a special role to play. "My first task was to put near my telephone a big, long yellow sheet or pads and establish a media-contact list, and anybody who came to my house and answered the phone was instructed to take down every person who calls and a phone number, and if they weren't a personal friend, what their personal title was and who they represented."

The work became a special comfort. "I wake up in the morning, especially if it is a dismal day. And I say, I'm not going to let the terrorists get my life." She invokes her daughter's memory by looking up in the sky, especially if a plane is going over, since her home is in a flight path. "I say, 'Okay, be with me today. Carry me forward.' Her cause was peace, so it is very easy to take up her cause and work with it — world peace."

Death in the family

The awful news reached many British families in their homes. Down a quiet country lane in a small village near Birmingham, a mother heard a bulletin on the television that a plane had crashed in the Scottish Borders and knew at once that it was the plane her daughter had been taking to America. "They did say it was the 6 o'clock plane out of Heathrow, a Pan Am plane," she recalled. "I didn't think there could be more than one. My reaction was the feeling of being kicked inside and out, all over — terror, a sort of disintegration, horror, numbness, pain, sheer pain."

She went to call her husband who was working in his study. But he could not believe it was his daughter's plane. "The timing didn't seem quite right. It seemed too late," he recalled. "(Her) plane should have been almost mid-Atlantic by that time." He said his wife had always been much more nervous about such things, more inclined to put a bad interpretation on news. "I was saying, 'It can't be the same plane.' But unfortunately it soon became clear it had been the same plane, the fact there had been a slight delay in takeoff and weather conditions that led to it being over Lockerbie at the time.

"I think how the truth dawned was that we realized that it had to be the right plane, but we weren't able to reinforce that by talking to anybody who could give us hard information," the father said. "I managed to get through to the emergency number that they'd put on the television once." He spoke with someone who identified himself as a representative of Pan Am, and asked if he could confirm that their daughter was on the plane. The representative said he had no passenger manifest, and so the father told him that the family would leave one of the two lines into their house clear so that he could telephone them back as soon as he got the passenger manifest. "He never actually rang back, for whatever reason, I know not," the father said. "When we tried to get him again, we were never able to get through to the number until the next day."

Although their other daughter called and confirmed that she had seen her sister off at the departure gate, the parents still felt the need for some official confirmation. "I think in these situations, you hope against hope that there's some excuse, some reason why the one you're worried about would not have been there," the father said. After several hours, he got through to Pan Am in JFK. 'A lady answered the phone and I said, 'Are you a Pan Am representative?' and she said, 'Yes,' and I said, 'I'm ringing about a possible passenger on your plane that's gone down over Lockerbie, Scotland. Can you tell me whether her name was amongst the passengers?' And she gave no answer, but put the phone down, and I got no further communication from the airline or anybody else at any time."

The first "official" word the father received that his daughter was on the plane came about 3 o'clock in the morning when he called BBC World Service, the radio service famous for its overseas broadcasts, especially in developing countries. He called them, following a broadcast he heard on the World Service. At that point, the media had very limited information about the victims; they did not know, for example, their addresses or nationalities.

"I don't remember the times very accurately, but very soon the list of names was published. It became clear that our daughter's name was amongst them," the father said. That brought the first flash of media attention. The family blocked the drive with a car to stop media from reaching the house. "We just didn't want anything to do with them at that stage. Nor did we want much to do with them for the first week or 10 days," he said.

As the mother recalled, "I had no energy really to talk to anyone at that stage. I was like an animal in pain, without words really. There were no words that could describe what I was feeling, so I didn't want to. I was quite bitter, and trying to cope with that. I had nothing to say. (All I could) try to say was what a beautiful, brilliant, lovely girl she was."

The family did agree to an interview with *The Times* of London. "We frankly weren't very impressed," the father said, "but he was a very junior journalist, who seemed to brush off the concerns of the family in the interest of doing his story as he saw it. We didn't feel at all positive toward the way he was handling it. I think he was a junior journalist; it's probably unfair to criticize him, but he didn't make us feel that we wanted to indulge in media cooperation exercises from then on."

Although British families, in most cases, heard about the tragedy more quickly than those in America, they did not become the targets of media attention the night of the bombing. As near as can be determined, the few relatives who did talk with reporters in Britain that night had responded to a Pan Am announcement that some sort of incident center would be set up at London Heathrow. Anxious families did travel to Heathrow, only to find almost no information was being given out, according to a London-based reporter who was sent there. The reporter said he exchanged information with some relatives, who seemed grateful for anything he could tell them.

The situation was very different in the United States, because a Syracuse television station had obtained a list of names of Syracuse University students from Pan Am and broadcast them on the 6 p.m. news, then shared them with other news media across the country. Immediately, reporters used the list to begin looking for anyone who might be related or know someone on the list. In some cases, the roll of names included people who never boarded the flight or who had taken earlier flights.

One family recalled a reporter calling and saying, "I don't know how to word this question because I've already spoken to two families who have said, 'No, he's right here in the living room.' So she said, 'By any chance is (their son) at home?'" Of course, he was not. His mother called his London landlord, whom they had met during a November visit, and said, "Tell me he left late and missed the plane." Instead, the landlord burst into tears and said, "Oh, no, in fact, he left very early."

A woman from a town near Camden, New Jersey, whose son was on the flight, said, "I think that (releasing the list) was just unforgivable, because the whole night we were getting phone calls, not just from our local media, but from the *Chicago Tribune*, the New York papers, all over. And that I think was horrible, absolutely horrible. And we still hadn't been notified by Pan Am that he was even on the flight." A Long Island mother saw her son's name in print as a victim of the disaster for the first time on the television screen. "This was before any kind of confirmation from Pan Am, the State Department or elsewhere. On one hand, I was grateful to see the name, on the other, I wondered should I really be informed by television of the death of my son."

As the news spread, family after family had to find a way of dealing with the media. Many relied on someone who volunteered to answer the phone calls, sometimes a friend or neighbor, sometimes a member of the clergy.

The family living in the Camden area had heard about the explosion of

Pan Am 103 on television, and immediately tried to contact Pan Am and the State Department. Soon their neighbors came over to see if there was anything they could do; a representative of the Camden *Courier Post* had already visited their house and interviewed them. The mother said a very close friend began answering the phone to intercept all phone calls. "All he was saying was that the (family is) not saying anything. They are waiting to hear officially from Pan Am exactly what is going on.

"Well, this television crew shows up (from Philadelphia) and tries to come in; in fact, they got as far as our porch, and (our friend) went out — and (he) is very tall and very big — and he said, 'Why are you here?'

"'Well,' the girl said, 'the (family) said they would talk to us.' And (our friend) said, 'You just called, didn't you?' And the girl didn't know what to do. Mind you, the cameras were starting to roll already. Well, (our friend) proceeded to call this woman some not nice names at all, and all of a sudden the lights went dim, the camera went down and that was it."

In another New Jersey community the brother-in-law of a woman whose husband had died in the disaster arrived with his wife to be with her. The brother-in-law recalled how he tried to protect the young widow from media attention. "I just went to her house and took control, and I wouldn't let them talk to her," he recalled. But one journalist kept him on the phone for 10 minutes and the brother-in-law finally agreed to let this reporter come to the house — without a camera. "I turned away all the news stations," he said. "With what she was going through, I didn't want her put through it, so I wouldn't let anyone see her. One local guy hit a nerve with me, so I allowed him to come over. He said, 'Look, I want to write an obituary.' And I said, 'Well, look (these are the) ground rules. We're going to talk about (the deceased) and nothing else. If you misbehave, I'm going to physically remove you from the house. No cameras. When I tell you to leave, you're leaving.' And so he was good, but I was very wary of the press." As he did with every major decision concerning the tragedy, the man recalled, he cleared his decision to meet the reporter with his widowed sister-in-law.

Some families, however, sought public acknowledgment of their loss. In Minnesota, the sister of one of the U.S. servicemen who died on the plane heard a radio report referring to two people from that state as Pan Am 103 victims, but giving no details about them. Her parents remember her announcing, "Mother, I'm not going to let my brother go unnoticed," and calling one of the local television channels. The parents said they did not want to do it at the time, but acceded to their daughter's wishes. The mother recalled the TV newsman telling them that he would be asking them some questions. "'If you don't answer, that's fine,' he says, 'but we'll make it basic. What we really want to know is how you felt at the time that you heard of the crash.' The guy was very, very good. He would ask us a question. We would answer it. And he says, 'If it's too hard to answer, we'll just cut it out. I won't ask it again.'"

The woman said he asked her husband, who had a heart condition, just one question, "How are you holding up?" "This was before I had my double bypass," the husband explained. "And he was really nice about this whole situation," his wife added.

The family soon realized that local police were keeping an eye on the house, questioning any one who pulled up in front about who they were and what they wanted.

In some other localities, grieving relatives found police playing a similar role. "From the moment it happened, police started cruising in front of our house," a Long Island, New York, man said. "And the following morning we got a phone call from the mayor — we live in a very small town — and she asked, 'Would you like a policeman stationed at your door to keep anybody away?' and I said, 'No, it's really okay, the media have been pretty responsible at this point.' She said, 'Well, okay, look, if you change your mind, and want somebody there to keep people away, you just call me.' Small towns, I think, respond that way."

The father recalled that phone calls started a little more than an hour after the family heard about the plane. "We were telling everyone we really were not interested in an interview, conversation or anything at this point. In every instance, in almost every instance, they backed off. 'We'll give you a breather, and we'll call you back.' or 'Let us know. This is so-and-so. Here's the number.' It was silly for them to even offer a number because the last thing I was going to do was take a reporter's phone number. But then they started to knock on our door. They started camping outside. They'd knock on the door and ask if they could interview...No, 'Well, do you mind if we take a picture of your house — outside.' That is ridiculous. What for? I guess they felt they had to do something. You can't stop them from taking photographs of the house, but..."

The following day, the father said, he began selectively to speak to the press. On the whole, he said, his family's experience had been very good. "A couple of them became a little bit persistent, but you got the feeling that they had a job they had to do, and they were going about it as best they could. They were sensitive about it, and they weren't real happy that they were intruding either."

But one mother came home to find that a reporter had entered her home while she was out. He was sitting in her kitchen. She ordered him out, and he then wrote an article that included criticism of her housekeeping.

Some American families felt compelled to go to Lockerbie. The brother-in-law of the New Jersey widow left for Scotland the next day. "I just had this need to see what had happened," he said.

Another man, whose businessman brother had been on board the plane, cited a sense of duty that stemmed from his family's values. His father had died a few months earlier. "I know that in my family, if it were me, my brother would go, my father would have gone. That's just the way we were brought up," he said. At the Pan Am terminal, airline personnel told him that the initial report they received was that there were no survivors. "The first thing I remember saying is, 'Can we go there?' And they said, 'Yeah, if you want to go, there's a flight that goes out tomorrow.' I said, 'Well, put me on it.'"

He returned home about 2 or 3 o'clock in the morning. "I didn't get much sleep that night. I was talking to my wife who was really shook by it. We started saying, 'Should I or shouldn't I go?' There was some doubt, and I remember at 7 a.m. on 'Good Morning, America,' I'll never forget. The show started with a picture of picking up a passenger off the roof who was still intact in the seat, and I jumped out of the bed and said, 'I'm going, and there's no ifs, ands or buts about it.' And that's what got me definitely, without any question, to go.

"And I went because of the factor that I would be able to identify my brother or... One thing that most of us who did go talked about a little bit later was that maybe it could be one of these miracle stories that you read about in the paper or you read in a novel, you know, there's one survivor. And so therefore, there would need to be someone there."

What family members did not anticipate was that the journey to Lockerbie would make them the focus of the international news corps seeking a fresh angle on the story.

The first man traveled with a group of 15 relatives on December 22, the second in a group of seven on December 23. Pan Am initially tried to keep the first group in London until the situation became less chaotic, but the first man and two others insisted on going to Lockerbie right away, while the others in his group arrived a few days later. Once he arrived in Scotland the man felt restricted by the way social workers were trying to protect relatives from the horrors of the tragedy. "I didn't go over there to sit around," he said. "And I more or less escaped from the protection that they had you under over there, and I went out and saw the sites on my own, and I blended in, in my work boots and my jeans."

When he came back from viewing the wreckage, he met the veteran police press officer who had come from Glasgow to take charge of media relations for the investigation. "They found out what I had done, and what I had seen, and somehow they brought Angus Kennedy to me. He happens to be a very close personal friend of mine now."

Kennedy, he recalled, asked him, "Since you've done all that and seen all that, how are you?" The American man said, "I'm okay, but I'm not going to sit here, I'm going to do something. And if you make me sit here, I'm going to go out and do what I did again." He remembered Kennedy said, "Okay, well, if you want to do something, we can hold this media off (from the other American relatives) for 36 hours. Will you go out there and do a press conference with me?" The man at first refused for fear it would expose his sister-in-law back home to media attention. Kennedy told him, "Well, you think about it for five minutes, and I'll be right back. You said you wanted to help and this is what you can do to help."

The man felt he should check with his sister-in-law before making any such decision. "So I got a plan in my head and I sat there for a few minutes, and I called (her), and I said, 'They want me to do this.' I said, 'I'm going to try to make a deal with this guy that if I do this for you, you'll help me get (her husband's body) real fast, and I can have access to all these rooms (in the Incident Control Centre, which served as the nerve center for the investigation) and everything.' So I said, 'If you don't want me to do this, I won't. And if you want me to, I will. I'll leave it up to you because it's not my right. I won't mention your name. Part of the deal will be that if I do this, you'll get my name but I won't say who I'm here for.' Because I didn't want the press banging down her door back home in Jersey. She said, 'Yes, I want you to do it.'"

When he explained his terms, he said Kennedy told him, "That's fine, we can do that. And I promise you can have the run of the place, and I'll help you as much as I can. I can't make any promises that I'll find him today or not. But I'll help you."

Once the man agreed to do the press conference, Kennedy briefed him on what would happen. "I was just very fortunate to have met up with (Kennedy), because he's just the consummate professional. And he took me into this room and we talked for maybe 10 minutes before we did the press conference." Kennedy explained the areas to avoid speaking about that might compromise the investigation under Scottish law, which is very strict about publicity that might prejudice the accused's right to a fair trial. "And he just told me, 'If at any point you're uncomfortable, that's it. Just let me know, and we'll end it.'

"And we went out there and it was like nothing I'd ever experienced before. I mean, it was the world press there. They took me in this room, and there's like — there must have been 70 people from all over the world, and I wasn't prepared for that. I don't think anyone could be prepared for that. So it was a very emotional time. It was a very hard thing to do. And I did it, and I did it for maybe 10 or 12 minutes, sat there, and then I couldn't take it anymore, and the press was very good. They asked me a couple of questions, and I got angry once. For the most part, the press behaved admirably from what I've seen and know of the press in the past, when things of this nature occur. And I was very wary of the press, but they did behave themselves admirably — at that point."

That was the last of his dealings with the media, although some members of the press did learn where he was staying and showed up at his hotel. The hotel keepers ousted them unceremoniously. Because the news conference was seen on television in Lockerbie, it gave him a chance to make contact with the local people. "Everywhere I went, 'Oh, I saw you on the telly,'" he said. That recognition also helped him bring about the release of his brother-in-law's body, in a way.

"I mean I immediately realized the power of the press and what it was getting me; it was getting me information," he said. "It was my allegiance with them that allowed me access to places that no other family member had, and I used that. I used it as a journalist would, I guess. And I used that clout, if you will, to gain access to areas, and to get certain things accomplished. So in that aspect, I had a good experience; it wasn't something I really enjoyed doing. It was a difficult thing."

The relationship he built with the Scottish police and the understanding he gained by having access to briefings inside the Incident Control Centre would become very important to the American families in the future, but at the time it allowed him to stay away from the media and work for the release of his brother-in-law's body. "I was hidden; when I went to Mass, I was able to go up the back door and I was able to stay away from (the media) after that. But what it did allow me was to actually get (his body) out of there."

While some people from Pan Am who were sent to Lockerbie were described by this man as very helpful, he expected more leadership from its management. "The real people from Pan Am who were compassionate and helpful were the rank-and-file. They lost people on that flight, too, who were their colleagues and their friends. And the people that should have taken over just totally collapsed."

He had been doing all the paperwork to allow the body to be released, when a Pan Am management representative came to him and said they would not be able to release the body to him until the next day. "I really lost my temper at that point. The memorial service had been set up (in New Jersey and could not be postponed). And I said, 'Well, that's it. I'm going to get him, and he's going to be at that memorial service. We're not having a memorial service without him.' And (Pan Am) just were of no help. When I finally decided my course of action, I walked into the Pan Am room and I just started flipping out. I said, 'You got 15 minutes to get that body released to me. Or,' I said, 'I'm going to walk out this door, and the press is camped outside and

I'm going to tell them what the hell you people are doing here.' About 15 minutes later I had the body, and I flew home on British Air — only because I threatened to expose what they were doing over there — what they weren't doing — through the media."

The other American relative who told us about his experiences in Lockerbie took a very different approach to the situation. In fact, the strategies the two men followed were so different that they never came in contact with each other during that initial stay in the small Scottish village, although later they were to become close allies. The group flying up on December 23 arrived in London and were immediately transferred to a British Airways Express flight to Glasgow, where they were put on a shuttle bus for the drive down to Lockerbie and after they had been riding for a while the bus stopped at what was described to them as a state college. "They had set up a buffet table of food for us, and there was a representative from the American embassy there and there were Pan Am personnel," this man recalled. "They set up some cots, and they asked us if we would like to have some food and rest and maybe go in the next day. And I said, you know, 'Well, how far are we from Lockerbie?'" When they were told it was about five minutes away, the man recalled saying, "You know, it's taken nearly 24 hours to get here. Our loved ones are most likely dead. There's no need for us to rest here. If we wanted to rest, we wouldn't have made this trip. So they put us immediately back in the little shuttle bus they had and they took us to Lockerbie."

That brought the group, which had been kept away from the media as it moved through the various airport terminals, face-to-face with news people. "When we were coming down the street to Lockerbie Academy, you could see that there was maybe about 20 to 25 people in the press, especially the TV press, and a lot of police," the man said. "At the time, we turned away from them and went down a side street, which I now know was just a side street to the ice rink, right across the street from the Academy. I was impressed. I remember sitting in the bus, thinking to myself, 'Gee, they've got their act together pretty much. They're going to take us in the back way.' And they let us off the bus, and that was not true. As we got off the bus, all of a sudden lights hit me, and the press had run down the side street to get to us, and we had the police escort us all the way up the street to the Academy. And this one fellow (from) one of the major networks kept trying to stick a mike in my face. You know, 'How do you feel, how do you feel, how do you feel?' And about halfway up, I just turned on him and said, 'Jesus Christ, how the hell do you think I feel?' And he said, 'Well, just give me a statement, just give me a statement,' and the police pushed him away. So that was the initial encounter, and we went into the Academy where people were all in a state of shock and chaos."

The next day this man and some of the other relatives went surreptitiously to Sherwood Crescent, the site of the huge crater created by the impact and explosion of the wings and part of the fuselage. "We realized at that point, on Christmas Eve around 11 a.m., there was no hope of anyone being alive," he said.

Then this man began working from the relatives lounge that had been set up in the third floor art room of Lockerbie Academy, going through the channels that were being established for the American families. "The key time of protection against the press was, I would say, December 23 to the day after Christmas. We were the story until they announced it was a bombing." So police barricades and escorts were set up and the group was housed at a secluded hotel about 12 miles south of Lockerbie. "The press didn't know where we were staying because (authorities) were concerned, and rightfully so, that if the press found out where we were staying, they would just have descended onto the place. There would have been no protection."

Although the relatives' lounge was off-limits to the media, some other entrances to Lockerbie Academy were unguarded and that led to this man giving an interview. On Christmas Eve day, he was walking with his Pan Am liaison to the cafeteria when the same television newsman who had been so troublesome when he arrived in Lockerbie came up behind him. The man recalled that the reporter said, "Do you remember who I am?" "I was startled for a minute and said, 'Yeah. What do you want?' He said, 'Look, I just need a short interview. If you give me that, I'll leave you alone.' I said, 'Are you sure?' He said, 'Yeah.' I said, 'Well, okay, let's go get it done with and then leave us alone.' We went outside and did a 30-second bite...and from that point on they never bothered us when we went out. Because every time we walked out from that point, the camera crews all said, 'He helped us. Let them go.'"

The man's brother-in-law went down on Christmas Eve to one of the little pubs in Lockerbie, where he met a couple of guys from CBS Radio who said they needed an interview and he said, "Why don't you interview my brother-in-law?" He came back to the Academy and told this man, "Look, now you don't have to do it. But I've set this up and if you would do it, it would really help the situation." So it was arranged that the interview would take place in the police station right across from the Catholic Church, just before the family went in for Mass. "So when we got off the bus and there was press all around there, the police quickly escorted me across the street to the police station and that's how I did the interview."

The news conference announcing that a bomb had been the cause of the disaster was held December 28. "That changed the whole focus of what the media were doing," the man recalled. Interest in the American relatives ceased;

the story in Lockerbie became the bomb. That meant the families who had been staying 12 miles away to help shield them from the media could move to the Dryfesdale Hotel, located on the outskirts of Lockerbie, where all the rooms had been rented to Pan Am. This man stayed there until January 1, the day his brother's body was positively identified and then released so he could accompany it home.

In retrospect, the man said, going to Lockerbie "was one of the biggest, smartest, and most prudent decisions I made. Because I did not know at the time (that) no one back home was getting any information.[8] In other words, I just assumed that I was getting what everyone else was getting. I just remember calling home — and I'd call home five, six, seven times a day because British Telecom had set up an open access line home without any charge to the relatives — and my wife kept saying to me 'Strange, you don't realize what is going on. It's awful,' and so forth. I couldn't understand what she was talking about. But if I wasn't there giving any information, it would have been even worse because there was no information going home to the people, either to the Pan Am employees in New York or to the relatives."

The announcement that there had been a bomb on board brought another round of media attention to the doorsteps of grieving families in America. A television newswoman, who had originally come out to Long Island to ask families the standard "How do you feel?" question shortly after the event, returned to the home of one family. The brother of the victim opened the door and she asked, "Well, how do you feel about it now that it is a bomb?" He recalled answering, "I've known all along. It's kind of obvious." She invited him to come outside because she wanted to talk to him, asked a lot of questions, then looked at her cameraman. "You got all that?" she asked. It was only then that the brother realized the conversation had been taped. "Maybe if I'd opened my eyes a little bit I would have seen the camera, but I just wasn't looking for that. I was just speaking one-on-one. It isn't so much that I would have refused to be on camera, had I known. I think she just wanted to make an impression on her superiors (with her reporting technique)." He said he was glad she had caught him instead of his mother or father because they were still shattered. "I'm sure in a lot of other households it would have been a big problem, too. So sometimes I think the press can go a little bit too far."

But his family soon began to see the media as a potential source of help, too, especially in gaining access to information. The brother remembered talking to a newsman who was doing a small profile of the victim, and asking the reporter if he had any access to a seating chart. This was a couple of days after the news that a bomb had gone off in the front luggage compartment, right under the Clipper Class. "We wanted to know where he was sitting, if he was sitting right on top of the bomb or if he had been in the last row, whatever," the brother said. "It was important to us because that's all we had at that point. And Pan Am just told us they couldn't tell us the information. I explained exactly the situation, and (the newsman) said, 'Well, let me get back to you.' Believe it or not, about an hour later he called, not to ask any more questions, just to tell us where he was sitting. "As it turned out, he was right over where the bomb was, and in those couple of weeks before we got the body back, it was comforting in a strange sort of way at least to know that he was right on top of it, you know."

Families reported that some friends and neighbors avoided them in the wake of the tragedy, apparently because they did not know what to say. One of the men who visited Lockerbie recalled that his family had been told by some friends and neighbors that they had driven around the block several times, trying to gain the courage to ring the doorbell and express condolences. A mother spoke about spotting a family friend in a grocery store who darted quickly down another aisle, apparently to avoid speaking to her. Such behavior left families feeling isolated, as did the attitude of the airline and the State Department. In some cases, being interviewed by the media or acts of kindness by journalists helped ease this sense of being alone. This same Long Island family agreed to being interviewed by an ABC newsman from New York on camera. "He also was just very, very friendly," the son said, adding that he recognized that it's easy to associate the press with being "right on top, reporting dirty laundry." But he said, "This event I think touched a lot of news writers' and press's hearts. I'm not sure if that happens a lot in the business or not, but it just seemed like some of the people really wanted to make us feel better and do something for us, and that was nice because I think, looking back, that we needed things done for us."

Funerals and memorial services took place at different times over the days and weeks that followed. Most received some media attention. Families varied considerably in their response, ranging from welcoming the media presence to deeply resenting the intrusion. It was important to them that the media respect the ground rules they set.

What happened at the funeral of the serviceman from Minnesota illustrates the kind of stress that can be added to this difficult day. Two television channels had asked if they could be there, and the family had given permission as long as they stayed at a distance. What caused distress was that a cameraman from a third channel showed up and was right beside the casket, taking close-ups of the family.

"Two of the military color guard walked over to this cameraman, and told him to take his distance," the father said. "What made me feel bad was that two people I'd told to be a distance were a distance, and the other cameramen were up so close, that they took pictures of my daughter crying and me and my husband," the mother recalled. "And everybody's saying, 'Why are they so close? They're not supposed to be this close.'"

This family was pleasantly surprised that the local newspapers waited until the funeral was over to approach them for interviews. "They took us one at a time and they talked to us and asked us what was the most important thing that we could remember that our son had done, that stuck in our minds," the mother said. "He says to my daughter, 'Okay, it's your turn.' My son-in-law went and told him. My husband talked to him. My brother talked. And it just seemed like everything was printed in the paper like it was said. And it was really a beautiful story."

For a Long Island family who had a memorial service on December 26, however, the media would have been more welcome at the service than they were when they visited the family in its home immediately afterwards. Crowds of people, many of who had come from great distances, came back to the house. Just as things were settling down, they received a phone call from a reporter. They remembered she said, "I'm in the neighborhood and I've interviewed other families. Can I come?"

"She did take us into a side room to talk when we wanted to be with people — some of whom had driven from Scranton leaving at five in the morning and people who had dropped Christmas right where it was to be supportive of us," the mother recalled. The family was also troubled by the reporter's approach, which they assumed to be the result of inexperience. "She didn't seem to know what she wanted of us, and then when a photographer came, she didn't want the photo inside. She had us come outside without coats and line up on the front stoop and then we came back in."

Although they felt her reporting was inaccurate — in some ways, for them embarrassingly so, they were surprised by what the victim's younger brother, also a college student, told her. "She had asked him things that we wouldn't have thought of asking him, which was good in a way because we were stunned by his answers," the victim's mother said. One of the priests had said that it was terrible that this should have happened at this time of year, and then he was quoted as saying, "and I wanted to stand up and stop him and say, 'No, it isn't terrible that it happened at this time of year. It's terrible it happened, but if it had to happen, this was the best time of year because we were all together.'" "And that to me was so original, and I didn't know it until I read it in the paper. So that actually while the girl, I thought, handled us clumsily, she certainly got something that she came after. If it was a surprise to the mother in the family, she was doing something right."

The report referred twice to fresh ham and turkey, when actually fresh ham would be pork. A local butcher and his wife had baked two huge hams and roasted two turkeys, which were being served. Also the Marriott Hotel, where the son had worked as a life guard, sent 40 dozen cookies, 40 dozen pastries, pasta salad, coleslaw, potato chips and several pounds of rolls and bread. But the newspaper article only mentioned cookies, so that the mother felt obligated to write a letter of apology to the hotel manager.

To her credit, the family said, the reporter did call the father's office the next day to apologize for the way the story appeared in print. "It turned out five of them had been sent out to interview families and then all turned in their notes and one person wrote it."

This family would have preferred to have the Mass covered, "but to come into the house toward the end of the thing when we already were exhausted was not great timing," the mother said. "But it was some sort of coverage; it was publicity for Pan Am 103. That is not what we were looking for at the time. Now I will phone a television station or a radio station. If I hear a word I phone right in and sometimes get on the air."

The family from the Camden area also had a memorial service on December 26, but arrived at the church to find the media waiting inside. "Our dear beloved pastor had allowed the media in already. So we had the three news channels and our 'friends' from the *Courier Post* again. We had a picture of (him) with flowers on either side, and (one of the reporters) wanted a picture of his girlfriend kneeling in front of this picture, which I thought was absolutely horrendous. (The girlfriend) said absolutely not now. Again, we had our friends doing all kinds of intercepting for us, which was wonderful. Finally, the photographer and reporter took some of (his) fraternity brothers from Syracuse and photographed them outside. I wasn't pleased even with that. You know, there is so much going on at the time that you don't really think clearly and having never had to deal with the media, suddenly you're dropped into this cauldron. When we watched the 11 o'clock news that night — and they did show some portions of the service — the one reporter said that knowing (their son) was in communications at the Newhouse School, he would have realized that this was the most difficult type of story to cover."

The family of a Central New York couple killed in the tragedy had very different experiences with the media at funerals on either side of the Atlantic — the wife was American and the husband English. The family was well acquainted with members of the New York media, and felt they handled the story sensitively, but in a little town in northern England, they faced the British tabloids. "Those were the only reporters we had trouble with," the wife's sister said. She said the husband's family had asked the press to stay away, but tabloid reporters snuck into the 400-year-old church. They described the wife's sister as her mother, and "they just didn't get their facts straight and didn't quote things right." Photos of the service, she said, were "smeared" across the papers.

For families of Syracuse students, the last major event of this initial phase of the grieving process was a memorial service in the huge Carrier Dome, the school's covered sports arena, on January 18. There they were seated far from the area reserved for the media, but for those relatives who wanted to speak to news people, news conferences were arranged.

Young people mourn: Syracuse University

In two days, exams would be over, and many students had left for home. But on the afternoon of December 21, the students still at Syracuse University were preoccupied with taking their finals or studying for them.

One recalled that she had been in her room preparing for a test the next day. "I heard somebody — I thought she was laughing at first and then I could tell that she was sobbing, and when you're in a sorority house, this happens quite frequently. So I figured that it was probably like a boyfriend problem or something like that, and so I went out and asked, 'Are you okay? Do you need somebody to talk to?' And she just like screamed out to me, 'You don't understand.' And she was sobbing in these little broken sentences, 'There was a crash.' And that's how I heard about it. Then I turned on the television, and it just was like a snowball after that. Everybody in the house started going nuts, and, I don't know, it was just like a snowball effect. I think that I'll always remember that moment. I mean it's going to be like, like I'm sure everybody remembers where they were when the shuttle exploded. I remember that so distinctly. My room-mate says it's just like my parents' generation remembering Kennedy's assassination. I remember it like it happened yesterday."

Another woman student who had studied in the London program the previous spring recalled hearing someone mention something about a plane crash out of London. "It didn't even hit me that could be any way connected to anybody being on that flight or that it was even headed to New York or anything. And I had two sorority sisters who were over there at the time. And then one girl came running into my bedroom hysterical, saying a Miss C. Smith was on that plane, and I'm saying, 'Now don't get out of hand. Smith is the most common name in America, and I'm sure there were hundreds of Smiths.'"

They immediately tried calling the university's Division of International Programs Abroad (DIPA), and asked how many C. Smiths were in the program. "Well, they wouldn't say a word. They wouldn't say anything. So then we found out from someone who had received a letter from her the day before, saying when she'd be coming home, that it was a sister in the sorority house." So they started watching television, and the local 6 p.m. news began scrolling a list of names they had obtained from the airline.

"I don't think it hit me until I actually saw the name going by on the television," the woman student said. "I was crazy. I was just hysterical. It just hit very close to home. I felt very personally connected, not just because I knew someone out there, but because I had been in London, and I had studied the same things that they had. I came home with my great stories, writing in my journal, what my last few thoughts were. I kept thinking, 'My God, it could have been me.' I should not have been thinking that. It wasn't me, thank God. But it was the fact there were all these other students who were just like me; that were also Newhouse (School of Public Communications) students, fellow Syracuse students who also studied in the same places I did, went to the same places I did. I was a wreck."

A male student had been working on a paper that was due the next day. About 4 o'clock he heard something on his clock radio about a plane crash. "They said it had fallen out of the skies...estimates that between 20 and 25 students were on it...Immediately I turned on the TV and all the networks had stuff on. I put everything aside and just watched TV." After a while he went to the student radio station, WJPZ, just to see if there was anyone there, and found student reporters. "Six or seven people just ran in when the 6 o'clock news began (on television). When they started rolling the names on, one after the other, people just started running out screaming and sobbing. That's really when it hit me, right then — people running out, saying, 'I knew that person.' It was just utter chaos.

"I called my father that night, maybe half an hour later. He hadn't heard it. He was just shocked." He called home again later and talked to his mother, who had heard it on the radio. She told him the first thing that had struck her was that they had wanted him to go to London that semester, and he had resisted saying, "I'm not too sure about leaving the country for a semester. I want to stay here." This student was affected even though he thought at the time he did not know any of the victims personally. Later he realized he had taken classes with some of the victims and that someone he knew had lost a sister in the disaster.

Another student had driven to a mall north of Syracuse that afternoon to get some Christmas cards. He was walking through the mall when he happened to glance at a television store and noticed that the star anchor for CBS, Dan Rather, was on the screen, even though it was not quite 5 o'clock and the regular CBS evening newscast does not start in Syracuse until 6:30. "I knew something must have happened, something bad, because they don't break in with anchors except when something really great happens." So he began watching as the television report told of a London–New York plane disappearing from radar over Scotland, more out of a "morbid fascination with plane crashes" than anything else. "So people keep coming up and ask me what's going on, and I tell them. Then this woman says, 'You know 20 or 30 SU students were on the plane.' "

That started him thinking, he said, about two students he knew who were studying in London, and he went back to campus. He ate dinner and talked with someone who said the names were being read on television and that only about one out of 10 students in the London program had been on the plane. One of the names was Shapiro, the last name of one of his friends. He called DIPA, but they would not tell him anything, so he went to the Women's Building, where the university public relations is headquartered, because he calculated correctly that media would be there waiting for information. "I gave a couple of interviews to the television stations," he said, explaining that he thought it was fair exchange for information he was hoping they could give him. After that he did a lot of phoning around, watching CNN, and finally learned that it was a different Shapiro who had died on the plane.

However, another student approached a television reporter, asked if the name of one of his friends was on the list, and was told that it was. The look of shock on his face registered with television viewers, especially students. The camera had been running throughout the exchange.

Some students learned about the tragedy in other ways. One, sitting an exam, saw his room-mate walk into the auditorium, speak to his teacher and then both point at him. "My room-mate came back to me and just said, 'Call your father,' and left. I sat there, thinking to myself, 'This is awfully strange, you know. I'm taking a final exam, and he comes in here to tell me to call my father. I think he means for me to call him right now.'"

He had some difficulty persuading his instructor that he needed to leave and then had more trouble finding a phone that worked. He finally found one and reached his mother, who told him that his brother's plane had gone down, "and to please come home as quickly as you can." "A friend drove me home just because he didn't think I should be driving. And I got home that night, and about an hour or two later, the phones started ringing — not the State Department, just the press calling, you know, every five minutes."

An art student recalled that she had been away from campus for three days and was feeling "very much on edge." She was on campus finishing up some projects. "The radio was on, and they mentioned a plane crash. It was funny. I heard the words England and Scotland. I just felt like something hit me, but then (I thought), it has nothing to do with me. It just never occurred to me that my friend — I knew she was in England — but it never occurred to me that she was coming home. I didn't know what day she was coming home. I just put it out of my mind."

When she got back to her apartment, one of her room-mates came home and said, "Did you hear about the plane crash?" "I said like 'Oh, yeah,' and he just kind of looked at me and said, 'Did you know there were SU students on board?' and I said like 'No, no way,' and he said, 'Yes, quite a few.' And so I ran over to the TV and turned it on and there was nothing on the TV. And I sat there waiting and waiting, being fascinated with it, and then remembering that (one of her room- mates) was over there and then figuring, 'Oh well, I mean there's nothing wrong.' But I had to see."

The room-mate who told her about the crash left and she was home alone. "Then the phone rang and I answered it. There was this woman who said, 'Is this (the name of her room-mate studying in London's) apartment?' And I said, 'Uh, yeah.' She said, 'Are you one of her room-mates?' And I said, 'Yes, she's away this semester.' She said, 'Well, I'm a reporter from the *Post-Standard*. I was wondering if you could update us on her condition.' And I said, 'What are you talking about?' And she said, 'Have you heard?' At that point I was just numb. I was stupefied to the point where suddenly I could have put pieces together, but I just refused to. And she just started asking me all these questions, and I said, 'Would you please tell me what you're trying to say?' And she said, 'Ma'am, have you heard what's going on?' and I said, 'No,' ...and I said, 'Wait a minute, are you trying to tell me that my friend's name was on the list of people who were supposed to be on that plane?' She said, 'Yes.'

"And at that point, I don't know what I did. I think I just hung up and passed out — or something." She called her parents, who decided she was too distraught to come home on her own. They drove to campus to get her. "I know that night, all night, I watched TV, but that from there on, until (three months later), I did not listen to the radio or watch TV."

A cheerleader had stayed on campus for the basketball game that night. She came off the elevator of her dorm and saw "all these people crowded round the television set...with stricken looks on their faces." She recalled that they sat in silence for 45 minutes or more. "Nobody's talking, nobody's saying anything. It struck me more like I was in a daze than anything else. I guess I was on auto pilot. I didn't know if the kids that I knew so well were on the flight or not — we had no idea, and we had to go to the basketball game. They didn't cancel it, didn't do anything about it."[9]

Many of the spectators arriving at the Carrier Dome had no hint of the tragedy until the singing of *The Star Spangled Banner* ended and the game's announcer handed the microphone to the Lutheran chaplain, the Rev. Michael Schultz-Rothermel. He asked them to remain standing and described very briefly the tragedy. An audible gasp swept across the stands from some of those hearing it for the first time. Then he asked them to join him in a moment of silence and a prayer: "God of compassion and love, in our frailty, we surrender ourselves to you now. Hear in this silence our deep felt concern and anguish for the lives of these students and all the other passengers."

Rothermel had been a target of media attention during those few minutes, but then their focus returned to the SU cheerleaders. They were after a picture for the front page, not a basketball action shot. One reporter asked the cheerleader who was part of this study for her name, her year in school and her major and then asked, "How do you feel about this?" "How do you think I feel about this?" she shot back. Reflecting on the exchange nearly a year later, she said, "That was a rude comment on my part, but I think (the question) was totally unwarranted. How did he think I felt?"

But the worst part, she said, was the photographers. "They wanted a close-up of our faces. They wanted to see us...lose our composure." She became determined not to give them what they wanted. She recalled fixing her gaze on "one of those stupid signs people put up" because it was a fixed point. "I looked at this fixed point — it was above this guy's head — I was blocking him out as best as I could — and I don't think I gave him what he wanted...because I never saw any pictures of me like that." She felt it was very important to contain her emotions. "I felt they were really exploiting the situation we were in. I mean, is that the perfect picture of the tragedy? The cheerleader in uniform is crying. And I wasn't going to give it to him. I wasn't going to give it to him."

The view from the stands was different. Many had arrived in the Dome not knowing about the accident. The chaplain's announcement and call for a moment of silence was stunning. Like the people who had played bingo in Lockerbie that night, most kept to their original plan and stayed to watch the game. But the university was severely criticized by many for letting the game go ahead, and Chancellor Melvin Eggers intimated on nationwide television the next morning that he probably should have canceled the event.

Students had started arriving in late afternoon at Hendricks Chapel, the interfaith center for the campus. The room-mates of one victim went after it was dark, but before the 6 o'clock news. "We avoided the big mass ceremony that everyone was invited to because we thought that it would be impersonal," one of them recalled. "I couldn't think of any other people; I could only think of myself. Grieving is a selfish thing. I didn't want to hear all the students."

The chaplains at Hendricks, responding to the phone calls and visitors to the chapel, hurriedly prepared an informal, inter-faith vigil. It seemed too soon for a memorial service, but not too early to pray together. They passed the word to the local media, many of whom had already been in contact with the chaplain's office, that there would be a vigil at 9 p.m. Broadcast media were the only way to alert the campus community and the people of Syracuse to the service. At 8 p.m., an hour before the scheduled vigil, little clutches of students sat in the white, straight-backed pews of the sanctuary. A newswoman slid in behind one such group and quietly spoke to them. A casually dressed man with a camera wandered down the center aisle to the front of the sanctuary, looking around, apparently sizing up vantage points from which to shoot during the service. Soon, from the rear of the chapel, where main doors open onto wide steps, noise intruded. A faculty member, going to inspect, found a cluster of television crews, their lights glaring across the darkened campus, focused on students as they arrived for the vigil. "As soon as I walked in, there was a girl hysterical on my shoulder," one student recalled. Then reporters spotted them. "I was completely aghast. I had three reporters asking me how I felt. It's like, well, what do you think — how do you feel?"

As the chapel filled, media were asked to stay away from the area in front of the raised platform, where chaplains and representatives of various faiths would lead the service. Photographers were asked not to use flash. But the emotion generated by the event, especially in the moments of meditation between scriptures and sacred music, created compelling pictures and the whir of automatic levers advancing film echoed from both sides of the sanctuary. Soon flashes began going off. Upstairs, at the back of one balcony, a local television reporter "went live" over the protests of students in that area.

An advertising major said the conduct of the media inside the chapel made her have second thoughts about her choice of profession. "I turned to a TV major and said, 'I'm ashamed to be a Newhouse student — truly embarrassed to be going into the communications industry. Look at this circus. I'm embarrassed to be part of it.' That was the scariest thing, knowing I had three months to graduate. I was so upset."

Another student called the media presence in Hendricks Chapel "a disaster." "One of my friends lost her best friend from childhood on the plane, and she was hysterical at Hendricks. And we're sitting next to her and kind of on the side where photographers were facing away from us. And when they saw (her) crying, they all turned around and focused on her. And just pretty much stared her down until she was like crying the most, and then took pictures. We were trying to make it clear to the reporters that we really didn't want them taking pictures of her. We were glaring at them, doing anything we could to stop it." At the end of the service, the student grieving for her childhood friend went to light a candle for her, and the young woman who was recalling the scene said that a reporter asked, "Would you like to say any last words to her?" The witness to the scene called it a "callous question."

A young couple sobbed in each other's arms, unaware that a radio newsman was holding a microphone by their faces to capture the sound of their grief.

A faculty member stepped between the newsman and the young couple. "Back off," she told him. "I'm only doing my job," the reporter protested, but he did step back and waited to approach the couple again when they regained their composure.

That kind of confrontation occurred repeatedly, not only that night, but in the following days, the Rev. Michael Rothermel said. Although he felt the media had an important and positive role to play in helping the chaplains minister to the dispersed campus community and the larger community, he himself became angry after the vigil. "We opened the doors and instead of the darkness of night, it was light! There was just light coming at you from every direction. People couldn't even get down the steps. I simply demanded that the TV people leave the steps. I said, 'Any story you get will be down there.' We just needed those steps, you know. You needed a transition space to go from the sacred space to the public space, where you were then kind of fair game."

Rothermel said he knew media would be there in great numbers. "My only hope was that (they) would be respectful about the way that they approached people rather than imposing themselves. That's why I got angry because some were, in fact, imposing themselves rather than being sensitive and kind. Others were marvelous, so sensitive and so tactful, so almost pastoral, in their approach, to students, athletes, others of us."

Student life during exam period takes on a special rhythm, irregular and less connected than when classes are in session. So some students did not hear the news for hours. One of the students who played a leading role in student-owned and -operated WJPZ radio, left the rock station to meet a friend about 5 o'clock, not knowing of the tragedy. "I got down the stairs, and the general manager was walking by and I saw the look on his face. Just an hour ago he was fine and happy. I couldn't figure out what was going on." The friends went to Cosmo's, a pizza place on the edge of campus, for dinner.

The young man went back to his room and about 8:30 or 9:00 a friend came down the hall and said, "There's been a plane crash and 35 or 40 SU students were on board." "It was really weird. I was just like, oh, wow! It didn't really like hit me, because I didn't know anybody who was abroad last semester." He borrowed a friend's television and sat there watching it. A friend across the hall from the Pi Phi sorority, which had sisters on the plane, came in and said she thought what the radio station was doing was really nice. Students at the station were putting together everything they could gather about the disaster and broadcasting it across the campus, even though regular newscasts on the station had ceased with the beginning of finals week. "Most of the kids had gone (home)," said the student-station executive, "and it didn't even occur to me that we had this news department. So I turned to the station and they were giving updates every 15 or 20 minutes about what was going on, and I was very impressed. In fact, I was very proud of the station and what we were doing." He called and volunteered to help, and about an hour later they did call and ask him to come down.

The next day notices went out to faculty that students who did not feel able to take exams should be treated with understanding. The chapel scheduled a noon memorial service, recognizing that many students, faculty and staff had not been able to attend the vigil the previous evening and, in many cases, had not been aware of it. But by then media had arrived from New York and other major cities. Based on the experience of the previous evening, the chaplains negotiated an agreement they thought would prevent the media from being so intrusive. "We had a rule that the media had to stay upstairs in the balconies, and they were to be stationary. They couldn't move," said Nansie Jensen, who directs counseling services for the chapel. She and another chapel staff member were in the balcony, trying to keep the media from moving around. "There was no way they were going to be stationary. They didn't pay any attention to us whatsoever. We had people asking us for interviews in the middle of the service...It was just chaotic, absolutely chaotic."

Students were leaving campus, anxious to be with their families. "On the plane, everyone was very somber. It was just odd. There was a bunch of students on board, and no one would talk," one remembered. Most of the students on the flight were going to the New York or New Jersey area. This student caught the shuttle to Washington. "It was like a normal flight. I was exhausted emotionally, physically drained, and the woman sitting next to me was trying to stuff this huge suitcase underneath," he said. After he helped her, she asked where he was from. When he said Syracuse, "immediately everybody within earshot looked over to me and then looked away. I guess they didn't want to talk to me. The lady sitting across the aisle gave me *The New York Times*."

When he arrived home, the first thing his father said to him was "I think you should go to London." The student remembers saying, "Right." Going abroad had been one of the factors that originally attracted him to Syracuse University, but after enrolling he became so caught up in working at the student radio station that he saw that as more important. The disaster made him rethink his plans. "Life is just too short to sit around. I figured I (didn't) wanted to be station manager for the rest of my life anyways. I figured I would go to London for an outstanding time — and live."

One student said her family wanted her to go home right away. "I felt more comfortable just being up here at school," she said. "This happened to my Syracuse family, not my family back home, and I wanted to get my life organized here first." When she did get home, her family tried to protect her from the tragedy. They made a point of going out to dinner while the 6 o'clock news was on or to a movie that coincided with the 11 o'clock news. "I couldn't understand why my dad was doing this. He didn't want me to see the coverage. All of a sudden, the newspapers weren't around anymore. CNN used to be on in our house all day. I think the only reason that he didn't want me to see it was because I was such an emotional basket case. He thought if I stayed away from the media, I would get over this faster. Well, I wanted to see it because I wanted to know what was going on. So I'd go downstairs at 2 o'clock in the morning and watch CNN."

After the cheerleader went home, her parents tried to plan activities to help her. "I was having a horrible time with the notion that someone deliberately set a bomb. It was murder rather than mechanical failure, and that's what I could not take. My parents were taking me to this movie I'd been dying to see — to this day, I can't remember what the movie was — and we were in a restaurant, where they've got a bar and a big TV screen." She spotted "News flash on Flight 103" on the screen. "When it said, 'Flight 103,' this bartender, a girl, lady, whatever, turns round and (said), 'Oh, not that crap again,' and switches the channel. And I jumped up and I let her have it, and that's the only time I've ever done anything like that in my life. I got up, and I said — keeping up the standards of Southern propriety — 'Would you turn that back on?' She looked at me (and said), 'What's it to you?' 'That's my goddamn school. Get it the hell back on.' She turned it back on. That just infuriated me."

Asked if she understood, looking back, why she reacted so strongly, she said, "Something affected me that much and somebody cheapened it, desecrated it. Of course, she had no connection to it, but my God, we've got a disaster of unprecedented proportions, and she's saying, 'this crap again.'" But the cheerleader was not happy about her own behavior. "There are things one doesn't do, and this was one of them."

On Christmas Day, two young women who had spent the fall semester studying at the SU London Centre had just arrived in Geneva, Switzerland, and were looking for the famous flower clock. The two room-mates had flown to Italy on December 21, four hours before Pan Am 103 left Heathrow. They planned to travel on the Continent until mid-January, then pick up the rest of their baggage in London and fly back to Syracuse for the start of the semester. They did not look at newspapers or television in Italy because of the language barrier.

While looking for the flower clock, they encountered an American student from Connecticut who was studying at the international law school in Geneva. They talked about the clock, about other major sites in the city and then he asked where they were from. They said "Syracuse University," and he looked at them and said, "You know what happened?" "No, what are you talking about?" one of them asked. As one of the young women recalled, he said, "Well, there was this Pan Am plane carrying Syracuse students that exploded in mid-air." "And I said, 'That doesn't happen. How many survivors were there?' 'You don't understand,' he said. 'There are no survivors. It exploded in mid-air.'" The room-mates looked at each other. He told them it had happened Wednesday. "My thought was, 'We've got to get out of here. This guy's crazy,' and he's like, 'No really, this is true, and I'll show you the newspaper.'"

So he took them to a university — the young woman wasn't sure which one it was — where the reading room was open, even though it was Christmas Day. He showed them a report with a partial list of names. They spotted the names of two people they knew for certain had been on the flight and several Steves, but like many young people who operate on a first-name basis, the room-mates weren't sure which of them had been in the London program. "That was bad enough," the young woman recalled. The law student cooked them spaghetti dinner in his apartment, and the woman's room-mate called her parents, who for some reason thought they were traveling in Scotland. A headline she saw back at the Geneva YMCA summarized the event for her. It said simply "Le Horreur."

The two room-mates kept traveling on the Continent because, they reasoned, the London Centre was closed between semesters. "We didn't go back because we didn't really think we could do anything." Travel became a blur, although the student remembered they did spend New Year's Eve in Belgium. At some point on the Continent they saw an *International Herald Tribune* and read a piece saying the passengers should have been warned about the bomb threats. They also saw an international edition of *Time.*

On January 6 they returned to London. "And when we got there, we just were too antsy there. We just didn't feel right. We went up to Edinburgh. We stayed there for four days, and we were much calmer there." In Scotland, they saw a newspaper story listing the bodies being returned for burial, and a friend was the first name on the list. "I don't think we read any further than that." They had no radio, and the place they were staying did not have a television. "We had thought about going to Lockerbie, and we were seriously going to do that." But they had the impression that the area was sealed off by then, so they stayed in Edinburgh. Each time they called home, they asked not to be told the entire list, because they feared learning about it in a strange place. "We were just waiting until we got to a safe place to find that information out."

They returned to London the weekend right before the second semester started. "We found out the complete list when we got back to the London Centre. And it was four pages long," the woman said. "I guess it was probably different for each one of us, but when I read (a certain friend's) name — that was it. I didn't get hysterical. I didn't freak out. I just kind of existed. And my room-mate and I never got upset at the same time. That's probably how we got through it," she said. "We just basically kind of sat there most of the time, and did what we had to do because there was nothing we could do."

In the weeks that followed the tragedy, many students went to funerals and memorial services. One attended a service for a friend whose body had not been recovered. "So many people were there, and it was like the whole thing was moving in slow motion," the student said. "Obviously it's an emotional thing."

One woman student became a special source of support to the mother of her friend, speaking about her to the media and the FBI. "Her mother couldn't really talk. At that point, I had it together. I knew I had to have it together if I was going to get through this. I knew there were things that I had to do that other people couldn't do. I lived with (her friend) for two years. I knew all her clothing, what her diary looked like. I wanted them to call so I could make her more than just a statistic," she said. "But the least they could do — they knew how hard this is — was to quote me right, quote the best things that I had said."

She gave the media a copy of the eulogy that she prepared and delivered at the funeral. "That took me two weeks to prepare, and I thought it was the most important thing that I had ever done, and probably would ever do. And the next day I bought every newspaper to see how it was dealt with and they misquoted me. I thought, 'All you're doing was standing there with a pen or a tape recorder and cameras at the back of the church, why can't you get it right? That's your job.'"

The two students who learned about the tragedy in Geneva spent their last weekend in London staying with a professor and his wife. That weekend a British Midlands Airways flight crash-landed on the M-1, the main north–south highway in England, after both engines failed. Forty-four died although 82 passengers and crew members survived. "A friend that we'd made in Belgium was supposed to be on that flight — he wasn't, but that was the last thing that happened before we came home," the student recalled. Flying home was "just horrendous." She recognized her grief was mixed with culture shock. "I was very worried about coming back to this country. I was really, really afraid," she said.

Her parents had saved newspapers for her, and she began to understand why they had thought it was a crash. That was the first time she had heard of the early speculation that it might have been structural failure. So she had a very negative impression of American reporting on the story. "I was still stuck with what I had first been told, which was that it blew up in mid-air, and planes just don't do that." She remembered calling her mother from Europe and arguing that it was not a crash, saying, "Well, what did it hit?"

The media did not seek her reaction to the tragedy itself. That aspect of the story was finished. It was just as well, because it was three years after the bombing before she could begin talking about the 35 friends and classmates she had lost.

When classes resumed, a memorial service was held in the Dome January 18, the only structure on campus large enough to accommodate such an event. One television station beamed the ceremony live to the Syracuse community and made the transmission available to other media. Still cameras and reporters were confined to one section. They could turn around and see students, faculty and staff in the stands, but they were behind the families of the victims and the students who had been in London with them during the previous semester. "I liked the way it was one camera — it wasn't that click, click, it was a constant thing," said one of the students who sat in the stands. "But, of course, whenever (the photographer) heard a sigh or a noise out of our section... There was a guy and he was (focused) on us the whole time and we knew it."

In the chapel, a memory book was placed by a candle for each of the student victims so that people who knew them or just wanted to express condolences could write messages. The books were eventually given to the parents.

One student recalled that one of the local television reporters was behaving at the chapel that night as if it were a regular newscast. "It was just like, come on, let's get going. It was joking around. I couldn't believe it, I was just sitting there staring. People were walking right by me."

The student said it seemed as if life on the campus slowed. "And I still think it's slowed down, right now," he said, referring to the end of the spring 1989 semester. "This is a haunted semester," another student in the discussion group said. "The consensus on my floor was that last semester never really ended," said a third. "We just left. We were going home but it wasn't like it was Christmas, I remember, because last year Christmas break was wonderful. You're going home, yeah! after a semester of college. And you're there for Christmas, family, everything. And this time like you were going home, but part of me — like I think everybody, most of the people on this campus, a little bit of them died on the plane."

One of them explained, "You think of the experience you might have shared with the person who was on the plane, and you know that's a part you gave to that person and they took it with them."

What survivors share

In the year following the bombing of Pan Am 103, the mother of one of the victims began a work of sculpture to capture the terrible onset of grief. Suse Lowenstein first photographed herself in the attitude she had assumed involuntarily at the moment when she knew her son Alex had died on the plane: kneeling, her face lifted to the sky, her mouth an open scream. Then she began asking other women who had lost loved ones on Pan Am 103 to come to her studio in Mendham, New Jersey, and be photographed in the position that each, without thinking, had taken the instant they realized their loss.

The sculpture created from those images, "Dark Elegy," testifies eloquently about the impact of Pan Am 103 on the lives of those women. It also makes an important statement about the process of grief. A journalist for *Newsday*, visiting the work, grasped the import immediately; she began her column:

> When a terrorist takes a child's life, there isn't a formula for the mother's grief. One raises her fists to the sky, another pounds them on the earth, yet another curls up into a ball, protecting her arms and legs. Not even a finger sticks out, because so much of her has already been cut off (Raver, p. 3).

Those whose work regularly brings them in contact with bereaved people know that grief is not a simple process. "We need to give each other permission to grieve in the way that's most natural for us. To some people, that means you go in, some people go out, in other words, some withdraw and some need to talk and be with people," said the Rev. Michael Schultz-Rothermel, a chaplain at Syracuse University who watched the grieving relatives and friends and the journalists who covered them.

Part of the problem at Syracuse, Rothermel said, was that many media people assigned to the story apparently knew little about grief, even though, like clergy, journalists must often face crisis situations. Although some news people were sensitive and kind, he said, others in the early days of the crisis appeared to be just out for the story. The latter group violated the space that is needed to grieve. "We all enter a period of first denial and then shock," the chaplain said. "It manifests itself in different ways, and then there's the anger stage... Not knowing that, (media people) were taken aback. There were students who had been crying one moment, and somebody from the media sticks a microphone in their face and the response they got was anger. Again, it was a lack of awareness, a lack of knowledge about really what's natural, what needs to take place, what's normal. It's not normal behavior for people generally in daily events to go around sobbing or screaming or whatever, but on something like this, it's perfectly normal. So give us the space to do that, too."

Several aspects of this tragedy heightened the reaction of families and friends in ways that could have been predicted either by those who work with the grieving or who have studied grief. The Pan Am deaths were violent, unexpected and caused by a deliberate, unexplained act, all factors that increase the distress of the bereaved (Fatah, 1979; Katz & Florian, 1987; McCann & Pearlman, 1990; Raphael, 1986; Shackleton, 1984). It also claimed many young lives, which hit parents and peers especially hard.

"Parents always say that the hardest thing of their lives is to lose a child, no matter how old the child is," Rothermel said. "Maybe they're 60 and the child is 40, or they're 80 and the child is 60. The child dies of natural causes — that's still their baby."

As a campus chaplain, Rothermel also knew that students would be profoundly affected by the tragedy, even those who knew none of the victims personally. "It hit them hard, and it hit them close, and it hit them because it was their peers. For people of the general college age, there is no bigger event, no bigger story, no bigger happening than the death of their peers, because this goes so contrary to their whole life style, their understanding, their sense of — they're young and they know they're not immortal, but they like to think that they can go on, and that these things don't happen to them, and they're invincible. And the consequences, the larger picture, the long-term ramifications, don't enter into their minds, so this happening brought the big things to bear on their lives in such a powerful way."

Research into the grief process supports his observations. Most empirical studies suggest that bereaved youth have a more difficult time recovering than adults (Shackleton, 1984). Raphael (1986) notes that in many ways adolescents' reactions to bereavement are like those of adults, but are colored by the young person's developmental crisis and by social and peer expectations. One study (Ball, 1977) found that younger adults suffered more psychosomatic symptoms, including sleep disorders, following the sudden death of a loved one than did older adults.

Most research on disasters by psychologists gives scant attention to the role of the media, and the few studies that do mention it cast the media in a negative light. Palacios *et al.* (1988) described a "psychological catastrophe" following the Mexico City earthquake, and said the "massive overflow of televised and radio-transmitted information and not the immediate physical impact of the earthquake" was the main traumatic agent (p.282). Another study followed the eruption of Mount St. Helens (Murphy, 1984) and reported that subjects who had lost loved ones believed that such factors as invasion of privacy, inaccuracies in reporting and extensive coverage contributed to delays in their recovery from the loss.

Studies of survivors and the media by communications researchers are relatively rare. A pilot study by Grotta (1986) consisted of 20 in-depth interviews about media coverage of violent crimes, but only four of the interviews were with victims and another four were with families of victims. Elliott (1988) interviewed 58 principal players in the hijacking of TWA Flight 847, including government officials, hostages, families and friends of the hostages, print and electronic journalists and executives. She concluded that some family members were abused by the media during the newsgathering process and that some used the media to try to influence the government or the terrorists.

Shearer (1991) summarized two studies commissioned by the British Broadcasting Standards Council. One was based on qualitative interviews of 54 survivors, 16 of whom had survived a disaster or lost a loved one in a disaster. The rest had survived rape, sexual assault or assault or had a loved one who had been the victim of murder or manslaughter. The other study was based on a random sample of the general public, one-fifth of whom had survived an act of violence. While many of the survivors found the media reporting both necessary and helpful, they also had some very negative experiences:

> These survivors told story after story of the hurt they suffered through the *timing* of media attention, *intrusion* into their privacy and *harassment*, through *inaccuracy*, *distortion* and *distasteful detail* in what was reported (Shearer, 1991, p. 14, italics Shearer's).

Our interviews with students, families and the people of Lockerbie echoed those complaints. To the people of Lockerbie and their relatives and friends, the erroneous report that the petrol station had exploded caused great distress. To family and friends of those on the plane, the lack of attention to detail in reporting biographical information about the victims and their memorial services was upsetting.

Shearer also reported that some survivors, specifically those who had lost a loved one in an auto accident, were distressed by the media's lack of interest in their tragedy. Media failure to recognize what survivors view as a disaster can have more damaging effects. A British probation officer related a case in which a train crash in the north of England was given only cursory coverage, and some of the individuals who had been involved suffered from what they regarded as denial of the trauma they had suffered. They reacted when the media covered subsequent tragedies while their own experience was ignored (P. Clare, telephone interview, November 1989).

Our interviews showed that survivors varied greatly in when they felt ready to talk to the media. Some were ready immediately, others took a day or two, others a month or a year, and still others may never feel able to speak publicly about their loss or reaction to the disaster.

Bert Ammerman, a leader of one of the American family groups formed in the wake of the tragedy to provide mutual support and to campaign for airline security, frequently lectures to emergency-management teams and crisis-management directors about survivors. He tells them that in disaster situations some relatives of victims will want to make a statement or express themselves to the media. "So instead of shielding all the relatives, and saying, 'No, under no circumstances can you see the press,' or telling the relatives, 'You shouldn't see the press,' the better posture to the relatives would be, 'Look, there are press that want (you) to speak and give a statement. We can set up a press conference each day. Any member who would like to do this, we can arrange it for you. We're recommending that, No. 1, you don't have to do it. And that No. 2, maybe you shouldn't.' Allow the relatives to make that decision."

Ammerman said by recognizing that news people are there to get a story and cooperating with them, "they will be much more humane with you. You can work a happy medium. Because if you'd gotten a couple of relatives to go into a press conference (at JFK or Lockerbie) and to make a statement, that would have sufficed a lot of the need of the press to get those 10-second bites, which they were desperately after."

The experience of the American relatives in Lockerbie supported this advice. As two recounted in an earlier chapter, once they cooperated with the media — one in a news conference and the other in a brief television interview — the media no longer bothered them and, in one case, told cameramen specifically to let one of them alone because he had helped them.

At both Lockerbie and Syracuse University, we learned of cases in which people voluntarily approached journalists. So far, we have heard of no such behavior at Kennedy Airport, where in addition to people who had come to meet the plane, there were family members who responded to a broadcast announcement by the airline that people who wanted more information could come to Pan Am Terminal A.

A man arrived about 7:30 or 8 p.m. and had difficulty finding where he was to park or go for information. "Not one worker outside had any idea that there'd been a tragedy or that there was a special relatives' lounge set up," the man said. Finally a porter told him to just pull his car over to one side and leave it. "So I went walking in, and I just kept asking, 'Where do you go for the Terminal A relatives lounge or a place that could be for VIPs?' Finally someone gave me some directions." He went round a corner, and realized he was at the right place because there were so many press people and camera crews. He recalled very quietly walking up to the ticket counter and whispering that he was a relative of someone on Pan Am 103. "It was just like the press had radar. Because all of a sudden, cameras were open, people were yelling things, and they quickly got some security people who ushered me into an elevator to keep me away from the press." The man called it a "dark day in the history of the press."

None of those we talked to who had learned about their loss in the presence of the media or from a media representative said that having news people there helped them personally. For some, what they perceived as aggressive media behavior clearly increased their trauma. The testimony from Kennedy Airport, where a reporter stood on the foot of a victim's mother, apparently to try to hold her in place, and from Lockerbie, where a newsman grabbed the coat tails of a potential source, showed that such journalistic excesses are not confined to one media market — or to one nation's media.

In two cases, young people at Syracuse were told of the death of a friend while a television camera was running, and the students' shock showed. We are less certain about the effect on students who encountered media people on campus and learned directly from them that a friend's name was on the list. How compassionately the information was conveyed could have played a role in how it was received. But no one came forward to tell about this as a positive experience, and the one young woman who told of learning about the death of a friend during a telephone call from a newspaper reporter was distressed about it.

The televised list of student passengers, shown in Syracuse within four hours of the plane's disintegration over Lockerbie, had an immediate and devastating effect on students who saw it. We have been told that a few family members also learned of their loss in this way. Most of the survivors we interviewed felt that media should wait until notification of next of kin to publish or broadcast the names of victims.

Those not wishing to be interviewed told us about ways they avoided the media. Some students went to the campus chapel during the afternoon because they believed the media would be present for the vigil that evening. Some people in Lockerbie spoke of the way they used body language to convey that they did not want to be approached. One man wore casual clothes, and did not don the garb that denoted his role in the community until he was ready to speak about what had happened. Families in many cases asked a relative, friend or member of the clergy to intercede with the media on their behalf. In one case, a businessman's employer released biographical information about him to the media and made it clear in its story that the family had asked for no further publicity.

All of those we talked with hated the question, "How do you feel?" And many reported being asked that question or something very similar. They described it as a "stupid question," and many saw it as exploitive, a way to use their emotions for the sake of the story. One of our colleagues, Frances Ford Plude (1990), who has begun research on the way audiences process tragedies they witness through the media, found some evidence that people in general are appalled when media ask that question.

The question may also be hurtful. The literature on grief shows that the initial sensation for many bereaved is numbness, a lack of feeling (Katz & Florian, 1987). Asking them how they feel may heighten their anxiety by making them feel guilty for not feeling worse. Alternatively, they may be struggling to understand what happened, and still not have the words for it — an experience to which many reporters can relate.

Those family members and friends who termed it "a stupid question" were right. It is a question that answers itself. One magazine professor at the Newhouse School commented, "A reporter who asks that question is at least as stupid as he is insensitive. His audience already knows the answer."

The person asking the question may intend to be empathetic. The reality is that the question is perceived as intrusive by those to whom it is addressed. While certain members of helping professions — doctors, psychologists, clergy, etc. — may be permitted to ask the same question, it is precisely because those professionals may be able to respond in a way that brings comfort to the grieving person. The journalist's role under such circumstances is very different. In fact, none of those we interviewed denied that the media have a role to play in disasters such as Pan Am 103. Most saw the media as an immediate source of information about the tragedy, and spent a great deal of time with television and newspapers following the crash, although a few found exposure to such messages so painful that they avoided them for weeks or months.

Media interest in the deceased, when it was handled sensitively, was also a source of comfort. The timing of such approaches was clearly a delicate issue. Some families accepted or even sought such interviews as early as the day after the tragedy; few were ready to speak the night of the disaster. Some families appreciated media interest in the funeral; others asked for privacy at this time or set specific limits on what would be covered. While one family welcomed an interview immediately after a memorial service, another found that timing troublesome.

A key issue for these people was control. Disasters (and other tragedies such as rape and murder) create a sense of powerlessness, of loss of control over one's life. How the media respond may either increase that feeling, thereby aggravating the trauma, or present the person who becomes the target of media attention with something about which he or she can exercise some measure of control. So, for example, the reporter who asks very politely for permission to talk with a family that is newly bereaved, and who agrees to abide by the conditions they set, may increase the likelihood of obtaining the interview. Such an approach, even if it fails, may help the bereaved regain their composure as well; they may have the sense that they were able to control that aspect of a terrible experience, and may be cooperative at some later time.

A similar conclusion can be drawn from the experience of people in Lockerbie. Townspeople were especially proud of the way they had been able to shield a young boy who had lost both parents and a sister because he had been at a neighbor's when part of the plane had slammed into his house. At one point, they said, a reporter had been asking where to find the boy, not knowing that he was in the room at the time. The way the townspeople asserted their desire with regional authorities to take responsibility for the recovery of Lockerbie was an even stronger sign of the need to re-establish control in the wake of a disaster. So it should not be surprising that, in the months that followed, they began considering how they would begin to take control over their own dealings with the media.

At Syracuse, the clergy had been very conscious of trying to use and control the media. As the Rev. Michael Rothermel explained, the chaplains wanted to get the story out so that they could pastorally serve the university community, including students who had already left for home. He was also conscious of the need "to try to keep the media within certain parameters so as not to infringe on that what I call 'sacred space.'" The guidelines that were set down for the vigil and for the memorial the day after the crash were meant to say, in his words, "We have something very important to do here, and to talk about, and to think on, and to pray about, simply to be together. Don't violate us. Don't invade our space. Don't get too close."

When many reporters ignored the spirit of those guidelines, their action left people at Syracuse University, not just students, feeling the situation was out of control. In his pastoral role, Rothermel had to deal with the anger generated by what he called "violation of that sacred space."

"There's something so important and so sensitive," he said, referring to the space people need to grieve. "Don't impose yourself on it, and don't exploit it. I think it was that sense of exploitation for a good story, or a story that's going to sell or whatever, that prompted a lot of anger, by students and by faculty, and so on, that I dealt with over those next several days. So part of our pastoral job was to be in tune with that anger. We were very aware of it. We had predicted it. So that's why we were trying to set these parameters."

3 Newsgatherers

On the scene: Lockerbie

In the Glasgow studios of Scottish Television, news editor John Kean had just finished his program for the night of December 21 when the phone rang. An excited Automobile Association patrol, calling on a mobile radio from the Lockerbie area, was describing a catastrophe: a jet plane had slammed into the town. "He told me that there were massive craters on the road, and houses were afire. He said, 'It looks to my mind like a jumbo jet.' It was obviously a very, very serious situation." Kean estimated the call must have come about 7:06 or 7:07p.m., three or four minutes after the initial impact.

"The moment that aircraft came down, there was no (telephone) communication with that particular area," the news editor said. He immediately instructed one of the reporters to get on to the Ministry of Defence and ask them to confirm the plane was a jumbo jet. "We did get it, off the record. They weren't actually too sure. They thought it was a military jet, but we got it established that it was a jumbo jet."

Kean estimated that shortly before 7:30 his station went on the air with its first bulletins, and dispatched three camera crews and the outside broadcast unit to Lockerbie. He also telephoned Independent Television News network in London, which broadcasts over the same television channel and had reported that it was a military jet. "We actually told ITN in London, 'Look, you're giving out the wrong information there. The real information is this: it's a jumbo jet. We're better off singing the same song.'"

The way a news organization first hears about a major story can be mixed with more than a little luck. More than three years later, Kean was still mystified about how the AA patrol had managed to get his inside phone number. At BBC News in London, the tip came quite differently. Richard Ayres, head of editorial development, news and current affairs, had lingered after hours. "It was purely a matter of coincidence that I was sitting gossiping with the woman who was the duty news editor of the day, and we were talking about old times when she lifted the phone and a voice said that a jumbo jet had come down in Scotland."

As he recalled it, the decision to go on the air was made within 15 minutes of that first phone call. "That may sound quite a long time in news terms, but remember, the first phone call was entirely unsourced... It might have been a hoax. We had no idea who was telling us. We just got this phone call.

"Having established that there was a genuine event to report — a plane had come down — the BBC's guidelines really say that your first concern in going on the air is to try to limit the (scope) of national concern as rapidly as possible. So a great deal of effort in the first few minutes is put into discovering which airline it is, what time it took off, where it took off from, and where it was going. So that ideally your first broadcast, although it will cause enormous distress to some hundreds of people in this case, should at least not cause undue alarm to some tens of thousands of people who've said good-bye to relatives at Heathrow within the last few hours." Ayres said the BBC would not refrain from going on the air with the news that a jumbo jet had come down on Scotland simply because it wasn't able to confirm which airline it was. "But we do our damnedest to find out as much as possible to limit the number of people caused distress," he said.

Wire services alerted to the story sprang into action. A key part of their work is to gather information from all available sources, so they monitored the television reports from ITN and BBC and quoted those organizations heavily. That meant the information of the disaster speeding to media around the world incorporated early errors from the scene, including the mistaken belief that the plane had struck a petrol station.

At the Glasgow *Herald*, a Christmas party was in progress. About 7:05 someone came from the newsroom to let the news editor, Robert Sutter, know a plane had gone down. The messenger thought it was a military aircraft. About 10 minutes later, he returned. The report was more ominous. Sutter went out into the newsroom, where the deputy news editor was checking with authorities and other sources. It was getting worse. Sutter went back into the party and approached newspeople individually. "Immediately, I told people — the reporters who were there — there was a major disaster and to just ease themselves quietly out of the party. Within five minutes, the only people who were left in that room drinking were management."

In retrospect, Sutter said the proximity of the Christmas party was fortuitous. It meant that even though the *Herald* was past its first deadline, it had a large staff on hand to work the phones and chase down leads, as well as reporters to dispatch to the scene.

Frank Ryan, a veteran newsman recently retired from the tabloid *Daily Record* in Glasgow and freelancing from his home near Dumfries, had just returned from shopping in Lockerbie when the telephone rang. He jumped in his car and headed back. Like other newspeople from neighboring towns, he arrived at a confusing scene. Darkness enveloped the town except for the fiery glow near the A-74, the dual carriageway linking Glasgow to Carlisle and the rest of England. As Ryan tried to get his bearings, he was approached by a man with a flashlight who asked him if he needed to get to where the plane had come down. Following his escort through back gardens and streets, the newsman soon found himself near Sherwood Crescent, staring at a huge, burning crater. Nothing in his long career could have prepared him for this or any of the many sights he would see in the hours ahead. It was as if he had arrived in the middle of a war zone.

The chaos of the first hour was captured on tape by a newsman from BBC Radio Solway in Dumfries, walking along the streets of Lockerbie with his microphone open, asking people what had happened. The confusion was clear in their voices and their terse responses.[1] They really did not know.

Soon John Kean received a call from one of his Scottish Television reporters who had made it to Lockerbie, and learned that the report that the plane had crashed into the petrol station was false. "Harry Smith actually called me from that petrol station using his own mobile phone, and, in fact, gave some of the very first interviews to be broadcast anywhere in the world." One of them was with the owner of the petrol station. The STV satellite transmission unit had not arrived yet, so Smith gave his videotapes to a stranger, a businessman who was headed for Glasgow, to deliver them personally to the station. "It was very, very imperative to get these tapes back because they were describing what we thought had happened, and we were actually very, very near the mark," Kean said.

Like the BBC, which has operations in Scotland, many national dailies could rely initially on permanent staff they had based there. Kerry Gill, who works out of Glasgow for *The Times*, was just settling down to supper when his newsdesk phoned from London to say there had been a plane crash in the Borders. Like many others, he thought the plane was probably a low-flying aircraft, because of the Royal Air Force training in that area. Then he heard the false report that it had hit a petrol station. "I immediately grabbed my things and got in the car and rushed down," he said.

At Moffat, about 10 miles north of Lockerbie, he was ordered off the highway, which had been closed to all but emergency vehicles. "So I had to take a sort of circuitous route through the countryside. I just sort of steered by natural instinct, and eventually came back to the A-74 (highway), down a disused cart track, used by tractors and things like this." The road was empty until "a whole convoy of ambulances and police came streaming by, and so I just tucked in behind them and drove into town that way." To those in the convoy, *The Times* reporter's car was just another pair of headlights in the rear-view mirror. "So I was quite lucky in getting there without being stopped or having any trouble."

Gill said he reached Lockerbie sometime between 9 and 10 p.m. "I don't think anybody actually remembers what time they arrived. You're thinking of other things. And when I got into town, I wondered what all the fuss was about. There didn't seem to be any commotion. Then I saw lots of ambulances on sort of side streets. They didn't seem to be doing anything, which I thought was strange. I drove into the center of the town. There just seemed to be local people wandering about."

He spotted three teenagers. "I went up to them and said, 'Where's the crash?' They said they'd take me because it was on the south side of the town. It was just a glow in the sky, possibly like street lights. We ran across some fields and over fences. Before we got to the crater site, I was running across these two fields and there seemed to be sort of white pieces just scattered all around, I suppose the effect from what natural light there was. Of course, when I bent down to see what it was, it was thousands of pieces of plane of different sizes from small to quite large pieces. And that's when, suddenly, I realized that this was something very, very big.

"When we got to the crater itself, all it seemed to be was a massive pit, aflame. You couldn't really see into it, it was just flame. Later on, of course, there was more and more debris. You would see things like toilet bowls and sort of stupid things like that in amongst all these pieces of fuselage and so forth. There was no sort of conception of how deep it was. All it was, was just sort of orange flame, flames going high into the sky. I seem to recollect there was a stench of avgas in the air."

Once he had been around the crater and had seen what had happened there, he went back to his car and filed a story on what he had seen. "Luckily I had a portable telephone because all the other telephones were out," he said. Then he spent the rest of the evening with his teenage guides finding where the other main parts of the plane had come down.

Graham Patterson, Glasgow correspondent for the *Express*, and Joe Campbell, one of its photographers, also received the news at their respective homes. Both recalled their initial reaction as disbelief. Patterson, who had phoned London with a story before leaving the house, headed along the two-lane roads that link Edinburgh to the Borders. About three or four miles from Lockerbie, he could see the sky was red. That's when he was stopped by the police, who asked where he was going. They said, "You can walk. You're not going to drive." Just then a friend of Patterson's, a senior policeman, came along, and the newsman dropped in behind him and drove right into the midst of Lockerbie. "What I didn't know was that the place I had stopped was 30 or 40 yards away from the cockpit," he recalled. "I didn't know that until the next day."

By the time Patterson reached Lockerbie, it was about 11p.m. and the streets were clogged with emergency equipment that had arrived from all over the Borders region of Scotland, as well as northern England. "You couldn't move anywhere, for fire engines, ambulances, everything like that. I parked outside the Blue Bell Pub, and I thought, 'Well, if there are any other journalists here, they'll be in the bar.' So I went in. There were none there. I grabbed the last room (to rent), and went out from there." He had arrived on the heels of the Scottish Office public relations team, which set up a press center in the Masonic Hall. That, said Patterson, was the first place he went.

By then Andrew McCallum, a veteran reporter for the Glasgow *Herald*, had reached Lockerbie by taxi — he had drunk "a couple of jars" before word of the disaster reached him and decided that was the most prudent way to travel. He found an open stationery store in Lockerbie while looking for a working phone, and came across some eye-witnesses in the process. "I had a quick word with one or two people who had come down into the town from one or two of the stricken parts, where there'd been an enormous amount of damage," he said. "Of course, people immediately after a crash will always speak very readily. The fact that you're from a newspaper is not right at the front of their thoughts. They just want to talk about it." But to relay his news back to the office he had to go out to a village about five miles from Lockerbie and call from there. "Communications were very difficult, and even officials were having a terrible time."

The *Express* photographer soon found colleagues from other tabloid papers. They agreed to meet back at a pub on Main Street where they exchanged information for about an hour and decided to go out again. They went toward the Rosebank area where the fuselage had come down between the rows of houses. "Shortly after that was the first time I saw a body that night," Joe Campbell said. The passenger was still strapped in the seat, which had wedged in a chimney knocked in by the impact. "One of the photographers actually got upset at that," he said. So the group retreated to the pub.

Kerry Gill spent the night gathering facts and phoning them to *The Times* as fast as he got them. "I was speaking to the locals and they were pretty incoherent really," he recalled "They'd no more idea than I had what had happened. I think I did something like 14 takes, 14 different updates of the story right through until early the next morning when I phoned up the news desk, and they said, 'Don't bother filing because everybody's gone home. That was our last edition.' And when I looked at the watch it was about 4 o'clock."

In London, the hub not only of British national press, but a major station for the international news corps, there had been a scramble both to get the news out and to send correspondents to Scotland. Maureen Johnson of the Associated Press was relaxing at home when the phone call came. The desk had already moved an urgent story quoting an Independent Television News broadcast that a Pan Am jumbo jet was missing over Scotland. She headed for the AP offices, where the bureau chief had arranged to send two photographers, a mobile darkroom, and a radio reporter aboard a chartered aircraft from an airport about 30 miles out of London. Accompanying them was a member of the AP staff in the traffic division because the chief of AP communications, John Mulroy, had been flying back to the States on board Pan Am 103. Accompanied by five members of his family from Britain, he was heading for his home in Long Island and a family reunion.

The AP contingent flew into Carlisle, a city just south of the Scottish border, and rented cars. The American television networks were doing the same thing. Dick Blystone of Cable News Network managed to get a seat on an ABC News charter. He got to Carlisle about an hour before his crew arrived, caught a taxi and went up to Lockerbie. "It was total chaos, of course. It was dark and it was raining. And it was cold. People were running around, trying to do their job."

After the AP charter reached Carlisle after midnight, Maureen Johnson shared a rental car with the AP radio reporter and the man from traffic, and they headed straight for the scene as fast as they could. "It was a filthy night, it really was. After quite a bit of losing the way and being turned around by cops and this sort of thing, we came over a hill. Suddenly we saw the (nose) cone of the plane. It was in a field, and there were not very many policemen around." They stood in the cold rain at the stone wall separating the field from the road and stared at the carnage.

Johnson needed to call in a story on the cellular phones, but first she had to decide what to report. The word picture she painted excluded the worst of what she saw, the detail of the carnage before her. "I don't think it would have been AP policy to do it. I didn't include (horrific detail) in a story. We didn't, as far as I know, take any pictures of it." She had some difficulty getting through on the cellular phone to the desk, where the stories about the tragedy were being pieced together, weaving in details from various sources who had been reached by phone. Making contact that time was easier than subsequent contacts would be, possibly, she suggested, because of the altitude.

Other London journalists found more mundane ways to Scotland. David Sharrock of *The Guardian* was told to get himself up there, and recognized there would be no chartered jets for him. "The obvious way was just to make my way to a railway station and catch a train up. I took a photographer from here, and we arranged to be met by a car at Carlisle." He estimated it was midnight or early morning when they arrived on the scene.

"The high street and the surrounding country lanes, whatever, were awash with car loads of press, TV, radio, newspapers, everybody, just driving around, trying to find out what had happened, where parts of the plane had crashed," Sharrock recalled. Here and there the fire brigade and police were busy surveying various sites where wreckage had fallen to earth and making sure they posed no further danger to the town. "I still remember there was a very strong smell of — I suppose it was petroleum, in the air. And everywhere was littered with small shards of metal. You'd come across larger pieces just embedded in the ground."

The *Guardian* team from London, which would work with Peter Hetherington, the paper's correspondent in Scotland, found their way to Tundergarth, the site where the nose of the plane had come down. "There were quite a few people there, the police had set up a cordon around it. It was an enormous thing in this field, which had dug into the ground quite a bit." Sharrock interviewed people from the farm at the bottom of the hill who described what had happened. "They had seen this sort of fireball, heard this enormous noise of the crash, run out into the field, and there (saw) one or two people, bodies on the ground," the reporter said. "They said one or two of them were still alive, but just on the point of death really. I mean no scream or anything, just literally (the witnesses were) on the scene to hear their last gasp."

Nick Cohen of *The Independent* also took the train north, reaching Lockerbie about 3 o'clock in the morning. Quite a few journalists were around, some of them in a pub watching the news. "I just started wandering around. There wasn't anything else to do," he recalled. "I went off by myself, just kept walking around by myself, and it got quite horrible because I started walking on a hillside, and I suddenly saw a body in front of me — a naked body on the hillside. I thought 'God.' And I thought, 'Well, I'm not supposed to be there.' Well, I assumed I wasn't supposed to be there. I thought, 'I better get off. The last thing police want to do is arrest me.' I turned back and realized I'd gone past lots of other bodies on the way up. There was wreckage all over the place and little bottles of wine you get on airplanes, you know those little bottles. They weren't even broken."

The opening paragraphs of his color piece in *The Independent* captured the scene graphically:

> In a field close by lies a seat with its safety belt still attached. In the woods alongside lies a twisted lump of fuselage the size of a tractor. And on the steep hill rising from Lockerbie to the golf course lies the body of a man.
>
> He is not burnt beyond recognition. He is not crushed. The clichéd descriptions which spring to mind when you hear that a 747 has disintegrated at 31,000 feet cannot distance you from him.
>
> He is whole, strong and unmistakably human. His arms are braced against the earth and one hand grips the surface.

> Around him are things which should not have survived when he did not. An unopened and unbroken quarter-bottle of Pan Am's claret. A green seat cushion with a gaudy cover (Dec. 22, 1988, p. 1).

Cohen said the day was "very peculiar" because in addition to describing the scope of the disaster, journalists were trying to work out whether it was a bomb or structural damage. He conferred with a colleague in London, an expert in aviation, who provided him with questions to help determine if it was a bomb. One was whether the radar tracking the plane had shown it going down in pieces. Another was what had happened to the flight avionics, the electronics that record and help to control the plane in flight. "Trying to get answers to those was just horrendous," Cohen remembered. "I'd been up for about 24 hours by then. I was trudging about in the rain the whole time. I was really quite upset by what I'd seen. And they finally had a press conference, a very short press conference, very illustrative in a way the sort of things go in journalism, because there were like hundreds of television cameras there."

Cohen made it clear that "hundreds" was an exaggeration, but he was exasperated by the way they set up right in front of the room and dominated the news conference. "The television people get their sound bites and then it's over," said *The Independent* reporter. "And I said, 'I've got questions,' and they said there'll be a press officer here to help you. So myself and a couple of colleagues — two guys from Canada — surrounded him. And I said, 'I want to know the answer to this, to these questions.' He said, 'Oh, well, I can't tell you.' I said, 'You must have some idea.' He said, 'Oh, well, actually, I'm a housing press officer.'

"I just snapped and went completely bonkers, stabbing my fingers at him like this and going, 'What are you fucking doing here, and bloody hell! We're being palmed off with all this nonsense, and you're supposed to be here to answer questions, and you're a housing inspector. What on earth are you doing at an aviation disaster?'" Cohen was clearly as troubled by his own behavior as he was with the temporary assignment of the housing press officer and his inability to answer the questions. Later the reporter would tie his own distress at seeing the bodies on the hillside to his anger at the press officer, which was prompted by what he considered at that time to be a "very casual, very contemptuous way" to treat the print media.

David Leppard of *The Sunday Times* jumped in his car and drove north as soon as he heard the news on television. "My job at that time was to cover major disasters, so I was on standby," he said, recalling that there had been a series of disasters in the United Kingdom in the preceding 18 months: the Zeebrugge ferry capsizing in the English Channel, the King's Cross fire that flashed through an underground station, the Clapham railway derailment, the Piper Alpha oil rig disaster off the coast of Scotland.

"I remember driving into town and hearing the sound of crunching under my car wheels," Leppard said. He got out and discovered he had been driving over pieces of airplane. He went through the back of the petrol station toward the Sherwood Crescent area, where he began to comprehend the scale of the disaster, and then up to Tundergarth. "I was going over to the cockpit, just to have a look, but was cut off by police officers," he said. "I went back down a little country lane, which runs away from the cockpit area over the hills from the church. And as I went up the crest of the hill, I first saw a dead body, and about that time a search party came over the crest." Leppard joined the search at that point. Over the next hill, an array of bodies was spread out across the field. In careful understatement, he described it as "not pleasant." "I spent the whole day with the search party," he said. "We discovered 60 or 70 bodies that day."

Leppard and Cohen described very different expressions on the faces of the victims they viewed. "It was quite shocking to see the expressions on their faces," Leppard said. "They looked as if they knew they were going to die." Cohen was struck by the peacefulness of the expressions, and felt good that he could subsequently convey that description to family members. Like many other aspects of the event, the reporters' observations raised unanswerable questions about normal reactions to horrific circumstances: To what extent was the difference in their assessment subjective, affected by their own way of understanding what they were seeing? To what extent was it objective, reflecting differences in expressions of the victims they saw?

Leppard could suspend his survey of the whole story and effectively become part of the search effort because his newspaper was not planning to publish the following Sunday, Christmas Day. He had 10 days to pull together a word picture of the tragedy; what he saw during the search would play a minor role in his story. Cohen and other daily reporters for the British press needed to write their stories by early evening, although they could feed late developments until the final edition went to press.

At Scottish Television in Glasgow, John Kean put in a rough night. His staff broadcast every hour, trying to update and rejig the news summaries whenever fresh interviews came in, including any new pictures they got from the area. "We changed it every hour. That was our job. We had to do that," Kean said.

Meanwhile, networks overseas had learned that Scottish Television had dramatic pictures and could transmit them via satellite from Lockerbie. "I don't know how many phone calls I took from America that night, but I can tell you it was a hell of a lot. I had all the major stations onto me, looking for pictures. A lot of the American stations were willing to pay big money, big money, for these pictures. They were screaming for them. And I said, 'Well, look, you know, if you need our pictures, then you will have them.'" In some ways, pressure from stations in the U.S., Europe, Japan, Australia and elsewhere kept Kean from reflecting during those hours on the scope of the tragedy his teams were covering.

"When it came home to me was sort of dawn the following morning. All our reporters obviously were checking in with me, every half hour or so to keep me informed about what we had and what we didn't have, people we'd been speaking to, eye witnesses." As daylight eased over the hillsides, the reporters' phone calls changed. They were confronting terrible sights, which they described to Kean and asked his guidance: what should they shoot? "I said, 'Look, film whatever you see there, film everything.' And all pictures came back to Glasgow and they were edited in Glasgow." That produced another kind of professional stress. "We had to be very, very careful, given that we're going out sort of prime time in this country. It was very, very important to make sure that we did not show pictures that were obviously too grisly to show on a news program at 6 o'clock. It was just out of the question. Although one or two of them came very, very near to that."

But the phone calls from around the world kept coming. "Eventually, I couldn't actually do my job of editing my own Scottish news, editing the fact that we had the biggest disaster in Scotland. I couldn't actually get on with my job for taking all these phone calls. I had to tell the (station manager), 'Please appoint one of the senior executives to handle all these calls from all the foreign stations.' Because it really was becoming beyond a joke. You know, 'We will pay $4,000 or $5,000 for two minutes of pictures.' Just crazy money. They were desperate for pictures from Scotland, and we obviously were the quickest avenue." Kean said part of the problem was that his station's satellite transmitter was set up for about five hours before the BBC unit began operations.

Hamish Campbell, the veteran photo editor of *The Scotsman* in Edinburgh, had sent a photographer to the scene as soon as he heard of the disaster. Campbell himself was ready to fly over the area as soon as light came up to photograph a panorama of the disaster. But authorities had declared a 10-mile exclusion zone, making the area off limits to non-emergency aircraft. "Which in this case was the right thing to do because there were helicopters flying about everywhere," Campbell said. That meant he had to drive down, "which meant I was later than quite a few others, and made it a bit more traumatic in some respects because we had to park outside the town and walk in. And it was fantastic. When I got to the town, there was windows smashed, and what got me was the streets and the pavements were littered with shrapnel. You know, just lots of shrapnel about, four inches square and even smaller. Everywhere, absolutely everywhere. Hanging on walls and window ledges, and on the pavements. Unbelievable!"

Campbell headed for the police headquarters, where he met colleagues who told him where the main sites were. One of his photographers had shot one side of the crater. He went out and shot the other side. Then he heard there was to be a "rota" or pool of newspeople to cover the arrival of Prime Minister Margaret Thatcher and the American ambassador. That meant photos from those visits would be shared with all media by the people taking them, so Campbell, having been told the nose cone was a couple of miles outside the town, decided to walk there. "I found, of course, that it was considerably farther.

"It was very strange. I walked up the hill out of Lockerbie, and looked down. You could see the mayhem where these houses were demolished," *The Scotsman* photographer recalled. He took pictures of the scene and walked on. "And I came to a point in the road — it's a country road — and I was walking along, thinking about this nose cone and exactly where it was, and there was nothing else in the road. And then I looked in the fields, and it was like sheep in the fields. Of course, it wasn't sheep. It was bodies in the field. And it was quite eerie, of course. There was absolutely nobody there, in this stretch, as it happened. I'd walked for about a mile on the morning of this disaster on my own and through this field, just bodies lying everywhere." Asked if he had taken any pictures of the bodies, Campbell was emphatic. "No," he said, "no, no. The only picture we did of bodies was a shot from the aircraft of exactly what I'm describing, and it looked even more like sheep from the air. No, we would never use anything (like that)."

Campbell got a lift in one of the rescue vehicles, then walked the rest of the way to Tundergarth, arriving just as the press contingent showed up to do its rota duty in covering Margaret Thatcher. "So I wasn't exactly popular. I had sort of gate-crashed," he smiled. He photographed the wreckage that would come to symbolize the tragedy. "The nose cone struck me, compared to the rest of it," he said. "It was quite different because it was — as everybody knows now, it was totally recognizable. It just looked like a cracked egg. That's what I thought when I looked at it at the time, a cracked egg. And everything else was just mayhem."

He also shot the arrival of the dignitaries. "Then guess who was first in the press bus back to Lockerbie? Me. I wasn't supposed to be on there, but it saved me walking back."

A team of regional journalists from *The Chronicle* in Newcastle used detailed local ordnance survey maps to find their way through a series of back lanes. "There was one way in effectively and we spent a long while finding it," said

Alastair McCall. "On the way into Lockerbie, we were stopping at various locations because we were traveling with a photographer. So we were taking photographs of material, wreckage strewn around a very large area. I think it was really at that point that the enormity of what had actually happened on a human scale hit you. I always remember seeing a Pan Am ice bucket lying in a field. I was imagining everyone was having a gin and tonic or whatever. It is being served up on the flight, and then suddenly the whole thing terminates."

McCall had been in the Underground at King's Cross when a fire in the escalator and ticket hall claimed 31 lives and injured 21; having escaped on another train, he returned immediately to cover the scene for his paper. "I mean, sometimes you have to be detached from these things, but I think the secret is also to retain an awareness of the enormity in human terms at what's happened at something like King's Cross or something like an earthquake."

Arriving in the town, the Newcastle team walked in past the school being used as headquarters for the search teams, dog teams, and police, and found quite a different scene. "People were ready in a way, prepared for what was coming in terms of media circus," he said. "And it was a phenomenon, media circus, all the TV crews, etc., and all the trailers, all being put into a made-up car park on a hill. In the high street, there were probably more journalists and TV crews than there were local people. It was organized chaos really. The police and emergency services were doing their best to lay on facilities, to feed out information. But obviously every journalist there was sort of trying to work off their own bat, and get their own stuff rather than just the official handout."

McCall had two stories to write, one a color piece on the aftermath and the other a factual report on what was going on. "So a lot of it was just wandering round and observing things, wandering round and noticing things like pieces of airplane embedded in household radiators, things like that, sort of scattered over a wide area. At one point I remember wandering up toward the golf course, which is where all the bodies were being collected. You couldn't get up there, but you could see, and the photographer could see with the aid of the lenses, that bodies were being piled up in body bags on the golf course. Things like that. It was horrible. Sherwood Crescent was shut off, but you could just about see that there was an enormous hole. You could see lots of gable ends standing both from the town itself and from the A-74. I didn't pursue at any great length a look into this smoldering great crater. I didn't think a lot would be gained from it. They clearly didn't want you to go there. Some things like that you can leave to the imagination."

McCall was also struck by the people he called "sort of ghouls." He said he couldn't think of any other word for people "who were coming for a day trip, coming up and around the town just to have a gander at the hole where the plane had come down. In instances like that you find some human beings can be very disturbing people. Why any one would travel to go and see it — you know, we do it as a job. We have to do it. You'd have thought that was enough to read about it, let alone go to see it firsthand."

Kerry Gill of *The Times* had caught about two hours sleep after his 4 a.m. conversation with the desk in London. By dawn's light he saw "the grisly aspect of it, not just fire and damage." He spent the day trying to put a piece together that would tell what happened to the town "from start to finish."

Other *Times* correspondents were working through official sources to try to explain the disaster. "At that time, we didn't know whether it was a bomb or the aircraft had broken up in midair." He could not remember exactly when he began to think it was a terrorist act. "If I remember rightly, most people seemed to think it would be a bomb. Just because it was a jumbo and it had obviously exploded so high up. I think most people know that most planes crash either on take off or coming in to land. Some people continued to think that it might be something structurally wrong with the 747. I think it actually was our paper that broke the news for sure that it had been a terrorist bomb. That was from our air correspondent in London."

Graham Patterson of the *Express*, visiting Tundergarth again by daylight, was struck by the impression that nearly all the bodies he saw, as he looked across the fields, had landed in a neat row. After that, he said, they saw "a lot worse," bodies on the golf course, bodies in housing schemes, bodies in gardens, bodies in hedgerows, horrific scenes. "That's a disaster. The easiest story in the world to cover is a disaster," he said. "There's so much stuff, you don't have to look for it."

Patterson said a major difficulty, however, was getting accurate information. He praised Angus Kennedy, who was brought down to help Lockerbie from the Strathclyde police force in Glasgow, where he had handled media relations on major crime stories for years. Lockerbie has the smallest police force in Scotland. "They obviously couldn't cope, through no fault of their own," Patterson said. "(Kennedy) couldn't tell us very much because the police didn't know very much, but from dawn onwards, information started coming and coming and coming."

Meanwhile, Kerry Gill moved around the town, talking to local people. "I think they were just completely numbed by it all. They were behaving perfectly normally, talking and speaking perfectly rationally, as one does in these things. I mean nobody seems to sense any sort of shock until days, weeks, months afterwards, do they? It was just sort of disbelief. They'd look out their window and where there was some line of houses, there was complete devastation."

He found many local people knew less than the media did. "Half the time they were asking us what was going on. They weren't just answering our questions. I think they were just numb with shock. But on the other hand a lot of people (in other sections of the town) hadn't seen anything of it at all. They'd have heard an incredible crash, but this was the remarkable thing I remembered in arriving at the time, if you arrived in the middle of the town, nothing seemed to be wrong at all. It was when you actually got to the edges that the devastation was."

Gill said hundreds of media were in the town that day, so many he joked that "it made it difficult because you'd stop somebody in the street to ask them what was going on, and they'd say, 'I'm from UPI' or...." Actually, he said he did not think the presence of so many interfered with the newsgathering at that point. "I never found any resentment of the press at that time. People were more than willing to speak to you, just to sort of share the experience or the shock or whatever, and ask questions as well as answer them. So I don't think it did create havoc. I think they just sort of felt, of course, everybody's got to be here. It's been such a disaster."

Gill suggested that the situation would have been worse if people had ignored it in any way. That came out, he noted, when some people expected a member of the Royal Family to attend the memorial. Prince Andrew, the Queen's second son, did arrive from Edinburgh that day but made a gaffe that has become part of the Lockerbie lore. He expressed sympathy to all the Americans who had lost loved ones in the disaster, ignoring the fact that Lockerbie people had lost their lives and that the community was struggling to cope with the crisis.

David Sharrock of *The Guardian* was amazed by the level of hospitality he found as he began interviewing townspeople. He recalled going up and talking to people on the street and them saying, "Where are you going to stay?" and "Have you had anything to eat? Well, come along, I'll make you a cup of tea." "Just talking to them was fantastic," he said.

Maureen Johnson found one of her best interviews when she stopped by a Lockerbie coffee shop about 9 a.m. Her subjects were a couple she estimated to be in their sixties. "They were lovely people, who were just sitting in that café," she said. "I just struck up a conversation with them from a nearby table. Now they had lost everything. And they made a very nice story because they'd recently built a house, and they'd been on Sherwood Crescent, where some of the houses were wiped out altogether. The Scots, you know, are not the most forthcoming of people, but they had a lovely way of telling it without any complaining about what had happened to them. It was, you know, what had happened to other people. By that time, news had come through that so many young people, young American university students, had been killed and that sort of thing." Johnson felt that the timing of that interview was important because "a lot of the British press are very intrusive. So that it's probably a rule of thumb in any disaster in Britain, if you're doing this kind of reporting, to get there before they do."

Johnson recalled finding people in Lockerbie "quite hard to talk with, and I don't usually. It's a lot easier for women to do these sort of things. I think it's much harder for a young man reporter." She recalled that the reluctance to talk coincided approximately with the establishment of the temporary morgue in the Town Hall. She remembered a woman who was organizing a church service not wanting to talk about it. She thought it was a combination of the Scottish reserve and the fact that "it really was a small place to have that many journalists around. (News) people were just on the street all the time or hanging round that press center that was set up, really because there wasn't anywhere else to go."

Johnson said the Lockerbie people she interviewed did give her very helpful material. "I mean you did get good descriptions, and being there early on helped. There was a man with a garage just by that hill who gave a description of this horrific sight of this plane just going to pieces, you know, coming straight at him over the hill." The man had described a fireball coming over the hill and the huge pieces of the aircraft. "And its wings had fallen off, and there was no front to it." Johnson called that "the most graphic description" that she obtained first hand and said it had "stuck" with her.

Dick Longworth, then the London correspondent of *The Chicago Tribune*, flew up to spend the day in Lockerbie and wrote about seeing "handkerchief-size pieces of cloth" covering tiny parts of human remains. The *Tribune* editors had trouble reaching him the previous night, and were so concerned about having their own reporter on the scene that they ordered Howard Witt, their Toronto correspondent, to fly to Britain. Witt handled the hard news angles, while Longworth wrote the color piece.

Longworth shared a rented car with Donna Foote of *Newsweek* and the two of them toured the stricken area. He recalled talking to people in the streets and knocking on a few doors in the Rosebank Crescent area, where people were "very hospitable." Then they drove out in the country and observed a field where bodies were strewn about. "It was horrifying, describing sickening stuff," he said. "We looked at pieces of fuselage in a totally amateurish way." They were looking for charred edges, for example, any evidence of an explosion.

Reporters had been flying all night from America. A reporter for the *Herald-Journal* in Syracuse flew into Glasgow in late morning, rented a car and reached Lockerbie in time to phone a description of the gaping crater for the afternoon paper's first deadline. After checking into a small hotel on the south side of the town, he hiked into the village center.

"When I first got there everything was panic," he recalled. It reminded him of a World War II movie, "You know, where the Germans are shooting and the Americans are shooting, and French nuns are walking down the street. So information was all over. People were very descriptive in what they said. So they were very open. It was like any accident scene, except on a grander scale. I'd been to murder scenes, where everything, even if you get there as you hear the police call come over, you get to a scene, it's always pretty calm by the time you get there. Even a fire, the guys have the water squirting by the time you get there. And they have their lines set up. But this was like there were no lines. Things were all over. It was of such magnitude... I'm from a small-town newspaper. So it struck me as: Wow! It's got to be some sort of a rush to cover a war."

Later the reporter would recognize that the scene before him was a battlefield, that the carnage and wreckage were caused by an act of war against innocent civilians, and that realization would trouble him deeply.

Peter Marks of *Newsday*, which circulates in New York City and throughout Long Island, had been at his newspaper's Christmas party Wednesday afternoon when his managing editor came over and asked, "Are you available to go overseas to cover this?" Marks said, "Absolutely," but he admitted later he was very nervous. Within three hours he was on a TWA flight to London with a photographer. "It was a very disorienting experience from the get-go, because I didn't know what to expect. I didn't know if we were going to get there and there would be no access. It just seemed like a very daunting undertaking. I didn't know if it was going to be bodies; I didn't know if we were too late."

Having flown to Glasgow and rented a car, Marks discovered the *Newsday* photographer was afraid to drive because traffic moves on the left instead of the right. "It meant like, after being up for 24 hours, it was on my shoulders. I'd been to Britain a few times so I knew how to drive there, but it was like having to deal with all of this and find Lockerbie." Fortunately, they ran into a photographer from England who agreed to drive the car in return for a ride to the scene, which, Marks said, "was excellent because I just was this space cadet." They reached Lockerbie in late morning and parked at a pub at the edge of town. As they were driving in they could see the crater beside the A-74, "and there's pretty much no aircraft left. I couldn't figure out where the plane was. It was like very weird. It disintegrated on impact."

Marks seemed to relive the experience as he recalled it. "I remember it was cold, and we were walking down the street," he said. "Up until this point it wasn't real to me, the whole thing wasn't very real. I'm walking with a guy — I think he was from the *Chicago Tribune* — and again I haven't slept, I'm on adrenaline here — and I start seeing pieces of the plane, in the streets, little tiny pieces. At this point you're not interviewing anybody, you're just trying to like scope out what's going on. And this little girl comes up to us, and she's talking about a finger — and I realized she was saying that her mother had found a finger in her garden. This is what people were talking about in the town that day. And I could see more and more pieces of this plane, like identifiable seat belts, just on the street. It was totally bizarre. And I felt at that point — " he laughed self-consciously, "I felt very excited because I suddenly realized we were going to be able to see a lot, even in the town. At that point I think you shut down. I suddenly stopped reacting emotionally. At that point I just went on overdrive, and just started reporting."

Marks recognized that he had a long day of work ahead of him because of the five-hour time difference. He could keep gathering information and writing until late that night, and still make his newspaper's first deadline at 6 p.m. EST. At first he couldn't figure out where the reporters were, although he saw plenty of photographers. Soon he discovered they were at the Masonic Lodge. "I went in and there was a press conference almost immediately. But the facilities were awful," he said.

Certainly, it was not what would have been expected in the United States. Angus Kennedy, the police public-information officer, was reading a press release. "He's reading nothing about the accident," Marks recalled. "He's just reading a condolence message from the Scottish police to the families of those who had died. Reporters are trying to ask questions about what happened, and (the police) were obsessed with the decorum of the event. That first day they didn't really want to speculate at all. But they were like obsessed with the mourning period for the families. It was almost like they were acting like the funeral home, I felt at first." Reflecting on that phase of the story's development, Marks said, "I mean it was understandable, very frustrating, but understandable. You could get little out of them that day."

He also was frustrated by the communications. He found one pay phone — and he had no British money yet — and one portable phone in an anteroom of the Masonic Lodge. "You had to wait a half-hour for it. It was horrendous, and I didn't know at that point what the story was going to be. I knew that they had sort of put together a first-day story with very little contribution from me. I called one of the editors at home and just sort of told him what was going on. He said basically, 'Look, just go out and do it. See whatever you can find.'"

Alastair McCall remembered another source of tension at the Masonic Lodge that day. "There was at times a fairly brusque atmosphere between some of the UK-based reporters and some of the reporters for foreign news media," especially foreign television crews. He recalled "one or two instances where people...turned round in the heat of the moment and said, 'Hang on a minute. This isn't your bloody country. This is a UK story. Take your turn.' There were a few very choice four-letter words flying around about who should have the priority or whatever, access to people or facilities, etc."

McCall recognized that many of the questions reflected the pressure from London and American newsrooms to find out why the plane had fallen from the skies. It was emerging from the news capitals that Pan Am had received a warning in early December that their planes were targeted for bombs. Thinking back on the day, the Newcastle reporter had the impression that the bomb theory was not "going around" among the press in Lockerbie until late in the day, although reporters like Nick Cohen of *The Independent* had begun pursuing that angle early that morning. "Obviously, the police were asked if there was any evidence this was a bomb," McCall said, "but it was far too early for them to say publicly."

The day was moving on, and McCall wanted to tell the story of the tragedy's unsung heroes. So he went back to the school where rescue teams who had been searching over the hills and fells, the barren mountains of the region, were resting and being fed. "The school was effectively a no-go area. They didn't want you in talking to the people who had been out on the hillsides, on the fellsides, looking for survivors in a fairly forlorn hope, also trying to round up all the bodies. You were completely denied access to them. So it was a question of sort of worming your way into the school through the back door, effectively starting at the kitchen door and getting to talk to the Women's Royal Voluntary Service, who were putting together all the teas, about what a wonderful job they were doing, getting quotes from them and wandering into the kitchens, talking to more and more people. Then you moved beyond the kitchens, into the dining room side, and that was how you got to talk to people, you know, who'd been out on the fells, who'd obviously seen very distressing things. You weren't milking it, but they'd been on a very odd mission. Normally fell rescue is when you go out with the intention of picking up someone who's injured. They knew before they started that there was no chance of picking anyone up.

"There were police in there and eventually they said, 'What the hell are you doing in here?' And you know, you explained you weren't doing any harm really," said McCall, who remembered the exchange that followed with a senior police officer as being relatively cordial. "You know, we agreed hadn't I got everything now and wouldn't I like to go back where I'm meant to be. So you're not doing anything any other journalist wouldn't do, but it raises the question of where do you draw the line. I don't think that went beyond what any journalist would do. You read afterwards that there were far worse things going on." McCall recalled that although he found people he encountered at the school were ready to talk, people in the town seemed to be "fairly media weary" by the end of the day. "Most people who moved around obviously were being interviewed by a lot of people. And some people would talk, some people wouldn't. Some people had had enough. Some people clearly did feel that we were preying on the misery of this little town."

By late afternoon, McCall had tramped over the town all day. His group pulled out about 5 p.m., and he wrote his stories in the car, on the way back to Newcastle.

For Peter Marks, working for *Newsday*, the day seemed to go on forever. "I just remember being out there for hours trying to find people who found pieces of the plane, or people who had witnessed what had happened the night before. I went to Sherwood Crescent. And they were keeping us pretty far away. There was another place where the whole engine came down. We spent the day chasing down plane parts. Trying to find people who saw the stuff come down. The story that day was the bodies falling out of the sky." He remembered another aspect of the atmosphere. "The Scottish police sort of set the tone. They made you feel like you were a ghoul if you were searching for that stuff," meaning carnage.

The *Newsday* reporter and photographer stayed that night in what Marks described as "freezing cold" bed-and-breakfast. "I was very depressed because you've just gone through this horrible day, and it started to sink in that night, how horrible this was. It was like 10 or 11 o'clock that night that I finally got into the bed and breakfast, and I had dinner and I was exhausted. And I went to bed, sort of like dreading the next day. I was not looking forward to this. It was not — I mean, I knew there was a lot of pressure to get stuff. I didn't know how long I was going to be there. It was Christmas time. My wife has been very supportive whenever I get these sort of assignments; I mean, I felt funny being (away)."

He had just fallen asleep when the owner of the bed-and-breakfast woke him up to say that his newspaper had called. The editor wanted him to contact some woman they had heard about, someone like the sister of an American relative of one of the victims. "Which could have easily been done in the morning, and I got up and I couldn't get back to sleep," he said. "I was so depressed. It was the lowest moment of the trip." He called his wife and said, "I want to come home. I don't want to do this." Sitting at his desk in one corner of the huge *Newsday* newsroom, he laughed at the memory. "You get really kind of crazy. It seemed to me it was getting more and more daunting. You know, they want me to find this person. How was I going to find this person? I can't even get to sleep." His wife told him, "Oh, shut up and go back to sleep. You'll be fine tomorrow." She was right. "In the morning, everything was okay. It had sorted itself out by the second day."

By the morning of December 23, authorities had established limits around major sections of the disaster, and were preparing to keep media focused with briefings and organized site visits. That made it easier for newspeople in some ways, but more difficult in others.

Don Singleton of the New York *Daily News* went to the Masonic Lodge the next morning. "They would put up on the sign board outside what time the next briefing was. So then you would fan out and do what you could do, interview people; I mean you'd do what you normally would do, find people who were involved in any way." By then, Graham Patterson of the *Daily Express* recalled, police had arranged for more phone lines to be put into the press center. "I thought the police did a tremendous job," he said, "in arranging communications and providing press conferences. And then Scottish Office did PR as well; they helped."

Peter Marks, having finally got some sleep, was anxious to get a first-hand story of what had happened. "The investigation story was kind of developing slowly. And I was trying to get the human side, which I love doing anyway." But when he got into Lockerbie, the media were told they should stay in town and not roam around the search areas. "I knew we had to get out to get some stuff, first hand stuff," he said. "So we just bluffed our way through the police." Marks remembered telling the officer guarding the roadblock he was just going a little bit farther, just to take some pictures, and the officer said, "Sure, go ahead."

"No other reporters were getting through that day, as far as I could tell," he said. The *Newsday* team went out through Tundergarth, stopped and took pictures, and Marks interviewed a couple of people. They noticed a couple of cameramen, but no print media. It wasn't what Marks was looking for, so they drove farther into the countryside. "This was when I started getting really emotional. I started realizing — it still hadn't hit me that there were all these dead people. And we drove into the countryside, and on the hills there were all these indentations, like one or two feet into the ground. I didn't know what they were at the time. There were a lot of these and there would be little red markers next to them." They were where the bodies had fallen to earth. "They had each made an impact. I also later found out that families had made pilgrimages to the impact spot, I mean, which blew my mind."[2]

As they drove along they found "this farm in the middle of nowhere," its fields covered in debris. "It was as if someone had taken a part of the plane and left it in pieces. I saw seat belts. I saw a seat. I saw a piece of a wing or something, you know, with letters. The whole field was covered with these things, almost like they'd been placed there. So we drove up to the farm house, and up to this point I had not talked to anybody really in depth," he recalled. He went around the back of the house and saw a man slaughtering a turkey. "He was literally with his cleaver up as we pulled up. And I said, hi, I'm from an American newspaper. I want to know —"

The man and his wife welcomed them. "They were just lovely, very simple Scottish people who were totally intrigued at the idea of Americans coming to — It was like they felt we were coming because we cared about them. And I certainly encouraged them to think that. I didn't lie and say, 'We're doing a story because we love you,' but I certainly encouraged them to believe it. They proceeded to spill the story of having seen the flash in the sky, and having watched this surreal event, watched pieces of a plane float down. I mean, they had no idea what was happening at the time. The way they described it was like *War of the Worlds*. I mean, it was like this strange invasion. But they accepted it in a strange way, too. They were not like freaked out." He had the impression that because they were so calm, they had not seen any bodies.

Then one of them said, "You know, you really should go talk to Jimmy, our cousin Jimmy, because he was the first guy into the cockpit." Marks could scarcely contain his excitement, but recalled asking quite calmly "Where is he?" and saying, "Yes, that sounds like a guy I'd want to talk to." The man said, "Well, I don't know if he'll talk. He's very shaken up." Marks remembers thinking, "He's my story. These people are good. But (he's) my story." The photographer got lots of pictures, and Marks began to relax. "I started thinking, yes, I'm a reporter. You know what I mean. I always feel like when I hit a new story that I'm not going to get anything. It's like my phobia."

So they went back to Tundergarth, and found Jimmy standing out alone, smoking a cigarette. "And he proceeded to tell me the most incredible story. He was clearly haunted — I guess this is now 50 hours after the thing. He tells me the story of watching, of sitting in his house watching TV, and hearing — again with the flash — and seeing... He actually ran into his back yard and saw the cockpit come down — that huge piece that you saw — and explained to me that he went out to the cockpit with a torch and he saw the bodies quivering. They were like all stripped of clothing, he said. I mean, he gave me the first real sense of what had happened. He said that one of them was still alive. He drove down into town (for help). It was so heartbreaking. At Tundergarth he found the local pastor of the church. He said, 'There are two wee bairn in the —' And they found the two babies strapped into seats."

As he listened, Marks said, it didn't hit him emotionally. "It really didn't. I just kept thinking, this is great detail. I mean, you think about it, God, what kind of person am I? Was I so just taken with the story? But I was proud of myself for having found him. I thought this justified the paper, you know, putting their faith in me. Anyway, so I wrote up this story, which became the lead story next day, the story of Jimmy telling the story."

Actually, he was frustrated that he had a lot more detail than he could put in the story. He was also writing a main story about the progress of the investigation, but the story he was proud of was the one from the countryside. "I thought I got something nobody else had."

Robert Barr of the Associated Press arrived to relieve Maureen Johnson, and was immediately struck by the impression that this was a very small place overpowered by the event. "There was an overwhelming media presence there. I was particularly aware that there was sort of this pack of us going up and down the street," especially in the few yards between the Masonic Hall and the Presbyterian church. "So, these people were coursing up and down the street, and I had the strong feeling that local people knew who was from outside and why they were there."

Within an hour of arriving in Lockerbie, Barr was taking part in a tour of Sherwood Crescent that Angus Kennedy arranged for a group of media. "I was in the press group which walked down the street. It was covered with aluminum shrapnel really, some of it rather large. But I remember the noise of things clanking underneath your feet. And I went down and looked at the crater, saw the dogs working there (searching for bodies). It was all very controlled. Everybody moved down in a pack and back."

Graham Patterson represented the *Express* as reporters were led up to the crater rim. "By then all the bodies had been removed, well, not of all them, most of them. They stuck garden canes by (where) each one (had been found). And it was just a row of canes right up the garden. It was astonishing. When you saw the canes, you realized just how many people had been on there. Astonishing." Patterson observed that such canes appeared for miles out in the countryside. "And if you were driving along, you'd see a cane and think, God, there's another body over there."

When the FBI arrived, Patterson said, "of course, we realized it must have been a bomb. We found out pretty quickly that they were there because they walked about with FBI on the back of their jackets. So they just had to admit it."

One problem was the number of potential interviews. "We had the army, the navy, the air force, the Red Cross; everyone was involved, so everyone had a story to tell," Patterson said. Covering aspects of the tragedy that affected Lockerbie the most directly, however, was difficult. "It was a case of getting hold of and approaching relatives of these people, for the obvious reasons, to see if they had photos of the deceased or any background details," Patterson recalled. But such information was hard to come by, and the highly competitive national papers cooperated in order to complete their coverage of that aspect. "So it was a case of really share and share alike. No one was doing the dirty on anyone. We just had to pool as much as we possibly could."

Patterson felt the reactions of local people had begun to change. "In fact, we were told on more than one occasion, that the people in Lockerbie spent more time (the day after the impact) watching the media at work, you know,

TV cameras that were there, radio that were there, reporters that were there. The first couple of days they were actually more interested in the media, and some people said that was a good thing. Because it took their minds off actually what had happened. And, of course, after a day, a day-and-a-half, they suddenly realized what had happened. And from being very helpful in the main, suddenly, (they) changed, and they realized just exactly what the media were there for, and what they were doing, and there was one or two scenes in the Main Street, things like that."

Pressed to describe what he meant by scenes, Patterson said, "Well, they were having a go at reporters and photographers and the TV people, and things like that, which I certainly thought very understandable. I didn't blame them for one little minute. In fact, I don't think any of the media did. It was perfectly understandable."

One incident that may have contributed to this change in attitude had taken place in Rosebank Crescent the previous day. Photographers and television cameramen had been there and recorded the process of lowering a body from the roof. The scene offended the neighbors, and the publication of the photograph in *Time* magazine prompted the only formal complaint made to the Press Council, the body then charged by British newspapers with taking complaints about press practices.[3]

At Scottish Television, John Kean studied the footage his crew had shot from that scene and used "only a very brief shot of the body on the roof, taking about two seconds."

The pictures of it being lowered were never shown on his program. "It was very tightly edited, but I did use part of it. I just felt it...would have been an absolute shock. Well, the whole story about Lockerbie was shocking. I felt we should use something. But my cameraman actually got a very, very close-up shot of it (the body). I thought we can't use this. I said, 'Can you imagine how the relatives of that particular person would feel if they saw that?' The cameraman, Harry Smith, agreed. He said not to show the close-up of the body," Kean said. "That was our decision, and I've stuck by that."

Although many live broadcasts were made from Lockerbie, the terrain itself in a way protected the town from some practices that would emerge in subsequent live disaster coverage. Because of the hills that surrounded the site, signals from the most picturesque locations were unreliable and so television crews tended to tape their reports and then transmit them. Live interviews, including one of a man in charge of Community Support with Breakfast Television in Tasmania, halfway round the world, had to be set up elsewhere, sometimes in a prosaic parking lot. Dick Blystone of CNN did a telephone report shortly after reaching the town, but recalled doing none of the live, on-camera telecasts that were to become his network's signature.

The search went on in the hills around Lockerbie. David Leppard would learn later that the rank-and-file police were very upset about the way some media treated the search scene. In his book, *On the Trail of Terror: The Inside Story of the Lockerbie Investigation* (1991), he quotes a personal report by a woman officer who, like most of the police assigned to the scene, had no experience with major disasters — or the media who cover them. She wrote about two police constables and an American CBS camera crew:

> Two PCs noticed a camera crew taking film, from about 100 yards away, of a corpse being lifted from the mud and put into a bag. They went to speak to the crew who admitted they had been told to go away, but had nevertheless ignored the warning. No one had stopped them coming to the scene because the road wasn't closed and anyone who wanted to could just drive up, have a look, take a picture or film, and basically do what they liked.
>
> This was particularly upsetting to us as we were aware that many of the bodies would be easily recognisable facially, and as a result of a long-range camera shot, someone sitting at home watching television could have been presented with a picture of a relative or friend they recognised being lifted out of the marsh. Even worse, they could go away thinking that because the person had a relatively soft landing they might still be alive. Other officers who spoke to the crew feel strongly that some sort of reprimand for their action is merited (p. 43).[4]

The woman officer also described how she personally confronted a different camera crew as they were filming the cockpit:

> When I saw these three guys taking film and making commentary right at the gate into the field, I told them to stop. They didn't, so I very gently pulled the lens of the camera down, and this American jerk started shouting at me for ruining the camera shot. I ended up having to apologise to them, because it turned out they had been given permission to film. What if relatives had been visiting the cockpit area and these b— had taken shots of their faces. I cannot see any reason why these leeches on society have been allowed virtually free rein to intrude on people's grief (p. 43).

Stresses from the scene combined with those from other sources. For some reporters, pressure from editors was a problem. Reporters from U.S. news organizations became very conscious of that fact as editors pressed them to get information about the cause of the disaster and for interviews with American relatives who had come to Lockerbie. "Every day I'm running back into town going to press conferences, interviewing people on the street, you know," said Marks. "Most editors have no sense of logistics, I think. When you're out there, they have no sense of what's possible and what's not possible, like, 'Find out what's going on in the investigation, you know,' like, 'All right, I'll ask at the press conference.'"

In many ways, the story was becoming "normal." As Don Singleton said, "It fell into the pattern of big, international stories where you get a large press corps, and it has to be systematized in some way because it's just too overwhelming. Quickly, the government agency, whatever it is, chooses a spot and a person to handle the press and then you get briefings. I was in that queue. I was among the press, and in that way it was like a lot of stories. It was no different."

The reporter for the *Herald-Journal* agreed that the story began to take on a routine. "I had a method where I'd walk through the village, and there were the golf course, the town houses on the east end of town where I think they found most of the bodies." He was referring to the council houses on Rosebank Crescent. "So I'd take a hike around there, go down where the sheep herding pens were. Check, did they get the engine out of the sidewalk yet? Who's down there? There'd always be people out. You know, you could stop and chat." Then he would drop into an antique shop, whose owner made a number of reporters welcome. "He was a friend of the Lord of Avondale or Baron of Avondale or whatever. He held some title but he still had holes in his suitcoat. But these two guys (the shop owner and his friend) took me everywhere, all around, got me through the police, everything. It was like a coffee shop. Well, actually, he just kept feeding everybody tea, and everybody would come in and it was just providence that I found the place. And I got a lot of information out of there, you know. 'They found that engine over there. Gee, they're looking for a suitcase.' You know, and bits like that."

That was especially helpful, he said, because the Scottish police system is founded on "you don't say anything. But these guys would go home, talk with their wives, their friends, and then their friends would go to the antique shop and, you know, so maybe I'd get information a day later. You always knew where they were looking or what was going on, and then these guys would jump in their car, and they'd be just as curious as anybody else here about what was going on. And they would take you all over."

In the early part of the story, the Syracuse reporter estimated that half of what he was reporting was "original," that is, based on observation and interviews, "and half what they were telling everybody at the press conferences. As time went on the press conferences became more and more the source of news. Townspeople got overwhelmed. There was less visual stuff going on...By the end it was completely spoon-fed stuff. They walked you through press conferences very tightly. They took you to scenes."

About the second or third day, he recalled, his mission became tracking down any American relatives, particularly family of victims with ties to Syracuse University or the Central New York area. "My priority became less reporting on developments in Lockerbie, but the search for anything with a local connection. My editors, rightfully so, thought it was important. It was impossible." Peter Marks agreed that gaining access to American relatives seemed impossible. "The Scottish police had no sense of our priorities, you know. Why should they? Some reporters don't understand that, I think. They think, 'Well, why can't they get us an American victim?' So I knew some people were pressuring them. I didn't feel like haranguing them."

The teams of counselors met the relatives at airports and escorted them into town and to discreet locations, keeping them away from journalists. "And at one point," the Syracuse reporter said, "everybody (in the media) began looking for family. The story became a little stale on the developments side, and the thing was everybody searched for family. People were hanging out at bars. If you had an American accent, producers from the networks would cozy up to see if you were family." When Angus Kennedy did produce the American family member at a news conference, Marks recalled the experience as "surreal." When the man walked into the room with the reporters, "he was clearly scared to death...and they'd only let us ask a few questions, so it wasn't very satisfying." The AP's Robert Barr remembered it as "just one of those grim things. Of course, it was useful to us, as reporters, to get anything from the families who were at the scene. They were, as I recall, very much shielded from the reporters, and I think the reporters were deferential about it. So anything was useful. As I recall, he didn't say very much at all. It was just one of those compromises that are made. People make a judgment about, 'I'll talk this much, and maybe this will buy me some space, and I won't have to talk anymore. The pressure will go off.' So it was that sort of thing."

Marks subsequently learned about the anger of the family members toward Pan Am and the State Department, and wondered aloud if shielding them from the press had been a disadvantage for the families. "It might have facilitated a lot, and made people's lives a lot simpler if we'd been able to get at that story."

The *Herald-Journal* reporter said one reporter from the *Detroit News* managed to interview a family from India living in Michigan. The Syracuse reporter tried hard to get in touch with families, even using the phone center in Lockerbie to call people in New York State and asking them to pass messages to their relatives who were staying in Lockerbie. He requested that they have the relatives leave a message at his hotel, so that they could "just talk for a while." He knew what he wanted to say to them: "I want to see what you're experiencing, what's going on, what you're thinking." He never made contact, even though people were making similar calls from his newspaper's office in Syracuse. "I came real close...I think it was an honorable attempt. I didn't portray myself as something other — like a tourist or family posed as somebody, which I suspect network producers were doing. They were going out, finding out where the families were staying, checking into the hotels, trying to cozy up to them."

He remembered that the CBS crew did manage to get a relative to talk to them. "They were kind of funny. They had limos. They had their own communications networks and everything. I thought they were really pretty aggressive in trying to track down families. And I don't know the tactics they used — but I know the tactics that the print people used, and I know the tactics that the local guys were using — and we weren't getting anybody. But they did. I don't know, maybe being from CBS carries some weight or something. But I don't see why being from the *Herald-Journal* would carry less weight with someone from Syracuse than, say, CBS. But it became pretty frantic as news dried up, and the search for families became the only thing really to justify people (reporters) staying there."

As the days passed, it became more and more clear that this was not an accident. The second day the *Herald-Journal* reporter had managed to call his home in Syracuse, and heard for the first time that his wife was pregnant. He found himself wanting to go home, partly out of a conviction that little additional information would be coming out of Lockerbie, partly because of the strong emotions the event was stirring in him. "I started thinking about the people on the plane. And they kept bringing in the bodies in the morgue," he said. "What I felt was just bad for what happened. I didn't feel bad that we had to do our jobs. I didn't feel bad for the people there because they had to endure reporters and stuff. I didn't feel bad about my role. I felt bad that the plane blew up. Family members and all that. It was the first time like — I'd been a reporter for seven years — a death was personalized. Probably because my wife (being pregnant). You know, I'd been to accident scenes; I'd seen a lot of blood and guts. I was one of the reporters that always covered murders and mobsters," he said, adding that he had seen firemen "carrying babies out of burning trucks. But, you know, I guess the holiday, being away, the toll (of the dead) — I mean, seeing bodies, the guys with the rubber gloves."

He was not part of the pool that went into the morgue. "Everybody shared it. You know, you saw the videotapes and well — Wow! You know, I just couldn't imagine...At that time, I think, they had 70 or 80 caskets. That is a lot. That is a lot. Eighty is a lot. And I was just from a small town paper. And it was tough. You know, I didn't dwell on it," he said. "I went about my job. I thought I wrote a pretty good story because of it." He called that piece, written for the Christmas Day edition "one of my best stories ever, really — probably because of the emotion."

Reporters noticed that tension was increasing between the townspeople and the media. Robert Barr, having arrived on December 23, said he soon realized "there was some antagonism simply because people had been interviewed too much." He remembered going into a shop. "Everything was very cordial until I identified myself as a reporter. And the woman sort of blew up at me. (She) says, 'No more. No press. Out.' So it wasn't a very happy situation to be in as a reporter." Barr did a Christmas Eve story about "whether people were really getting down to the celebrations. You hated to go and ask people these questions."

Many of the British newspeople were able to spend Christmas at home, although Nick Cohen of *The Independent* remembered that he arrived and collapsed with exhaustion, sleeping most of the holiday. His wife, he recalled, was not pleased.

Don Singleton remembered Christmas morning in his hotel in Dumfries for two reasons. A tape of Christmas music sung by a boy's choir was playing as the *Daily News* reporter went down to breakfast, and then he heard some American accents of people who had not been there the previous day. He assumed they must be relatives of victims, but decided not to approach them.

A Syracuse *Post-Standard* reporter arrived in Scotland Christmas Eve. He had been sent to Kennedy Airport the night of the tragedy, then traveled to London to interview students at the Syracuse University center. He reached Carlisle by train and eventually found a taxi driver to take him to Thornhill, a 35-minute ride from Lockerbie and the nearest place he could find accommodation. The taxi driver asked about the reporter's heritage and when he said his grandmother came from Scotland, the two reached instant rapport. "We got along great because of that," the reporter recalled. The taxi driver, who had been in Lockerbie the night of the tragedy, became the Syracuse reporter's guide and drove him to the scene the next day. That night the *Post-Standard* reporter stayed in Thornhill to rest. He was tired and lonely. He opened his suitcase and found a tiny parcel his little daughter had tucked in. It was a key ring with his initial on it. "That and watching the BBC were my Christmas," he said.

In the morning, the taxi driver came by. He was delivering some tape for Scottish Television and offered the reporter a lift to Lockerbie, dropping him in front of the Town Hall. That two-storey building had become the focal point of the town's mourning; as victims were identified, their coffins were placed in neat rows in the upstairs meeting room. Floral tributes were being placed along the front of the structure. "The first thing I did was look at all these flowers. I was trying to take notes and read what (the messages with the flowers) said." The guard saw he was having difficulty, "and let me inside the barricade so I could read all the cards."

He walked around the town, and within a few minutes, bumped into the *Herald-Journal* reporter. Normally, the two men see each other as rivals; their newspapers are headquartered in the same building but the morning and afternoon papers compete vigorously. Here, however, the *Herald-Journal* reporter told his newly arrived *Post-Standard* foe how frustrating the search for news had become. "He had gotten the same thing that everyone else was getting. He just found out his wife was pregnant while he was over there, so we were really commiserating about what a great Christmas we were having."

The *Post-Standard* man trudged out to the ice rink, where the morgue had been moved. "The pathologists were coming out in their surgical gowns, and they were walking back and forth. They appeared pretty unapproachable." The reporter read the body language of the townspeople and decided they did not want to talk. "They would avert their eyes and walk a wide bend around you. I was carrying a briefcase around with my computer in it. Pretty much everybody would have recognized you as a reporter." It did not seem logical to him to press people to talk. "The other thing was that it was the 25th, and everybody had done the what-you-saw story to death, so that really wasn't a priority."

Filing the story from the bar of a hotel that night turned into a nightmare. "I almost got beat up," for tying up the phone, the reporter said. "The phones in that area were just overtaxed with what was going on. So I ended up having to dictate the story; it wouldn't 'take' from the modem. It was a satellite — like a ship-to-shore radio. If they made any noise, it would cut you out and it took forever."

Peter Marks had a much different Christmas experience. By then he was staying in Glasgow, driving down early every morning and back late at night, because as he said, "I wanted some amenities," and the ability to file right from his hotel room. "Christmas Day was a big day in Lockerbie. I knew I had to do a big story that day, and I wanted to find other ways to tell this story. I knew there was going to be all these services; they wouldn't let us into the Catholic church. Because when you have like 500 reporters, it ruins everything. We all step all over each other, and all you need is two assholes, and the whole thing collapses. I would hear these stories about people claiming we were vultures, and I think if you acted like one, people reacted to you that way, but if you were pleasant and gave them space, they responded. I never had anyone slam a door in my face, and say, 'You're a vulture.'"

So Christmas Day, he went to the Church of Scotland, a Presbyterian church. "I talked to the pastor, who was extremely nice, and explained that I wanted to hear his sermon." He arranged for the *Newsday* reporter to sit in an annex, where the service was piped in. "So I could actually take notes and get the sense of what he was doing. And that was okay. I mean, I didn't have to have hundreds of people. I would have liked to have a little more access, but that was fine."

Marks thought he had finished reporting for the story, which was to be about a town in mourning on Christmas. "This man comes up to me, and just out of nowhere he said quietly, 'It's a sad day.' He didn't know me, and I didn't know him. We fell into conversation and he, it turned out, had lost some friends, and we went into a pub and talked for an hour. Wonderful. He turned out to be a great little vignette in a piece. I'm always amazed at people trusting reporters like that. They'll sit down with them — you don't know me from — you don't know if I'm from the *National Enquirer* (an American tabloid sold primarily at supermarket checkout counters). I mean that's the other thing, you can say *Newsday* in Scotland and nobody knows what the hell it is. It's almost different if you say I'm a *Syracuse Post-Standard* reporter. You can say Syracuse, New York, you know what I mean?" he said, referring as well to the tie that was already developing between Lockerbie and Syracuse as the site of the university that had lost 35 students. "Long Island is not a place people identify with as a real place. I was always amazed that people would just open up to me, as this stranger. They just needed someone to talk to."

The AP's Robert Barr also attended some of the Christmas services, which were very simple and very somber. "Again, I think it was a matter of people just being overwhelmed. There weren't the real ritual expressions that you expect after a tragedy. They were just sort of coming to terms with it."

Two days later, however, Barr witnessed a quiet tribute as the first bodies of the American victims left the town. "They just came in a couple of vans down the High Street. And it hadn't been announced, but it seemed like people in town knew that this was going to happen. People came out on the street. They stood there in absolute silence." Then the vans passed along the street and out of the village. "Everybody melted away. It was terribly moving to see that. It was sort of this natural response from the town, of doing the proper thing. That was very impressive."

From the *Newsday* point of view — and for many media — the story of what really happened seemed to be unfolding, after a few days, in Washington and London. "We hung around (Lockerbie) because we were waiting for the story of the why question. You know, why did it blow up? What happened to the plane?" Peter Marks said. Information was still coming out, but not the answer to those questions. So Marks went down to London after Christmas. "The idea was to talk to some experts, people who may have had contacts in the Scottish police. And I talked to a couple of guys who were experts in the field and they speculated, basically. Yes, it was a bomb. No, it wasn't a bomb. You know what I mean? It really was inconclusive. We were sort of fishing in those days."

One of the stories he filed from London actually was based on an appearance by Oliver Revell, executive assistant director of the FBI, on the CBS-TV program, "Face the Nation." "New York ended up sending me the transcript and I wrote it and sent it back. But I was trying to write it all — I felt it was important to keep the story in Scotland. And by this point, I felt very competent. I had a few stories under my belt. The story sort of did fall into place. The big thing was the investigation."

The last day he was in London, he flew back to Lockerbie "on a hunch because somebody had said to me, 'There's something brewing up there. They're going to announce something.'" Marks figured the most likely place for such an announcement would be Lockerbie, and he was right. "It was the most information the police ever gave us." The *Herald-Journal* reporter was pleased about the timing of that particular news conference. It came early enough to make that afternoon's paper in Syracuse, which meant he had a scoop over major American newspapers, most of which are published in the morning. Graham Patterson of the *Express* said the news conferences leading up to that announcement had become more and more detailed. "Of course, once it was announced that it was a bomb, that was it. That was really end of story."

Like most British media and many of those from abroad, however, that was not the signal for the *Express* team to leave. They still had funerals and the memorial service in early January to cover. Some of the most touching and troubling parts of the media coverage would occur around those events. Atholl Duncan of BBC Scotland had the unenviable task of setting up cameras inside the Church of Scotland so they could broadcast the event without disrupting it. He found a way of hiding them behind a cloth hanging and, after the service, was very surprised when some local people came to him to express thanks for his efforts.

But a few media representatives offended both the townspeople and the rest of the newspeople covering the story by using subterfuge to gain access to the funerals. The most frequently heard complaint concerned two reporters who allegedly dressed up in dark clothing, as if they were mourners, to cover the first funeral of a Lockerbie victim. None of the people interviewed for this study were able to name those involved in this breach, so that we were unable to explore the rationale these reporters used to justify their action.

Behind the barrier: Kennedy Airport

Tom Brook was working at a computer in the Manhattan office of the BBC when someone rushed by saying a plane had gone down in Britain, probably an American airliner. Using the computer, Brook checked the wire service reports and learned it was a Pan Am plane. "I can't really remember what happened immediately after that, but we soon learned that the plane was headed for Kennedy, and had apparently gone down in Scotland — I suppose it was a knee-jerk reaction. We figured that if it was going to Kennedy, there'd be some sort of story. We were not quite sure what the story would be, a press conference or whatever." So the broadcast journalist grabbed a taxi and arranged to meet a crew out there. "It was a rather eerie afternoon, because it was wet and cloudy. It just was ominous, the whole thing, going into the airport. It was just before Christmas...and I think there was a feeling of palpable anxiety."

Mike Santangelo was at the *Daily News*, essentially finished for the day. He had completed his story for the next morning's edition. "I was sitting around reading the wires, which I do compulsively — a lot of newsmen do that. And I saw the bulletin, 'Plane crash,' and, of course, a 747 goes down, you're interested, immediately. When I saw 'bound for Kennedy' I went to the city desk. Immediately I said, 'She was bound for Kennedy,' and they said, 'Go.'" Santangelo went to his car and drove himself and a photographer through heavy traffic. It took them almost an hour to reach the airport.

As soon as they arrived, the Daily News team began looking for families. "It took us a little time to find them, but we knew they were there," the veteran reporter said. He recalled that two or three families were already in what he referred to as the VIP lounge.[5] "Then Pan Am said, 'We're going to have a press conference,' and then they jerked us around. Press conference was supposed to be here. Then it was supposed to be there. Then it was supposed to be at this time, then it was supposed to be at that time. I remember we did a lot of running back and forth. And we were getting kind of annoyed about when the press conference was going to be." Pan Am opened the regular press room, and provided coffee, soft drinks and sandwiches. "Which was smart — get the press the hell out of the way, put us in one place," Santangelo said. "If you can, that's the best way to handle the press. They gave us something to eat. We were getting something free, and we were in one place."

Arriving at the airport, Brook and his crew were also told to go to the press room. They joined other media waiting around for the news conference. "And what happened then, I think, was that it became clear that Pan Am were not going to hold a press conference. Which seemed a bit silly because we'd all been waiting there about an hour, been told to go there. Consequently, there were all these TV crews, reporters, hungry for information, who suddenly had no information. And actually thinking back on it, I suppose that was the start of the problem. Because then we began to — and I do use this word deliberately — stalk the airport, looking for victims, so to speak." They went down to the First Class lounge, also described as the VIP lounge, "which Pan Am had cordoned off and made the kind of bereavement center for people," Brook said. "Somehow, I don't know why, but I didn't think that there would be many people arriving who didn't know about this (crash). Because it was all over — I say it was all over, I mean I heard it on the radio; it was all over the TV by that time."

Brook remembered that he felt under pressure to get a story. "I realized this was a very big news story. And I was frustrated that there was nothing official from Pan Am, that apparently the press conference was taking place at the Pan Am building in midtown Manhattan. It was also strange because Pan Am was trying to pretend that nothing strange was going on. You'd ask people about information and they'd say, 'Don't mention that there's a crash.' Which seems bizarre because there were people checking in for flights all over, to go to Europe and everything."

Brook estimated probably between 10 and 15 television crews, as well as print reporters were hanging around the bereavement center — and they shot some pictures of relatives being escorted into the lounge. "I don't think that at that point we were being particularly intrusive," the television reporter said.

As Bill Douglas, who had been working out of the Brooklyn office of *Newsday* when he got the call to go to Kennedy, remembered, "You had a hard time finding family members because Pan Am's a big terminal; you don't want to go up to just anybody and say, 'By the way, was your relative on this plane?' That's a bit rude." Douglas said he walked around for a while, searching for people who looked worried. "So we went up to worried looking people, and asked why they looked worried. They said, 'You know, I've got so-and-so on the plane.' About four or five of the people said, 'I'm not sure what's going on.' And they didn't want to talk about it.

"Pan Am people didn't want to talk about it. They were trying to, you know, shoo the media, or usher them out of the terminal," he said, referring to the scheduling and cancellation of the press conference. Luckily, he said, someone he knew from the Red Cross was there. From that person he learned about the bereavement center. "So that way we knew that there were enough people there who were concerned, who were family members. The Red Cross did extensive stuff, lodging for people who didn't have lodging, and they were helping to break the news to people."

Douglas recalled that Pan Am representatives said nothing official until well into the evening, when he understood they told people in the bereavement center. He remembered being in the middle of the terminal lobby when "Pan Am made the announcement that the plane had indeed fallen out of the sky. They didn't explain what happened." He said the word was passed by people "circulating around and telling people."

About that time, Santangelo noticed a man and woman "sort of wandering around." He thought someone must have told them to come that way. As they walked into this area, they looked up at one of the monitors. A sign was flashing on the monitor, Santangelo recalled, saying something like "People meeting Pan Am Flight 103 please use the house phone."[6] The woman waited, while the man went to one of the white wall phones and identified himself to Pan Am, the reporter said. "By this time I knew I had something. I knew this is a live one. Let's try and move in on this."

He motioned to his photographer, who was up a flight of stairs. "I signaled him, pointed to the woman, figured that's where the action was. I moved in behind her, came in on her flank, figuring I want to see what happens, and if I can, I'll talk to her. The guy put down the phone. It was really pretty emotional," said Santangelo, who admitted to feeling emotion even as he told the story more than three years later. The reporter said he could see the look on the man's face, "like a condemned man, walking to the gallows, almost. And here's this woman — it was a daughter I think they were going to meet — and he walks up to her. I couldn't hear what he said. She just looked at him, gave him a look, 'no.' And then she said it. She gave him the look first, and then he repeated it. He said it very softly. I couldn't hear. And she said," Santangelo emphasized the word the way he recalled she had, "'No.' Just very certain, 'No.' He said something else, and she says, 'Not my little girl.' Then she began to shriek. 'Not my little girl, not my little girl.' And she fell over.

"I never saw anybody collapse like that. She stiffened up like a board, and she went, again like a board, on her back. She just fell straight back," he said sadly. "I never saw anything quite like that. And he, of course, was very upset, and he went down on his knees next to her. He was saying things to her, but I couldn't really catch what it was. It was like great garble, very emotional. And she was just saying the same thing, repeating over and over, 'Not my little girl, not my little girl.'[7] She put her arms up and she tried to push him away. He tried to hold her down. And then she began thrashing around."

Tom Brook recalled it a bit differently. The television crews were cordoned off, and he remembered seeing a woman coming up, talking to an airline official and "then hearing this terrible noise. And I didn't really know what was going on. I didn't realize that this was someone who'd come to the airport, had her daughter on the flight and had just discovered it. It just was very strange. I'd never heard anything like it. And, you know, I was with the crew the whole time, and it was something that I have a lot of conflict and anguish about, because I just had an automatic reaction, 'Look, just get it.' Then I realized what was going on, that it was a horrible event really, because she lost control, and she fell to the ground, spread eagle in a way, and she was screaming. It took me a while to realize what it was. I didn't know whether she'd been assaulted at first; it was so strange."

He estimated that while she was on the floor "there could easily have been 10 cameras" capturing her distress. "And after it became clear (what was happening), people did back up a bit, but they still wanted to get that shot and there were print cameras, too. And I remember realizing there was something wrong about our behavior. I'm not quite sure what exactly at that stage, but someone went past and hurled some kind of epithet at the press, saying, 'Don't you have any morals?'"

The security guards helped the woman's husband take her to the bereavement center, leaving the members of the news media shaken. The emotion as New York television reporters spoke to viewers that night was so striking that the *Daily News* media reporter devoted a column to it (Mirabella, Dec. 23, 1988). He quoted Matthew Schwarz of Channel 9 who called the mother's collapse "one of the most emotional moments I've ever experienced." Schwarz said:

> ...At that moment I didn't like this business very much at all. There were all of these cameras and people were fighting and jockeying for a position. An airport staffer walked by when that was happening and said to us, 'Merry Christmas, you ——holes.' And I thought she was exactly right (Mirabella, p. 80).

Mike Santangelo and his photographer had the picture. "I didn't get to talk to anybody. There was no way to talk to anybody, but I put it into the story," he said. "It was a terrible thing to see. It's one of those things you really wish you hadn't seen. It was hard to tell the rewrite man about it. You felt very bad for her."

Bill Douglas, the *Newsday* reporter, recalled how the woman fell right at his feet. "And you just sort of stand there and you wonder, 'What do you do? Do you get down on the knees with her? Do you start interviewing her, or do you just let have her moment?' I sort of opted for letting her have her moment." Douglas thought she was wailing in Spanish, although no media reports that were examined as part of this research mentioned her using a foreign language. The *Newsday* reporter remembered, for example, "When she got up, I tried talking to her, but I don't speak Spanish."[8] Asked if this could have been a different woman, he said, "I think it's the same lady because I think those were my shoes in the *Daily News* (picture). She was just crying, really, really crying. You know. That's when I realized that this was a big deal."

A reporter for the Syracuse *Herald-Journal*, who had flown into Kennedy in time to see the woman collapse, recalled, "I was just so amazed — something really hit me. I don't know what I did think when I saw that. I just thought here's a first-hand case of grief. I thought, 'What a great story!'"

Tom Brook stayed another half hour, and shot some other pictures of relatives. "We weren't intrusive after that point." He told the woman colleague who was coordinating the BBC coverage from its Manhattan office,

"Look, well, you know, there are some people turning up here, and I did just get on tape something which is very dramatic, and I don't know whether we should use it or not." Reflecting on that statement, Brook said, "I think now I would say I wouldn't have even questioned whether we should have used it. It's really thanks to (the colleague) that it didn't get used, her judgment. Because I brought the tape back to the office, and she looked at it, and she said, 'No, we can't use that.' She was quite clear about it. I wasn't at that point so clear. I would be now, though." Brook could not remember his colleague's exact reasons. "I think she said it was just too disturbing. I think that was her justification."

Mike Santangelo stayed at the airport. The reporters were mostly lounging about within the roped off area, he recalled. He was looking for more sources to help him tell the story of human tragedy. He saw a family emerge by a side door of the VIP lounge, and very quietly went toward them. "I don't know why I spotted them," he said. A woman reporter from one of the smaller papers, possibly a New Jersey newspaper, saw he was going to approach them. "I guess she figured if I was doing it, it might be worthwhile to see what I was up to. Because there was really nothing going on."

The two reporters followed the family to a long corridor leading to another part of the terminal. "I began speaking to them at that point. And the woman did speak to me. The husband was kind of subdued, almost embarrassed about the whole thing. I think he was a little bit embarrassed at his wife's bitterness; his wife was extremely bitter. I can't remember exactly what she said. It was basically, 'Yeah, I'll talk to you. Why not? My daughter's dead. I've got nothing more to lose. This is all your stupidity, all your — you and the government and the media and everybody else. She's dead and there's no good reason for this. You can all go to hell. You want me to say some more?' Just a very bitter thing. Which was terrific for me, because I was the only one that got it. It was great for my story. It wasn't good for my feelings. It was a very emotional night. She got to about three-quarters of the way down that corridor when the TV crews spotted her, and spotted me and spotted the other reporter, and the TV people came in. Once the cameras spot you, it's like being in a feeding frenzy of sharks. The cameras came in, and she collapsed. She hadn't made it out of the airport."

The woman had to be carried back into the lounge, he said. This incident was clearly stressful to witness, but not as difficult for the reporter as the first woman's collapse had been. "If you'd seen that, you wouldn't forget it," he said of the first woman's collapse. "I still choke up when I think about it. That had to be the most horrible experience of her life. Dying is not going to be as difficult as that. I'd never seen anyone stiffen up like that. I've seen people killed. I've seen people terribly injured. But I've never seen anything like that. This woman just went rigid, absolutely rock hard rigid. And fell. It's amazing she wasn't injured. I presume she wasn't injured. I've never seen anything (like that). I never want to see it again.

"The second one was bitter. I mean, she really was just dripping bitterness. She hated at that point. I think if she could have figured out who to kill, she'd have killed somebody. There's no place to focus it. What do you do when you've got that kind of pain inside? I was there and she was bitter towards me. It didn't matter. I was getting my quotes. It was my job. I was delighted. To tell you the truth, I could almost say I wasn't unhappy that she went down after she spoke to me. Nobody else got it. I got it. Again, when you're a reporter, you close yourself off from things like this. There are certain things you've got to do. With the *Daily News*, talking to the families is a big thing. It's not a great job sometimes, but that one was okay. We got that."

At least twice, some media tried to enter the lounge where the family members had been taken. Both Mike Santangelo of the *Daily News* and Bill Douglas of *Newsday* told about such episodes.

Santangelo described how reporters had found a way that they could see into the lounge and then how they tried to come in an outside entrance. "It's the kind of thing, you know you aren't going to do it, but the boss expects you to try anyway," he said. "What I usually do in a situation like that is I find out who's going to try that stupid thing, and I get four feet behind him, and if they make it, I'll make it. If they get arrested, that's their problem. I don't like to get arrested. I always manage not to." This description seemed to fit the incident that was so terrifying to one of the mothers in the lounge. Told that it had been very frightening to this woman, Santangelo commented, "I can see where it would be."

The *Daily News* reporter said he thought some news media tried to get in another way as well. "Which is stupid. You're not going to get anything. You'll get arrested, whatever. I wanted to watch. I had no thought of getting in. That was too well controlled."

The *Newsday* reporter could not remember who had led the effort he witnessed, but thought it was a television crew. "They tried the ever-popular 'the public has the right to know' while the camera's flashing, and the what I call 'do you still beat your wife' play: where the camera's rolling, you're arguing with the Pan Am representative, 'Why are you hiding this from us? Why are you hiding this? The public has the right to know!' You know, as the Pan Am guy's trying to shut the door. I can't remember who that was," Douglas said. "So I didn't try to sneak in. I just don't do that."

Santangelo said that it took Pan Am a while to "crank up." After about three or four hours they provided a priest, a rabbi, a nurse and, he thought, also a doctor. "So we had people to talk to, which you need in a situation like that. You need an authority figure who can talk to the press. You need a clergyman first off to say, 'These people are devastated.' What did they say? You don't even have to give a name. 'One woman just said this,' and give us something we can write. What happened. Give us something that allows us to tell our readers and our editors," he said, emphasizing the editors. "You know, we're being whipped by editors. We've got to produce a story. If we can't produce a story, we're going to go crazy...You're going to have people who, you know, wrap themselves in lead and catapult themselves through the window to get it — who get real desperate. I don't do that. I've been at the *News* too long to do that. I figure I'm going to get something. I've done these things before."

Overall, the public relations was handled well, Santangelo said, "once it got cranked up." He said the presence of the clergy was critical. "The TV people had a talking head with a Roman collar. A rabbi showed up later on. So we had a priest and a rabbi. The priest, I think, was an assistant chaplain with the (police department), so he just showed up. The regular airport chaplain was ill that night or had been ill for some time. I don't know what the situation was. So they didn't have immediate clergy response, which I think in a situation (is) very important. You get somebody who's a clergyman, the press can't beat him up."

The Syracuse *Herald-Journal* reporter was struck by the strict security in place at Kennedy Airport. "At one point, I think I remember this right, some reporter had gone behind the barrier, the little rope, and some cop just shoved him back. You could tell the security people were really pissed at the reporters. They thought we were real ghouls."

Soon, some of the families were taken out of the VIP lounge so that they could go to hotels or, in some cases, to their homes. Most were escorted past the waiting reporters, photographers and television crews, who shouted questions at them. The *Herald-Journal* reporter found that being part of the media crowd made it impossible to try to interview anyone. "I guess I joined in the yelling, but I don't think my questions were heard," he said. "The closest I got was when people were being escorted out (of the lounge), and I followed them." Security guards protected the families from the trailing media corps. "Everytime we started to ask a question, they'd say, 'Shut up and get out of the way,'" said the Syracuse reporter, who became so frustrated he shouted, "How do you feel?" at one relative. His question went unanswered. In fact, his story, which ran on the front page of the next day's afternoon paper, was based on his description of the scene. Only officials were quoted, except for the unidentified mother who collapsed on the floor, crying, "Oh, no. Oh, no. Not my baby."

A reporter from the morning Syracuse newspaper, the *Post-Standard*, witnessed many of the same scenes, but stayed away from the media crowd.

He held a hand-made sign that said "Syracuse," which he had prepared on the plane, in hopes that someone would come forward to talk to him. He tried to spot some representative from Syracuse University. "I wasn't looking forward to having to try to Sam Donaldson my way with grieving people," he said, referring to the aggressive interviewing style of an ABC television correspondent. "I don't really think I would have done that if I had an opportunity to."

From his vantage point, the *Post-Standard* reporter said the location in which the media were cordoned off appeared to be the worst from the standpoint of the grieving families. "Someone would come through being escorted, and cameramen, who were waiting for something to happen, would turn around." This reporter decided on his own not to try to interview the bereaved because he could not approach them quietly, and the wire services would cover that scene. He also knew what was happening at Syracuse University and reasoned his paper's reporters would find plenty of grieving people there to quote. He covered a news conference finally held in a narrow, crowded room and managed to get an answer to his one shouted question: "How many from Syracuse?" He filed his story from a pay telephone.

Shortly before 10 p.m., a taxi carrying a Syracuse television reporter and cameraman from La Guardia Airport pulled up outside the terminal. They had not been able to make a connection directly to Kennedy. Then the cab got stuck on an expressway, behind a traffic accident. "I'm sweating bullets, having the guy (taxi driver) flip from radio station to radio station to hear the different coverage to give me a sense of what was going on at Kennedy and what was going on with the story in general. We were out of touch in the air for 45 minutes and developments kept happening so quickly. And by then, information was coming out of Syracuse on the New York radio stations. So I was getting a sense of what was happening back at home so I didn't sound like a total idiot when it came to going on the air."

Arriving at Kennedy, the reporter located the live truck that belonged to a fellow network-affiliated station. The reporter guessed that he had been given the assignment because he "spoke the best TV to go to a place like New York," meaning that he understood the technicalities and jargon for satellite transmission. "I'd be able to walk up to a live truck, knock on the door, and say, 'Hey, put me on the air.'" The reporter was worried about the time — he knew he would be expected to go live during the 11 p.m. newscast — but he could not rush into the terminal to get information, as he would have liked. He claimed that while his station provided him with the name of a contact, it had not actually set up his live shot. "They had not confirmed a slot, a window (referring to time on a satellite). And that was some hairy times — this before I had even been in the terminal."

While he was making the arrangements, his photographer went inside to shoot pictures. When the reporter walked into the terminal, a little after 10 p.m., he found the media penned into a fairly tight space behind police barricades. "By then, somebody had decided that the media needs to be taught its place, and its place is penned up inside this little wooden barricade area on one side, and on the other side, there's a stairwell that went up a couple of steps to a little landing. And there were cameras on both sides, still and video, and radio reporters on both sides. The networks were there, which means not just a cameraman. It's a cameraman, a light guy, and a sound guy. And there must have been 70 reporters and technicians."

Reporters and photographers did their jobs from this space, he said. "Every now and then, someone would come up this walkway and look a little bewildered...and bam, three dozen lights come on. Boom mikes go out in front of the person; they get even more bewildered. Somebody comes out with their little red jacket on or a Red Cross volunteer ushers them into this room (the VIP lounge). And everyone captures the picture, and the more aggressive, or the people who were out in front, try to ask questions of the person — not only of the family, or whoever it was who was coming to the airport, but somebody inside. 'What's going on in there?' And so that would happen five or six times every half hour."

But according to this journalist, this scene would have been different if Pan Am had not essentially ignored the press. "They just walked by and the Red Cross people gave us dirty looks. 'How dare we?' How dare we? Well, I think if they were prepared to send someone out to tell us what the mood was inside (the VIP lounge) we wouldn't have to do that (yell questions at those walking by the press)." The reporter did not realize, of course, that such statements had been made before he arrived. He had an hour or less before he had to do his live report, and still had little information. He had spent time traveling, time arranging the satellite time for his live shot, and then time getting no word from those in charge at the airport. He began moving from print to radio reporters, offering what he knew from Syracuse in exchange for information about what had been going on at Kennedy.

Bill Douglas remembered the pressure he felt from *Newsday*. "The editors were very driven. They really wanted this very badly, you know. At one point, someone literally on the phone said, 'Don't come back unless you get me some sort of survivors.' He just wanted some drama, the heartbeat, you know, the impact. So we milled about and we got survivors and we got the drama. But it was difficult. It was a zoo, definitely a zoo. Print people, you know, are lucky because we can fall in and about a crowd," he said, adding that the presence of television crews made the job of newspaper reporters harder "because, you know, if anything moves, they immediately flash lights and start aiming cameras, taking pictures, which makes people nervous. You know, you had a lot of TV there. And that made a lot of people antsy, anxious. It made Pan Am real nervous. And it made finding survivors difficult because they're busy ducking TV cameras, because they don't want to be seen on television."

Douglas said it is important not to get into "a pack mentality because on a story like that, if you do get involved in a pack, TV tends to take over, and you're at a distinct disadvantage. Because TV, all they've got to do is shine the light and camera on somebody and just ask questions. You know: 'How's it feel to lose your family member?' If the person breaks down and cries, great video. They've got their five seconds. I need words, and I can't ask, 'How does it feel to lose a loved one?' I need more than that. I need to know who the loved one was, why they were on the plane, what they were doing in Europe, how they found out about the crash, the whole nine yards. I need more than five seconds. So I think a lot of the print people were trying to subvert the video people...I just don't like dealing with the TV people en masse."

Douglas said he thought that he had been involved with worse "media feeding frenzies," but added, "everybody in the media was antsy because nobody knew what was going on at the time. So if anybody from Pan Am walked out and looked official, lights would go on, notebooks would start coming out. You know, people'd follow people. Stuff like that. It was testy more than anything else."

A group of Hasidic Jews arrived, and spotted Mike Santangelo. The *Daily News* reporter had developed a special relationship with this sect of the Jewish faith from a story he had written many years earlier. Although Santangelo is not Jewish, members of the New York press corps were used to seeing him talk with these men with their long, curled sideburns and flat black hats. "People were kidding me, 'Where are your Jews?' And all of a sudden, perhaps 12 Hasidics that I knew came marching into the area where the press was waiting. Of course, they recognized me, and they all came up and started talking." That was one of several stories that never got printed that night — the disaster produced so many angles that not all of them could be published — although Santangelo thought a reporter for an Israeli newspaper might have written a story. "It turned out that there were supposed to be 40 Hasidics on that flight."

He explained that Hasidic diamond merchants regularly took Pan Am to London, Brussels and back, but this particular flight was supposed to be carrying a wedding party. The son of one of the more prominent rabbis affiliated with the Safar Hasidic sect was to be married that weekend, so the grand rabbi's oldest son, his daughter-in-law, and the oldest grandchild and

37 others from Europe were booked on 103. "The Hasids were absolutely horrified," Santangelo said. The Jewish sect leaders had cellular phone communication with London, and they passed along information to him as they received it. "They were the first ones to give us a count of the people on the plane. I presume they got that out of the London airport. They were the first to confirm that it was a bomb, I think." The 40 Hasids from Israel had come into Britain via Brussels and had been on a bus that went to Gatwick instead of Heathrow Airport, Santangelo was told.

The *Daily News* reporter also found another, much smaller group of Hasids at the airport that night. It was a man with two children, a girl about nine and a boy about a year older. "I asked him what he was doing," Santangelo recalled. "He said, 'I thought it would be a very good educational experience for my children to see how one of these things happened and how the press reacted.'" The family group stayed at the airport until 1 or 2 o'clock in the morning. "He kept them out of the way, and he would give them little commentaries, 'See what that person's doing. See what this person's doing.'" The father explained how a few weeks earlier, he had taken them to another big event — Santangelo remembered it as a building collapse — to see how the police and the fire handled a disaster. "So now they were seeing how the press handles something like this. He knew there'd be a lot of press."

Santangelo remained in and around the terminal all evening. "At one point, we went outside and almost got somebody," he said, recalling how he met the uncle of one of the victims while standing with two other reporters out behind the VIP lounge. "A tallish guy with white hair — he found out on the car radio coming in, as he was approaching the airport. He was very businesslike...dressed for business, wearing a trench coat. And this guy kind of came in walking up the street, the outside route to the VIP lounge. Somebody must have told him, 'If you're with Flight 103, go to the VIP lounge; it's over there.' They didn't provide an escort, and he just looked (at us) and said, 'Look, I just found out about this.' That was it, very calm. No emotion, or not a lot of emotion. Just that, 'Leave me alone.'" The reporters watched as the man went into the bereavement center. "You could see what was going on. People comforting one another. There were a couple of clergymen there."

Santangelo saw the crowd of media grow and wane. "It got to be kind of a circus atmosphere, which these things do. I would guess better than a hundred press at one point. A lot of cameras, an awful lot of TV cameras. I don't know if there weren't 25 TV cameras there at some point. The New York press corps — to use the vulgar name — is known as the 'gang bang.'"[9] So, he was asked, the woman who fell on the floor was correct when she likened the news media behavior to rape? "That's exactly what it is," he said.

"Exactly what it is. I don't mean to condemn myself. The term 'gang bang' is going out of style now, and it's being known as the 'wolf pack.' It's not much different. You get this sort of — everybody needs to get a story. You've been sent out to get a story. Until you get a story, ravenous. Somebody gives you a story, you calm down. Then you sit down. You see a lot of people — we all know each other. It's like old home week. We're all buddies, or a lot of us are buddies. We talk: 'How ya' doing? How's the kid? How's the wife? You get divorced yet? Yeah. Oh, you bought a new car.' It's like a sewing circle. But we can't do that until we've got a story. We're all crazy until then."

Santangelo was under orders from the *Daily News* desk to stay at the airport until around 3 a.m. Personally it had been a bad night for him. "I had dinner plans. It was a wedding anniversary. That didn't do me any good. There was nothing I could do about it. It happened. These things always happen when you don't want them. I don't think that ended the marriage, but it didn't help."

He and other media representatives drifted out of the terminal, leaving behind the ropes and barricades that had been so ineffective in shielding grieving people.

Some of those who had been at the airport that night later did other stories related to Pan Am 103, perhaps a profile of one of the victims or an interview with family members angry over the lack of what they considered a real investigation.

Months later, Tom Brook was still thinking about the scene at the airport, particularly the collapse of the mother on the floor. "I was troubled by my own behavior, really," he said. "I was angry about it as well, that I'd engaged in a destructive process of news collection." So he began work on a reflective essay for the BBC as an attempt to examine that behavior. As part of the piece, he sought out the woman who had collapsed on the floor and did an on-camera interview with her. He also did an interview with an editor who defended publication of pictures and others who argued for use of television footage of that scene.

Brook acknowledged that newspeople are divided about showing that incident. "But I cannot find a valid journalistic reason for showing that footage. I'd be prepared to debate anyone that could. I think I was troubled by my own behavior, and that I came so close to thinking that would be okay to broadcast. But I can only say that in hindsight. I learned that from doing it. I learned that it was a wrong decision, and it clarified the issues for me." He said he recognized that his reason for doing the reflective piece was selfish, "but many times that kind of journalism can be very productive. Because I think a lot of people — viewers — don't know why that was wrong."

Brook asked why, in covering a story, is it necessary to cover private emotion. "I mean, in a way, you're assuming that the audience is really stupid if they have to see that people are grieving after a tragedy like that. I think it's compelling TV, there's no doubt about it, but for very unhealthy reasons. It's bit like seeing somebody being incontinent, in a way. It's a private thing; you turn away. Whether you see their face or not, that's not the issue. Because I think it has an impact on the audience, too. The consequence of doing this is that you really desensitize people, so you don't think that there's anything horrific. The other thing that I think is very dangerous about it is you engage in a process in which you're objectifying people. This becomes compelling TV and it'll get people to watch. But it's not really the way you treat, I hope, your neighbor or someone you knew."

Brook leaned back in his chair at the BBC's Manhattan office, and spoke slowly, deliberately. "You see, the interesting thing is I know that I did realize on some level — not a very conscious level — that there was something wrong about us being there, and I think I've learned to listen to that more. You know I'm sure a lot of the other reporters did, but we all know we've got to do our job. So to me it opens up a whole internal debate, one I've externalized actually, about what is private and what is public in journalism."

Brook pointed to related cases; for example, the *New York Times* deciding shortly after William Kennedy Smith was charged with rape to name the woman who accused him. He also suggested that the issue of "outing," in which prominent people who are homosexuals were named by publications, had to do with what is private and what is public.

Speaking of the woman on the floor of the airport, Brook said, "I don't think anyone would dispute that this was a very private moment. People justify it in the most bizarre way, that it happened in a public place." He said he thinks that the media need to be really careful about invading privacy, "unless there's an overriding public interest, which I can't see in (this) case." In fact, he argued that it was in the public interest *not* to show it on the grounds that it was insulting to the audience to think that they have to see such stark grief to know that a disaster has happened. He suggested that, in a way, such depiction of grief takes away the focus of what should be the issue: A plane went down. Why did it go down?

"I suppose the thing is people in TV feel they have to have pictures with everything, because it's television. Well, I don't think that's justification, either. Anyway, I feel very strongly about it."

Richard Ayres, head of editorial development, news and current affairs for the BBC, said the leadership of the news organization had talked about Brook's footage of the woman "a good deal on the night, and a great deal in future days and weeks. We're not ashamed of the Tom Brook decision," Ayres said three years later. "We still think it was right."

The reflective piece that Brook prepared was shown originally by the BBC and then as a segment on "The Eleventh Hour," a program on media criticism produced by WNET, a Public Broadcasting System station in New York (December 21, 1989). That meant media people who had been at the airport that night had a chance to see it. Brook said he recognized some of his media colleagues think that he is being "holier than thou...Or that I'm being dishonest in a way. A lot of people disagree with me. I don't quite see why they feel so strongly about it the other way. I'm not blind to their arguments, but they don't make sense to me. They don't seem rational."

Producing the reflective piece raised the issue anew: Did he need to show footage of the woman collapsing in order to convey the problem it posed? For the original piece, he had asked the woman herself about it. Consequently, his crew shot it as it was being shown on a television monitor, so that viewers could not dwell on it. But when "The Eleventh Hour" wanted to run a shorter version of the BBC piece, he had second thoughts. "I reflected upon that, and with the help of some other people, realized I didn't want to fall into the trap of repeating what I'd already done." So he told the program's producers, "Look, I'm only going to put it together if we don't use the footage."

Brook said he understood why newspeople used that dramatic scene at the airport. "Because they want to dramatize the story, but I think it's corrupt, you know," he said. "I think that it undermines what they're doing, really, personally. The way in which you go after an audience ultimately corrupts what you're trying to get across. And if you're going after an audience by pandering, it's going to, very often, just affect the message, the integrity of the message. It's a bit like a lot of advertising, in a way, using very devious means to get people in ultimately corrupts the whole process — you wonder if what's being given to you overall can be trusted. It's hard though, given that things are so competitive, in a way. I can see the pressures people are under."

Brook, who works freelance, although mostly for the BBC, is familiar with the pressures to deliver a story. "And it's hard not to hype things, at times."

Asked if he had ever been in similar situations before that night at the airport, Brook said he could not think of specific examples but was certain that on some occasions he had intruded more than was necessary. "It certainly made me much more reflective of what I do now. I'm not prepared to objectify people so easily and intrude. Unless — even if there's an overriding public interest — I'd have to think about it. It gets very complicated with some issues. This case though, I think is pretty simple. It wasn't at the time. What I think is a problem is that everyone is really so unprepared to deal with an event like this. I wonder how much you can teach. I think there could be more instruction on ethical issues."

In Britain, he noted, the tradition of teaching journalism does not exist to the extent that it has developed in America. Although increasingly aspiring journalists do attend a university, they study some liberal arts subject. Professional instruction tends to come on a training scheme. Brook said he had never had an ethics course and he imagined that few British journalists would have had. He acknowledged that there is a code of conduct of the National Union of Journalists, and the BBC has its own guidelines. "They really are pretty good on this kind of issue," he said of the BBC guidelines.

Brook recalled that when he originally went through a BBC training scheme 15 years ago, "We weren't taught much about this kind of thing. But I think things have changed. They have become quite enlightened in a way. But with all these things, you can have a lot of training, (and) it still comes down to you operating as an individual and not being too dominated in a robot-like manner by professional strictures of having to get the story. That's why I'm saying it's so hard, it seems, for many journalists to listen to their own humanity at times." Brook said he did not mean that reporters have to get emotionally involved in the stories they cover. "I mean, you see people who pretend there's nothing emotional about it. It's another story. I don't know what it is — a kind of macho thing. And these things are disturbing, and that is very hard for people to reflect."

The BBC reporter suggested it is difficult for any professional group to admit that they don't do things right some of the time. "I don't think journalists are that different from surgeons or any other profession. I don't know how you'd measure it, but I suppose 80 percent of them do a relatively decent job and then 20 percent don't."

The movie, "The Doctor," which had opened in New York the week of this interview with Brook, provided a similar self-examination of the medical profession. The surgeon who wrote the book on which it was based saw the callousness with which his profession could approach patients when he checked into his own hospital for treatment of throat cancer. The author, Ed Rosenbaum, argued that hospitals and doctors in particular need to be more sensitive. He told *People* magazine he could understand why patients are treated coldly: "When doctors are seeing 20 to 30 patients a day and dealing with death and dying, they're not going to survive unless they build a shell around them (Hauser, August 26, 1991, p. 71)." But he argued for a more compassionate treatment of patients, a goal that colleagues told *People* Rosenbaum had advocated long before he contracted cancer.

"As a journalist," Brook said, "I find some of the most interesting stories I've done are when people who do jobs are prepared to question the manner in which they do them. I always find that very interesting, very compelling, somebody admitting that they made a mistake, and there were a lot of mistakes in the way Pan Am 103 was covered. I think (it's) a healthy thing to try to learn from it. It upsets me that I don't think that much has been learned, really. I don't think, for instance, if another flight went down we'd see anything different." He said he thought some of the people who had been at Kennedy might do things differently, but those who had not been exposed to that scene would probably behave the same way. "I don't mean to sound like Granddad. I'm 38."

Reflecting on why he was so disturbed by the behavior of the media at Kennedy Airport that night, especially the moment when the mother learned her daughter's plane had gone down, he said. "You're taking advantage of people at a moment when they have no control. I think that's the issue." In other words, he explained, something that happens when a person has no control is private, while something that someone does voluntarily is public. "I suppose with people in grief — or when there's a lot of emotion involved, when people aren't in control — it is very primitive, it seems to me, to take advantage of that situation. It goes without saying, it's unfair.

"I mean I don't like being out of control. That's what (the woman who had collapsed at Kennedy) said to me, that she's a health-care worker and she's always been aware of being very much in control. This is a moment in her life when she lost control, and to have that invasion of privacy going on, I do think it's tantamount to rape."

A tale by two newspapers: New York

While television and radio broke the terrible news of Pan Am 103 to the American people on December 21, newspapers made it concrete the next morning. In New York City and its suburbs, where a relatively high percentage of papers sold daily are purchased one copy at a time, potential readers faced very different treatments of the tragedy. Especially striking was the contrast between the *Daily News* and *Newsday*, both tabloid in format.

Huge block capitals in the *Daily News* quoted the mother at Kennedy Airport crying "NOT MY BABY!" and a full-page picture showed her collapsed on the floor.[10] *Newsday* headlined "New York-bound 747 crashes in Scotland" above a quote from Lockerbie, "The sky was raining fire." The bright flames of burning houses in the Scottish village shone in color above another headline: "Jet with 258 Aboard Hits Town; 38 Syracuse Students on Passenger List."

Front pages sell newspapers, especially tabloid newspapers. Front pages compete with each other for buyers' attention, and with other sources of diversion for any attention at all. When Flight 103 was blown out of the skies over Scotland, the two papers were locked in combat, along with Rupert

Murdoch's *New York Post*, in the so-called Tabloid Wars. The great, gray *New York Times* printed all the news it saw fit without entering into the fray; its readers tended to remain loyal, day-in, day-out, no matter what the three tabloid-size papers carried on page one.

Clear champion of news-stand wars at that point was the *Daily News*, although its one million copies on an average day was nowhere near the roughly 4.7 million apex it had reached in 1947, twenty-eight years after its founding by Joseph Medill Patterson. *Newsday*, started on Long Island by Patterson's daughter Alicia in 1940, had developed into a respected daily for suburban readers and then as part of the Times-Mirror chain had launched a Manhattan edition as *New York Newsday* in 1985.

The two papers were very different, and not just on the day following this particular disaster. F. Gilman Spencer, then the editor for the *Daily News* and now editor of the broadsheet *Denver Post*, once called *Newsday* "a tabloid in a tutu." During this interview, he said, "*Newsday* is a serious, upscale, aimed-at-the-*New York Times* kind of newspaper, whereas the *Daily News* is your standard, total, typical street, blue-collar tab. They're very different animals. They approach things from their own gut."

But it is the black-and-white front page picture of the woman on the floor at Kennedy Airport that Spencer and other editors elected to run in the *Daily News* that is remembered, not the colorful flames on page one of *Newsday*. Even some key editors at *Newsday* had no vivid memory of the picture they carried that day; they tended to remember it as being the cockpit, lying on its side in a Scottish meadow, which was the picture they used the following day.

In the months that followed Spencer would be called on again and again to defend making the mother's grief the focus of his front page. "Now it wasn't a violation of her privacy...because it was a public number," he told Tom Brook when the BBC newsman was preparing his documentary on the issue. "We weren't sneaking into her house or doing it through a window. It was there in front of everybody. From where I sit, I'm a professional and I am not exploiting that woman. I am picturing a tragedy and I'm doing that in a way that's going to convey — this isn't a rationalization. I believe this." (The Eleventh Hour, WNET-TV, Dec. 21, 1989)

During a televised roundtable moderated by former CBS president Fred Friendly, Spencer said that the number of deaths, the fact that many of them were college students and that it came right before Christmas helped to justify it. "I can't imagine anything that would rivet attention and sympathy to that particular situation as much as that picture. It was taken at the time. It was an honest picture. Certainly, it was an honest reaction." Friendly challenged him: "Did you think at all about this woman's agony?" "I think that was all about her agony," the editor shot back. "And I think it's about the agony that's in all parents and all people when you have something like that happen." (The Other Side of News: Entertainment News or Entertainment, PBS, April 12, 1989)

Asked during this interview if there was a lot of discussion about the picture or if it seemed a "must" for the front page once editors saw it, Spencer said, "You had a huge, huge story. And now you've got the pieces of that story laying all over the garage floor, and you're trying to get it back into the automobile. So what you're doing at that time is that (picture) comes up and you look at it, and you say, 'Is this fair? Is this an invasion of privacy? Is this something that ought to be in the newspaper?' We didn't have a picture of the plane going down at that point," he recalled. "We didn't have a picture of what was happening over there as such. We did have a picture of a grieving parent in a moment of total agony, which would have riveted, absolutely, the feeling of the country in terms of true dismay and anguish that anybody would relate to. In terms of that picture, any parent, any person, any human being would relate to what that was all about. That may be a cheap rationalization, but I don't think it is. I think it makes absolute sense in terms of riveting the tragedy and the feeling that it inspired. And you could say, 'No, we aren't going to use that because this woman, you know, was unprotected.' Of course, there's no question about that it was public. It was in a public place. It was, in essence, if you just wanted to take the cheapest route, fair game. But I think there was more in that decision than just 'Okay. We got a picture. Let's use it because it's a great picture.' I think the feeling and the understanding and sensitivity was there."

Spencer suggested that other papers might have been more apt to use the picture, if like the *News*, they had a shot by their own photographer. Although the photo moved on the AP wire, and some newspapers used it on inside pages, in our examination of major American newspapers we found none that treated it so dramatically.

The *Newsday* photographer at Kennedy Airport did not get the shot, but most editors at the Long Island headquarters did not see that as a factor that played much of a role in their decision. Managing Editor for News Howard Schneider remembered seeing and discussing television footage of the woman on the floor at the airport. "When I watched it I was kind of horrified, professionally and personally, and it became really an object lesson, a real case study, of how far you go," he said. Ken Irby, who was one of two night picture editors at the time, recalled vividly the long discussion about the photo. "We thought it was very intrusive. We didn't use that picture, although we had the opportunity to. We had a photographer there that did not make it, but the wire picture we did see, and had every opportunity to use."

The strongest images of grief in *Newsday* came from Syracuse University. A good friend of Irby's, Toren Beasley, was director of photography at the

Syracuse Newspapers, and their personal networking meant that pictures shot on campus were also available for *Newsday*. "We didn't rely on the wire service (for Syracuse coverage) because we weren't really thrilled with what we had (from them)," he said.

What makes readers buy one newspaper rather than another may be determined by their reaction to page one, but with a tabloid, what will help them understand an event is found inside. There, too, the two papers were a study in contrast. The *Daily News* focused on the impact of the disaster, both in terms of what had happened in Scotland and the grief, especially at Kennedy Airport and Syracuse University. *Newsday* concentrated on the crash itself, particularly what might have caused it, giving less prominence to the grief, including the bereaved at the airport.

The *Daily News* story out of Lockerbie, by Frank Ryan, the Scottish freelancer, was the one he had filed with the Glasgow tabloid, *The Record*. It was headlined "Death from the sky and sorrow below." It began:

> The blazing crater was a scene from hell, all that was left of the fireball from the sky.
>
> Shocked residents who an hour before had been Christmas shopping stumbled around in the pitch darkness, staring at the smoking crater and a section of plane sticking out of a bedroom window.

Spencer explained how they got that story. "It didn't matter where a huge event occurred, if it was out in the country or aboard, we would try to find a newspaper. You'll call a local paper and see if you can give a guy $500 or whatever it would take to help with the immediate, quick coverage that you can't get yourself, and you're not going to get from the wires very quickly. So you'll have your person there, who has been a sort of conscripted stringer."[11] The editor described that as a practice at the *Denver Post* and other papers where he has worked.

Right next to it was "A terminal of tears" by Mike Santangelo and Stuart Marquez, accompanied by a close-up of another crying relative. It was captioned: "A WOMAN WEEPS at the Pan Am terminal after it was learned that Flight 103 had crashed in Scotland." To the right was the main story summarizing the major facts of the event. Two big photos across the top half of the two pages showed Lockerbie burning. On other pages the *News* carried stories about a family that had lost six members on the flight, a Syracuse student who had switched to another flight at the last minute, and a piece on Syracuse University headlined "A campus in shock," accompanied by pictures of weeping cheerleaders.

Asked about the emphasis on the disaster's impact, Spencer said, "It goes hand-in-hand, when you're talking about a tabloid newspaper, with sensation.

People will usually use sensation instead of impact. But impact would be basically your tabloid (approach) — any paper can look at it a whole bunch of different ways and the best kind of coverage is where you get all the factors. You get the impact of it to the humanity involved, the people, and then you get the issue itself, as to what really happened here in terms of the technical aspects of what happened. And that's a whole different search. On a lot of papers you'd have an aeronautical person, who specializes in airlines etc., and so forth. The aeronautics writer would be looking at that. Or you'd have a generalist looking at that in lieu of a specialist." The *News* at that point had no aviation writer, he said.

William Goldsweig, national editor for the *News* at the time, was responsible for handling stories coming in from Scotland and Washington. "As serious incidents go, the sheer toll was one of the worst I remember during that whole period of terrorism," he said. "The fact it happened, who it happened to, a lot of innocent kids from universities, the fact that it happened close to Christmas, and the controversy about the warnings, elevated it to a special story." Goldsweig suggested the emphasis on what happened at Kennedy Airport was natural. "At a New York City newspaper, you'll have an emphasis on New York coverage when something is happening in our town. It's a quite natural and sensible way for us to cover something. I mean, that happened here."

Inside *Newsday* the focus of the two-page opening spread was on the crash itself and the tie to Long Island: "NY-bound jet crashes in Scotland. LI residents among 258 victims." The story, carrying a London dateline, was by Timothy Harper, the paper's special correspondent.[12] AP photos showed burning buildings in Lockerbie and Syracuse cheerleaders crying after the moment of silence. A story headlined "Sorrow in Syracuse" quoted university officials confirming the loss of students from the study-abroad program. A dramatic shot from a vigil in Hendricks Chapel showed many more grieving students.

The paper used a Reuters story from Lockerbie on the effect of the crash on that small Scottish town, and on page 16 began its coverage of the victims and their families, along with a piece about the same student who had taken a different flight. The paper also carried a piece by aviation correspondent Glenn Kessler about *The Maid of the Seas* having been rebuilt after a troubled record, as well as a piece from London headlined "Possibility of Sabotage is Raised" by Timothy Harper. In some editions, a piece from Kennedy Airport about the families was played on page 17; in other editions, it was moved back to page 34. The piece by Katherine Foran and William Douglas told of the sorrow in the terminal as relatives learned of the tragedy, and included a description of the mother collapsing on the floor. But that story was not accompanied by pictures; no grieving family members were included.

Editors at *Newsday* recalled that on December 21, they originally viewed the disaster as a crash. The kind of decisions they were making would have been made irrespective of what caused the 747 to fall from the skies. "Plane crashes are big stories in general," Schneider said. "This one we could tell early on because of the nature of it — everybody killed, over Lockerbie. The fact that it's coming to New York heightens obviously our interest. Even though any international flight might stop over, this one was coming to New York. When it became clear that there were a bunch of college students on here the level of interest rose because from an identification point of view, we have a lot of kids here, a lot of parents, who would identify with this. So for a lot of reasons, it became obvious that this was going to be a very good story, an important story, that we're going to have to cover with multiple people."

Schneider said he sees two key elements when a plane crashes: Why did it happen, and the human dimension.

"Why did it happen is a crucial question because, as Glenn Kessler (the newspaper's aviation safety correspondent) likes to say, there are no kind of laboratories in air safety. Each crash is its own laboratory for pointing out systemic, potentially systemic problems that affect everybody. Which is why plane crashes are big stories, not because 80 people die or 100 people die, but because really that's the way we learn about potentially systemic problems that are patterns in the planes we fly."

The human element varies, he said. "Maybe eight people survive and have an incredible story," or it may be the grief the crash causes. How those two elements combine affects the news decisions. For example, he said, if the cause had been relatively predictable, such as a snowstorm in which the pilot tried to take off and could not, the editors might have given more prominence to the grief. This particular story had two windows to the grief, the people arriving at the airport, and the campus community at Syracuse. The latter struck close to home for Schneider, both as an alumnus of the Newhouse School at SU and as a parent of college-age children. "You could not read the story the next day and be a parent without feeling heartsick."

Many decisions at these two newspapers, the *Daily News* and *Newsday*, in those early hours seemed remarkably similar. Each dispatched a reporter and a photographer to Lockerbie; each sent a reporter to Syracuse; each had at least one reporter and photographer at Kennedy Airport. The approach taken by the reporters on those various scenes seemed to reflect their individual judgment and experience more than it did their respective newspapers' editorial attitudes. The reporters who flew up to Syracuse University demonstrated both differences and similarities in their methods.

Mark Kreigel, who left the *News* at the time of a strike in 1990 and now writes sports for the *New York Post*, remembered particularly his visit to a fraternity house. "To see a kid on a lawn outside a frat house grief-stricken...it was surrealistic. Most of the young people I'd covered grieving were poor kids from lousy neighborhoods where dying is not anything (unusual), young people who get killed over drugs or just the endemic crap." The scene at the fraternity touched him deeply. "I wanted to cry," he said.

He flew in Wednesday night too late to attend the service at Hendricks Chapel, and met up with a friend from the *Miami Herald*. "We were still seeing kids at the bars (in the Marshall Street area), and then there were these pockets of grief. What added to the story was this campus, not a place where grief belongs. There was this wonderful, untouchable college life."

The strangeness of the atmosphere, he said, showed again in an SU news conference the next day that began not with statements about Pan Am 103, but "something about the eligibility of a basketball player. It was completely off...It certainly did not make it any less surreal or screwy."[13]

Kreigel noted that the story was different from "normal" disasters in which "you're thrown right into the scene of the tragedy. There was no focus, no fulcrum for the tragedy. It had happened literally in thin air on the other side of the earth." He paused. "There weren't any police lines."

Elizabeth Wasserman, who had worked in Syracuse before going to *Newsday*, caught a flight that left New York around 7 o'clock that night. On board were other reporters and television crews. "A few TV crews had actually started interviewing people on the plane," she said. By the time the plane landed, the reporters on board realized they had traveled with a story, a Syracuse University student who had originally been scheduled to fly home on Pan Am 103. "So I knew I was in for a pack journalism experience as soon as I got off the plane. There was an immediate press conference with a couple of students who had taken an earlier flight," she said. "You know, the TV cameras set their equipment up, and we all just interviewed these people and phoned in our notes because we knew that was the only thing that was going to get in the following day's editions."

Then she rented a car and headed for a supermarket to buy a toothbrush. "I know I was up pretty late, making phone calls to different campus officials, to find out, you know, what was going to be going on the next day." About 9 o'clock the next morning she headed to the campus and met up with a reporter from the *Philadelphia Inquirer*. "We kept running into each other."

They went to Pi Beta Phi sorority because they knew three of the victims had been sisters there. "Someone answered the door — I don't believe it was one of the students; it was an older woman — and said that they were upset, they didn't feel like talking to us." So the two reporters started walking to another place on campus, and then noticed some young women leaving the sorority. "We approached them and they talked to us. And it was very emotional. They were very upset. I certainly didn't feel that I overstepped the bounds, or that the other reporter I was with overstepped the bounds at all, because if they had said, 'No, I'm too distraught. I can't talk about this,' certainly we would have said, 'Fine.' Several other people that I had approached on the campus said that they hadn't felt like talking about it. Fine. I wasn't about to press them.

"The reason I led with them in my story was they had kind of touched me when they said they had chipped in to send flowers, and this type of thing was not supposed to happen to people their age, who had all their life to look forward to. Yet it did, and they were going to have to come to terms with it."

Although Wasserman recalled having dealt with young people involved in sad news events before, she added, "I guess I never dealt with students who had seen so many of their friends perish in a way that was inexplicable, where they still had so many questions."

Wasserman recalled that the young women told them about the intrusive behavior at the sorority house by some media the previous night. "They were telling us that someone had tried to photograph inside the house."

Less obvious than the differences in the way that the two newspapers dealt with grieving families was the attention they gave to the possible cause of the tragedy.

In the main story of the *Daily News*, the Scottish Secretary Malcolm Rifkind was quoted as saying, "The aircraft clearly experienced some form of explosion," but he declined to speculate on the cause. The story also quoted Pan Am as saying that there had been "an incident at altitude." That was followed by Jeff Kriendler, Pan Am's vice president for corporate communications, saying, "We have no indication of an explosion."

The *Newsday* story from London noted that there was no definitive word on the crash, but cited indications that the jet may have begun to disintegrate before hitting the ground. The paper reported that Pan Am and British authorities said there was no evidence of sabotage, "but aviation experts said the possibility could not be discounted." It quoted two such experts briefly in that story. Jim Ferguson, aviation editor of *Flight International* magazine, said it could be structural failure or it could be sabotage. John Galipault, president of the Aviation Safety Institute in Ohio, told the paper that earliest information from the disaster scene suggested either a bomb or a catastrophic failure inside the plane or its engines as the primary cause.

Kessler's piece revealed that *Maid of the Seas* had been the fifteenth Boeing 747-100 ever built, but had undergone extensive renovations the previous year. The rebuilding was part of a federal program to convert such planes for airlifts during a national emergency. His story incorporated reports from the *Los Angeles Times*, which like *Newsday* is part of the Times-Mirror newspaper conglomerate, that the plane had a history of trouble that included cracks, corrosion, an on-board fire and smoke in the cabin.

Kessler quoted a former deputy director of the National Transportation Safety Board, the U.S. agency in charge of investigating major air accidents, who told him that such experts normally check for the possibility of structural damage or incomplete repairs during major overhauls when they are trying to determine the cause of an aviation disaster. The last major crash involving a 747, Kessler told his readers, had been a Japan Air Lines flight in 1985 that flew into a mountain and had been partly blamed on faulty repairs; a crack in the rear cabin wall caused a sudden loss of cabin pressure. But, Kessler said, safety experts viewed the 747 as having "an enviable safety record, making yesterday's crash even more puzzling."

Harper's piece on the same page about the possibility of sabotage also quoted the aviation editor of *Flight International* magazine, but it focused on the puzzling circumstances of the disaster itself. The story led with speculation about the way, apparently without pilot warning, it had crashed to earth from cruising altitude. It noted the only time that a 747 was known to have been brought down by a bomb was in 1985 when an Air India flight from Canada crashed into the Atlantic off the Irish coast. That crew had issued no distress signal.

The story also quoted a statement from Britain's Civil Aviation Authority as saying authorities were "puzzled" by reports from witnesses that the plane trailed flames before it crashed. Harper said that was not ordinarily associated with the "nose-region structural failure" found in other 747s. His story reported that ITN (Independent Television News) in Britain had speculated that if the plane had been sabotaged, likely candidates would include Arab groups intent on scuttling recent efforts toward peace by Palestine Liberation Organization Chairman Yasser Arafat.

Kessler, who works out of the New York *Newsday* office in Manhattan, joked about the pressure to explain the "why" of an aviation disaster. "It takes investigators a year to figure out the cause of a plane crash, but my boss on Long Island wants me to tell them what the cause was two hours after it happens." In this case, however, he remembered the case as having all the earmarks of a bomb very early on. "In airline safety, you're always reinventing the wheel. You know, everyone reruns the last campaign; everyone reruns the last plane crash. And that's why you suddenly had everyone worried about structural failure. Because it might have been structural failure. It might have been a bomb."

So he focused on the Air India bombing. In talking with the retired investigator from the National Transportation Safety Board, he learned about the key investigator of the Air India tragedy and even obtained the man's home telephone number in Britain. He found other experts as well and was able to quote in his second-day story a British investigator, who spoke anonymously, as saying that the air controller had seen the primary blip that represented the plane split into smaller blips shortly after the flight number disappeared from the screen. He also quoted Eric Newton, former chief investigating officer of the British Aviation Investigation Branch, as predicting that investigators could have tangible clues of an explosive device by the weekend. Newton told *Newsday* that the presence of small craters on the metal fragments of the aircraft and shrapnel in bodies of passengers would point to a bomb — although he stressed that in at least two cases, 747 jets had survived attacks by explosive devices, so that the accident could have been caused by a structural flaw.

In fact, Newton's prediction proved accurate. David Leppard, the *Sunday Times* investigative reporter, recalled that on Saturday, Christmas Eve, he overheard the crash investigation team in the bar of the hotel where he was staying talking about something that had been discovered. On Monday, the major news from the press conferences in Lockerbie was an announcement that pieces of the jet and a suitcase found among the wreckage were being taken to the Royal Armament Research Establishment, a weapons laboratory at Fort Halstead in Kent, to test for evidence of a bomb.

For *Newsday* editors initially the concern was logistical, Schneider said, "getting to the right places to try to get access to people." That is a matter of choosing the right reporters and having confidence they will handle themselves well, he said.

"The other question is the uncertainty early on in this kind of story of just how big it's going to be, and where it's going to lead...You feel it as an editor in your stomach more than your head. There's a lot here we don't know. There's a lot going on. This is a big story." On this story, Schneider felt, they could be going in three or four different directions. "You leave feeling uneasy that night. You don't leave feeling we've got things under control. You leave feeling...we're going to have to scramble on this one. We're going to have to get in the next day and really say where are we going and where we're heading."

Asked if he lay awake on a night like that, he said, "You feel heartsick. I mean, you sit here, you scroll the wires all night, you're on the phone or you're talking to our editor. You're watching television. In that sense, you are no different than most people. But the other dimension is, you're saying to yourself, 'God, how do we figure out what happened? Do we have all the right people? What's the angle on tomorrow's story?' It's the kind of story that you think a lot about...and once you deal with an area like international terrorism, now you're dealing in such a shadowy area where there's so much disinformation, where there are places where we have absolutely no access to do reporting...You're a little concerned that our government has an agenda, other governments have agendas, and therefore there may be some fingerpointing here. That becomes clear early on, and yet you've got to pursue the story.

"When you see something like this, you also ask yourself, 'Are there other incidents that are likely to happen? Is this part of something that's now going to happen, and are we doing enough to look at security? Am I going to come in tomorrow and is there going to be an explosion somewhere else? And are we now going to see an escalation of the kind of terrorism, the air terrorism we saw in the seventies? How do we get ready for that?'

"You know, you're on that roller coaster. All those kind of things go through your mind. As a newspaper, you look for what you can bring to the story that the other media can't bring to the story," he said, adding the newspaper asks itself, "'What is our role in this particular story? Is this a *Newsday* signature story? Is this the story that *Newsday* has to make a difference on because it's so important to our area? Is this a story that we can handle?' But it was clear to us because of what happened, because of our circulation area, because of its dimensions...This was a full commitment story to us, a full commitment."

Schneider said he thought the way *Newsday* handled the story seemed natural as the decisions were being made. "I was almost surprised when I looked at the coverage (in the *News*) and saw this other way of handling it (with the focus on the human emotion). But the *Daily News*, of course, has their reasons for saying it the way they say it. It makes an interesting contrast in approach. But in retrospect, and no newspaper's perfect, our thrust was the correct one given the way the story would grow."

For *Newsday*, in many ways, the more dramatic treatment came on the second day, as Marks began reporting from Lockerbie and Kessler helped pin down sources willing to speculate that it could be a bomb, including the International Air Transport Association, which called sabotage "the most likely explanation." Adding credence to the theory was the news from Washington that on December 5 an anonymous caller had telephoned the U.S. Embassy in Helsinki with a warning that a bomb would be planted on a Pan Am flight from Frankfurt to the United States within two weeks. Word of the warning, the story said, had been passed to the Federal Aviation Administration, which then notified Pan Am and other airlines, the Pentagon and some U.S. embassies. In Moscow, the notice was posted on the embassy's community bulletin board where everyone, including journalists, could see it.

"Now it became even a bigger story when there were indications there may have been sabotage and given the international climate and who might have done it and why and the concern about terrorism, it was a quantum leap of a story, " Schneider said. The fact that the warning had not been passed on to potential passengers heightened its significance.

In contrast, that day's big news on page one of the *Daily News* was something quite different: the acquittal of former Miss America Bess Myerson on charges she had conspired to fix her boyfriend's divorce case. The Pan Am headline on the front page was much smaller, and referred to the warning note posted in the Moscow embassy. *Newsday* treated the Bess Myerson story with a similar smaller headline above the nameplate.

The Myerson saga, dubbed "the Bess mess" by the tabloid press, had been a New York soap opera played out on front pages for months. Myerson had been City Cultural Affairs Commissioner in the administration of Mayor Edward Koch, and had given a $19,000-a-year job to the emotionally troubled daughter of the judge in the divorce case. The judge's daughter, the key witness, had secretly taped telephone conversations with her mother to help the prosecution's case.

Gil Spencer saw it as a natural *Daily News* decision, even though the paper carried six pages of news inside about further developments in the Pan Am 103 tragedy. "Well, I mean you had Bess Myerson, former Miss America, indicted and tried on fascinating charges. Bess Myerson was news. I mean, she was bigger than life, period. She was total New York. And if Bess gets acquitted, that is a New York story that is major league, and particularly for a paper that had been following that sequence, and we had excellent reporters doing that. So I would say that...short of an assassination at a very high level in this country, Bess Myerson was going to dominate that front page," he said.

"I mean, the whole game — there are millions of choices you make every day. And the choices (for) a newspaper in terms of what it displays on its front page, and particularly (for) a tabloid where you don't have much room (are difficult) ; you know, (you're) basically talking two stories, three possibly, but basically two stories and one picture. That's a tabloid front page. There's a reason for that, as you know. We're selling them on the street. Whereas *Newsday* had a home delivery base, we did not. We were selling a million papers on the street, 200,000 home delivery. So that front page meant everything in terms of impulse buying. Therefore you are looking at the story that is going to affect that town as much as humanly possible. And I would say that would be the decision in why Myerson dominated the page."

Spencer conceded that a person with an international perspective reading a tabloid over a number of days would probably find it more local in scope than the reader expected. "I think the tabloid is doing a different thing. The

New York Daily News is a local newspaper, in effect. It will deal with the world through its wires, etc., but we had no foreign correspondent. They did in the old days, but we did not. So basically we were dealing with New York, and then what was of interest to the country. Now when the Los Angeles riots occurred recently (in 1992), that would have dominated the front page. When (Democratic presidential candidate Bill) Clinton and Gennifer Flowers appeared, well, of course, the tabloids would go nuts over that. Basically, you're constantly juggling what is of immediate impact, and interest, and what is important — to you as an editor and to people you're serving and also to the country and world at large. I think we can get awful cheap sometimes. But I think you gave me an easy one with that Myerson. There are others you could have given me where I'd have had more trouble defending."

Ultimately, Spencer argued, the battle that tabloid papers like the *News* fight is for people who might not read any newspaper if the tabloids cease to exist. Such papers are a dying breed, he said. "There are very few of the character of the *New York Daily News* or, for that matter, the little sister character of the *New York Post*, who are, basically, sort of, out of the side of the mouth, hot-shot, straight New York-style tabloids." He started a run-down, naming papers in Boston, New York, Philadelphia and then had to think hard to come up with more. "It's a dying animal, but it shouldn't die in New York. Because New York deserves that. I think New York has to have that. Because those readers are not going to read *The New York Times*. And I don't think they're going to read *Newsday*. They might out of self-defense in the absence. I think you'd lose a whole bunch of readers. I think what will happen is that New York hopefully will end up with one tabloid; I'm assuming it would be nice if it ended up with two, but I don't think it will have two. I think it's important (for) a blue-collar (audience), the mass of New York, the strap-hangers, that whole wide swath of people who look for a slightly different kind of paper based more on the human condition, and that's a fancy way of just saying people. I just think that's really important, and they write it in such a way that it's accessible and it's fun and it also deals seriously with serious problems, with people like (Jimmy) Breslin[14] and others who are quintessential."

Spencer made it clear that he saw a big difference between a tabloid like the *News* and the British tabloids. The editor, who retired from the New York tabloid in 1989 following a fight with then publisher Jim Hoge over the latter's decision not to endorse David Dinkins' candidacy for mayor, said the real struggle between the two men came when Hoge wanted to transform the paper into a British-style tabloid.

Hoge came to New York from the *Chicago Sun-Times*, which, Spencer said, was a different kind of tabloid from the "gritty" *New York Daily News*. The new publisher "was enamored with the British tabs. He was extremely interested in that, and he decided that the *News* should go downscale." Rupert Murdoch was in his heyday of trying to remake the *Post*. "So Jim wanted to take us down, and how far down was hard to figure," Spencer said. "But he definitely wanted to take us down a few notches. He wanted to bring in some Britishers and what not. Which he did, a little bit. And at that point, it's the thing I'm probably the most pleased with in terms of anything I contributed to that newspaper because I fought that, almost desperately, because I felt that the *News* owned the middle. And that the *Post* owned the area down below us. Here was *Newsday* nibbling at us, just at the beginning of *New York Newsday*. And *The New York Times* was looking down on all of us like we were bugs. So the issue to me was fight or leave, because I just couldn't see that happening to the paper. And so we fought that one out. In essence, I won that one. I think Jim ultimately understood that, although we never really discussed it in terms as you and I are talking about it. But I think we didn't do what he was aiming at doing, (although) he brought in a couple of Britishers. And I (permitted) that just as a mild compromise, but only on the basis that it would last as long as I wanted it to, and it didn't last long. They left, and then we got back to what we were doing."

Spencer made clear his disdain for the most controversial of the British tabloids. "The London *Sun*, you know, it's just excrement, from everything I've seen of it, and I don't think Jim would have ever taken us down or wanted to take us down that low. But I do think he saw things there that, you know, intrigued him from the standpoint of reaching more people, doing more with circulation, all of that. And I thought we were doing pretty good where we were, and I was terrified if we began playing Rupert's game, that we were going to lose it, our franchise, and could also give him one. So anyway that was where I came from as far as that whole British approach."

Spencer said the weekly tabloids sold in American supermarkets provide some of "that really low-down cheap gutter stuff," and he sees their approach as less defensible than the British tabloids. "I think (editors are) trying to do a little more news over there, but they're spinning it, and they're taking the piece they want. They don't care about the whole so much. They're taking little bites and they're making it into sort of another version of Mad comics a lot of the time. As Sinatra said, 'Whatever gets you through the night,' but that isn't what we do, what I was brought up to do. Lord knows I've made my mistakes. Maybe including the woman on the floor of the airport. You know, I could revisit that a million times a day. I don't. But I would say that maybe everything I told you about how we arrived at that decision was a rationalization. And maybe that was all fueled by a desire to get a picture on the front page of the paper that people would look at. But I don't believe that."

When it was suggested that part of the problem may be that editors in their offices cannot see what actually happens on the scene, Spencer disagreed. "Basically, I don't believe that. Or let's say, maybe I don't want to. My feeling about that is if you aren't sensitive enough to know what the problem with that was — and there was a problem, no question about it — maybe you ought to be working for McDonald's. Because once you saw the picture you knew what you were dealing with. This woman was unprotected. There was no way — we had a picture she didn't know about." Spencer said that it is the job of security and police to protect people in such circumstances. "The journalists are going to get as close to the heat as they can. That's their job...In a question like this, I'd hope that the airport would provide enough quick protection, but on this she collapsed, and I suppose there was no way to prevent what happened."

Told about the situation in which a mother inside the VIP lounge had been terrified by being able to see the media, especially as they tried to get in a door, Spencer commented, "Well, they're like animals at that point. And I understand that...and there is a certain kind of journalist who would have stood back." Informed that some journalists did stay back, he added, "I'm not sure I would want one of them working for me. I'm not asking for a savage beast who's going to be up there pushing a microphone in somebody's face and saying, 'How do you feel about your kid getting killed?' I mean, I think that's outrageous, unspeakable. But I also think that where something like this is occurring, these people are out there to do a job and basically they have to work within the constraints of some semblance of decency, but they also have to get what they can get. And then it becomes, how frenzied the situation, how big the story, all of that. And you're going to have things like happened to this woman. It's happened in less cosmic situations."

Spencer cited the way media has been called on to handle rape stories and women's issues with more sensitivity. "So I mean, we're growing up! And papers today are very different than they were 25 years ago. I mean there were things that were in newspapers 25 years ago, racial stuff and what-not, sexist stuff, that isn't in papers today. It certainly isn't to any degree. But when you get into one like this and we're just talking about that one picture (of the woman at Kennedy), that's the way people try to work their way through those things. I probably made it sound like we gave it a lot more thought than we did at the time, but maybe it's because I've thought about it so much since." The picture has become a classic which newspeople can use as a reference point to discuss issues of sensitivity. "You have a whole bunch of cases you can compare to this," he said.

At one point, Spencer said, "I'm glad I never had to talk to her," then immediately reversed himself. "As a matter of fact, I would be delighted to, because I understand exactly where she's coming from, but she wasn't running a newspaper in New York at the time, and the question was whether that might have made people think a little more about what happens when you lose a kid at Christmas time. And what happens in terms of airlines and mess-ups and all of that. And I don't know. The great question is: Would you do it again? And I'd say, yes, sure, yeah. The same deal, knowing what I know now."

The rivalry between the two newspapers reached all the way to Lockerbie. When Peter Marks of *Newsday* interviewed the farmer who had seen the cockpit float down into the field, he relished what he saw as his competitive advantage. "The *Times* didn't have anything quite like that the next day. And the *Daily News* had somebody there. A guy named Don Singleton, who's a terrific reporter. He didn't have anything like that. He was the guy I was paying attention to. I mean, if there was an element of competition, he was the guy I was worried about. He probably doesn't remember this, but whenever I'd see him I'd try to figure out where he was going. I wanted to know, you know? And he'd do the same thing with me, asking, 'What have you found?' And I wouldn't tell him anything. But he tried a couple of times — he wanted to know if I was going to do this or that. And I didn't play along. I didn't quite trust him. Why should I?"

Back on Long Island, *Newsday* was struggling with the fact that this was a story of global dimensions, and that it was so difficult to find the answers to critical questions, such as exactly what happened and why.

"To get our arms around it," Schneider said, "it seemed overwhelming at first. The nature of reporting out from Europe, of getting our sources here," along with the Frankfurt angle and the possibility of terrorists being linked to the Middle East, "you needed almost global resources to quickly jump on the story." He contrasted it with the Avianca plane crash 13 months later when the Colombian airliner ran out of fuel and smashed into a residential neighborhood on Long Island. On such a story, the newspaper dispatches 20 or 30 reporters to sites that essentially are in its backyard. "This one was tough, it was like managing more of a global story. This was also very painful, so that the sense of outrage, the sense of what happened, the feeling of the pain of the parents and the relatives of the survivors and of the people of Lockerbie were so intense that that drives even more the question of trying to get the closure." He likened it to the assassination of President Kennedy, and all of the pain associated with it. "The drive for closure is so intense and so unanswered (in that case) that it will never go away during our lifetime."

Schneider said that it became clear early on that the Pan Am 103 tragedy was going to endure in the news. "There is frustration after two days or three days when the story begins to wind down, the investigation begins to wind down, and the human stuff — you've played it a couple of days and there's a limit. You get frustrated about, you know, you can't wrap the story up. It's not going to be in a week's time."

Editors recognize that the attention span of their readers is limited, even on such a huge story. "We have an editor who teases me about how his wife goes to the supermarket and she stands on line — he came in one day and said she was standing in line and there was *Newsday* for sale and she said to her friend, 'Oh, that story again on page one.' We'd played it too long on page one; it wasn't Flight 103, but you can almost feel when you've got to back off."

The story moved inside on both papers after the second day, although on most days, one or both did feature a headline calling attention to a story inside. On December 29, the day after the announcement that the cause was, in fact, a bomb, both newspapers made it their lead page one story. Then the tragedy became an inside story again.

The local story: Syracuse

The downing of Pan Am 103 assumed special importance in many locations around the world, as media learned someone with ties to their nation or community had perished on the plane. But in Syracuse, the media realized early on that this story was of exceptional local import. Although the city is not the stereotypical college town, a number of factors make Syracuse University central to community life: it is the largest employer in the city; its faculty and staff are active in civic and cultural affairs; its students play roles ranging from sports heroes to volunteers in local charities and interns in area businesses. In addition to the students lost on the flight, a couple from the northern suburb of Clay and two other victims were from neighboring counties.

A city of 163,860, Syracuse sits squarely in the middle of upstate New York. Surrounded by suburbs and villages, it counts 545,100 in its market area, which ranked it 67th out of the 262 markets in the nation identified by *Broadcasting Yearbook* (1991). In fact, Syracuse is considered such a typical American city that it has frequently been used as a test market for new products.[15]

It has three network-affiliated television stations, one for each of the major networks, ABC, CBS and NBC, and their television news teams engage in intense competition, as well as two independent television stations, one public broadcasting channel and two active cable television operations. Its two daily newspapers, the morning *Post-Standard* and the afternoon *Herald-Journal*, compete for news, although both are owned by the Newhouse chain and operate out of the same building. Each has a healthy circulation — 89,185 for the *Post-Standard* and 93,449 for the *Herald-Journal* — primarily in Onondaga County of which Syracuse is the county seat, although approximately 33 percent of the former and 17 percent of the latter are distributed in three neighboring counties.[16] A variety of other local media cover news, including several radio stations and a weekly tabloid. In other words, the media environment is fairly typical for an American city of its size — except that most such cities have only one daily newspaper.

So the experience of Syracuse news people may mirror in many ways what might happen in other American cities under similar circumstances. But it also shows how local coverage is related to national and international media systems, how interdependent communications has become in the global village.

Syracuse television: out in the night

It's hard to imagine a worse time for a tragedy to happen, from a local television news perspective.

While no time is a good time for a disaster, late afternoon in a television newsroom is often a nightmare, even without a late-breaking story. During a "typical" day, reporters back from the field would be busily forwarding and reversing videotapes, looking for the right "sound bite." Other reporters, anchors and producers would be dashing off scripts. Producers would have already made big headway in "blocking the newscast," that is, deciding what order stories would appear in the early newscast.

On December 21, local journalists had already expended extra effort planning coverage of a Syracuse University basketball star's appearance in court on fourth-degree criminal mischief and harassment charges. Then Pan Am 103 was blown out of the sky. Although the bomb's blast came shortly after 2 p.m. EST, and it initially appeared to be a story primarily for the networks, Syracuse television journalists recalled that they began to realize that this was going to be a big local story at about 4 p.m. — just one-and-a-half hours before air time for two local newscasts and two hours before the third was to begin its broadcast. Not only did local news managers have to quickly decide how to juggle the tragedy with their already planned newscasts, they had to plan coverage of a story that happened thousands of miles from the city and about which only sketchy information was available.

Newsrooms immediately scrambled to learn how many people with local ties might have been on board. Published accounts verify that during the hours immediately following the crash, finding out just who was aboard Pan Am

103 was a problem even for relatives of the victims. A special edition of the Syracuse *Post-Standard* told of the efforts of a mother to get information:

> She put on her coat and went home. Once she was there all she could do was dial and redial the constantly busy Pan Am information number...When Peggy put down the phone, Robyn (the victim's sister) picked it up and tried again. She got through and gave Pan Am her sister's arrival time in New York City.
>
> "Can you tell me what flight number that was?" Robyn asked.
>
> There was a pause and Peggy watched her daughter pull the receiver from her ear...
>
> "Flight One-Oh-Three."
>
> Peggy redialed and tried without success to learn the names of the passengers. ("The Darkest Day," May 1989, pp.12-13)

But one reporter was able to "crack" the Pan Am bureaucracy before her station's early newscast. Obtaining passenger names that early in an air disaster was an unusual "scoop," and one that would have far-reaching consequences. A second reporter, from a different station, later got Pan Am to confirm those names. Both reporters used different tactics. Both scenarios raised important ethical questions: How far should a reporter go to get information? Are there circumstances that justify a reporter misrepresenting his or her identity in order to get the story?

The television reporter in Syracuse[17] who obtained the names had called up Pan Am and said, "Hello. I understand that there were some SU students. I need the names." The reporter recalled, "The person on the other end of the line — I don't know if it was a new hotline that had been set up or if it was volunteers trying to react to getting these calls with names — whoever it was on the phone called up the names on their computer and gave them to me." Asked if she identified herself, the reporter said, "I don't know if I did or not. I don't think I said I was anything. I think I just said, 'Are you so and so at Pan Am? I understand that there were some SU students on board. Could I please have their names?' And I don't really think that I said who I wasn't. I didn't deceive her." The reporter was pressed for clarification: "You didn't say that I'm — from a (network) affiliate?" "Right," the reporter responded. "I don't think I said that. But I have the list — the original list (of student names) that I wrote down because she just said, 'All right,' and she called it up on the computer and started giving me the names, and all she gave me (was), in alphabetical order, last names, first initials, which was all she had at the time."

This reporter felt that withholding her identity to get information was acceptable journalistic practice. As a result of her efforts, the last names and first initials of the students aboard Pan Am 103 were aired during her station's early newscast.

A reporter at a second station was asked by his management to confirm that list and to get whatever other information he could from Pan Am. This reporter said he called up Pan Am and lied to them. "I told them that I was with the International Studies Program (at SU) and needed to confirm the list of names and they gave them to me. Because the first question they asked me was, 'Are you a media person?' I wasn't about to tell them." The reporter also admitted that during his deception, he played on the sympathies of the Pan Am representative to get the names of the students. "I was able to call some type of security number, and they wouldn't give it to me at first. I said, 'Hey look, you know, none of your people have been able to confirm and these are people in our own program,' implying that I was (with the university). And the person felt bad about it at that point, went over and got the list."

The reporter justified his subterfuge by what he perceived as Pan Am's ineptitude. "It was clear to me that they (Pan Am) didn't know their ass from first base when it came to handling the media." The reporter added that his phone call was transferred to several people and at one point he was told that those he needed to talk to were "all home now." "I wasn't going to stand for that," the reporter said. "Yeah, I lied and I don't feel ashamed about doing it. And if presented with the same circumstances, I'd do it again."

Under what circumstances would the reporter have truthfully identified himself? "If I felt that they (Pan Am) had an adequate staff on hand to handle it," he replied. "A person might then say, 'Well, that's a disaster. What's an adequate staff?' It's obvious this airline never made any plans in the event that they had a crash of a plane to staff extra people, which most airlines I know of do have. At least they have a game plan in place. And Pan Am didn't have the foggiest clue."

Management's decision at the first station to air the Pan Am passenger list ran counter to a rule of thumb of good reporting: one source is not enough; two sources are better and three or more are better yet. The names and first initials given to the first reporter were from only one source, a person who answered the telephone at Pan Am and whose position was unknown to the reporter. While the reporter reasoned that this was not just any "source off the street" but someone with access to a Pan Am computer, she still labored over whether the names should be aired. "I came off the phone, and it was very close to 6 o'clock by that time. And I said, 'What do we do? Here are the names.' And our news director and our executive producer — thank goodness there was someone else there to make that decision because I didn't want to make that decision. I said, 'Here they are. What do you want to do with them?' At that point, there was no other confirmation other than me getting these names on the phone and putting them on the air."

Another reporter in the same newsroom also questioned whether the student passenger list should have been aired: "As it turned out, it was correct.[18] But I think in a sensitive situation like this, you should have two sources and make sure they're trustworthy and reliable. And we didn't have that. I think we kind of got lucky that we didn't do terrible damage to the people who thought that they might have some victims in their family."

Within minutes of the names scrolling up the screen on the station's early news, the newsroom was flooded with calls. The reporter realized that modern technology was carrying her unconfirmed student passenger list, from one source, around the world. "I answered those calls from Boston, New Jersey and places I never heard of. All of a sudden, I remember looking up during the night and I see (our executive producer) faxing these in my handwriting, who knows where... And I'm thinking, wow! I was getting a little nervous about that, because we really didn't have a lot of confirmation."

Later, on network news, the reporter saw a list of the student passenger names with first initials. She believed that it could have been her list, because it contained a misspelling she had made. "I know that what I did would change the course of that whole night...not only for us, but for a lot of other news agencies and a lot of people that night...You can see how fax machines and satellites and everything just changed the course of this."

Some faulty information was used in Syracuse. One of the three local stations did report on its early newscast that there might be survivors on Pan Am 103. During a newscast aired in the same time period, the station that had obtained the list from Pan Am was running a scroll of student victims. Among the scores of phone callers to this newsroom were those who saw a loved one's name for the first time and wanted to be sure, and those who heard about the list and wanted to know if someone they cared about was on it. This posed a dilemma for people in the newsroom who were answering these phone calls. Reporters may be somewhat used to their role as the bearer of bad news via the air waves, but being the personal bearer of bad news, specifically the names of victims, was something else. If a reporter decides to release the name to an individual, is he or she prepared for, or responsible for, dealing with that individual's reaction?

One reporter called reading the list of names to a young drama student, who phoned her station, "probably the most horrible thing I've ever had to do as a reporter or as a person. (She) knew half a dozen people on the list and would just get a little more hysterical with each name. And at one point, I stopped and asked, 'Are you with anybody? Are you sure you want me to do this?' There's nothing quite like reading the names and realizing that the person on the other end is close to that person, and you have just told them that they are dead. It makes you sick to your stomach." But the reporter felt that it was necessary for her to be the personal bearer of bad news, because the callers couldn't get the information from Pan Am or the State Department hotline. "But, of course, they were frustrated because they couldn't get through. In that sense, I think what we did was somewhat of a public service to these people."

Another reporter told of a young man who also asked for a reading of the names: "We read off some of the names and I remember reading down and I was reading, 'Boland, S., Bolanger, N., Carwell, T., Cohen, T. as in Tom.' And he said, 'No, that was Tim.' It was just an initial to me, but to him, I was just saying 'T as in Tom.' And like, 'No.' And he knew the person. And that's when it hit me...when he said, 'No! It's not T as in Tom, it's Tim.' ("T." Cohen was actually "Theodora" Cohen. The reporter later said she remembered the incident, but not which name caused the young man on the phone to stop and correct her. She added that she was using her anecdote for illustrative purposes.) "He was a friend, a frat brother or something in Massachusetts, and that's when it really (hit). I said, 'I can't do this anymore.' It's one thing to put them on the air, but I can't — then you'd hear them — the grief on the phone, the people who weren't even around here. And it really ripped me apart."

At that point, the reporter says she also realized that she and others in the newsroom had been answering questions about loved ones in a less than empathetic manner. The pressures of a newsroom came into play. Additionally, she said, they weren't prepared to be counselors when the person at the other end of the phone reacted. "We were answering these calls, not in the mindset of someone prepared to answer calls from friends and loved ones. We were still running a news show. We had to get the show on the air. We had affiliates coming. We had networks calling. We had (a New York City station) flying a crew up and they were wanting our time... And so we weren't like a Pan Am volunteer, saying, 'I'm very sorry...blah, blah, blah.' We were like, 'Give me the phone! What do you want? See you later!' You can't do that. You feel like you're cheating these people and you — when I talked to these people and this guy — all of a sudden you're working at this frantic pace and someone says something like that (the guy who knew the first name of someone he thought was a victim), it knocks the wind out of you, and you sit down and say, 'What am I doing? What am I telling these people? How do you separate that emotion from your work?' They're people. You just can't be brusque with them. (But) the only option we had was to be brusque with them. Because we didn't have the time. We didn't have the people here that could sit in a quiet room and talk with them. We were in a newsroom!"

The reporter decided not to continue being the personal bearer of bad news. Like several other reporters that night she had to make a critical decision on her own; the station had no policy to follow. "I just wouldn't take any more phone calls," the reporter said. "At that point I made the decision, and it was difficult because there was no newsroom edict saying we're not giving out these names...It was every man or woman for him or herself in answering these calls."

Wresting the names of the victims from Pan Am was just one of a number of ethical dilemmas that 13 Syracuse television reporters faced during the afternoon and evening of the crash. Twelve of the 13 were interviewed and responded to a written questionnaire for this study. (The thirteenth reporter was on leave. An attempt to contact her, through her management, was unsuccessful.) They had more than 100 years of combined experience in dozens of broadcasting jobs, mostly in New York state, but also in other Northeast states, New England and the Midwest. Some reporters were relatively new to the profession; others would call themselves veterans. Eight had undergraduate degrees in either journalism or communications. All had taken at least some journalism courses.

These journalists largely reported that neither their current news managers nor their past managers played significant roles in helping the reporters prepare for the ethical dilemmas posed by their coverage of Pan Am 103. All 12 said that none of their news managers, in any of the stations where they had worked, had ever discussed ethical coverage of tragedies in a formal session, such as a meeting or an in-house training session. Seven reported informal discussions, but said that these sessions were largely reactive and not proactive. One reporter linked the need for input from management to his age: "Young — not a lot of life experience. I don't have kids. I don't have a wife. I don't know how (such a tragedy) would impact me."

For the most part , the journalists also reported that their college professors had played minor roles, if any, in preparing them to make ethical decisions. Nine journalists said that significant discussions of the ethical considerations of covering tragedies were not part of their college journalism courses.

Reporters said they were primarily guided by personal morals, by their coverage of previous tragedies and their own assessments of their performances, or by life experiences, such as the loss of parents. That meant these journalists were out in the night, making critical ethical decisions essentially on their own.

If being the personal bearer of bad news, via the telephone, was difficult for some local journalists, two other reporters delivered it face-to-face that night. One journalist delivered the news after getting what would be considered a real break. He learned of a local student who, only days before, had shared a few smiles and a little conversation with those who had just been blown out of the sky. She had studied abroad with the Pan Am 103 victims and could have flown back to the States with them. Instead she came home to Central New York a couple of days earlier. The student and her family agreed to talk with the journalist in their home. He went there with a photographer, camera equipment — and the list of the names of the Pan Am 103 victims tucked inside his coat pocket. The reporter said he brought the list because the student's brother, on the telephone, had said that the family wanted to know who was on it. But the journalist decided that he would not show the list unless the student specifically asked to see it while he was at her home. If she asked, the reporter would answer.

"So, we went ahead and did the interview," he said. "She told me about how she got on the plane early, decided to come home early, how she would have been on that plane, how she knew the kids, how she felt about being spared the tragedy. Then I talked to some of her family to get their point of view, how grateful they were. (The photographer) came in and at that point (he) was shooting the table. (The student and her family were sitting at the dining room table and the photographer was taking some shots of them talking.) This was unintentional, but at that point she asked me if I had the names and I said, 'Yes.' She asked me if there was a certain name on there. She identified that name, and I was looking on the list for it. And I stopped at that name, obviously. She saw the look on my face when I was reading through the list and I saw that name. I looked up at her and kind of nodded, and at that point, she broke down crying. It was a fiancé of a friend of hers, a very close friend."

In response to a written questionnaire that followed up the in-depth interviews, seven out of 12 reporters said that they would willingly be the personal bearers of bad news. One reporter added, "but only if I was *100 percent* certain. Otherwise, I would have said, I don't know." Some said that it would be difficult to lie and say that they didn't know who the victims were. One noted that he "hates people who sugar coat things and I hate people who lie to me. I want everything in very honest terms." Another reporter said that whether he would be the personal bearer of bad news would depend on the people involved. Four others said they would not be. Two of the four said that they would refer the questioner to an appropriate agency. One reporter said she could not break the news face-to-face because she is not a counselor and would be unable to go back to the person's residence and cry with him or her: "It's almost like inflicting pain that you're not equipped to cope with. And I don't know if that's our job."

The reporter who confirmed the name of a victim for the student didn't have to deal with her reaction. The young woman left the room. But does a reporter have a responsibility to comfort a person whose question prompts bad news to be delivered? Four reporters who answered this question in the written survey saw their responsibilities as "limited," "few," and "very little." Said one reporter, "If people call or ask in person, most realize that they may get bad news." Three reporters said they would comfort the questioner somewhat, but one said that he "wouldn't become pro-active." Two reporters described more extensive obligations to the person to whom they had just delivered the bad news. One reporter said she "did it gently and then tried to give comfort and support." Said another, "To be compassionate, make sure that they are okay or have someone to help them. Being a reporter doesn't alter these responsibilities."

Another dilemma surfaced for reporters who gave bad news face-to-face: Should that reporter allow his photographer to take pictures of the person reacting? Should the reporter use those pictures on the newscast? One reporter said: "(You don't) set people up for a terrible reaction and then shoot it." But if it happened in the course of the interview, she said she'd let the photographer keep rolling. She was unsure if she'd later air the picture.

The report on the student who escaped tragedy by flying home a couple of days earlier ended with the shot of her in tears, leaving the family dining room. A caller to the station accused the reporter of confirming the student's fears so that he could make his story more emotionally gripping. The reporter denies this. "If it happens during the course of gathering news, let somebody learn something, as long as it wasn't intentional...I wasn't trying to stage something to make my story better. And I feel comfortable with it."

On two other stations, audience members viewed a young man learning for the first time that a friend was dead. The dark-haired student was surrounded by reporters. The shot showed several microphones near his lips. "Her name was on there (the list)?" he asked. A moment of silence was interrupted by a voice (presumably that of one of the reporters): "I saw the list." "Oh my God," the young man responded softly. His head dropped.

Meanwhile, reporters from all three stations were waiting at the SU Women's Building, which housed the offices of SU's Vice President of Public Relations, Robert Hill, and his staff. This, they had expected, would be the place to be to get the official word from the university. Instead the situation developed into a confrontation between Hill, who had been on the job barely six months, and representatives of the local media. One after another Syracuse newsperson criticized the SU public relations effort, in contrast to the few who praised it. A number from both print and broadcast singled Hill out for criticism. In interviews with print and broadcast journalists on both sides of the Atlantic, no other public relations or information officer personally prompted so many complaints. For some Syracuse newspeople, the animosity lasted for years after the event.

The problem, according to three journalists who spent the early hours of the story at Hill's office, was that university representatives were not saying much to the local media. Independently, the three journalists reported that the university's public relations staff, in their opinion, did not do its job properly. As these reporters saw it, this was to the detriment of the reporter's job and of the public's right to know. In those afternoon hours leading up to their early local newscasts, two journalists separately recalled waiting for any word from the university's chief public relations officer.

"So I remember sitting outside of Bob Hill's office and just waiting. And finally he (poked) his head out of the door. I don't know how long it was, but it was at least an hour and a half. And he said, 'Why are you here?' The other stations were represented, as well. And I said, 'I'm here to get some information.' Nobody was giving any information at all and then finally he comes out, and he said, 'There's no reason for you to be here. You might as well go back. We'll call you when we find something out.'"

A second reporter said she thought Hill's request that reporters leave was "absolutely absurd!" She said, "I told Robert Hill that I simply wasn't going to be leaving, and I wasn't going any place, and I'd appreciate the information as soon as possible."

The first reporter said she felt that rather than looking cooperative, the public relations department seemed dictatorial. "If they had just come out periodically and said, 'Look, I'm sorry, we're trying to compile information.' But it's not that way. (Essentially they said:) 'We're in charge. We'll do what we want!' And so, you wait."

As a third reporter recalled: "They weren't very forthcoming. They wouldn't even admit...that that was a possibility... that (students) were on the plane. They had no comment." This journalist also remembered security guards being present at the public relations office, something she said surprised her. She called them unnecessary. "I felt that Robert Hill was very new on the job. He was almost afraid to talk to us, especially when the guards appeared," she said. With a laugh, she added, "What did they think we were going to do, storm the building, his office...? Most people who have worked with us — we've got pretty good manners for the most part, if you know your local media. I know in other cities some pretty outrageous things have happened. But I would say we're pretty courteous. I just think that he was so new that he didn't know what to expect."

Some reporters said that the lack of information and communication was stressful for them and unfair to the public. Said one reporter, "At a time when the public was demanding answers, (university officials) were silent."

Reporters are often trained and counseled not to take no for an answer — at least not the first time they hear it. They tell how many interview subjects agreed to appear on camera after initially declining. To them, part of a reporter's job is to try to understand and address the person's objection. How many times or how hard a reporter tries seems to be an individual matter.

That was particularly true for Syracuse television reporters confronted with the task of approaching grieving students on the evening of December 21. The spectrum ran from one reporter who refused to approach students at all to one who felt he was justified in aggressively following a particular student. The latter felt he had the right to be persistent because he had witnessed an SU student from the London program give an interview to another television crew. The student originally held a ticket to return home to Central New York on Pan Am 103. But his mother changed his ticket for one on a flight that brought him home a few hours earlier. In fact, according to the reporter, when the young man arrived at Syracuse's Hancock Airport, he held a ticket with the words "Pan Am 103" still on it.

The Syracuse television reporter said he was determined to "keep following him; keep asking him questions. If he would have said, 'No,' and belted me, I still would have kept asking him questions." The reporter's justification? The student gave an interview to another television crew. "By God, then, he was going to give it to me. It's not incumbent upon him to talk to anybody to begin with. But once he does, then I feel he's fair game at any price...Once I see somebody being selective, I'm going to stay on his tail until he sees me in his dreams." According to the reporter, the student had been interviewed by a crew that the reporter surmised was from a network or at least a big city. "They got off the plane and he gives them an interview, and he gets to me and he says, 'I don't want to talk about it.' At that point, I didn't say it like this, but, 'Hey Buddy! You talked to those guys. I'll shove my mike up your ass until you talk to me.' And he did. But I was very persistent."

The journalist said his previous reporting experience influenced his decision to pursue this student. "I guess I started out in this business as a nice guy, very understanding of people and these types of situations. And I just got walked on by other reporters, even people who were grieving, for understanding. In other words, the reporters who were not understanding got the story; I didn't. So I learned very quickly that this business has no room in a situation like that for someone who is understanding. I mean, you don't have to go up and be obnoxious, but you do have to pursue. And that's what I did."

When covering deaths in the news, it is standard practice for broadcast and print reporters to try to locate someone who knew the victim, someone who can at least add a brush stroke to the portrait the journalist hopes to paint. It is common, for example, for journalists to knock on the doors of neighbors of a murder victim. It wasn't that easy in the case of Pan Am 103. But it became apparent early in the evening that reporters had a better shot at finding someone who knew victims if they concentrated on "Fraternity Row," a neighborhood of a dozen or so fraternity and sorority houses. Like the reporter at the airport, those sent to "Fraternity Row" had to decide how to approach those grieving and how hard they would press them for an interview. Two reporters from different stations described a "low-key" approach.

"I've always tended to try to be less aggressive in a situation like this, as opposed to more aggressive," the first reporter said, "in first offering my condolences or whatever the situation might call for and then see if they have any desire to talk to us...If they do, fine; if not, just sort of back off. That was the tone I tried to use that evening."

The other reporter echoed, "If a person feels like talking, fine. If not, then you try and pursue another angle."

On arrival at the Greek houses, this reporter said she and the cameraman tried not to add to the trauma of the evening. They had agreed on how to proceed before arriving at the fraternity house. "We only wanted to talk to people who wanted to talk to us. We didn't want to force ourselves on anybody. Both of us — I mean the photographer, you know — felt that in this situation you should use some discretion, a little bit of sensitivity. We both had agreed, before we head in there, we are not going to blare our camera's bright light and microphone."

The reporter recalled how the team had put that philosophy into action: "I remember getting there, walking up to the fraternity, knocking on the door. And we left our camera and our equipment behind, because we knew people would be upset. So we just proceeded with caution. When we went up to the fraternity, a young man came to the door and we identified ourselves and told them we are from Channel — and we understood that a member of the fraternity was on board the plane. And he confirmed that for us. He looked kind of distraught, but not distraught enough where I felt we should leave. He invited us in and we chatted for a while. He told us about the fraternity member. I think his name was Steve. I'm not 100 percent sure. And then I said, 'Well, being with the television station, would it be all right if we came in and did an on-camera interview with you? We know you don't have a lot of information, but perhaps you can tell us how the tragedy is affecting this fraternity and your feelings on your friend.' That sort of thing...He was very receptive to that. He said, 'Sure. No problem.' We went back out. We got our cameras and went back to the fraternity. We set up in an area where other fraternity members, who looked a little upset, wouldn't be upset by the presence of our cameras."

What was the first question that the reporter asked, during the on-camera interview? "I think I asked, 'I understand you've been trying to find out about your friend, Steve? Can you tell us what you've been able to learn?' He said that we know he is on the plane; we don't know his status; we are trying like heck to find out. I said, 'Well, tell me a little about Steve?' And he told me that he is a broadcast journalism major, how long he has lived at the frat, what kind of guy he was. And then I said, 'This must be terribly upsetting...It has come as a shock to all of us.' And then he responded by saying, 'Sure it has. I can't believe this.'"

By the time the second reporter headed for "Fraternity Row," she already had conducted one interview. An intern at her station knew several of the students on Pan Am 103. The intern had a yearbook with her. As they looked at students' pictures, the reporter asked her to tell any anecdotes about her friends. With this interview "in the can," the reporter headed out for what she thought was an interview with a specific person at a sorority house that had been pre-arranged by her newsroom. She felt that pre-arranging the interview was the most sensitive and sensible way. "I didn't want to knock on people's door cold and say, 'By the way, did you know any of these dead people?'"

But when she reached the house, she was told over the intercom that no one by the name the station had given her lived there. The reporter will never know if an error was made back in the newsroom or if the contact suddenly decided against the interview. But she said what happened at the door of that sorority house made her "feel terrible" and convinced her that students were "in a state of shock." "They were quite upset that we would even come and ask. And some of the students who were going into the (sorority house) would go in and brush past us and sort of swear at us and call us bad names...They wouldn't even answer us and a couple more said, 'How can you be doing this? This is terrible...You should go away. You should be ashamed of yourselves. Don't you think we feel bad enough?'"

According to the reporter, the pressure on her was compounded by instructions that she was getting over the two-way radio from her newsroom. "While we were walking around from house to house, we would get calls on the two-way radios and they would say, 'Go to this house. Go to that house. Did you hear about this?' And I think that a lot of their information was wrong, because we didn't get very far. And that was very frustrating because here you are like old man death, walking to the door with a TV camera and you've got the wrong information. So we felt somewhat angry at the people who were supposedly in charge back at the station. We felt that they didn't know what they were doing, and that they were giving us bad information, and that we were the ones paying the price."

Finally, the reporter was able to get someone to talk. At a fraternity house, the reporter asked to speak to the president. She recalled that the president and three other brothers, dressed in mourning clothes, descended a staircase bordered by dark wood paneling. A fraternity brother had died. They were willing to talk. This reporter's approach nearly mirrors that of the first reporter.

"I interviewed them one at a time. They all sat together, but we did them one-on-one. Well, first of all, I said, 'I'm terribly sorry. I hope this won't be too difficult for you.' But they all seemed fairly composed, and I asked them to tell me about their friend. I asked them how they first heard about the news and what their reaction was." The reporter said that she and the photographer came in with portable equipment, including a portable light mounted on the camera, but didn't set up a tripod or any extra lights. According to the reporter, she wanted to make it "as easy on them as possible. Yes, they talked about him, what kind of guy he was. It was interesting. They didn't use the past tense at all: 'I'll be really happy to see him.' Obviously it hadn't hit them that they would never see him again."

The fraternity brothers in mourning clothes were on their way to the vigil at Hendricks Chapel. Although many students had left campus for the holidays, hundreds remained. A number of them walked to the chapel with one hand carefully shielding the flames of a candle from the cold wind. One reporter described them as "the most frail human beings I had ever seen."

Two reporters sent to the chapel had the same mission as those on "Fraternity Row" and the reporter at the airport: Get reaction. Find those who know the victims. As before, they had to make critical decisions on how to approach the students and how hard to press for an interview. One reporter described her approach: "I just walk over and introduce myself and say, 'I understand if you don't want to (talk), but if there's anything you'd like to (say)...' Most people just walked right by."

But this journalist said she did get two interviews by planning ahead. Earlier in the evening, she had called the president of a fraternity house. "I told him I knew that it was a very difficult time and that we would be up there (Hendricks Chapel) later on for the service. If there was anything that maybe he or the house wanted to say about the person they had lost, any of his good qualities or anything at all that they wanted to express or wanted people to know, that they would be welcome to talk to us. We certainly would hear them out. I think that he was happy to hear that. He thought about it for a little while, and I called him back later, as I told him I would. And he said, 'Yes, we'll be all set. We'll look for you.' That was the interview I got when I was at Hendricks Chapel that night. A couple of guys, who had time to talk about it, about themselves...they were able to approach me. I didn't have to go after them with a blazing camera light or microphone."

Setting up these interviews ahead of time relieved this reporter from some of the pressure to get student interviews that she says she otherwise would have felt. She tried to interview other students anyway because "you want to get whoever you can get...(also) I always want to try as hard as I can." But after about ten students turned her down, she stopped asking. She had her pre-arranged interviews on tape, and she realized that more were not "crucial to my story."

In response to the written questionnaire, local reporters described how they approach grieving people:

- Nine out of 12 said the camera is either not in sight or not rolling when they walk up to a grieving person. (One said she might have the camera rolling if the interview were to happen in a public place. The other three respondents didn't comment on the instructions they give their photographers.)
- More than half of the respondents said specifically that they approach in a sympathetic manner, actually express sympathy or say something comforting.
- More than half said that they simply ask the grieving person if he or she wants to talk or "share their account" or if there is anything that he or she would like to say.
- One reporter cautioned never to ask "How do you feel?" There are other ways to get the message.
- Another reporter said the journalist should never be argumentative.
- "I try to put myself in their place. They should be handled carefully," wrote another reporter.

But one journalist stressed that reporters do need to approach grieving people for interviews: "The more timid...reporter would say 'Leave them alone.'"

The second reporter outside of Hendricks Chapel would undoubtedly dispute that "timid" label. She decided not to approach the students there, even though her management expected her to do so. Many field reporters can empathize with her situation. Many can recall being at the scene and being overruled by someone miles away. It is a classic reporter-management struggle. This reporter decided to go with her own judgment. "We called back to the live truck and they asked me, 'What do you have to put in your package?' I said that I had this, this, and this. And I said, 'I don't have any kids!' I don't...usually stand up first and say something to (management). I'll defend something, if they ask me. But (in this instance) I said, right away, 'I'm not talking to these kids tonight! I've seen other people do it and I'm not doing it! You can yell at me later if you see it (on the other channels) but I'm not doing it!'"

What prompted the reporter to come to her decision? "There was more than grief. These kids were seriously in shock. They were walking around like zombies. When I was walking out, I saw radio people and maybe a TV person...It was —— from radio. And I was so embarrassed. There were these three girls bawling and being comforted by one of the ministers. And (the radio reporter) stuck his mike in the middle of the huddle...and they were crying and I thought, 'It's not worth it.' Yes, this is a huge story, but this was one night for us. For these kids, this is the biggest thing that has ever happened to them. They're in shock! Why do it? I don't think I can tell the story any better if I have a girl bawling. If people can't get the feeling and the sense of loss and grief from the nat sound[19] in the church and just the pictures and the pictures of these kids' faces....It told you more than anything that they would be able to blurt out if they had a microphone stuck in their face. When I saw that, and then again when I saw the kids walking out of the chapel, I just said, no!"

The 23 steps of Hendricks Chapel extend onto the Quad, a grassy rectangle lined with academic buildings at the heart of the campus. Those steps had been in the news before, often as the scene of student protests. For Syracuse students attending the university in 1988, Hendricks Chapel will be forever linked to the Pan Am 103 tragedy, etched in memory as the place many went to try and understand what could not be understood.

Up those steps that December evening flooded not only students and members of the university community, but members of the print and broadcast media. Certainly the vigil at Hendricks was newsworthy. And members of the media correctly assessed that this was a tragedy that would sadden the entire community. But of all of the Syracuse media coverage of Pan Am 103, that at Hendricks Chapel would receive the most vehement criticism.

The chaplains, by reporters' accounts, were gracious and understanding of this need for coverage. And the chaplains reportedly shouldered the entire responsibility for initiating the service, planning and conducting it. No university public relations representative served as their intermediary with the media. One technique that those experienced in planning for media coverage of sensitive occasions sometimes put into place was not used that evening — a pool. What that means, simply, is that stations agree to share resources and manpower so that a minimum number of cameras and people are shooting the event. And all stations get the same video and audio feed. Such a pool is common in courtrooms, for example.

The Hendricks chaplains did set boundaries within which the media were to conduct their business, but without a pool the number of reporters and photographers became a crowd. In hindsight, some members of the media and many critics of the media's performance agreed that a pool would have substantially reduced the intrusive nature of the coverage.

A number of those attending the service described the media as too noisy, too close with their cameras to those grieving. Some reporters who were there admit to some problems.

One reporter said that she was unsure why, but her news crew was late getting to the service. That only added to the tension. "We had walked in and it had just started, but our live truck wasn't there yet. We were supposed to be taping it live, just like everybody else. Everybody else was up and we were panicked. And still the seriousness of the situation hasn't set in, because you are just frantic and the adrenaline is flowing. I am trying to quietly run up and down the stairs to run cable in the chapel and running outside and telling the live truck where to go...So then, we were running up and down and we got it hooked up. It was hard because there were people, of course, who didn't want their picture taken and you are trying to be sensitive. And I had shoes on that made noise. I had to kick them off to run up and down the stairs because these people are praying and crying, and I'm running up and down the stairs, trying to yank this cable up and then quietly pull it the length of one pew to get it into the photographer's camera."

This reporter had some harsh words about the conduct of some of her colleagues. "We certainly didn't want to barge in there, which is what another station did and it was even worse than the whole rest of us. I think it was Channel —— and they just came in like you'd come into a news conference, like with all the stuff over their shoulders. And everybody else — still photographers and video photographers — were all set up. They just came in — it was just like we were already being obtrusive. And the still photographers were using flash, which is a debate which goes on among photographers, whether that was really necessary. But that was just so intrusive."

One reporter defended her photographer and others who used zoom lenses to shoot those weeping . "I think that they were doing their job. I think that people can criticize them for it, but just because they're zeroing in doesn't mean that they're close to them...It was easy to get close-ups of them without having to move. I had no problem with that." The reporter did say, however, that sometimes her photographer was closer to students, but she added that "he was very mindful of their grief."

For some reporters, this mixture of prayers, tears, and their own adrenaline produced a conflict of major proportions: should reporters act as their personal morality dictated, even if that interfered with getting the assigned job done? This conflict between what the individual felt should be done and what he or she was paid to do was apparent in this reporter's testimony: "You walk in and you think that nothing can curb that adrenaline. And all of a sudden, it comes over you like a cold chill, and you realize how many people have died and how serious it is and you're knocked off kilter for a second. But then the adrenaline comes and you don't have time to feel just yet... You're sitting there and you're listening for key (sound) bites, and it almost seems so crass and unfeeling, because all you're thinking about is these good emotional bites from a person of (the) cloth."

Asked if she felt ambivalent about this, the reporter said she went "back and forth...because I'm a semi-religious person and it was real hard to, one minute, not pray with them and the next minute think, 'Oh, what a great bite that was! That's going to look wonderful in the wrap[20] that I have to do later!' It was hard to go back and forth and you didn't know what to do. Half of you wanted to maybe pray, at least for the people who were there, if not for yourself and for those who died. But in your professional side, half of you wanted to pray because you wanted to look like you were certainly caring and that you respected what those people were there for. And then the other half of your professional side was going, 'That was a great bite and I have to hurry up. We only have so much time. We have to get out there.' It was back and forth. It was hard."

The struggle between a reporter's own morals and the demands of the job surfaced in another incident at Hendricks Chapel. In this case, a reporter had been assigned to do a live report from the chapel while the memorial service was in progress. "We went inside and the place was packed," this reporter said. "And it was difficult because we wanted to do a live shot. And we went up in the balcony. It was very dark and the people, the students there were upset. We were the targets. We had cellular phones; we had live equipment; we had cables. And we were going into this service and people were screaming at us...just things like, 'Get out of here. What are you doing here?' These people were really angry. 'Don't you understand that this is a memorial service to our friends?' And, yes I did understand. And yes, I didn't want to be there. But, yes, I had a job to do that I had been told to do."

The reporter did the live shot, but then realized that the shot was not worth doing from a technical standpoint. She couldn't speak in a normal voice, so the audio was lousy. The shot was done off the photographer's shoulder, not a tripod, so the video was not the best. According to the reporter, "Everything was bad about this live shot."

But for this reporter, the conflict, the inner turmoil, did not end with the conclusion of that first live shot. Within moments, a producer from a large, network-owned-and-operated station in another city was on the cellular phone, asking the reporter to do a second live shot. The pressure, she remembered, was tremendous: "They were on the other side of the country and they were saying, 'Are you ready? Can we do it?' I said, 'Listen, this isn't cool exactly.' And I remember the producer, who made me think of *Broadcast News* (a movie about television journalism)...This woman on the other end of the phone was just like, 'Are you going to do it or are you not going to do it? Tell me!' I didn't really feel comfortable...She didn't want to hear that, but I was the one who was in the situation. I heard her say on the phone, 'Are you going to do it or are you not going to do it?' And I said, 'No, I'm not.' And she said, 'Okay!' and hung up and that was it.

"As a reporter, again thinking journalistically, it would have been great for me to do a live shot for —— in San Francisco. It would have been a nice little bit to do as a reporter in this kind of market.

"But I didn't do it. I would make that decision again, too, because that was, I am sure, the right decision to make and we should never, in my mind, have been up there doing a live shot to begin with."

Back at the Women's Building, the three local television reporters, along with print media representatives, were still waiting. In the early evening hours, the vice president for public relations, Robert Hill, did speak with them. Then an announcement was made that Chancellor Melvin Eggers would make a statement before 10 p.m.

Sometime after 9 o'clock that evening, a fourth television reporter relieved another from his station at the Women's Building. This reporter was sent to get the Eggers statement. While reporters who had been waiting were highly critical of the university's public relations effort, this reporter saw it in a different light. In the written survey, he rated the effort as "excellent." He wrote: "They helped us set up our coverage and never gave us a hard time."

He described what journalists were doing when he arrived. Some, he said, were eating pizza. Some were joking; some were not. He understood the joking, but couldn't participate. "Frankly, mind you, reporters have to step away from a story. You have to do that or otherwise you go nuts. But I was involved in this story. I had seen people; I had seen hurt. I was really running around. Some of these others — I don't know what they were doing that night. Obviously, they were dealing with it as journalists would normally. When you are waiting around for something to happen — we all know each other — we all joke around with each other, and that's the situation I was thrust into."

But along with the joking, the reporter said the pressure of competition was very evident. "There was a certain amount of competitiveness. (Reporters were asking:) 'Did you guys get this? Did you get this aspect?' Or 'I hear you got the list. You got the list. Let me see the list.' And I wasn't going to give them the list. They were all looking around for somebody who had a family here in the area. 'Do we have a family? Do we have someone who was directly affected?'"

Perhaps it was this sense of competition, perhaps it was desperation for information, perhaps it was the fact that the 11 o'clock news was near that fueled what this reporter observed next: journalists swarmed around Chancellor Melvin Eggers as he appeared to make his statement. "It was like a crush," the reporter said. "We tried to get some order...And the chancellor was just watching this all take place, and you could tell that this man was really going through the wringer. He was having a tough time, but he was kind of watching all the newsmen crowd around him with microphones and trying to trip over each other. I wonder what went through his mind."

These local television reporters, gathered around the chancellor, had collectively covered thousands of stories and had collected, in their careers, at least an equal number of sound bites. Yet they reported that the chancellor's statement was one that would stand out in memory. "It was probably one of the best statements I think I've ever heard...after a tragedy like this. It was just wonderful...I think it was totally off the top of his head. I think he called (them) 'our best and our brightest.' It was one of the lines that I was particularly struck with. You could tell, not only by what he said, but by the way he said it that the man had really gone through hell that day."

Across campus was another important site for the story that night. The curved edges of satellite dishes create a soft contrast to the straight lines of Syracuse University's S.I. Newhouse School of Public Communications' broadcast facility. One of those satellite dishes could do something none of those at Syracuse's three affiliated stations could. While the affiliates' dishes, known as "downlinks," could pull a picture down from a satellite, Newhouse's "uplink" could beam pictures and sound *up* to a satellite. From the satellite, those images could be transmitted to the networks or to other stations across the United States, and relayed around the world. The woman in charge of booking the satellite transmissions at the university recalled 25 reports were sent during the evening and nighttime hours following the crash — normally the number transmitted in a two-week period.

By evening, the networks, large local stations affiliated with the networks, and independent stations had swarmed to Syracuse to get the SU angle on the tragedy. They were making heavy use of the Newhouse School satellite dish, as were the Syracuse stations sharing their material.

Among the transmissions via satellite that night were some campus "live hits" beamed to a New York City station. The reporter for those "live hits" was a seasoned Syracuse journalist, who was described by several of his colleagues as "one of our best live reporters." Local management had made the decision to put one of their best to work, not for their own station and their own community, but for a station outside the Syracuse market. It was an example of what several local journalists, from one station in particular, complained represented management going too far to accommodate larger outside stations and the networks.[21]

That excellent live reporter was not the only "human resource" local management loaned to others. Accompanying the live reporter was a field producer, another pair of eyes and ears to gather information, another person to weigh what should and should not make the air. One reporter, serving the local community, said her audience would have been better served if management had sent field producers on key *local* assignments.

Some journalists reported that their managers should have been more careful about allowing the networks to share limited equipment. One trouble spot was the editing booths at the stations. Inside those closet-sized spaces a reporter and an editor turn a series of unsequenced pictures and interviews into what the public has come to accept as a finished report: sequenced pictures and an accompanying reporter's narration, carefully selected "sound bites" from the interviewees and perhaps a reporter's "stand-up," the reporter's opportunity to show the public that he or she was on the scene and had some information to convey personally. Anyone who has ever worked in local news knows there are rarely enough booths for the number of teams waiting to edit stories. Teams with lead stories often "bump" teams that are editing stories that will appear later in the newscast. Sharing such limited resources with the networks, according to some local reporters, put "much more" stress on them. One reporter said she understood that it was part of an affiliate's duty to help the network, but it was local management's duty to coordinate it all in a way to avoid further stress on local reporters and to prevent jeopardizing the local product.

Another journalist reported that her local station's "hospitality" was not reciprocated: "Interestingly enough, (the network) sent a reporter up here, and when I got in that night, she wanted to know if I got anything from Mel Eggers. I said, 'Yes.' I pointed her to a very good bite. But she didn't tell us that she had a bite from somebody who was supposed to be on the flight. That they didn't share with us...but we gave them everything, including somebody's typewriter and seat."

Whether it was management's fragmented attention, the lack of a plan for covering disasters, or a combination of these and other factors, at least one reporter felt that her managers were confused as they labored in their newsrooms on that December evening, and that in at least one case, it affected the news product. This reporter claimed that she sent a tape back to the station with four or five good sound bites from SU students that, she said, never made it on the air. "Well, as it turns out, the tape gets back and nobody ever relays the message to whomever was producing...It was so crazy back here, I was told. We had it. That's the shame of it. We had it and we just didn't use it. They were befuddled back here. This was bigger than all of them."

The Syracuse television reporter who went live from Kennedy Airport would probably agree. He claims he was on his own making ethical decisions because his managers were "all out doing other things." For example, the reporter said while he did not personally witness the mother who had fallen to the floor earlier in the evening, he did see the footage later on an airport television monitor. He talked about the incident during his live shot, but later asked himself: "Did I make it seem like I saw it? Well, I did see it. I saw it on videotape…Was I wrong to use that information and make it sound like it was my own?" The reporter concluded that what he did was acceptable because he had used the information just as a journalist would use information supplied by a wire service.

But, according to the reporter, someone back at the station should be in charge of making or helping make such editorial decisions. "There needs to be somebody in editorial control of television. In some shops, there is. But I would venture to say that in 80 percent of TV shops, there is nobody. And the first time the line producer (who has responsibility for what's in the show) sees it is when it's going out on the air. And that's too late." The reporter said that at least part of the reason he didn't get the support he needed from his station was that his management was too busy serving the network and other out-of-town stations.

At 11:30 p.m., local television news studios concluded their reports. For that night, at least, the reporters' work was done. From "Fraternity Row" to Syracuse University's public relations office, from Syracuse's Hancock Airport to New York's Kennedy Airport, from the private homes of students to the public sanctuaries for community mourning, the reporters had covered the news. It had been a tough night, asking questions under difficult circumstances, facing criticism about the way they did their job, struggling with the technicalities of communication and in some cases, with a lack of support from their own newsroom. But above all, they had been dealing with young people grieving over a terrible tragedy. Speaking about the experience two years later, one journalist said, in a voice so soft that the interviewer had to ask him to repeat his answer, "I cried a couple of times that night."

In fact, eight of the 12 journalists reported emotional reactions they experienced after covering the Pan Am 103 tragedy. They described a range of emotions from sadness to depression.

One reporter talked about the way journalists are often pushed by management and by teachers to believe they have to have nerves of steel: "Maybe someone should have told me, 'You're going to have the adrenaline rush when you're out there. But when you go home that night and you're taking your bath, you're going to feel lousy…and you're going to want to bawl.' If someone had only told me that, maybe that would have prepared me."

Another reported a reaction, not on the night of the crash, but a few days later: "I just sat there and started crying, because there was all this pain and grief we had seen…You're not supposed to be showing this pain and grief because you're the big…distanced teller of the facts."

Two journalists reported that while they were able to remain professional and do their jobs, the gravity of the tragedy weighed upon them as they were out in the field. As one veteran reporter prepared for a live shot with the grief-stricken Chancellor Eggers, she wondered if she would maintain her composure. "My only reservation about it (the live shot) was that I was very emotional about this," the reporter said. "I was not very sure if I could go on the air and not start crying." Later, she added, "When I did the interview, you could clearly hear in my voice that I was very upset over this."

The second journalist reported that she was unable to erase her emotions during a standup at Hendricks Chapel, and that she was later criticized for it. She explained that she is used to doing what the profession calls "hard news," factual stories that must be relayed quickly, and stories devoid of "personality" and emotion. "But that's what my story was — to somehow help viewers understand the grief at the chapel," she said. "I was criticized by someone at another station a couple of days later for saying too much."

But the other reporter said that journalists should not feel compelled to disguise their emotions and she encouraged them to lose "that reporter's voice," the voice of authority. "When John Kennedy was shot, Walter Cronkite cried when he made that announcement. It's perfectly okay. And if we as reporters think it's not okay to shed a tear or to have our voice shake, well, then we're dead wrong." The reporter later added that it was the sincerity of her words and emotions that made the difference. "You could see that this was not a reporter acting."

Long after the television studio lights faded that evening, this reporter felt that the story was not over on the Syracuse University campus. She and another reporter and a photographer, taking a ride around campus, came upon what the reporter called "the most amazing shot." Silhouetted against the night sky was a young fraternity brother, lowering the fraternity flag to half-staff. "And he was kneeling in prayer...and I said to myself, 'This is not a private tragedy. This is a public tragedy.' I've not wanted to invade on private moments, but I made the decision that this time it was the right thing to do. We took the picture. The kid came running down. He was hysterical crying. He was screaming. As it turns out, he happened to be a communications major...Very interesting (that) he didn't think we should be there. I talked to him. I grabbed his hand. I said, 'Look, you know I'm sorry. I understand your pain. I've lost friends.' He didn't want to know from anything...He was really hysterical.

"We started to leave. He went back up on the hill...up on the fraternity lawn. And then, there was another picture. He was kneeling in a different kind of way. It was just the most amazing picture in the way that the light was coming off the fraternity." But at that moment, the reporter said she decided not to have her photographer take that second picture. "It was enough. I had invaded his private moment enough. I had my picture and there was nothing more I wanted out of him...I couldn't drain him. He was already drained. And I remember the photographer and the other reporter being very happy that we were going to get out of there. And the photographer (said) to me, 'I really have newfound respect for you.'"

Syracuse newspapers: writing history as it happens

One of the editors of the Syracuse *Herald-Journal* had just sat down with a reporter to edit a Christmas-week series about people who give of themselves to help the dying, the homeless, those in need. Although it was mid-afternoon, it was late in the day for the editor, who had started his long workday on the afternoon paper at 6 a.m. He left the editing job in mid-sentence to take a call.

A reporter was phoning to tell him a plane had crashed in Scotland and some Syracuse University students might be on board. The editor remembered his first thought was to send a reporter to the scene in Scotland as soon as possible if the report was true. He never finished editing the Christmas series.

On the other side of the building, in the offices of the *Post-Standard*, a photographer interrupted the daily news budget meeting and announced to the editors that a bunch of SU students were on board a plane that had crashed. The editors were not even aware that a plane had crashed; wire service bulletins had just begun to arrive. The logistics of covering the story were very difficult, a *Post-Standard* editor said, because it was "a major local story that was nowhere near where we were." He wanted his newspaper "to bring home this distant tragedy and to reflect the local aspect in a significant way."[22]

The paper's university reporter began calling offices and sources to try to learn what was happening and to develop angles to hand off to other reporters. The editor also sent a general assignment reporter to camp out at the university's public relations office. Another reporter was dispatched to Kennedy Airport where, the editor reasoned, family members might be waiting.

The task that faced newspaper journalists that night was similar to that of their television counterparts in some ways, very different in others. The print reporters needed to provide all the kinds of information that would be broadcast, but they also were expected to provide something more: a permanent record of the event that would be delivered to homes across the circulation area the next day. Many people would save those editions the way they did when John F. Kennedy was assassinated. Pan Am 103 would be an important page in Syracuse history.

At the *Herald-Journal*, the editor chose a reporter to send to Scotland and asked him, "Do you have a passport?" After explaining that he might be leaving for Scotland if SU students had been killed in the crash, the editor told the reporter to call a travel agency, book a flight, and then stand by.

Reporters were rounded up to start making calls: Had there been a large number of SU students on the plane? Were there any survivors? The reporters called SU, Pan Am, Kennedy Airport, the State Department. They were getting nowhere.

A newspaper columnist who called Robert Hill, the university's vice president for public relations, described the spokesman as upset. "He's always that way, whether he has a reason to be upset or not. He never says, 'Gee, we're in a panic here and really can't help you' — he's never like that. I wouldn't have expected any help from him or any of his people. For a person who is hired by the university to deal with the press and be helpful, he's certainly the most unhelpful person that I've ever run into in that business. He seems to be seething with dislike for me and my colleagues."

The editor's superiors told him not to send the reporter to Scotland unless the story would be big locally. They couldn't afford it. But the final flight leaving Syracuse that could make the overseas connection would leave shortly. Finally, frustration mounting, the editor called the Syracuse University London Centre. "As calm and unthreatening as I could, I explained that we had heard there was a plane crash, and that we also understood that there were quite a few SU students aboard, and what could they tell us about it? The person at the other end said they had already been told by SU not to say anything to reporters about this. Of course, I found that absolutely mind boggling. Why do you want to withhold this information? Why would you not want to answer a perfectly reasonable question and either put minds at ease or let people know they should brace themselves?"

The editor tried to convey that he was "a reasonable person just trying to find out what's going on. Were there students aboard the plane?" After a little more conversation, the person in the London office said that he had seen several students who were supposed to be getting on the flight. "It was enough evidence to tell me that yes, there were a significant number of SU students aboard the plane."

The reporter arrived at Syracuse's airport ten minutes before the last connecting flight. The editor met him and gave him $200 from his own wallet, money for Christmas shopping he had planned to do that day, along with a box of pens and notebooks.

The *Post-Standard* also sent a reporter to Scotland, but had him cover the scene at Kennedy Airport en route. The *Herald-Journal* sent their newsman to Kennedy Airport on the same plane with a ticket for Glasgow.

Back in the newsrooms, reporters were still calling in search of information.

But the phones were ringing, too. People had heard a broadcast bulletin, saying a plane had crashed with SU students. Was it true? By early evening, the newsrooms were flooded with calls from students, friends, faculty members, concerned relatives. Soon out-of-town papers were calling, too, especially to see if the Syracuse reporters had been able to obtain any biographical information on the victims.

The *Herald-Journal* assigned one person to handle the incoming calls. Her job was to try to give out as much information as possible, as well as take down names and phone numbers of people who were calling in so that they could be phoned back when information came in. If they knew someone on the plane, they might be interview subjects.

The editor at the afternoon paper believed one reason the newsrooms received so many calls from relatives, friends and other news organizations "was because no one was getting any information from SU." Students who went to the public relations office had no more luck than reporters who were sent there. "They wanted to know if someone they cared about was on that plane, and they ended up by contacting reporters, if they saw them there, or calling our newsroom." Sometimes the news given out over the phone was reassuring. Sometimes it was painful. "I think there were several people for whom we broke the news," the editor said, but he added none of them was a parent or other relative.

When a list of passengers appeared — the editor did not remember its source — the big task became verifying the names. "I think it's important to know that we didn't just put it in the newspaper and publish it, and say, 'Well, we got this list from somewhere, God only knows where, here it is.'"

Reporters used telephone directories, newspaper clippings and school yearbooks to find families, friends, teachers and colleagues of people on the list. They rang up family and friends to ask, "Have you heard anything?" The editor chose two reporters for the task: a woman he described as "an empathetic person — she isn't going to get on the phone and say stupid things to grieving relatives," and a man in whom he had "great confidence not to be rude or callous."

The woman reporter said most people she telephoned spoke with her, although some asked clergy or friends to speak for them. "When those people said, 'Don't talk to me,' I didn't. And from my perspective, anybody who felt that my questions were too private to deal with, all they had to do was tell me and I would have gotten off the phone." She described her approach: "One of the things I always do when I'm trying to write a story about someone who has died, I try to explain to people what we want to do is to be able to let our readers see the deceased as a real person, not just an anonymous name on the list. And the only way to convey that to people is for those who knew them to share with me his life, his interests, his accomplishments. And they were willing to do that."

The male reporter described a similar method. "I remember almost getting into a routine of identifying yourself, apologizing for calling at this time and say, 'We really want to tell people that these just aren't statistics, that these are people. Is there anyone there that can talk to us?' I always would say that we don't want to just let this person be forgotten; we don't want this person to be just a name — and that often worked." He thought giving the person an option to pass the phone to somebody else gave him an edge. In some cases, a parent, too shaken to talk, would pass the phone to a brother of the deceased. Another time he was referred to a pastor who spoke for the family. A best friend answered the phone for one family and told him all about her girl friend.

It was hard duty. The woman reporter remembered looking across the room during the middle of the calling and meeting the eyes of her male colleague. He slowly shook his head.

As the night wore on, more reporters were given five or six names of family members and asked to call them. A police reporter explained that if the person she reached refused to talk, she would ask if she could call back later, and if they said no, she would wait an hour or so and call back anyway. "We had to get this stuff on time," she recalled. If they said no a second time or hung up, she made it a rule to leave them alone... We weren't the only ones calling them. They had the whole world calling them. Once they hang up on you or something...(you) shouldn't waste your resources on that. Go to someone else that maybe would be more promising or leave them your number and say, 'Look, I know you're kind of shook up now, but call me back.'"

This reporter, who had covered many tragedies, said she also explains to bereaved people that she wants to tell readers about the victim. She tries to be positive. "It's happened. You don't want to sit there and apologize for it, just deal with it. They're dead, and we have to keep that in mind, but at the same time you just explain we're still going to be doing a story and we'd like to include your memories of that person, and some of them come around. Most of them come around just like that. If you think about how you'd want it done to you...you are bound and determined that you are not going to call and say, 'How do you feel now that your daughter is dead?' So you have to come up with your own approach. They're crying on the phone, and you have to let them cry. And you can't talk when they're crying, but you just have to reassure them: 'I know that this is upsetting. I know this has just happened.'"

People did call her back. One was an SU student who had studied in the London program and knew many of the victims. The reporter called Germany, where the student was visiting a friend, and left a message. The student called the reporter back and gave an emotional interview. "She was so vocal and her story, in her words, was so good...I couldn't say it any better."

The *Post-Standard* also had the list. The editor thought it probably came from local television, a list which he said Pan Am had released early and then tried to retract. About a dozen reporters were pulled off other assignments to help on the story. Some of them called for information about names on the list.

One reporter for the morning newspaper called an editor of the student newspaper just to see what she knew. "And it turned out that she was very upset because a good friend...was apparently one of the victims," the reporter said. That, in turn, upset the *Post-Standard* journalist, who went to the lounge to collect herself and smoke a cigarette. "I was all alone, and I was just thinking, okay now, you know a lot of calls are coming. You know you've got to do it. Pull yourself together."

She received a variety of responses from students she called that evening. "Some people really are anxious to tell their stories to a reporter. Others have to be coaxed a bit, and still others will absolutely refuse," she said.

This reporter did not have to call relatives that evening, but one of her colleagues did. The colleague, who was assigned to cover the university regularly, said her initial telephone approach was to ask the people who answered if they had been contacted by the university or the airline. "It is an awful job to call up a family and say, 'Have you heard?'" she said, but explained she was helped by a veteran obituary writer whose desk was near hers. He told her that families often don't know what is going on and suggested that she offer them some information. So she asked families if there was anything that she might be able to help them with. She gave out the State Department hotline number, "and that did help in reaching a couple of families."

Some people told her they couldn't talk and hung up. "I wouldn't call them back. Anyone who didn't want to talk or was upset on the phone, I wasn't going to push."

Most people knew something about the crash, although many were confused and one or two seemed not to know anything about a crash and asked why she was calling. In two cases, the person answering the phone was a student whose name was on the list, obviously in error.

The reporter said she had tried to call the State Department to confirm the list, but reached only a recorded message. "We had no choice. We didn't want to wait to try to confirm an official list because the university was not giving us anything either, so (the editors) said that we (would) have to come up with our own list somehow, and that means calling families, playing detective." Several reporters were using the list to make calls at the same time and some families were called by more than one reporter from the same paper. One reporter said some calls were made by reporters for the "Neighbors" section, who had no experience with such stories.

The reporter who regularly covered the campus went to Hendricks Chapel to help at the vigil. Her assignment: to talk to people. As students walked away from the service, she decided not to interview anyone in obvious distress. She saw a couple of students she knew because of her university beat, but they did not know anyone on the plane.

"I stopped people who were not broken up and who were coming out by themselves or in a small group. I said, 'Excuse me, I'm with the *Post-Standard.* Would you like to talk about this? Did you know anyone on the plane?'" Of the five or so people she approached, only two or three talked to her, she recalled. The others refused or said nothing as they walked by. One sorority group emerged and refused to say anything except that they were not talking to anybody. A fraternity group gave the same response. "I remember standing on the steps of the chapel feeling lost — what do I do now? At this point, I said, 'The heck with it. I'm not going to stop anybody else. I don't care if they get mad at me. I don't care if they fire me. I'm not talking to anybody else. I'm going back to the office with what I have.' People were just so upset that I didn't see how it was my right to interrupt these people and as a total stranger, ask, 'How are you feeling now?'"

The *Post-Standard* assigned its religion writer to cover what happened as the grieving students gathered inside the chapel and to talk to the chaplains. This material was combined with those quotes the campus beat reporter had been able to get from the two students who had spoken to her.

The *Herald-Journal* asked its star columnist to do a reflective piece on the service and the sorrow within the chapel. He remembered deliberately sitting toward the back because he wanted to be as inconspicuous as possible. "I've done this before — it's like going to a funeral as a reporter," he said. "And you really don't want to upset anybody by your presence. All I need is a small notebook and a pen. So I can sit down in a church pew with a lot of other people and blend in, which is what I did that night."

The columnist saw his role as becoming part of the audience. "I knew from experience I could get enough material by just sitting there and watching what happened." He did not talk to anybody until the service ended. Then he made contact with a friend who teaches in the S.I. Newhouse School of Public Communications, and that faculty member introduced him to some of the people there. "Really we were just sharing thoughts. I don't know if I was taking any notes at that time."

His column focused on the shared experience, which he emphasized by writing in the first person plural, beginning with the simple statement, "We cried." In the column, the writer called the television cameras and microphones that lined the sides of the chapel "sextons." Asked about that, he recalled, "It's kind of stretching the image here, but I saw the camera people as the grave diggers — the professional mourners, the people who weren't there because they really wanted to cry, but there because it was their job to be there." The columnist said the media were polite by comparison with their behavior in other situations he had been in, but he did remember becoming conscious of the still cameras. "There was this period at the end when nobody was talking — everybody was finished doing what they had to do and there was this film advance — click, click. There were 10 or 12 of these (cameras) clicking at the same time, and it made this noise. It's not really anything offensive — it's just an unnatural sound."

One of the photographers capturing the scene was shooting for both Syracuse newspapers. He had been scheduled to cover the basketball game, but before the tip-off he went to the Division of International Programs, the university's office in charge of the study abroad program. "They told me to go away, so I took some pictures from across the street of people in the windows because it looked like a kind of moody scene."

On his way to the Dome to shoot the game, he saw a student in an oversized military coat and a pair of shorts, although it was cold out, which caused him to wonder. "Interesting. So I walked up to her and asked, 'What's going on?' and she was crying. We began to talk, and she said a friend of hers might have been on the airplane." The photographer, who had graduated from the university only five years earlier, took no pictures of her at that point. "It was dark out. Crazy. People rushing to get to the game. There's cars and horns and lights. And there she was in this weird outfit. The thought went through my head that she was distraught. She was wearing someone else's clothing. I thought that I should talk to her." He asked if he could come over later and "just hang out and talk to her." She agreed, so he took her address and phone number and headed for the game.

Inside the Dome he met up with other Syracuse newspaper photographers also assigned to the campus that night. He assigned each of the photographers a different angle. "I chose the overall. I tried to get pictures of people in the crowd and to shoot an overall (picture) at the moment of silence." Another photographer shot the players and still another focused on the cheerleaders.

Once that was over, he remembered saying to himself, "I'm out of here. I'm not going to photograph a basketball game." He stayed in touch with the office by cellular telephone, and then went to the chapel. "I got there well before it started. If you get to something on time, you're 15 minutes late. There's pictures to be made before the thing starts, and those could be the best pictures of the day. That's the way things work."

He began lighting the chapel interior. "It was dark in there.[23] Rather than blast people with direct strobe, I decided to put a couple of lights up in there and pop the whole place — so the whole place was illuminated." The photographer said he was criticized for that action by his competitors who were using direct flash. "But shooting someone with direct flash, in my opinion, is worse than illuminating an entire area. I can move around a shoot without it being known that those are my lights. I feel that if you illuminate a large area you are more transparent because you are not actually emitting the light that's illuminating the subject."

The photograph that ran across the top of a section page two days later, and was shared with several other publications, demonstrated the result of his lighting technique. It presented grieving faces amid a sea of students embracing each other. "You can see that everyone is illuminated in the picture, unlike a direct light that would have just illuminated the people in front and it would have been black in the background."

By this time, the photographer had learned that he knew some of the people on the plane, photography students from the Newhouse School. "It was pretty hard to do (the pictures). But I'd do it again." He regretted that he did not have time to set his lights up in the balcony instead of the floor level; that would have provided better overall illumination, he said. "I didn't feel I was going too far," he said, but added, "There were times when I think I upset a few people. You're talking about people walking around in shock." By then the ceremony was over, and the photographer began approaching some of those in his pictures to ask their names. "People were very reluctant to give names. And so the pictures that I ended up with from that memorial service were without names."

He acknowledged that a number of photographers were present, but he said, "It was not a wild media scene — I can tell you that, having been in wild media scenes. This was an 8-to-10 person media crew, which in the world of media is not a wild media scene. A wild media scene is 40 or 50 people clawing at each other. Most people have never seen that, and most people never will. This was not that kind of scene. This was a small, relatively polite group of media people."

The photographer recalled that five television stations were present, as well as about five still photographers.[24] "There were also print reporters — reporters disappear into a crowd. You don't even see reporters. But photographers stand out. They've got all this stuff."

The photographer remembered no one setting guidelines that night. "The way that I deal with people like that is that I'll agree to anything I have to do in order to get into a location, and then I'll do whatever I have to do to make pictures in that scene — whether or not it's consistent with what I agreed to.

If what I've agreed to prohibits me from making pictures, then I've obviously made a mistake. At that point, I'm going to renege on my agreement."

The atmosphere in the chapel had been intense. "It was a pretty emotional scene," the photographer said. "Initially, people were just freaking out. It's not like a funeral where an individual has died, and people's grief is focused. This was disorganized, unfocused. Just craziness."

He gave his film to a runner who took it to the newspaper offices, and used his cellular phone to call the student he had met earlier in the evening. She agreed that he could come over and "hang out." He was there when the occupants of the apartment learned that their room-mate who had been in London had, in fact, been on the plane. He took a roll of film in the apartment. "I didn't walk in the door and start firing. I didn't come in like a commando photo guy. I came in and hung out, had a cup of tea — no, I had a beer. They were drinking beer. And then I kind of just slid into the corner, drinking my beer, and I took pictures — one bounce flash, one flash shot (aimed) up into the ceiling." He asked the woman student if she would mind talking to a reporter. When she agreed, he called the newspaper and they sent over a reporter. "I hung out until I felt that I had the pictures that I needed, and when I felt that my presence there was not enhancing our reportage anymore, I left. I tried to be as personable and nice and understanding in that situation as I could be. But still doing my job."

By then it was after midnight and the police reporter, who at one point had to interrupt her work on Pan Am 103 to cover a murder-suicide, was sent to the apartment. "We had been sitting here looking for one just like them." The students talked freely, while the reporter listened and took notes. "Anything I could ask them wouldn't be as good...It was like I was a little mouse in the corner and absorbing the things they mentioned." The reporter felt particularly good about one part of that interview. The student's room-mate had said that the victim had trouble expressing to his father that he loved him. "I put that in my story. I thought to myself, you know, 'His dad knows that now because he read my story.'" She returned to the newspaper, wrote up that story, and her editor sent her back to the campus area for more reaction from students. "I said it's 4 o'clock and they're not going to be out. He said, 'Find them.' I said, 'Great.' I hate it when (he) does that. And I was wrong. There were some out."

She went to Marshall Street, a strip of shops and bars along the north side of the main campus, and found some students who had spent the night in one bar. "I tried to fall into the mode that they were in, and just kind of said, 'It looks like you guys have been up all night.'" She already had her notepad out and asked if they knew anyone on the plane. "I know that up on the Hill (the university neighborhood) at that time this was the kind of conversation going on. Kids were turning to each other, 'Did you know anyone?' and sharing that." One of the students did know one of the victims and she did an interview.

The newspapers, like the television stations, also sent reporters to "Fraternity Row." One *Herald-Journal* reporter was turned down at both a sorority and a fraternity. Students at the door of the sorority house told her they couldn't talk with her. "When I get what I sense is a very firm, definite 'Go away — I will not talk with you,' I go away," she said. "I don't know if that maybe makes me not as good a reporter as other people are or maybe it doesn't. It's not anything that I ever worried about."

But her approach paid off with a lengthy interview at another fraternity house. She had met brothers from the fraternity on the way to the chapel vigil and had walked along with them. By the time they returned from the service, they were willing to let her in. She sat in a chair by the fireplace and listened to them speak about their friend. She wrote in her notebook and asked questions, but for long periods they would just talk. Her questions were specific, about such things as his accomplishments — never "How do you feel?" The reporter said, "I wouldn't be able to get it out without laughing — it's such a ridiculous question. You sort of rephrase it. 'Do you remember where you were when you found out? What did you say to the person who told you?' A very specific question like that — not the generic 'How do you feel?' Of course, they're sad, shocked, etc. You know that."

The front pages were beginning to take shape. The morning newspaper headline would read: "Fiery Jumbo Jet Crash Kills 38 SU Students in Scotland."[25] The largest picture showed an SU cheerleader crying during a moment of silence before the basketball game. "It was somehow moving," the editor said. "The cheerleader said Syracuse University. It's local, it's SU and it's grief. You can look at it in hindsight and analyze it in all sorts of different ways. That was very appropriate because the plane crash was remote — it happened somewhere else. But this was a local thing. It covered the local angle of the story and that was very important."

The fact that it came in early was also important. It was in color, and by the time the dramatic photos of the vigil in Hendricks Chapel arrived, it was too late to run them in color. The morning paper carried four stories about the tragedy on the front page, and devoted all of pages 8-10 of the first section to the event.

As an afternoon newspaper, the *Herald-Journal* would have more time to present readers with a record of the tragedy. Photographs of 11 students were spread across the top of the front page over a banner headline that stated: "SABOTAGE SUSPECTED."

The idea for displaying the student portraits that way had come from an issue of *Life* magazine, which had used the device with casualties of the Vietnam War. "It was a very effective device to show these are flesh and blood people," the editor said.

Three major stories dominated page one, and five inside pages were devoted entirely to Flight 103 stories, four of them containing no advertising.

Late on the night of December 21, the *Post-Standard* reporter flew to London and by mid-morning Thursday arrived at the big white Victorian house that serves as the Syracuse University London Centre. The facility was closed; it had been besieged with reporters and camera crews during the night. A sign on the door told reporters to call Robert Hill, the university's vice president of public relations, in Syracuse. But the reporter sounded the buzzer, explained he was from Syracuse and was admitted. After conducting an interview with the London program's director, Roy Scott, he learned that a memorial service was about to take place at a church across the street. He asked and was given permission to attend. He was the only reporter there.

"I was very uncomfortable. I was trying to be very discreet about it — no taping or anything. I think I just recorded the ceremony. I was not trying to be secretive of who I was," he recalled. The reporter said it was very draining to sit there. One woman student collapsed behind him. "When someone is collapsing you don't ask them how they're feeling. It's a stupid question anyhow. By being there it was just as good as talking to them."

Afterward, he tried to talk to a few people outside. He told them he didn't want to intrude, but that he had just come over from a Syracuse newspaper, and he wanted to get a better idea of what life was like for students in London. Would they talk to him about that, he asked. No one would talk, other than small talk. One professor said he would talk, but then changed his mind. "I think they felt intruded upon," he said, "but it was outside the church, and they were talking so it wasn't in the middle of the ceremony."

The reporter returned to the London Centre along with the students and staff. He sat in a corner watching groups of students carefully and trying to pick out those who might be receptive. He had brought copies of New York newspapers with him and showed them to a couple of students with whom he struck up a conversation. "They wanted to see them," he said. One student saw the picture of the woman on the floor at Kennedy Airport and recognized her as the mother of an SU student. "I didn't know that was the mother of one of the students, so I felt badly about that. I felt really terrible." The two students became a group of five and he interviewed them. Then he met a former student who had remained in London to work as a bartender. He took the reporter to the students' haunts where he talked to people who had known them. While out, he met a British professor who had taught several students and interviewed him. On Christmas Eve, the reporter went to Lockerbie.

Back in Syracuse, the newspapers' reporters continued to call relatives and friends. The story would be with them a long time; they wanted their readers to have the big picture, including details they could not provide the first day. A reporter for the *Herald-Journal* put it in perspective:

"You've got what turned into a whole international incident with terrorists blowing up an airline and killing all those people, and I think it's worth telling the world that the victim of the dispute is a girl who wanted to study drama and who just wanted to maybe start her own business and this is the kind of life she lived, and she's a victim of some stupid dispute 5,000 miles away. I think that's what you're trying to do. The only way you can do that is to talk to the relatives and ask what was this person like, and what did she want to do, and tell me about her. And then you read the paper and see that it is not just numbers that got killed, but there were people who were just enjoying London and just starting their lives."

An editor for his paper agreed. "What we were trying to do was find out about the person who was killed, the event that has occurred, about tragedy. This is obituary information we gather every day about people. I think that's part of the responsible newspaper's job — to tell the community who died, so that all of the people sitting home at night can say, 'Well, look, Joe's sister died, the person I used to work with died.' That's the kind of news that to a community our size is important and that a lot of newspapers have forsaken."

The editor for the other paper added, "Sitting in the office we didn't have a good feel for what was going on there (on the campus). We knew there was news there, and that there were people there who in some degree were involved in the story. Who were the students? What were they like? To say, 'It's Billy Jean, 20, from wherever,' I don't think does it. When somebody suddenly becomes a tragic figure, people want to know who they were, what was their life like. I think we must see that story is told."

One editor said, "People are saying how can you portray grief publicly? That ought to remain private. I've heard from others who will say it's that sort of emotion, that sort of portrayal of grief, that brings the story home and helps people understand in a more powerful way than almost anything else can do. It really is a global village. That sort of grief used to be felt village-wide or clan-wide, (but) is now instantaneous around the world."

A journalist who had to call families back several days after the tragedy, in order to get more complete information for a special supplement put out for the memorial service in the Dome on January 18, said he was afraid they would not talk because he knew they had been "hounded by media" for days. "But my worst problem was getting off the phone because the parents and the other people wanted to tell you their kid's life story," he said. Later he met many of them at the campus memorial service in January.

Although many connected with the university felt the restrictions placed on coverage of the memorial service in the Dome, which was aired live on television, kept the media from being intrusive, the episode left bitter feelings with local photographers. They particularly resented not being allowed onto the floor of the arena, where seating was provided for family members and students who had spent the semester in London with the victims.

The photographer who covered the vigil on the night of the tragedy said, "Because of their restrictions, I have chosen not to cover a lot of regular SU events." The service, which featured a musical tribute by the Syracuse Symphony and massed choirs, as well as tributes from representatives of the faculty and student body, brought reactions that differed according to individual perspectives. Many described it as very moving. This photographer, still bitter over the restrictions, called it "a very large ad for Syracuse University. It was so controlled, so contrived, so manipulated by the university that the reality was sucked right out of it. To control the media is to control what the public sees — and in as much, control people's perceptions of reality. We basically pulled out of that arrangement," he said, explaining that since then the newspaper's photo staff has refused to provide photographic coverage of events at the university it views as optional, such as famous speakers. "That's it. No coverage. Boom. If we don't cover it, it didn't happen." It now covers the university photographically only if editors of one of the papers say they want pictures. "If you need to cover it, then you do it."

Weeks after the tragedy, the reporter for the *Post-Standard* who had been so shaken by her initial call to an editor of the student newspaper wrote letters to family members for "The Darkest Day," a newspaper supplement developed in the six months following the bombing. Her assignment for that project was to track down the stories of victims not from SU; the paper wanted to include the larger perspective.

She began with the little girl in the red dress, the victim described in a note on a bouquet of flowers outside the Lockerbie town hall. Who was she? Then there was Colonel Charles McKee. Who was he? Was he a spy? There was the co-pilot, too, as well as two other families. Although she wrote many letters, she called the son of the co-pilot in California and got "the classic angry response. 'You people have no business doing this. Get your noses out of it — the family and I have nothing to say to you — how dare you call?' Bang went the receiver."

The reporter remembered closing the letter to one of the mothers by saying, "Please accept my sincere sympathies," which she thought was appropriate at the time. She remembered vividly the mother's response. "She called me up a few days later and she was sobbing. She was just sobbing and sobbing and talking rather heroically about why she wanted to be interviewed and tell (her daughter's) story." They agreed to meet in the office of the woman's husband. "She would talk and then it would digress into tears and we went through this over and over again for a couple of hours."

With the father of the victim, the reporter used "a certain technique where you take a person through step by step whatever experience they had. You make them explain what the sky looked like; you make them explain what the temperature was. You get them to tell you the first thing (they) saw, recall (that) and give you a very descriptive account." The father had been to Lockerbie. "He went and looked for his daughter's body in a part of the plane where he thought he might find it, and he was telling me about this, so calm, as though he were reading from a book. And I was sort of thanking him mentally — not verbally — because you want to come across as a professional person. But I was thanking him in my mind, saying, 'Thank God, he's not crying.' And then he cried. We had been talking for two hours, and then he cried. And I was immensely guilty for that. I felt I had no business in his grief. The person side of me felt that. The reporter's job is to be there and get into that grief. The person side of me was embarrassed to be there, and was ashamed to have brought it to the surface.

"This kind of thing happened again and again." She went to visit the uncle and newly married aunt of the victim believed to be the little girl in the red dress. "He showed me pictures, and he's a doctor and he's extremely used to grief, and so I went to see them in their apartment. Here's a couple who've just been married, and they find out that all of his family is essentially wiped out. All of their family in America: his parents, his sister and her children, all gone." The couple had also been to the scene of the tragedy. "You hear the scene from their perspective, how body after body had to be identified." When he spoke about lifting up a blanket and recognizing one of his loved ones, he started to cry. "He went into the bedroom and came out with pictures and started showing them to me." Then his wife went into the bedroom, and when she came out, asked the reporter to end the interview. "I respected that. I said, 'Okay, thank you.'"

She went to see Colonel McKee's mother in Trafford, Pennsylvania, a small town on the western side of the state. Relatives had told her that this was a remarkably strong woman. "She showed me pictures, and we talked about what he was like. I asked her outright, 'Was he a spy?' And we went through this series of questions, and she said, 'I just cannot believe that is what he did.'[26] She was also at the time very, very angry at the State Department; she viewed them as callous regarding her son. That interview went on for four hours, and the lady served me lunch, and that was so sweet of her and she was really together. Then I was leaving and she said, 'I want to show you something else.' And I said, 'Okay.' We went up to his room. His nickname was Tiny, and he was not tiny. He was a big, big guy, really huge, about 6 foot 7 and 250 pounds. Well, his room was tiny, no bigger than a closet, and there was a plant by the window, and she said, 'This is Chuck's plant' — I think of it as Tiny's plant. There was this very nice philodendron in the window, and I guess he hauled it along in all of his assignments. He had bought the plant for his wife at the time when his daughter was born, and then they broke up and got a divorce, and she gave him back the plant and he took the plant wherever he went."

She got a feel for the victims through the eyes of those who loved them. "I had to keep reminding myself: Don't grieve yourself, but it was almost inescapable. After a while, I felt myself, in a sense, personally grieving for people I never knew and never met."

The reporter never cried in front of the people she was interviewing, even though at times she felt intense sorrow. She remembered catching her breath with one mother, asking where the bathroom was, and not letting the breath out until she reached the bathroom. "I didn't want to cry, but I felt so bad for her — to lose a 16-year-old. She affected me more than any of them, and to this day I think of her. There's nothing I can do."

One night she cried in her living room because she was "letting things pile up," and she talked to her sister about it. "She pointed out something to me I hadn't even thought of — that our father had died the December before, and she said, 'Maybe that's it.'" That helped the reporter realize that she had perhaps been making an unconscious connection with her father's death.

By the time she was ready to begin writing, her distress was "pretty much squelched." She had come to terms with her own feelings, "the way you have to (in order to) separate self from job."

Reporting reviewed: perceptions, practices and ethics

Not quite two months after the tragedy, students and media representatives returned to Hendricks Chapel.[27] It was a tense evening. Those on stage ranged from a news editor of the student radio station to the city editor of one of the Syracuse newspapers, from a veteran anchor of a local television news team to a freelance photographer. Those filling the pews were, for the most part, students who had been troubled by some aspect of the coverage of the story, especially on the night of December 21.

The students waited with some impatience as each speaker gave a brief description of the role he or she had played — or in some cases, elected not to play — in the coverage. The showing of video highlights of some of the coverage, intended to help focus on specific problems, was so disturbing to a few in the audience that they left the chapel. Then came the opportunity for students to question the media.

A young woman stepped to the microphone in the center aisle. She said she just wanted to ask Channel 5 anchor Bob Kirk, "if you feel you have the right to stick your camera in someone's face? How do you get to that point? You know, have you been in the business for a lot of years, and then you just get hardened to it, and then it just becomes very easy to stick your camera in a grieving student's face?"

Kirk, a veteran of many years in the Syracuse market, did not reply directly. Instead he looked out into the audience and asked: "How many people did radio reporters and television reporters run up to and stick that microphone in their face and demand an answer? How many?" He watched hands go up. "Somebody did not give you the opportunity for you to turn them down, to say 'No, I don't want to answer?'" The way Kirk asked the question suggested that he was sure of the answer, and that in his mind students must have overreacted. So he pressed the point with the students who had raised their hands. "They insisted?" he asked incredulously. The hands stayed up. "Well, that shouldn't be," Kirk said, clearly embarrassed. "You obviously have the right not to answer questions. If somebody's that aggressive and needs the story that badly, well, they need some talking to or..."

The young woman was not going to let him off that easily. "Did you ever feel awkward doing that though? That's what my question is. Did you ever feel awkward when you came to Hendricks Chapel that night? Did you maybe feel a little bit uncomfortable with your camera looking for grieving students? Or does it just not faze you? I'm just wondering. I mean, I would like to be a reporter, but I don't know if I personally would be able to do that. Do you ever just feel a little bit uncomfortable, you know, before you ask students how they're feeling and...?"

Kirk explained that his role that evening had been as anchor, so he was back in the studio. "But I've been in similar situations, and it's awkward, to say the least, and you have to be really aware of sensitivities."

The exchange was one of a number that evening that helped illustrate the differences between the way journalists see their profession and the way they are seen by others during a disaster, particularly in the early hours and days of the story. Newspeople want to believe that they have done a careful, compassionate job of gathering and processing the news under very difficult conditions. They want to think that their colleagues, even their competitors, will work in a way that brings credit to the profession. They have a hard time accepting the possibility that excesses do occur in the rush to get the story, especially to get it first and to tell it dramatically. They find it easier to write off some reports of journalistic malpractice as part of the mythology that grows up around any disaster.

For example, at the forum in Hendricks Chapel, media representatives heard a young woman tell how a journalist had climbed up on a window sill of the sorority which lost three sisters in the tragedy. Some newspeople said privately that they could not believe that had really happened. We looked for the man on the window sill during this research project and found no one who would admit to such behavior. Scores of journalists came to campus that evening and, as far as we have been able to determine, the reporter or photographer on the windowsill never published whatever he saw from that viewpoint. But we are inclined to believe he existed, not only because a sorority member repeated the story during our initial round of interviews the following April, but because the morning after the disaster four sorority members told the story to reporters from *Newsday* and the *Philadelphia Inquirer*. At that point, it hardly had time to be passed around and built into mythic proportions.

But that is an extreme example. Lockerbie is a more subtle one. Many newspeople arriving in the disaster area behaved with exemplary decorum, engaging in self-censorship when they felt certain facts of the situation would harm more than inform, approaching townspeople respectfully, trying to work out the mystery of what had happened from what they could learn from witnesses and what little police could tell them initially. That assessment of the behavior of media people comes from experienced public information officers who worked with journalists at Lockerbie, as well as the journalists themselves.

Some mistakes were made in the early reports from the scene, but the media there performed a critical service in gathering and transmitting information that was needed around the world — and in Lockerbie itself. Explaining what had happened and how it happened was daunting because the event itself was, in many ways, unprecedented. The disaster was so confusing that journalists on the scene found themselves trying to answer questions from the Lockerbie witnesses they were interviewing. Some local people, such as the man who learned his family had been listed as missing *after* the news had been received in Australia, would have appreciated *more or different* information via the media.

In a sense, Lockerbie provides an instructive example of how a population devastated by a disaster responds to media attention when *most* of those operating as journalists conduct themselves according to generally accepted news practices. News people who arrived the night of the disaster found helpful interview subjects and guides although many local people were confused or caught up in trying to contain or assess the disaster. Townspeople were staggered when they found so many newspeople in the main street the next day, but many of them responded to journalists' questions and provided accounts of the disaster so vivid that they "stuck" in the minds of their listeners years later. Some townspeople even offered hospitality, a cup of tea or a lift to a hotel, something which journalists remember with gratitude.

As will be discussed in the section on institutional response, several factors contributed to the degree of journalistic discipline exhibited at Lockerbie: the horror of the event itself; the relatively senior journalists that most media assigned to the story; the arrangements made for regularly scheduled news conferences and special access to important sites and sources.[28]

Yet the journalistic presence did add stresses in Lockerbie. One reason, of course, was that in a journalistic throng as large and diverse as the one that descended into this tiny Scottish town, everyone would not be equally mindful of professional conduct. Only a few "rogues," knocking on doors in the middle of the night, lifting sheets that cover bodies, pressing people to talk about things they felt were better left unsaid, are sufficient to poison the atmosphere for all journalists.[29]

Another reason is that even if each and every journalist operates as a model of deportment, the modern newsgathering methods that allow rapid dissemination of information about a tragedy bring additional and, in many cases, unavoidable stresses to the disaster scene. The mechanics and urgency of transmitting news means that even the most considerate reporter will tax an already overburdened communications system; the reallocation of telephone lines for emergency services and the media may mean local people cannot reach or be reached by family and friends. The fact that so many reporters are looking for witnesses means that people may be interviewed over and over again, reliving the terror or feeling pressed to come up with additional details. The way coverage of such a disaster develops its own routine, with news conferences, press pools and news people rushing to meet deadlines, can add to the disruption caused by the original catastrophe and the efforts of rescue workers.

But the experience at Lockerbie also demonstrates that what may be acceptable journalistic practice under other conditions can be very distressing to people caught in a disaster situation. An example can be found in what townspeople, newspeople and editors said about the bodies on the roof. The sight of the body still strapped into the passenger seat and wedged into a chimney had been so horrifying to four tabloid photographers on the night of the disaster that when one of them became upset, all four had returned to the pub. The photographer who told that story was not there the next day when the body was lowered from the roof, but many other photographers were, along with many television camera crews, including the BBC, Scottish Television, and probably ABC.[30] The way people in that neighborhood remember it, photographers were jockeying for position, running through gardens and up on steps to get as close as they could for a picture. Angus Kennedy, the police superintendent who directed media relations on the disaster, said many photographers and camera crews were shooting the scene, which was too large and visible from too many vantage points to be cordoned off at that stage. But, he added, very few ever used the pictures. In Britain, only one national tabloid used a picture of the young woman being lowered from the roof. The *Daily Star* ran it on the front page under the headline: "She and 275 others paid the price of a bomb warning that slipped the net." The caption under the photo spelled it out, "The body of a young girl is lowered from the roof" (December 23, 1988).

Apparently journalists on that scene were obeying an edict that many editors and news directors view as standard operating procedure: "Shoot everything and we'll decide here what to use later." That may be logical in some situations, but it was one of the incidents that helped to change the attitude of Lockerbie people toward the media.

Most editors who considered using that picture or footage probably went through a discussion similar to the one that Richard Ayres of the BBC described: "The age-old trite debate is: If you show it, are you being sensational? Are you causing unnecessary distress? Are you degrading human life? If you don't show it, are you sanitizing violence, disguising what it is like for a jumbo to be blown up at 27,000 feet or whatever it was? There isn't a right answer for the two. It seemed to us that for our coverage in totality those pictures were — and hours and hours of live coverage was — sufficient to convey the awfulness, the horror, the indefensibility of what had happened. And that it would have been truly, truly distressing to people who were already sufficiently distressed. It was a real trauma in the nation, as I'm sure it was in the United States. It didn't need further graphic illustration, in our judgment."

Ken Irby, working on the photo decisions at *Newsday* in Long Island, remembered that picture clearly. "We had an opportunity to use it," he said. "There's an interesting policy at different newspapers that different photo departments go through, as to whether you should use this picture because of the magnitude of the story. At the time, we knew that there were a lot of families on Long Island and the Metro area that had lost loved ones there. We didn't know whether they knew yet, but it potentially was a victim, a loved one of someone who we'd be showing this picture to, and we opted not to use it. It was mostly a taste issue. We do have a pretty standard policy; we don't use body pictures, unless it's a major need."[31]

The concern that bodies shown in a picture might be identified by a relative or friend was justified. A student who had spent the semester in London with the 35 Syracuse University students killed in the disaster saw the two pictures

Problems facing editors

from that scene in *Time* magazine. She said the one of a body lying face down was a girl, "and the reason why I know it was a girl was because it was my friend—. She was wearing the clothes that I had told her to wear home...That has never been a doubt in my mind." Other friends and relatives may have had a similar experience. The possibility of exposing the loved ones of victims to such sights is increasing as the population becomes more mobile and the reach of news media widens. The young woman who identified her friend's body in *Time* saw it in the international edition while traveling in Europe.[32]

But there is evidence that audiences as a whole recoil at such scenes. Studies commissioned by the British Broadcasting Standards Council showed that more than three-fourths of those polled felt the media should not use "the scene of a major incident showing dead or seriously injured people who are recognisable." By comparison, only 23 percent objected to seeing a "scene of a major incident from a distance so that bodies are not recognisable" (Shearer 1991, p. 36).

The only complaint made about the coverage of the Lockerbie disaster to the British Press Council, at that time the authority to which complaints about the printed press were submitted, concerned the pictures of the bodies in *Time*. The Council commented that decisions about whether to publish pictures of disaster or tragedy "which may intrude into grief, add unjustifiably to the emotional stress of those affected, or offend readers at large" are difficult to make; but the council ruled that the editor was justified in publishing the pictures to illustrate "the awful nature of the tragedy" (Press Council Adjudications, p. 232).

More media might have shown something of this scene if they had worked from a distance instead of competing for vantage points close to the action. Most editors and news directors of major news organizations who saw the close-ups decided they were unusable.

The "shoot it there, we'll decide here" rule also played a part in media conduct at Kennedy Airport. That scene was unique in the sites we examined in this study: none of the journalists who were present when the mother collapsed expressed pride either to us or to the *Daily News* columnist (Mirabella, 1988) about the way the media behaved there. It is no secret that such packs form on major stories in big cities, or that they will pursue those subjects they think their managers expect them to find. The situation apparently was exacerbated by what journalists found — or, in the case of the expected news conference, did not find — at the Pan Am terminal or at Syracuse University.

But public relations failures or other circumstances that complicate coverage do not remove the obligation of editors and news directors to work with their personnel to minimize harm caused to victims and survivors by intrusive equipment and methods. They can begin by seeking a way to work without the bright lights that families at the airport found so distressing. The tougher question is: how can the "wolf pack" be tamed? That question is not intended to imply that the media should become a collection of whimpering lap dogs; it means helping them collectively and individually to perform the watchdog function on behalf of the public in such a responsible way that they can operate without external restraints.

The competitive fervor with which Manhattan media attack a story is not a new development; it is tolerated and even demanded from above. Bob Teague, who worked for WNBC-TV, the New York station owned and operated by NBC, tells of a woman reporter covering a plane crash who found a state of chaos in the hospital where casualties had been taken (1982). "We took pictures of the injured, some of them barely conscious, struggling to live," she told him. "I didn't want to bother any of them. Just being in there meant that we were increasing their chances of infection. So we just took pictures, talked with one of the surgeons, then packed up to leave." At that point a reporter from a rival station showed up and started interviewing victims, including a man whom the first reporter said was obviously dying. The woman reporter returned to her station, but when the executive producer saw those interviews on the rival station, "He wanted to know whether I'd interviewed the same guy or even somebody else who was dying on the spot. When I said I had decided not to as a matter of decency, he damn near had a fit." So the producer called the rival channel and begged a copy of their tape, which ran with a credit line describing it as courtesy of the originating station. "I was so mad I couldn't even cry," the reporter told Teague (1982, p. 71).

The journalistic pack is not unique to New York. Alastair McCall, who covered Lockerbie for *The Chronicle* in Newcastle, had an intense experience with the London version of mob journalism after he escaped the fire in the King's Cross underground station, and then returned to cover it. Most of the 31 people who died in that tragedy on November 18, 1987 were caught in the flashover[33] that swept up the escalator and into the ticket hall (Frost, 1990). "I got out of the station only after coming fairly close to the ticket hall where the flashover happened. And so (it was) literally four or five people in front of me where they cut off and said, 'No, don't go up there.' Otherwise I would have gone up there, and may well not have written the piece at all."

The clash between journalists and the authorities was very strong at King's Cross, McCall said. He was standing outside the station with a crowd of onlookers when "suddenly, literally from every corner you could see photographers and cameramen, TV people, come running. Suddenly there were dozens and dozens and dozens in the space of literally about 10 minutes." That was before most of the national newspapers had moved out of Fleet Street and its environs. Adding to the intensity was the timing, about 7:30 p.m.; newspapers were close to early deadlines. "There was a lot of argy-bargy that evening, certainly early on between journalists who felt they were not being given the access to the station, to what was going on, that they felt they should have, and police who were being perhaps unnecessarily antagonistic — sort of, 'You stay there, and do as you're bloody well told.' And there was unnecessary agro on all sides, and there was a lot of pushing, shoving and an occasional fist flying, which isn't an exaggeration."

McCall said that happened especially as the London media tried to get access to fire crews that were sitting, recuperating from having just come up from the underground, or ambulance crews who were standing by after searching for those who needed hospitalization. Reporters wanted to know what the emergency personnel had seen, what they had done, to flesh out the story. "It's all the sort of things that newspapers feed off, apart from the official statements. It comes back into talking to people, and talking to people who are going to talk to you, not in an official divisional commander capacity, but as Joe Fireman or Joe Ambulance Crew or whatever. It was the initial denying of access to that sort of thing, and the desire for information."

McCall remembered reporters "standing around saying, 'Are there any eye witnesses?' People screaming, 'Somebody find an eye witness!' Within moments, dozens of journalists crowded round. You couldn't hear a bloody word anyone was saying. It was all agreed afterwards by the people at the front (of the pack) to the people at the back, 'Well, they said this, this and this.' It was the frantic desire for information, the fact that it was on a newspaper deadline, mid-evening anyway, and the fact that there were undoubtedly going to be people screaming at you in an office, you know, 'For Christ's sake, file some copy.' And so that produced that fairly unseemly argy-bargy."

While F. Gilman Spencer, formerly editor of the *New York Daily News* and now of the *Denver Post*, is correct when he says that security and police have a responsibility to protect survivors and victims from the media, a disaster can overwhelm resources that would provide protection under more normal circumstances. The fact that it is, in the words of Charles Dickens, "the worst of times" does not provide the media with permission to make it even worse. News executives can begin to change that by rethinking their instructions to "shoot it there, we'll decide here." They can decide, for example, to work with their journalistic staff to come up with and enforce a code of practice toward grieving and injured people.

One such code, covering victims and relatives following accidents or other tragedies, is described in the CBS News Standards, originally adopted in 1976:[34]

> Although it is not feasible to set forth hard and fast rules that will cover every contingency, these policies are generally applicable to such interviews:
>
> — Avoid them, normally, except when they are essential for the story; for example, when they throw light on what happened or drive home a point which might help avoid future tragedies.
>
> — Exercise restraint in soliciting and conducting them.
>
> — Do not interview, or attempt to interview, a person who appears to be in a state of shock.
>
> — Do not attempt to conduct an interview until permission has been obtained from the interviewee (1992).

Such a code should rule out, for instance, being part of any attempt to storm an area where family members are being helped while they try to come to terms with the awful news. It should prevent a journalist from physically trying to restrain a potential interview subject. It should prohibit the shouting of questions at such subjects.

"Should," of course, does not mean "will." The CBS code predated the 1979 crash of a DC-10, which lost power shortly after take-off and fell into a mobile home park adjacent to Chicago's O'Hare Airport, killing 275. An analysis of network coverage of that crash found that only CBS reported on how families and friends of the crash were reacting to the disaster (Nimmo and Combs, 1985). The first rule of the code, to avoid such coverage unless it provides some insight into what happened or drove home some point that might help avoid future tragedies, apparently was violated. The Los Angeles-bound flight was carrying many writers and publishers to the American Bookseller's Convention, including the managing editor of *Playboy* magazine. Much of the report focused on the reactions of those attending the convention and told how the convention gala planned at the Hugh Hefner mansion had been canceled.

Today such coverage of the bereaved sounds very tame. It could be easily argued that CBS was right in breaking its own rules to seek the human dimension of what was, at that time, the highest death toll from any domestic airline crash in the nation's history. As a matter of fact, the news organization did wait until the second day to broadcast that angle; nothing in the analysis of its coverage suggests that it raced to family and friends in the hours immediately following the tragedy.

The BBC guidelines on covering disasters and emergencies contain other language that might be useful in developing a code of practice for disaster coverage:

> It is inevitable that pictures of a disaster will be distressing to those personally involved, and perhaps to other viewers too. But we must not lower our standards

> of what it is proper to show just because of the volume of explicit material which becomes available, or the speed with which we receive, edit and transmit it. The reporting and camera teams at the scene may be working under the most difficult circumstances, and a further process of selection and editing in the newsroom must take matters of taste and sensitivity very seriously.
>
> Acceptable standards will change from time to time reflecting, among other things, changes in society. Current practice demands that we do not linger needlessly on pain and suffering, keeping shots short and angles wide; that we do not zoom in to shots of blood, but rather pull away from them in deference to the victim. Reporters or producers who feel there is a case for departing from current standards in order to properly reflect the nature of the event *must* refer to their programme editor.
>
> In some cases, an event may produce such scenes of suffering and bloodshed that they simply cannot be shown on television. But our motive in withholding such images must never be to conceal the true extent of what has happened. We must find other ways of conveying the full impact of the event with words and sound — even if that sometimes means television doing without moving pictures at all.

On the subject of intrusion, it says:

> If people are dying, we allow them to die with dignity; we do not seek to capture their last moments on tape, and if they are captured unwittingly, we do not broadcast them.
>
> In the early stages of a disaster we should be particularly mindful of the distress we will cause if we show identifiable pictures of dead or injured people before their relatives have been contacted.
>
> And remember that our audience is sometimes offended by what *they* believe to be intrusion, even when *we* know the cameras were welcome. A few words of explanation in the script will sometimes help allay their fears…
>
> Interviews, too, are a common source of difficulty in the confusion and distress that follows a disaster. Interviewees are at their most vulnerable, reporters at their most pressured, and the audience at its most critical. Thoughtless, unfeeling questions cause great offence: often they are asked by other reporters, with the BBC merely eavesdropping, but the audience does not know that. Sometimes it may be better to use the interviewee's answer without the question that prompted it: but our technical ability to do that does not excuse insensitive questioning. (1992, p. 3-4)

In developing or revising their codes of practice, media should consider a conservative standard for the depiction of bodies. Codes that express concern about relatives not having been notified are correct. Showing such scenes to unprepared family members could be potentially traumatizing. Treating a body as an object can be deeply distressing to anyone who recognizes the deceased, *and* to the general public. The problem presented by the bodies on the roof was that there was no way to retrieve them — or to depict them — that preserved the dignity of the dead. The same can be said of a close-up of a body shrouded by black plastic and marked by flags that ran across two pages in the British tabloid *The Sun*. It accompanied the only story we have read in either U.S. or U.K. newspapers entirely devoted to graphic descriptions of the carnage (Murray, December 23, 1988).

We would caution against the reasoning that bodies should not be shown only because relatives might not yet have been notified. While that is a valid argument, it can be used to justify using dramatic footage or photography of bodies once the initial phrase of coverage is over, which can be deeply troubling to the grieving. In this research, the authors learned how much journalists have to understand about the grief process. One of those lessons began in Syracuse the night of the forum when media and students faced each other in Hendricks Chapel. Local TV representatives offered to bring tape of their coverage so they could discuss specifics with students, many of whom had left Syracuse before the tragedy and hence had not seen that footage. That seemed logical. But none of us, including the students planning the forum, anticipated how difficult that would be for some of the young people still struggling with their grief. Those who left the chapel as the tape rolled were clearly in distress, and some of those who stayed spoke about how troubling it was for them to see those scenes. As will be discussed in a later chapter, the authors have since learned much more about post-traumatic stress, and the kind of stimuli that can trigger or aggravate it.

The producers of *Frontline*, a public affairs program offered via the Public Broadcasting Service in the United States, probably had no idea of the hurt that might be caused by showing the scene of the body being lowered from the roof as part of an in-depth piece on the tragedy more than a year later (February, 1990). It lasted only a few frames and added nothing to the telling of the story. It was presented as just one of the images of the disaster, something to look at.

There is, however, an argument for showing the bodies being lowered from the roof in Lockerbie. Mike Oniewski, a freelance photographer who took part in the forum at Syracuse University, told a student who asked why those pictures should be shown: "This is the United States of America, and I'm going to be real blunt here because that's the kind of guy I am. Sometimes you've got to hit Americans over the head to get their attention, to have them change things. We wrote a lot of stories about Vietnam, soldiers getting killed — the French were there — it wasn't until we started bringing it home into your living rooms, your parents' living rooms, every single night while you were eating supper, that the war stopped. And now we need to continue that, to stop all the craziness and the madness, and yes, let's run the pictures.

If that upsets you, I'm very sorry, I hope you remember it — because I think we would still be in Vietnam, I think we'd still be playing all those games over there and have brothers and cousins and friends who'd be off for a year on a tour of duty and getting killed unless people got really shocked about seeing bits and pieces of bodies being put into black plastic body bags while they're eating supper."

That response was made just two months after the downing of Pan Am 103. With the benefit of hindsight, the authors believe it was *not* the pictures of the body being lowered from the roof that led to those positive changes that have come from this terrible tragedy — or that may come in the future. This scene was troubling and did, for example, convince the brother of one of the victims to go to Lockerbie, but it was seldom mentioned in editorials, letters to the editor, or the flood of letters and offers of help to both the Scottish community and Syracuse University. Most people seemed to relate to the disaster in more general terms.[35]

In the long run, one picture seldom makes or breaks a story in the eyes of the audience. The cockpit in the field would come to symbolize the tragedy, and the great gaping crater gouged out of a quiet residential neighborhood would stand for the impact on the town. On this particular story, if there was one picture that summed up the human tragedy in a way to which people responded, it was the sight of the mother on the floor of Kennedy Airport. At one point during the Syracuse University forum, as it was becoming clear how difficult it was to draw a line between what is and is not acceptable journalistic practice, a student rose to tell the panelists that the scene of the mother on the floor helped her to understand "how dependent we all are upon you for our information source, for how we feel or how we react to situations."

On the night of the tragedy, she had been studying for her last final exam, when her mother called her after watching CNN and seeing the woman on the floor of JFK. That was how the student learned of the disaster, which claimed the lives of three of her friends and four of her acquaintances. That scene struck the mother so forcefully that she immediately called her daughter to see if she was all right.

"My comment particularly after hearing everyone of you express your ideas here today, is 'Yes, the media stepped over the line many times,'" the student told the forum. "I think all of you know where and when you stepped over that line. But it's also important that you (were there), not only for those of us who experienced grief, and needed to share their feelings, but for the rest of the world to share our experiences. I think one of you mentioned all the other plane crashes that happened very recently. I think about how often we hear about plane crashes and we don't realize that it's somebody's mother, somebody's father, somebody's sister, particularly when the Soviets knocked down the Korean airliner — well, that was someone else's problem, somewhere else in the world. And then when the U.S. bombs some place in Libya, we got (the Libyans) back (for the Berlin attack, but) it was still somebody else's family, just on the other side of the world.

"I think what happened with Flight 103 is no different from what's happened at any other point in the history of covering these types of events. It brought (the tragedy) home to us. In fact, it's essential that it brought it home to us, because it shows how (difficult it is for) human beings to share each other's experiences. If there's anything we've learned from this experience, it's how to feel compassion, and how to feel sympathy for others."

That does not mean, however, that people who did not see the mother's collapse failed to connect to the tragedy. There is no indication that those who stayed tuned to the BBC, which did not use that footage, felt less sympathy for those affected by this tragedy because they did not see that scene.

One other image from the disaster deserves special consideration. That is Lockerbie in flames, which television on both sides of the Atlantic tended to use to symbolize what had happened. John Kean of Scottish Television volunteered that he received complaints from throughout Scotland, not just Lockerbie, "for months on end and maybe even up to the year after," about the fact that they showed pictures of the houses burning around the crater. "The same sort of thing kept coming through, 'Why are you continually showing pictures of Lockerbie, all the houses destroyed, and that kind of thing,'" Kean said. "My answer was this: This was the vivid image of the night. And that's what I said, and you can't get away from that. It happened." Other broadcasting organizations in Scotland were getting the same complaint, he said.

When Scottish police traveled to America to meet with relatives several months after the tragedy, they realized that many of these people knew very little about Lockerbie or the police investigation. The dominant image they had was of the houses in flames, according to Angus Kennedy, the police superintendent who led the delegation and who had directed media relations in Lockerbie.

That leaves a mystery: Why were the scenes of the burning homes so distressing to Scottish people?

The answer to the question is suggested by Frances Ford Plude (1990), who has written that audiences, viewing reports of a massive tragedy, may react as survivors. Certainly the people of Scotland had good reason to identify with what happened to residents of Lockerbie, who had been spending a quiet evening at home when huge pieces of plane descended on them, engulfing a whole neighborhood in flames. The distress of those who called to complain about images of burning houses may have reflected very real fears or other emotions brought on by the tragedy.

Covering a disaster and its aftermath can have legal as well as ethical ramifications, as a reporter for the *Cleveland Plain Dealer* learned a few years ago. He lost a suit brought by a woman who had been widowed when the Silver Bridge across the Ohio River collapsed in December 1967, killing 44. Joseph Eszterhas' long article for the Sunday magazine was based on coverage of the funeral of Melvin Cantrell at Point Pleasant, West Virginia, and a visit to the Cantrell home when Mrs Cantrell was not there. He talked to the children and wrote in detail about what he perceived as the family's poverty. His story, published for the anniversary of the disaster, implied that he had seen and perhaps talked to her. A passage critical to the lawsuit read: "Margaret Cantrell will talk neither about what happened nor about how they are doing. She wears the same mask of non-expression she wore at the funeral. She is a proud woman. She says that after it happened, the people in town offered to help them out with money and they refused to take it" (Cantrell v. Forest City Publishing Co., 419 U.S. 245, 95 S. Ct. 465, 42 L.Ed.2d 419 (1974)). The lawsuit, alleging that the article placed Mrs Cantrell and her family in a false light, went all the way to the U.S. Supreme Court, which called the descriptions in the article "calculated falsehoods" and upheld the $60,000 award by the original jury (Goldstein, 1985).

The United Kingdom and United States differ considerably in the legal environments they provide for the media, and American courts currently provide more protection for the privacy of individuals. In Britain, which has more restrictive libel laws but no law of privacy, individual members of Parliament drafted legislation in 1989 to protect against intrusion and guarantee a right of reply, as well as establish a statutory press council with power to wield enforceable legal sanctions. The Conservative Government and Labour Opposition signaled a growing willingness to support some legislation along these lines. To fend that off, the old Press Council was disbanded and a new Press Complaints Commission was established early in 1991. It was financed by a levy on the newspaper and periodical industries, the same way the British advertising industry financed the self-regulatory system it developed in the mid-1970s.[36] As the new Commission explains in a briefing document designed to describe its workings, "the press and the Commission were both put on probation until the middle of 1992." If the new attempt at self-regulation failed, a statutory system of regulation would supplant it.

An important difference between the old Press Council and the new Press Complaints Commission was that the latter was charged with enforcing a Code of Practice, which was drafted by a committee of editors chaired by Patricia Chapman, editor of the *News of the World Newspapers and periodicals committed themselves publicly to adhere to the code, which makes newsgatherers and editors both responsible. As the code's preamble states:*

> Editors are responsible for the actions of journalists employed by their publications. They should also satisfy themselves as far as possible that material accepted from non-staff members was obtained in accordance with this code.

The code prohibits or discourages several methods described as having been used in covering Pan Am 103. Specifically, it states:

> In cases involving personal grief or shock, enquiries should be carried out and approaches made with sympathy and discretion.[37]

That would seem to rule out the sort of mob scene that transpired at Kennedy Airport if a similar event occurred at a British airport. One does not require a medical degree to recognize that someone collapsing is probably in a state of shock, or have to think very hard to recognize that storming a room where bereaved are being comforted is not an exercise in "sympathy and discretion." Certainly, it should be clear that a person learning that a loved one has probably died or been seriously injured is in a state of grief, even if he or she is in denial and exhibiting little emotion at the moment.

The guideline that Tom Brook suggested, that the media treat as private those moments in which an individual has lost control, even when they occur in a public place, is not part of the Code, but seems to speak to the "discretion" criterion in the Code's language. But there may be cases when "loss of control" is difficult to determine, or when media behavior prompts the individual to lose control, as it did when television cameras zeroed in on the woman Mike Santangelo had been interviewing.

The issue of control is important to the bereaved, as we discussed in an earlier chapter. Let grieving people decide for themselves when they are ready to speak publicly, when they prefer to speak through an intermediary *and* when they wish to remain silent. To achieve "approaches made with sympathy and discretion" may require much more cooperation than has been customary among newspeople on such stories. For example, in the absence of public information officers or corporate communicators, journalists may need to send a small committee to negotiate with emergency support personnel.

Such requests would need to suit the particular situation. In a Kennedy Airport-style scenario, it would be logical to ask to speak to clergy and Red Cross personnel. Under conditions which might be worked out either directly or indirectly with one or more of the grieving, it might even be possible to set up a brief interview with one of them. A mother who was at Kennedy Airport said she would have been willing to do this if someone had explained the significance of the event to her and had been willing to talk to her under carefully controlled conditions. This may sound idealistic and overly simplistic, especially in the face of criticism that the New York media vie to top each other in portraying the "bizarre and grotesque" (Maneholt, 1992, p. 50).

But a procedure for controlled access to those grieving who wish to speak to the media would be more productive than shouted questions — as well as being compassionate. The clergy and others who were aiding the bereaved at Kennedy did help flesh out the story, and a quiet interview with a relative or friend of someone caught up in the disaster would undoubtedly provide more information and less stress on everyone than shouting "How do you feel?" at grieving people who are trying to reach some sort of privacy in an open airline terminal.

The concept of "controlled access" may not appeal to editors and news directors used to having their own reporters present even if they agree to a "pool" arrangement. But meeting two or three reporters in a quiet room may be all that a distraught relative can manage. He or she may not even feel up to facing a camera. Such an arrangement, however, will provide more information to share among the media and will be seen by the audience as more humane than the style of attack that took place at Kennedy Airport.

The media and, in some cases, those serving as intermediaries, need to recognize that it is very important to be open to what people who are suffering may *wish* to say. There will be some people in most major disasters who have something they want to share with the public. Being open to that desire may be important to the story, as well as to the person wishing to speak to the media.

At Syracuse University, most journalists were looking only for students who knew victims on the plane. Many of their stories missed the impact the disaster had on the entire student body, and several students told us informally that they would have been willing to discuss their reactions with reporters although none of their close friends was killed. The *Post-Standard* captured some of that mood indirectly by quoting one of the chaplains, the Rev. Paul J. Kowalewski, who told of a student who came up to him after the vigil and asked: "Why does it hurt so much? I didn't even know any of them." (McKeever, 1988, p. A-10)

Some of the press overtures that bothered people in Lockerbie or bereaved families in their homes would also seem to be prohibited under the Code of Practice. It generally rejects "intrusion and enquiries" into an individual's private life without his or her consent, obtaining information or pictures through "misrepresentation or subterfuge" or "intimidation or harassment." It notes that normally "journalists should not photograph individuals on private property without their consent; should not persist in telephoning or questioning individuals after having been asked to desist; should not remain on their property after having been asked to leave and should not follow them." It also sets forth four criteria of public interest as the only justifications for invasion of privacy, misrepresentation or behavior that might be construed as harassment:

(1) Detecting or exposing crime or serious misdemeanor.
(2) Detecting or exposing anti-social conduct.
(3) Protecting public health and safety.
(4) Preventing the public from being misled by some statement or action of that individual or organisation.(p. 6)

Such criteria, it could be argued, would have been met by journalists who posed as cleaners and gained access to airliners at London's Heathrow Airport to test new security measures. A *Daily Express* reporter and a London Weekend Television researcher separately gained access to planes at Heathrow Airport in January 1989 by hiring on as cleaners (Dudman, 1989; Fisher, Jan. 14, 1989), and the following April a *Sun* reporter used false references to obtain a job as a baggage handler with Pan Am (Pascoe-Watson, 1989). Their action was designed to demonstrate a danger to public safety. But the criteria would not have excused the methods used by at least one of the two Syracuse stations to obtain the list of students from Pan Am. Telling Pan Am personnel that one is with Syracuse University's international study program qualifies as misrepresentation. The methods used by the reporter who called initially and did not identify herself are more debatable. Some would argue that such methods fit the dictionary definition of subterfuge: "deception by artifice or stratagem to conceal, escape, avoid or evade" (Webster's, 1981).[38] Others would defend this technique, arguing that the reporter was justified in representing herself as a person, a member of the general public, and that the error in giving her the information before next of kin had been contacted was made by Pan Am. The reporter said that she did not *deliberately* withhold her identity. The Code of Practice recognizes that the use of subterfuge and even misrepresentation, under certain conditions, can be justified by journalists, but the circumstances in the immediate aftermath of the Pan Am tragedy would not meet its criteria.

Both stations aired the list, assuming it was accurate because they had obtained it directly from the airline. One of the co-authors argues that the second station had two sources for the list: the names that appeared on the first station and the confirmation it received by obtaining the list itself from Pan Am. But neither of the reporters said the airline told them that next of kin had been notified. Such notification serves two purposes: It provides the terrible news to the bereaved in a more compassionate way than seeing it in the media or hearing it from a reporter, and it provides a check on the accuracy of the passenger manifest.

The original list of 38 did contain errors; newspaper reporters learned that when they began to call families and found in at least two cases that they were talking to students named on the list. Obtaining an early estimate of the number of SU students on board the plane was very important: Syracuse news organizations needed to make informed decisions about the coverage of the event, and they had an important responsibility to alert the university and the surrounding community to the extent of the tragedy. It is hard, however, to justify the transmission of an unverified list of victims before enough time had elapsed to permit notification of next of kin.[39] As newspeople at those stations soon learned, broadcasting the list made their job more difficult; the phones began ringing almost immediately from people who had missed the list or were looking for verification, followed by out-of-town callers who heard the station might have the names.

The experience of reporters in Syracuse suggests that a code of practice should also address the issue of covering vigils, memorial services and funerals. The reaction of the students demonstrates — as does that of the people of Lockerbie — that even reporting methods which by normal media standards would be considered polite and relatively unobtrusive can be very distressing to those shaken by tragedy. More assertive journalistic behavior adds to the trauma.

The newspaper columnist and photographer assigned to Hendricks Chapel generally saw the media as more subdued than normal. The columnist recalled they had "kind of grouped themselves out of the way. You could see them, but they weren't in their usual configuration that you would expect at something like that." His story told of the shutters clicking as still photographers shot their pictures and he recalled that sound during the interview for this book. The photographer also compared the media presence to other stories that he had been on, calling them "a small, relatively polite group of media people."[40]

Most media people who were at Hendricks Chapel saw that scene very much the way journalists who were sent to Lockerbie did. Initially, they were caught up in the excitement of a very big story; they saw themselves as trying not to add unnecessarily to the distress of those they were covering. With a few notable exceptions, they saw most of their colleagues behaving responsibly, and they did not attempt to defend those they felt had stepped over the line of acceptable journalistic practice.

The reaction to media in Lockerbie might have been much worse if most journalists had not agreed to pooled arrangements at memorial services. Television stations in Syracuse could have shared a single feed from the chapel, transmitting the service itself, with less disruption and a better quality picture. That is, more or less, the way it was handled at the Church of Scotland in

Lockerbie. The public relations office at Syracuse University could have arranged for such a shared feed by being more pro-active in response to this event. That would have avoided the worst excesses brought on by competitive pressure among local television media. We can only agree with the Syracuse television reporter who came to the conclusion that her attempt to do a live stand-up from the balcony of the chapel was wrong; others can learn from that mistake. Likewise, walking into a service with cameras ready to roll, as if this were a standard news conference, is hard to defend. Although it may seem normal conduct to television reporters, the "ready to roll" posture of camera on shoulder signals intrusion to potential targets of media attention.

Although some very moving pictures resulted from photographers' attention to grieving students inside the chapel, the coverage raises two issues, one about methods and the other about privacy.

The move to color photography in newspapers makes the work of photojournalists much more demanding. Lighting sufficient for black-and-white is inadequate for photographers to shoot color. Those hoping to sell their work to magazines must go for high quality color. Overhead lights were on in the sanctuary at Hendricks during the vigil. It was not a candlelight service, although candles were lit on the stage. But most photographers, seeking color pictures, felt they needed more light and so used some form of flash or strobe. That distracted the audience, especially those who were alerted by the lights to the fact that their grief was the object of a photographer's attention.

The motor drives that advance film automatically allow photographers to work very quickly, zeroing in on their subjects without pausing. But those motors create a noisy distraction, especially to those nearest to them, who are most apt to be photographed. If photographers want to argue that they should be allowed access to such events, even on a pool basis, they need to demand that their suppliers create affordable equipment that allows them to be unobtrusive. That change is needed, although it will not guarantee the kind of access they might wish. Those in charge of such an event may determine that the only photography permitted will be a wide shot of the service from the back of the audience.

Solving the problem of technological intrusion does not answer the issue of whether photographing the grieving in such circumstances is appropriate. If the grieving cannot have privacy during a memorial service or vigil, when can they expect it? Is this not, as a chaplain argued in an earlier chapter, sacred space?

At least two photographers did refuse this assignment. One was Larry Mason, a Newhouse School professor who is also a freelance photojournalist. Asked by United Press International to cover the chapel, he declined in advance and covered the basketball game instead. Mason told the forum Hendricks Chapel that his refusal stemmed, in part, from his recognition that many of his own students would be among the mourners. He reported that a photographer from the *Rochester Times-Union* also rejected the assignment although he tried initially to cover the Hendricks Chapel service. Mason said the photographer left the game and went to the chapel, but returned quickly. "I asked, 'Well, what happened?' He said, 'Well, I went in and I shot without strobe and I shot without a motor drive, and I stayed in one location and I used a long lens and I made a picture of a young woman grieving in the front row. And as I shot a couple of frames, she heard the camera go off, and she looked up at me. She didn't say anything, but her eyes said, 'What in the hell do you think you're doing?' And he said, 'That was too much for me.'"

Interestingly enough, none of the Syracuse journalists who reached a personal decision that night *not* to cover grieving people told of any reprisals by management for refusing to do this particular assignment. Although some journalists felt driven by their editors or news directors to go after this aspect at one or more of the major sites of the story, it is not clear what would have happened if these reporters had also refused.

Let us be very clear on one point: arguing against covering people in their most personal moments of bereavement should not be interpreted as advocating that news media ignore the grieving. They should consider when, where and how they approach them. To prevent some of the excesses of Pan Am 103 and other disasters, news organizations should work with the personnel they will send into the field or assign to telephones to develop a code that will guide their newsgathering. In some cases that training might involve the discussion of hypothetical situations and/or role-playing.

While one way of preparing for future disasters is by developing or revising a code of practice, it is not the only way. Interviews with journalists on both sides of the Atlantic indicated little or no planning for disaster coverage, especially for what might be called a "worst-case scenario." Even major news organizations were less than fully prepared for an airline disaster that did not meet the criteria of standard problems associated with landing and take-off. In Lockerbie, local people and those scattered across the United Kingdom who were familiar with the little town heard the report that the petrol station had exploded repeated as fact during the main BBC news telecast at 9 p.m. Many of them never expected to see people who lived in that part of town again. The BBC anchor spoke with two different people reporting from the scene during the newscast and never attempted to ask about the report of the petrol station exploding. The BBC guidelines now state:

> The first things our audience need to know about any disaster are when and where it happened, the scale of it, and whether anyone near or dear to them was involved. Sometimes those things are not immediately clear, because disasters are often attended by a high degree of confusion and contradiction. So our first job must be to define or limit the area of concern as far as we can.
>
> That means giving any detail that we are certain of: the name of the airline, the time of the train, the exact area of the explosion, and so on.
>
> And in the absence of information about exactly what *has* happened, it may be helpful to make clear what *has not*! Thus: "There are no reports of any injuries..." or "It's thought no civilians were involved..." or even "There were no British passengers on board." (There are times when that is entirely appropriate, and there are other times when it sounds like the worst sort of jingoism — you must judge the circumstances and be able to justify your decision!)
>
> For the same reason, it is important to keep reporting the number of known survivors even when the number of victims remains unclear.
>
> We have a positive duty to allay people's unnecessary alarm as well as to confirm the worst fears of the minority who are directly affected.

This failure to zero in on and narrow the area most affected by a disaster is not unusual; researchers following the Mexico City earthquake claimed that the failure of broadcasters to let audiences know that much of the capital and the surrounding region were relatively unaffected exacerbated the psychological impact of the quake (Palacios *et al*, 1988). A similar complaint was voiced in an informal poll of college sociology students about the 1989 quake in the San Francisco Bay area, especially of "images of the Marina district that suggested the whole city was in flames and collapsing" (Gitlin, 1989, p. 33). A San Francisco broadcaster said local television provided a context for the most dramatic scenes (the Marina, the collapsed section of the Nimitz Freeway and a tourist's videotape of a car plunging through the top deck of the Bay Bridge). The problem, he said, was that some of the networks left the impression that those scenes represented the impact of the quake on the entire area. Residents in unscathed areas told of calls from frightened relatives across the country, some of whom thought everything from Santa Cruz to San Francisco was demolished (Laufer, 1989).

Given the immediacy of television, it is especially striking that disaster planning was either non-existent or unknown to all but one of the 12 TV reporters interviewed in Syracuse. Not only had their current station never talked with them about a disaster plan before the downing of Pan Am 103, neither had the management at any previous station where they worked. One journalist did report that her station had a plan for covering plane crashes, but she wrote, "few newsroom members have been briefed on the plan." She was right. None of the other journalists interviewed from her station knew it had a plan.

Newspapers, even though they did not have to transmit immediately, also showed signs of being caught off-guard. The Syracuse editor who gave his Lockerbie-bound reporter $200 intended for Christmas presents demonstrated the need to anticipate the unexpected costs that can come with disasters. The first reporter Howard Schneider approached at *Newsday* and asked to go to Lockerbie did not have a passport.

The importance of even a little planning was illustrated by the TV newsman sent from Syracuse to Kennedy. He said his station had no real plan for disaster coverage, but his news director had informally discussed with him what the reporter's role might be if tragedy struck. When he got the assignment, he raced home. "I always kept a bag packed with the essentials, just in case something happened...because (my news director) and I talked that if anybody ever had to go, it would be me."

Television reporters from two Syracuse stations largely described their newsrooms as "chaotic" or "somewhat hectic." Those who described it as somewhat hectic agreed that some clear directions were given, but often reporters were operating on instinct. Those who called the newsroom chaotic said they were not always sure who was in charge. One of them said four different people held the reins that evening; the news director failed to respond quickly enough to the news, and did not make solid news decisions until late that evening.

A reporter at a third network affiliate said that their newsroom seemed organized, that it was clear who was in charge and what each person's job was. One reporter at that station praised his manager's ability to make decisions and to execute them: "Decisions had to be made, and we didn't have a lot of time for vacillation."

The television reporters in Syracuse were asked for suggestions about what should be included in a disaster plan. Five recommended that one person be in charge. Said one of these, "Our newsroom was a mess, duplication of effort, no communication. Someone to 'direct traffic' and assign tasks would have helped a lot." Another of this group wished for a "disaster coordinator," who would check with each reporter, the producer and assignment editor to find out which stories were being pursued. This information should be passed along to reporters in the field: "I was a reporter in the field and never was clued in fully on what the 'big picture' was, as far as our approach to covering the big story." "When time is so critical, it's more important to have people 'working smart' rather than frantically working," said another Syracuse TV reporter.

Several of these reporters suggested the assignment of specific duties. One suggested having business-side personnel handle incoming calls, relieving journalists for reporting duties. That may be an answer in some disasters. If the disaster creates a demand for information from a list of fatalities, it might work to contact local clergy to take calls. *This would need to be part of a disaster plan, not a last-minute thought.*

A different telephone assignment helped one of the Syracuse newspapers and could conceivably be incorporated into disaster plans of other media: taking calls from those seeking information and noting their name and phone number and reason for calling. Ringing back with information as it becomes available can lead reporters to a situation in which they are being helpful and perceived as less intrusive. This can set the scene for an interview, either at the time of the callback or at some future time.

Two television reporters suggested designating a "field producer," who does nothing but coordinate the crew on the scene. This person would communicate with the newsroom on behalf of the crew. One reporter said a counterpart to the field producer should be present in the newsroom, taking in information from the crews.

The Scottish Television experience would add another function to a disaster plan. When executives there reviewed their Lockerbie coverage, they decided that any disaster plan should include a business-side person to deal with networks and stations calling for satellite feeds. Some Syracuse reporters thought such demands also distracted their supervisors.

In preparing a disaster plan, news executives should review their own organization's experiences in covering major stories and seek out sources that might be particularly helpful. One shared with us by the *Newsday* aviation writer Glenn Kessler is *Air Accidents and the News Media*, a pamphlet published by the Aviation/Space Writers Association (1988). It would be particularly helpful for American media because it provides a basic list of U.S. sources to call in an air disaster.[41]

Careful planning should result in quality coverage, not just an adequate effort. A widely used broadcast reporting textbook describes the award-winning coverage of the Flight 191 crash at Chicago's O'Hare Airport by a local station, WMAQ-TV. The book says that the fine coverage was made possible, in part, because the station's news director, a veteran of stories ranging from the Robert Kennedy assassination to California earthquakes, had what he called a game plan. It contained several of the elements the Syracuse newspeople suggested. For example, it provided for a "producer of facts," one person responsible for taking in all facts and details; he would look for angles and direct the in-house staff of reporters and researchers. Also important was an "assignment desk manager" to take charge of the logistics of assigning the live and tape units, and assigning reporters to execute the angles, previously determined by the "producer of facts." (Yoakman and Cremer, 1989, p.295–96)

Such a plan needs to include ground rules for use of the latest technology. Pan Am 103 was one of the first major stories, and apparently the first disaster of international proportions, in which reporters were able to use cellular telephones. In 1988, the device was just coming into its own; many areas still were not covered (Levine, 1988). Although some reporters, like the AP's Walter Mears, had used the portable phones to cover the presidential campaign (Guttenplan, 1988), those organizing communications for the Democratic Convention in Atlanta in July were surprised that the heavy cellular telephone traffic for which they had prepared never materialized (*Communications Daily*, 1988).

Many regions of the world — including wide areas of North America — were not yet served by cellular telephone, but all the major sites of this particular story were ready for the hand-held units. In fact, the United Kingdom and the United States had adopted the same standard for cellular phones.[42] That both simplified and complicated the work of reporters with access to one of the hand-held units. It certainly sped up contact with a reporter's home office, and reduced the scramble for telephones that had been part of the journalistic routine on big stories (Crouse, 1972). The AP's Maureen Johnson could stand in the rain and look at the nose cone at Tundergarth, and decide what she would dictate without having to search out a traditional telephone. Scottish Television reporter Harry Smith could call John Kean from the petrol station that supposedly had exploded, and correct those erroneous reports. A photographer for Syracuse Newspapers could confer with his editor about what he was shooting at the Dome and Hendricks Chapel, and when he finished there could call a young woman he had met earlier and arrange to cover a group of grieving students in the privacy of their apartment.

But the cellular phone added to the stress for a Syracuse television reporter at the chapel. Although prior to this technological advance, she would have had two-way radio communication with her station, it would have been impossible for a San Francisco station to call her in the middle of a quiet vigil and press her to do another live "hit." The tendency for editors and news directors to drive their staff in the field is probably a natural one; both television and newspaper managers monitor broadcast output during such crises and so are keenly aware of the competition. The temptation, even with traditional telecommunications, is to call out to the field too often, to direct too much. That is why Peter Marks was awakened half-way around the world with a tip that he could not follow up. That is why some reporters felt driven to talk to families at Kennedy Airport. The cellular telephone provides the means, especially in the hands of a nervous editor or news director, to make the work of the news people in the field much more difficult. The temptation may be strong because it is common practice, especially among news organizations with limited staff, to send the less experienced reporters into the field to gather information while keeping more experienced journalists where they can help package and, in the case of television, anchor the breaking report. A call on the cellular telephone, however, can interrupt not only the quiet observation of action related to the disaster, but a delicate moment in an interview the reporter has obtained with considerable difficulty.

Geography — and the sensitivity of most of those involved in the coverage — shielded the world from live pictures of many of the worst sights stemming from the Lockerbie disaster. Townspeople, public information officers and journalists all spoke of seeing a parking lot one block off the main street of Lockerbie filled with satellite dishes. They did feed transmissions to Europe, back to the States and as far away as Tasmania, but the way the town is nestled in a valley played havoc with telecommunications, so live broadcasts from the scene were generally stand-up interviews or straight narration from a relatively neutral site.

Live interviews under such circumstances can be particularly risky, as veteran CBS anchor Dan Rather learned during earthquake coverage in San Francisco less than a year later. Rather was standing in front of the collapsed Nimitz Freeway during a CBS special the night after the disaster. He was interviewing a survivor of the Nimitz collapse, Chris Mitchell (Laufer, 1989). The exchange started:

> Rather: Chris, when the earthquake was underway, what did it feel like?
>
> Mitchell: Well, I didn't know there was an earthquake for about 20 minutes. All I knew is that the freeway fell on me. At that time it was nothing but confusion. I immediately climbed down and sat on the ground far from any structures, and somebody later told me it was an earthquake and all I knew (was) there was a freeway that hit me on the head.
>
> Rather: What did it sound like?
>
> Mitchell: Silence...there was silence...nobody...there was nothing...there was silence. When I got out of my car, quiet and...it was quite graphic, though. But there was no sounds.
>
> Rather: Quite graphic meaning?
>
> Mitchell: There was blood all over the road as I got out of my car. In the front of me, there was a brain of a person quivering on the ground by itself. You asked, that's it. (CBS, Oct. 18, 1989)

People in Lockerbie could have told tales as harrowing, but from their own recollections and published accounts, most of them chose not to, and so far we have found no evidence that they were asked to do so during a live interview. It can be argued that disaster survivors should never be interviewed live. A taped interview places less strain on the subject, who is trying to give a coherent account of a very traumatic experience, as well as less pressure on the journalist, who in a live interview must be simultaneously listening to the story and cues from the production team. If some parts need to be eliminated, they can be edited out. If a veteran reporter such as Rather can run into difficulties, imagine the problems an interviewer with much less experience might encounter. The issue is not simply a matter of taste. How audiences, especially young audiences, are affected by graphic reporting of traumatic events, needs more research but this study found evidence that interviewing survivors in a tragedy can cause a sort of "vicarious traumatization" in journalists, and it is possible that broadcast interviews could have a similar effect on members of the audience.[43]

Certainly criteria might be developed that would provide exceptions to such a general proscription against live interviews of survivors, but increasing the theatricality of the news program — some might say sensationalizing the coverage — would not be a justification. That would seem to be the trap into which Dan Rather wandered when he did the interview the night *after* the earthquake, not knowing the trauma that his subject had experienced.

Elmer Lower, former president of ABC News, once noted that live television is "the only journalistic medium that does its reporting and editing right in front of the audience" (Yoakman and Cremer, 1989, p. 296). The issue of when to transmit live became more difficult in disasters that occurred during the months after Pan Am 103. Two that happened while cameras were focused on sports events illustrate some of the problems: on April 15, 1989, the surge of Liverpool soccer fans into a section of the Hillsborough stadium in Sheffield, England, crushed those in the front against a high wire fence; and on October 17, 1989, the Loma Prieto earthquake shook the San Francisco Bay area just as baseball announcers were beginning the pre-game show before the third game of the World Series.

At Hillsborough, the BBC was transmitting the FA Cup semi-final between Liverpool and Nottingham when authorities began to realize something was very wrong in the Leppings Lane terraces at one end of the field. Terraces, a traditional feature of British football grounds, provide standing room on elevated rows, separated by waist-high iron barriers that are intended to contain fans in small sections and resist the pressure of overcrowding. Many of those barriers bent as fans surged forward, so people behind them were shoved forward or onto the ground. (McKibben, 1989)

What had happened was that police outside the stadium, confronted with an estimated 4,000 fans without tickets demanding access, opened a 16-foot wide gate leading into the already overcrowded section. Those trapped inside by the perimeter fence struggled to escape or just to breathe; some managed to scale the 10-foot mesh or climbed onto the shoulders of friends and were lifted out of the crowd by people seated in the stands above them (Fisher, 1989).

Millions of sports fans watching on television and many of those in other sections of the stadium were not immediately aware of what had happened. After six minutes of play, the sight of fans escaping onto the field prompted referees to stop the game. Police used wire cutters on the perimeter fence so that fans could escape onto the field, where many of them collapsed on the grass. Then rescuers began carrying those who had been critically injured out of the section. BBC, staying with its guidelines, showed the crowd crushed up against the fence, but kept sufficient distance so that individual victims could not be identified (Tan, 1991).

The legal ramifications of straying from such guidelines can only be estimated, but a test case arising from the Hillsborough disaster suggests they could be significant. The case was filed against the Chief Constable, as the party responsible for crowd control, but explored the law's attitude toward mental suffering by relatives and friends who learned of the tragedy under various conditions. Of the 16 seeking redress for the post-traumatic stress they had experienced, four had been in the stands; one heard a radio report while listening to another game; another learned about the tragedy from a friend. The remaining 10 had watched the event on live television. Initially, many of the claims, including those of parents and siblings of victims, were upheld by Mr Justice Hidden, who specifically recognized that live television was equivalent to being present at a scene or actually seeing it and awarded damages. The viewer, he said, knew that the camera lens was augmenting his eyesight but that he was seeing images of what was actually happening at a distance (Tan, 1990).

The case was appealed all the way to the House of Lords, where it was overturned. Lord Keith said that the Chief Constable, aware of the ethical guidelines of televising identifiable victims in disasters, was not responsible for the effects on those watching television. A summary of the ruling said, in part, that the viewing of those scenes could not be equated with:

> ...the viewer being within "sight or hearing of the event or its immediate aftermath," nor could the scenes reasonably be regarded as giving rise to shock.
>
> They were capable of giving rise to anxiety, and undoubtedly did, but that was very different from seeing the fate of the relative or his condition shortly after the event. The viewing of the television scenes did not create the necessary degree of proximity, and the appeals would be dismissed. (Tan, 1991)

Both the original ruling and the House of Lords decision to overturn it appeared to be guessing at the effects of the live transmission. Mr Justice Hidden had limited such damages only to close relatives, and so little research has been done on such cases that it is hard to understand how the Lords' opinion could state so positively that the scenes at Hillsborough could not "reasonably be regarded as giving rise to shock." The attitude of the courts may change as more evidence is gathered about post-traumatic shock and the extent to which it may be affected by media images, especially those in which individuals can be identified.

In fact, photographs in which Hillsborough victims were identifiable appeared in many British newspapers and triggered the most complaints received that year by the Press Council.[44] Its investigation determined that more than 30 national and regional papers used pictures, taken from a distance, that showed the crowd through the steel fence, "the front row crushed against it, many of them recognisable and in attitudes of distress, pain and fear." It ruled that publication of these pictures was justifiable, noting, "They were horrific; they portrayed an horrific event." Public interest was served by their publication because "they brought home vividly the danger of a dense crowd under pressure packed behind an immovable fence." It did condemn, however, photographs published in a few newspapers that focused on a single individual or a small group, "sometimes with features cruelly distorted by its steel mesh," and those depicting "single, often clearly identifiable, individuals lying on the ground, being treated or being carried away" (Press Council Adjudications, 1989, p. 226).

Codes of practice and disaster plans should consider the kind of live coverage that may be needed and the resources that will be required. The reporter and camera crew going live need to function as their own editors; they will do that better if they know in advance what their organization's policies are with regard to showing horrific sights. In a massive tragedy, long shots may be more informative in helping the audience grasp the extent of the damage than graphic close-ups. A station's traffic watch helicopter may be put to good use. In the Lockerbie disaster, airspace was closed to all but emergency aircraft, but hills above the town offered a spectacular vantage point.

The public does not always understand what happens in the newsgathering process, which makes it difficult for them to offer constructive criticism. Although some stations showed the television crews and photographers crowding around the woman who collapsed on the floor of Kennedy Airport, others did not. A woman caller to a Syracuse talk show apparently saw the scene cropped in a way that eliminated the media. She said she had heard criticism of the photographer who took that picture, and wanted to speak in defense of the photographer, whom she assumed was a woman. "This picture moved me more than anything else that I had seen," the caller said. "She didn't ask silly questions about how the woman felt; she simply took the picture and that was it. And I think that picture must have moved other people as well." (WCNY-TV, 1990)

The public also does not necessarily understand that reporters, photographers and camera crews may be affected by what they are covering. That helps explain why a *Daily News* columnist thought the emotion television reporters showed at Kennedy Airport was worth writing about. In fact, a number of reporters we interviewed about covering Pan Am 103 went through considerable distress in the process — or had some reaction afterwards. Al Michaels of ABC told one interviewer that covering the Loma Prieto earthquake was difficult because of the way he felt about the San Francisco Bay area. "I thought of the families in Oakland waiting desperately for someone to come (home), and that someone never did," Michaels said. "When I got back to the hotel (the next) morning, I sat down and cried for those people" (Martzke, 1989).

Asked how they would advise a reporter who was going to cover people caught up in disasters, a number of newspeople stressed the humanity of the process. Don Singleton of the *Daily News* now draws on a tragedy in his own family, the suicide of a brother. "I remember when my brother died...all I wanted to do was talk. To anybody," Singleton said. "I mean, you just felt like crying out for human contact. I'm like that. So I think that kind of sets the pattern for the relationship between me and a (grieving person)."

He said he doesn't go to a potential source in such circumstances as a reporter, but just as one human being to another. "In fact, I always say when I write a story, I write it first to please God, second, me, third the people who pay for the newspaper, and four, for the editor. That's how I approach it. I do it as a human being, not as a journalist." "So you can look yourself in the mirror the next morning and feel okay?" he was asked. "I hope so. And if I didn't, my reaction would be to get right back to wherever I did something wrong and straighten it out, make it right. Because I couldn't stand walking around, knowing there's somebody out there hating me."

William Goldsweig of the *Daily News* recalled covering a USAir flight that went off a runway and into in the water off LaGuardia. Although he was already an editor, he was asked to go because his home is fairly near the airport. He arrived at the terminal just as they were bringing in survivors, soaking wet. "I'm standing with my notebook and a tape recorder. I don't walk up to them and say, 'How do you feel? How do you feel? How do you feel?' Those people are suffering." But he was looking for people to tell him what had happened. "I see a middle-aged man who's shaking and trying to light a cigarette. I light a cigarette for him. I try to calm him," Goldsweig said. Then he saw a flight attendant who was concerned because there weren't enough blankets to go around. "She asked me if she could have my jacket. I gave her my jacket to put around someone. Actually the jacket ended up disappearing in the incident. But, as a human being, you try in a way...if possible, to be comforting.

"And then, you're not going to make these people feel worse, and these people are more often than not quite willing to express themselves because they have a need to. They need to verbalize and to vent, and let out what they're going through. But you have to approach them in a sympathetic way, and — you know, some people can fake sympathy, but I think you really have to have genuine sympathy. Because fake sympathy is going to look fake. So if you've got to talk to somebody who's had somebody killed in a terrorist bombing of a plane, you don't turn off your emotions, you turn on your emotions," he said. "If you turn your emotions on, you will approach them in a compassionate way. You'll hopefully not cause injury. And if they don't want to talk, you don't stand around and press the point. You move on to somebody else. Or you give the person more time. If somebody clearly does not want you to be part of a private moment, if it's clear that you're only inflicting pain, then that's the time you back off."

Goldsweig recognized the pressure from editors to come back with something. "Odds are you're not going to come back with nothing. Because if you approach it right, you're going to find somebody willing to talk. They will vent and feel better for having had that opportunity. You will have done your job, and they will not feel any the worse for it."

None of the newspeople interviewed said they like to cover grieving people; a number of them volunteered that the chore they dread most involves approaching a family member who has just been bereaved. Howard Schneider, managing editor for news at *Newsday*, was asked if editors at his papers talk with reporters about such coverage. "We try to set a tone for how we expect our reporters to handle a situation where they have to deal with people who have experienced a tragedy or have lost people," he said. "It may range from reporters who go to funeral homes or wakes, to reporters who knock on doors. We don't have a written policy."

As an example, he said, *Newsday* editors tell reporters and photographers they should not go to a wake or enter a funeral home if they're not invited. "Our reporters know that, in covering tragedy, part of the story is the survivors. Their job is to go and try to talk to the survivors and put the human face on the story...They'll go to a funeral home, for example, and stand outside, try to meet someone in the family, introduce themselves and explain why they're there and what they're doing. And if the family says, 'Please, we do not want you in,' we tell them not to go in. At the same time, we tell them to be as resourceful as possible in trying to make contact." Schneider said if reporters are dealing with a family under great duress, they should find someone like a member of the clergy who can make the contact. "We'll tell them, if they go up to a door and get it slammed in their face, they can write a note and leave it outside with a card." The note can explain that the reporter recognizes that the family is under great pressure, but if anyone can call and would like to talk, this is how to reach the newspaper.

"So that's how we try to set our tone. The level of discussion is often between the city editor and the reporters going out. In time, I think it filters down to the newsroom (so that the staff has) a general feeling of what our guidelines and policies are."

Many experienced newspeople told us they avoided being the personal bearer of bad news. Schneider remembered being a reporter during the Vietnam era when the newspaper received killed-in-action reports. "After every KIA, we'd call the family. I remember once calling a family and for some unfortunate reason, the family didn't know. I got the grandmother or the grandfather. You don't forget that as a reporter."

Journalists interviewed in this study clearly believe that notification of family should take place through what they considered more appropriate channels, specifically the airline, an official governmental body or, in the case of students, from Syracuse University. But in Pan Am 103 many saw these sources as highly disorganized and those people who asked for such information as terribly anxious, so they often felt obliged to share what information they had been able to obtain. The idea of showing the reaction of the survivor was even more troubling to them, especially if there was any sense that this person was "set up" to react on camera.

The cross-cultural and multi-media nature of this investigation helped us see that problems caused are not inherent in a given medium. It would be easy from the American vantage point to look at the behavior of some television camera crews and assume there is no way that broadcast journalists can conduct themselves that would be compassionate. But television outlets in Scotland and England came in for much less criticism than did the British tabloid press.[45]

It would be equally plausible to look at the tabloid press from the British perspective and conclude that those reporting for that market must operate under a set of rules inherently different from those at the so-called "quality papers." Yet the New York tabloids studied here came in for relatively mild criticism. The criticism tended to focus on the decision by the *Daily News* to feature the full-page picture of the grieving mother prostrate at Kennedy Airport. While newspaper coverage was criticized in America, those using a tabloid format, or even what might be called a tabloid approach to the story, came in for no more criticism than the broadsheet publications.

Within each nation's media structure, however, those working in the print and broadcast media do see each other quite differently.

A number of those interviewed at the Syracuse newspapers noted differences in the way print and broadcast media approached the story. All told, each newspaper had between 30 and 40 people directly involved in gathering information the night of the disaster. Each sent a reporter to Scotland and one to Kennedy Airport during the initial phase of the coverage.

The dozen broadcast journalists interviewed for the chapter on Syracuse television, each accompanied by a photographer, represented most of the news people sent out on the story; others, of course, worked in the newsroom to help gather information. One television station did send a crew to Kennedy Airport, but none sent one to Scotland.

In Syracuse, newspaper reporters seemed much more conscious of broadcast reporters; the television journalists, on the other hand, seemed to pay close attention to what crews from rival stations, as well as the networks and out-of-town stations, were doing. One newspaper reporter recalled seeing a network reporter "preening at 5 o'clock in the morning in front of the chapel." She said, "It's like they were putting on a performance. He said something to the effect that it looks good for us to be here. It made me a little sick to see him. Then I thought, I'm here doing the same thing."

One of the reporters who went to Hendricks Chapel to try to interview students remembered television reporters and their crews "running around with cameras and trying to stop people as they were walking by." She contrasted that with her own situation as a print reporter holding a notebook. "I could walk along with somebody. I didn't have to jump in front of them and turn on the lights."

Some print reporters disdainfully called the "how do you feel" question something that broadcast reporters might ask. One recalled a pack journalism situation that involved a different story, one in which reporters were trying to interview a defendant leaving a courthouse. "TV reporters were chasing after her. She wasn't saying anything. Some of the questions that were shouted were to get a reaction out of her. 'How do you feel knowing that your son is dead?' I heard a TV reporter ask that. To be perfectly honest, all TV journalists are the same. I think it's lousy journalism."

But a *Herald-Journal* reporter who joined the crowd of journalists at Kennedy Airport said that at one point, out of frustration, he thought he shouted out, "How do you feel?" He did not seem particularly proud of the fact, and we found no journalists — either print or broadcast — who defended the practice of using that question with grieving people. A few said that they wanted to know how people were feeling, but argued that emotions would emerge more naturally by asking less aggressive questions.

The perception of many reporters who went to Lockerbie was that it was important to reach the scene rapidly in order to find people who were ready to talk about what they had seen and experienced. They generalized that most people will talk immediately following a disaster. Yet our interviews suggest that there were many people who were initially reluctant to speak about what had happened. The Lockerbie people were bothered by what one journalist called the "overwhelming media presence," but they were also bothered by what they saw as the pursuit of "gory details" and the way packs of journalists would descend on them while they were talking with friends in the street.

This raises the question: was it the media or their methods that bothered people in Lockerbie? The answer seems to be primarily the methods. That conclusion is based partly on the fact that, as time passed, many American family members were willing to talk to Syracuse newspaper reporters in response to a carefully worded letter or phone call, and a number of close relationships developed from those contacts. Similar relationships also developed eventually between some British families and individual British reporters. Lockerbie people tended to remain media wary after their community was overrun by hundreds of journalists and news crews day after day. They had had enough.

What was the basis of ethical decisions made by newspeople covering Pan Am 103? Two precepts seemed to play critical roles: the utilitarian concept of the greatest good for the greatest number, and the Golden Rule, Do unto others as you would have them do unto you. Not surprisingly, both these themes and their applicability to journalism have been discussed explicitly or implicitly in writings on media ethics. Fink (1988) notes, for example, that John Stuart Mill "interpreted utilitarianism to mean that ethical conduct should aim at general well-being, creating the greatest happiness for the greatest number of people," although he also defended the rights of minorities (p. 7-8). Mill argued that it is the outcome or consequence of an act that counts, not the intent behind it. Fink adds:

> The seeming contradiction — or shall we say, flexibility — in Mill's argument is no stranger to newsrooms today. For example, should a newspaper or TV news team invade the privacy of an individual — thus inflicting unhappiness — in order to serve the larger populace, the larger good, with a story that should see the light? Mill probably would counsel looking at the consequences and determining what would serve the greater number (p. 8).

The Code of Practice that British newspapers have agreed to uphold seems to be based on Mill's principles, but at least one code, recently adopted by the tabloid *Daily Star*, incorporates the Golden Rule. Brian Hitchen, editor of the *Star*, told the *Financial Times* that the new code of practice places considerable stress on avoiding intrusion. He said the paper's staff had been told, "Don't do anything you would not like done to you"(Snoddy, 1992).

In a sense, news people showing compassion in connection with Pan Am 103 seemed to be operating from the Golden Rule, deciding that the feelings of the individuals they were dealing with did not have to be sacrificed to the "greater number," their audience. Those deciding to press ahead, in some instances, seemed to have concluded that the interest of the public at large was paramount. Gil Spencer can argue as firmly that the *Daily News* was acting ethically in using on the front page the picture of the woman on the airport floor, as can editors at *Newsday*, who decided not to run it at all.

The other theme relating to justification of media behavior was less philosophical. It was the "I'm just doing my job" theme. Sometimes this reasoning laid responsibility at the feet of media management; sometimes it looked to the audience.

Said one journalist who was at Lockerbie: "There was so many press in town I'm sure there were people who could go over the bounds of human acceptability. But with a major disaster you're always going to get a media circus. If people didn't really want to read about it, we wouldn't be sent there. People go out and buy the papers the following day, and they want to know what it was all about. I think, in many ways, that is justification enough for what we do. You're there obviously preying on people's misery."

The photographer at Hendricks Chapel sounded a similar theme. Asked what he would say to those who complained that he was invading people's privacy as he confronted the grieving with his camera, he said: "I tell those people: Don't watch CNN. Don't buy the newspaper. Write letters to the newspaper and tell them you don't want that kind of coverage. You don't want to see people in Afghanistan who got their legs blown off. You don't want to see the people in LA getting their heads beat in. You don't want to see earthquake victims and flood victims. If you don't want to see it, then that's fine. If you do want to see it, then when it's your time, it's time to take your turn to be involved. I understand that some people don't want to be involved. But I find most people's behavior to be inconsistent, and inconsistency is something that I don't admire."

Again, this theme is not unique to Pan Am 103. In the early days of the controversy over publication of the biography of Princess Diana, Jonathan Dimbleby of the Radio 4 program "Any Questions?" asked for a show of hands from an audience in Cuckfield. How many would boycott the *Sunday Times* because it was serializing the Andrew Morton book about the princess? Dimbleby reported the majority of those present raised their hands. So the program sent a reporter back to Cuckfield to look for unsold newspapers. Not only had readers bought all the copies of the *Times*, they had also cleaned out many of the other papers with related stories (Leapman, 1992).

But by and large, news people believe that something good can come from what they do. Ideally, they see benefits both for those who become the subjects of their stories in a disaster, and for their audience. The same British journalist who argued that the media would not be sent to places like Lockerbie if people didn't want to know about it, said he thought the media did not do that bad a job in covering the crash site. He explained: "There was an enormous appeal raised for Lockerbie itself, from which the community benefited. We brought home to people the enormity of what had happened. You can argue that television does it even more. I think we have a job to do in that sort of situation, but you have to know where to draw the line. Providing you do, people respect that and they'll answer questions, within reason."

4 *Institutional Response*

The Scottish Office

The odds of a 747 jetliner falling from the skies onto a quiet market town in the south of peace-loving Scotland as the result of a terrorist bomb must be 100 million to one. In fact, investigators believe that the masterminds of this act intended that no trace of their deed would ever be found; if all had gone according to plan, the remains of Pan Am 103 would be deep in the Atlantic. Crisis management experts, who specialize in anticipating the worst fates that might befall their clients and then help them to prepare, could never have developed a scene as devastating as the one that faced Scottish officials at Lockerbie.

Like most of their countrymen on the evening of December 21, the staff of the Scottish Information Office (SIO), headquartered in Edinburgh (and now known as The Scottish Office Information Directorate), were enveloped in the warmth of home and family and dinner when the first reports came across Scottish television, shortly before 7:30 p.m. That incomplete bulletin was enough to trigger a pre-established alert system within the SIO, drawing the staff back to their offices at New St Andrew's House, where they immediately notified their colleagues and Scottish ministers in London, who, in turn, notified British government departments. In the first wave, six members of the Press Office staff converged back in the offices and took to the phones, already ringing furiously. With little more information than the fact that a plane had crashed into Lockerbie, 70 miles to the south, two press officers raced down the highway, knowing that reporters would converge at the crash scene. They kept in touch with their Edinburgh office by cellnet phones.

Two key officials of the Scottish Information Office — Deputy Director David Beveridge and Senior Information Officer Brian Reid[1] — speak with mixed emotions of quiet sadness and professional pride about their part in what could be considered a classic in crisis communication management. Indeed, in 1989, Beveridge was invested with the Order of the British Empire by Her Majesty Queen Elizabeth II for his work in civil emergencies, especially at Lockerbie. Beveridge had ten years' experience as a journalist before joining government service in 1966. Reid, who is responsible for Home Affairs and Crown Office matters, joined the SIO in 1978 after a career in Australian civil service.

The Scottish Information Office, Beveridge explained, is the "presentational arm" of the Secretary of State for Scotland. It serves all Scottish governmental departments, which constitute in Edinburgh a miniature version of the government in London's Whitehall. The role of these information officers (who recoil from being called public relations practitioners) is, according to Beveridge, to "service the activities of the Scottish Office Ministers, and the presentational activities of the departments." The office also looks after the interests of United Kingdom ministers, including the Prime Minister, when they travel north of the border and require presentational activity. The office provides a similar service for the Royal Family when members are in Scotland.

In the late 1980s, the staff of the SIO numbered 52-and-a-half persons, approximately half of them with professional backgrounds in journalism or broadcasting, and the other half coming through the civil service system and trained on the job. In addition to the Edinburgh office, they maintain offices in London to meet the needs of the Scottish ministers during the sessions of Parliament, and an office in Glasgow, focused primarily on the country's economic and industrial issues.

SIO has two major divisions, Publicity and Press, and it was the latter that went into action at Lockerbie. The Press Division, grouped into six teams of 2-3 individuals, is supported by clerical staff and serves assigned governmental divisions. All offices are linked electronically for the rapid exchange of information and counsel; the Press Office operates 24 hours a day, 365 days a year, with staff on rotational call.

The Scottish Information Office also is responsible for planning for civil emergencies and for disasters, Beveridge explained. While no one in the office had ever seen anything on the scale of the Lockerbie disaster, Beveridge and his staff were no strangers to emergency planning.

Beveridge traces the real beginnings for governmental crisis planning back to 1975 when the Ekofisk Bravo oil platform blew out in the North Sea. The experience of this event, reinforced by the nuclear power plant disaster at Three Mile Island, the Iranian Embassy siege at Prince's Gate in London, Chernobyl, and a series of hostage takeovers in Scottish prisons, further impressed the government of the necessity of crisis planning, and, says Beveridge, "they brought the Scottish rehearsals for dealing with disaster to a very high state of order."

Beveridge plays a key role in developing a full range of crisis scenarios, complete with rehearsals and role-playing. Depending on the type of crisis, drills are also routinely run: "two to three times a year for civil nuclear emergencies, oil spills, rabies outbreaks, civil disasters, perhaps once a year for police/government exercises." Integrated into these emergency drills is a media plan.

Beveridge contends that while each and every incident is unique, "nevertheless, we will clamp a template onto these incidents...and simply adjust the scale...We had become very skilled at what we were doing: When Lockerbie happened, we knew exactly what we were going to do...there was no uncertainty."

Speed also played an important role. Beveridge's press officers, Bill Hoy and Allan Thomson (who was celebrating his 40th birthday), arrived in Lockerbie shortly before 10 p.m., and entered the Police Station "right at the back of John Boyd, the chief constable for the Dumfries and Galloway Region." There, said Beveridge, "they immediately began the process of handling the media: you've got to brief them, get the information flow going, keep them warm, keep them dry." Pre-planning and speed are essential; a bit of ingenuity doesn't hurt. Seeing that a large number of reporters were already on the scene (close to 100 by the press officers' count), the SIO officers swung into action: the doors of the Masonic Hall were forced open, and, instantaneously, it became the media center.

In the darkness and rain, the press officers accompanied Boyd on a tour of hellish scenes, weaving their way through the mass of emergency vehicles, fire trucks, volunteers, and townspeople to assess the scope of the disaster so they would be able to brief the media. "The basic ground rules remain the same, no matter what the incident; that is, you need to get the flow of information going. One has to get into the business of communicating *quickly*," Beveridge said. "We, that is, Brian and I, think that there is a very narrow window of opportunity...If you don't get your people on the ground quickly, you can lose that...and therefore, the information flow can go awry." Somewhere between 1 and 2 a.m. on December 22 (reports conflict as to the exact time), the press officers assembled their first news conference with John Boyd as the spokesperson for the investigation.

By 1 a.m., Beveridge, who was still in Edinburgh, decided that he needed assistance. "The media were assembling in larger and larger numbers: the crowd of 100 reporters at 10 p.m. had swelled to nearly 400 by that time, so I talked to Angus (Kennedy, the force information officer for the Strathclyde Police headquartered in Glasgow). I told him that he was going to have to go to Lockerbie, simply because of the sheer number of reporters who were assembling."

But Beveridge wanted Kennedy there for other reasons, too. "The decision was made that we (SIO) would pull back and put all the local organizations who were dealing with it up front, which was proper." The police, meaning Boyd and Kennedy, had to speak on behalf of the investigating authorities. According to Beveridge, "The State fell back into a position behind" and, Reid interjected, "We really took on the role of advisors to all of the various bodies." (In the ensuing days, the list of these bodies grew steadily: Lockerbie town officials, the Dumfries and Galloway Regional Council, the police and emergency services, the Crown Office, the Procurator Fiscal, the British Department of Transport, Downing Street, Buckingham Palace, the U.S. Department of State, the Federal Aviation Administration, insurance carriers, and on and on.) Pan American World Airways representatives, of course, were there, too.

Kennedy arrived early the next morning by Chinook helicopter; Beveridge and Reid arrived later by car. With Kennedy now supervising the flow of police information to the media, Beveridge and Reid were able to deal with "the political consequentials: plans for the arrival of the Prime Minister and of Prince Andrew."

Beveridge interjected that the Scottish Office and its Information Office have kept careful watch on the "presentation of Lockerbie-related events, not only because it was, and is, a major international news story, but because of their responsibilities to maintain the image of the Scottish police, the UK government and Britain overseas." Indeed, Beveridge and Reid stayed with this event through all the memorial services, the criminal investigation, the commitment to burial, and the Fatal Accident Inquiry. Even in 1992, nearly four years later, they continued their involvement as media advisors to the Lord Advocate and the Crown Office which he heads. The intense media pressure that Lord Fraser of Carmyllie, who held the office at the time of the Lockerbie disaster, came under as Scotland's senior law officer with ultimate responsibility for the international criminal investigation would make a case study in itself.

Again and again in the research phase of this book, the authors were told by family members of the victims and by reporters that "if this horrible thing had to happen, it was 'lucky' that it happened in Scotland." Most were referring to the enormous sensitivity of the Scottish people and the great outpouring of concern and human kindness by the citizenry for the families of the victims. But this "luck" had professional overtones as well.

Beveridge is convinced that "few organizations could have tackled Lockerbie quite so efficiently as the Scottish Office, the Scottish Information Office and the Scottish community." He attributes this to the fact that "lines of communication are shorter here; people know one another here. It was rather a collection of chums who teamed up to deal with it. There was no contingency plan to deal with Lockerbie — certainly nothing on this scale. But the groups who went there, at least the key groups, had rehearsed together in other circumstances, and therefore, for them, Lockerbie was...I hate to say it...they were just doing their job. You were not conscious that you were doing any more than we would normally do. Sometimes you had the feeling that you were in the middle of a big exercise...and you had to shake that feeling."

Reid commented, "Every disaster is unique unto itself; you can rehearse different scenarios, but you cannot rehearse the real thing. Our training in other areas helped us with Lockerbie." Beveridge, referring to planning that goes into crisis management, added, "The basic ground rules remain the same: You've got to get the flow of information going; the information needs to be accurate; timing becomes important; you've got to be aware of whom you are serving. All of a sudden we jumped from servicing the Scottish media to the international media. Suddenly you're conscious of people working in other time zones." The deputy director said, "You also have to make sure that your photographic opportunities are properly planned; you have to make sure that they're not causing distress to relatives."

Beveridge called it "fortunate" that leading up to Lockerbie, the Scottish office had coordinated media coverage of a series of hostage takings. Also, he described as helpful the fact that "we're reasonably closely integrated into police operations and exercises." That meant that the SIO had observed the media in a number of tense situations. In Beveridge's opinion, "With a few notable exceptions, the media tended to behave themselves at Lockerbie. They were affected by the incident themselves. This is quite an interesting psychological point: I think there was a certain amount of self-regulation or self-policing going on. We would also, if we felt it were necessary, not hesitate to discipline reporters who we thought were being difficult."

Asked to define his term "discipline," Beveridge said, "We have access, in the normal course of events, to a higher editorial level (to both United Kingdom media outlets and London-based foreign media), therefore it does not have to be face-to-face confrontation (with a reporter), though we would certainly not hesitate to do that if necessary. One might want to speak to management level in the industry itself. In certain circumstances we will issue editorial requests for restraint for the newspaper or broadcast station, but whether they want to take that — after all, it is a democracy and they're not taking orders from the State. But, on the other hand, in the area of hostage-taking incidents, the media has been quite good to us and held back information that in the negotiating process we did not want front-ended at that stage. Prisoners have access to radios and certain information can affect the negotiations. Media can be an important factor here, so therefore the media's access must be controlled on the basis that we do not want them (the prisoners) negotiating through the media...So essentially what I am saying is that there is access for us at various levels within the media if we feel that something is undesirable and we may want it to change."

Asked about differences in reporting style among the various nationalities who converged on Lockerbie, Beveridge's perception was that the British reporters seemed more difficult than the international press corps. "I was quite interested to see the American media because I had always envisioned them as being terribly aggressive. But surprisingly, they are not. They have a differing style: the British interviewing style on television is much more aggressive; the American interviewing style is just as perceptive, but more laid back; they tend to pick on you with a stiletto, while the British ..." Reid finished the thought, "...kind of brain you." "So," Beveridge continued, "we were conscious of the differing styles and approach. There was also advantage in the fact that the international correspondents who came were, by and large, fairly senior figures: in other words, they were experienced, they were out of London or out of the States, and so therefore, you tended to have less difficulty with experienced journalists than you do with characters who are new." Beveridge added that freelancers were particularly difficult.

The SIO officials were sympathetic to the pressures of the reporters. "It's like everything else: these fellows are down there to do a job, you have to recognize that. They are driven by terrible competitive pressures, and therefore, one tries to understand in these situations the demons that are driving them, and to try to manage the flow of information to them...It's quite important...because you do have a major event. The public at large is wondering what's going on, and the State cannot regard the event as being exclusively theirs. One has to get into the business of communicating."

Beveridge said that he and Reid are convinced that "if your team comes on the ground late, you can lose that little slot of opportunity." In the case of the SIO's performance, "because of the speed at which we moved, we captured (that slot). The mechanism was ready, it was there, and that's because of the speed at which SIO operates in the normal course of events. This is a very busy office. We issue about 2,200 news releases a year, and we are involved in most of Scotland's events, so the teams here are used to operating at very high speeds. We simply translated our experience and our methods of operation and the speed at which we work onto the Lockerbie operation. It was just 'there it was. . .*let's go*!' And there wasn't much questioning."

The level of cool professionalism exhibited by Beveridge and his staff throughout the Lockerbie disaster should not be confused with cold indifference. "Lockerbie, for us, was not just another event," the deputy director said. "We became emotionally involved in Lockerbie — we still are. Lockerbie produced on the press officers — and I'm not a great man for post-traumatic stress disorder — but there was a psychological effect on the staff. Some refused to be sent back; others had flashback activity; others couldn't sleep. The stress of dealing with that — and stress is, part of the job, you know, working here, we sign on for a stressful life — but there was an effect I think on everybody who went to Lockerbie. If people went to Lockerbie and said 'It didn't affect me,' then I'd say they were liars...It had an effect, and it still does. I feel it whenever I have to talk about it."

Beveridge added, "It also had an effect on the journalistic community. Now we can argue that because we work in this life that we are pretty hardened people, and somewhat cynical — working journalists tend to be that way — but I think there was an effect on journalists themselves. One journalist said to me he would not go back to Lockerbie, he just couldn't. And that aspect has never been truly studied — the effect on the people there who had to deal with that."

Beveridge compared it to the experience of soldiers who had served in the Falklands or in Vietnam.

Reid remembered receiving phone calls in ensuing months from journalists who had been at Lockerbie on the first day who said, "Look, we realize that you've been under tremendous pressure; come out, have a cup of coffee." What the news people were doing was "anything to get us out of the office, and these were the journalists, those nasty cynical people out there, who had enough compassion to phone us and say, 'You're under too much pressure; come out of the office,' which I thought was very good of them to do."

The incident had physical ramifications, too. Reid said that one day, eight months after the bombing, it suddenly occurred to him that neither he, nor Beveridge, had had a free weekend since the night of December 21. Weekdays were very hectic, with about 70 percent of their time devoted to the developing criminal investigation and monitoring the content of worldwide media stories. Work days stretched to 8 or 9 o'clock in the evening. At home, sleep was often interrupted by phone calls from journalists halfway around the world in pursuit of a new lead. As developments unfolded, meetings were hastily called — at 3 a.m. if necessary. "Weekend after weekend we'd be on the phone to the Lord Advocate or to the Crown Office officials, or there would be a new development, I'd get a phone call and then I'd be on the phone to David, or he would get a call, and he'd phone me so that we would be speaking with the same voice," Reid said. "This went on and on and on, and suddenly we realized that we had not had a break."

If the SIO professionals were cognizant of the special needs of reporters covering disasters, they are even more sensitive to the concerns of survivors and the families of victims. Touring the smoking neighborhood of Sherwood

Crescent in preparation for an inspection by Prince Andrew, Beveridge and Reid were made painfully aware of the toll in very human terms: college sweats, holiday gifts, school books and sneakers were strewn everywhere among the rubble of a destroyed plane: "My God," Beveridge remembered thinking, "these are kids."

In planning a tour for the media, who were clamoring to get closer to the actual sites, Beveridge and Reid were in agreement. According to Beveridge, "we made a conscious decision that we couldn't take the media into certain areas because we already knew, for example, that the kids from Syracuse were there, and we certainly weren't going to have them photographed, so we tried to 'sanitize' that which people were seeing. I think that so far that has been the approach of Lockerbie, to spare the community at large and the public as much of the scenes down there as possible; we felt that there were certain things that the people who went to Lockerbie saw which we felt should not be seen. We were particularly distressed by one national newspaper because they showed the people who had fallen and who had left the imprint of the bodies on the ground...We were particularly annoyed with that newspaper for showing that because none of the other British papers or television had carried any of that sort of material, and also there was an unwritten rule that they would not show this insensitive material. There was a great deal of annoyance among the journalistic community with that particular newspaper for showing that. There were several harsh words exchanged at the time about it."

Beveridge pointed out that it was impossible to cordon off this entire area. With 845 square miles of countryside included in the search for victims and debris that might hold critical clues, there was not enough available manpower. Some journalists did wander off on their own, he said, but when they got into certain areas they realized themselves why the police did not want them there.

At one point, Beveridge continued, the media were agitating to go down to the crater. The SIO officer in charge, Bill Hoy, had told his colleagues that, as he took the media party to the site, "there was a great hush, and the great agitation disappeared. They all just stood there, and stood silently, because... there was a huge crater and the visual impact was terrific, and you could smell the kerosene, and there were small fires, and there was nothing left of the aircraft." Reid interjected: "It was vaporized." "Bits of human remains and...the smell was terrible. That was the scene," said Hoy, "and I think they (the journalists) were greatly affected by that."

Conventional wisdom among crisis communications experts calls for the selection and training of a spokesperson in advance of a crisis, centralization of information from that spokesperson, and a common willingness to co-operate with the media. The SIO press officers think that they scored on all three levels.

Allan Thomson, who along with Bill Hoy was the first SIO press team at Lockerbie, said, "We were so fortunate to have John Boyd; he was very receptive to interviews, and that certainly helped head off any potential media criticism that we were not readily forthcoming, or that we were withholding information." Early on the morning of December 22, Thomson recalls that he personally witnessed Boyd agreeing in rapid succession to five television interviews and six radio inquiries.

Since Boyd did not have his own press counsel in Dumfries, Thomson and Hoy served that role until Angus Kennedy could arrive. "We had unlimited access to everything. This was great, because as you might suspect, the natural reaction of the police is to not let outsiders in. But we were acting as Boyd's press officers. We went everywhere with him during the early tour of inspection of all of the different areas."

Boyd, like most police chief constables and other key Scottish government officials, had experienced sophisticated media exposure during training exercises. These media sessions are videotaped and played back for review and critique. Beveridge feels that in addition to gaining the necessary skills in public relations and media relations, the participants in these exercises bond together as a group. When the "real" crisis hits, there is already a working relationship established.

Beveridge advises that the public information staff must stay close to their sources "so that you are not misleading journalists, you're giving them the best information." But Beveridge sees a very limited spokesperson role for information officers. "Even with Angus (Kennedy, the police public information officer), the media don't necessarily want the monkey — they want the organ grinder; they want the lead character."

The SIO officers described themselves as particularly fortunate to have had John Boyd as the spokesperson for the Lockerbie operation. Beveridge explains:

> If you get somebody who's no bloody good, or not in charge, or who freezes up with the media, or if your experts whom you have brought in aren't comfortable...this affects how you are perceived...and the media will simply...well, as individuals they are very nice people, but as a group, they're a wolf pack hunting, and this can be frightening for people who are not used to that; it can be very alarming. The key decision-makers have got to feel comfortable and have some presence.

Beveridge notes that in the crisis exercises, "you can downplay information — but in reality information becomes one of the major factors they're dealing with. We tell chief constables and other decision-makers: 'How the media perceives you can make or break your career. If the media senses that you're not performing — if you don't appear positive and aware and on top of things, your career will be broken.' Very few people have got the skill to do that."

Looking back upon Lockerbie, Reid said, "It would be a very unwise chief constable...who did not appreciate the fact that the disaster which has befallen on his patch does not belong to him. There are people affected by the disaster — either on the site or across the Atlantic. It is his *duty* to keep them posted...He cannot take the disaster to his bosom and exclude everyone."

Crisis communications experts usually insist that the organizational leader arrive in person on the scene, and Beveridge and Reid subscribe to that theory. During the early hours of December 22, they learned that Prime Minister Margaret Thatcher would be coming to Lockerbie that morning. While the arrangements required much forethought and detailed work, they felt that her presence helped the situation. The symbolism is important, they say, because it conveys that the leader is concerned, that the leader has fully understood the gravity of the problem, and that the leader has sympathy for the survivors. On a very practical level, the visit of Margaret Thatcher had another advantage: by her seeing the degree of devastation first-hand, "there weren't going to be any problems with the Treasury." Manpower, supplies, equipment and funds to rebuild the destroyed neighborhoods of Lockerbie were quick in coming.

In retrospect, Beveridge and Reid suggested the performance of the press officers could be improved. "One of the lessons we learned was that it was not entirely satisfactory to have just the police and government together," Beveridge says. "We'd have all of the public information people from various organizations grouped together in one place for better coordination." During the Lockerbie incident, the public information officials of the various agencies were scattered throughout the town; in the case of the Department of Defence, public information officers for the Army and Air Force were headquartered in Fife. For Beveridge and Reid, having all of the public information officers in one place would have allowed them to speak with one voice when it came to granting media access to various sites, accuracy of facts, and official statements.[2]

"Second," Beveridge continued, "we'd want improved telecommunications because if you lose that, you lose the ability to know what's going on." In Lockerbie, the crash knocked out the local telephone lines, so officials turned to cellnet telephones. But this alternative also had difficulties: heavy use overloaded the cells in that area.[3]

Third, they would improve the "handover" process when one shift relieves the next at the 12-hour mark to ensure that the information flow is not distorted or interrupted.

In closing, they again stressed the importance of having trained, capable spokespersons willing to meet with the media because "information becomes one of the major factors" in a disaster. "This was reinforced by the Lockerbie experience where we had very capable spokespersons."

Beveridge warns that in crisis emergency exercises, the topic of information is often downgraded far below others such as rescue, food, etc., as almost an afterthought at the end of the agenda. "In reality, you cannot do that," he stressed, meaning that information should never be treated as secondary in a crisis situation.

Asked to recount the areas of performance in which they take the greatest pride, Brian Reid said that "in a very general sense, I suppose it's the fact that we have not encountered any direct criticism for the Scottish operation — there's been minor ones — but on broad base, I think our involvement as part of the overall team, our contribution has perhaps helped in spotting potential disaster areas that could have erupted, and we've been able to change the course of events so that didn't happen."

For Beveridge, pride comes from knowing that "when we were faced with the ultimate test, we were able to make it work, to cope with that pressure, and to achieve that which we had all planned and trained for...It will for me, I think, represent the high point of my career."

Scottish police

The man pedalled his bicycle as fast as his 70-year-old legs would allow. He bent forward, fighting a gale wind blowing across the Hebridean island of Coll, but he had a mission to complete. For him, it was an honor and a pleasure to carry a very special telegram to his neighbor, the vacationing Angus Kennedy: he had just been awarded the Queen's Police Medal for his service during the Lockerbie disaster. Kennedy was cited by Queen Elizabeth II for "his calm and immensely professional manner...under the quite exceptional pressures from the media." Kennedy's low-key response to the news was quite in character: "This comes as a surprise and a very great honor."

Kennedy, as a police superintendent and spokesman for the Strathclyde Police Force, headquartered in Glasgow, was well known to journalists in Scotland. The force he represents is the United Kingdom's second largest in terms of manpower, with an authorized strength of 7,000 officers and 2,000 civilian staff, and it covers the most area geographically. London's metropolitan force has more officers to cover less territory. For the past 13 years, Kennedy has served as the Strathclyde force's public information officer, an assignment that originally was to last only two years. When Kennedy was thrust into the international spotlight as the official spokesperson for the investigation into the bombing of Pan Am Flight 103, the attention revealed a highly skilled communicator.

Like most Scots, Kennedy can remember exactly how and when he heard the news. He was at home, off-duty, when he heard the television flash that an aircraft had crashed near Lockerbie. Kennedy knew immediately what that would mean for his department. Few newspeople outside Scotland would have any idea where Lockerbie was. "From past experience," Kennedy said, "if it's something that's vaguely Scottish, then they tend to phone Strathclyde Police, because we are the largest police force."

So Kennedy pressed the call-out button, and phoned his staff in their homes. As he made his way into the center of Glasgow, the streets were lit up with blue flashing lights. Emergency services were headed towards Lockerbie, exactly 70 miles south. Kennedy was in his office within 20 minutes. "Of course, the phones were ringing," he said. "I started handling media calls because they were pouring in." Media were looking for confirmation and information, even though Strathclyde Police suffered along with news organizations from a lack of solid information. "The roads were blocked, telephone lines were down; it was physically impossible to get accurate information back up the line over that distance."

Soon Kennedy was operating under a system known among U.K. police as "mutual aid," which permits a police force faced with a major operational problem requiring an abnormally large manpower commitment or specialist support to request aid from other forces. In this case, the smallest police force in the United Kingdom was asking for help from the second largest. "So we initially, on an ad hoc basis, provided a very basic kind of service to the media, and as it built up quickly, our lines were fully engaged." The flood of phone calls overwhelmed Kennedy and his department, even though within a half-hour, the staff included himself, an inspector who was his deputy, a sergeant and four officers, as well as a civilian clerk acting as an information officer. More staff came in as each hour passed. At the height of the operation about a dozen were working on media calls.

"Our main difficulty was going to be actually getting to Lockerbie," Kennedy said. He and his staff decided in the early hours they would be more useful as a satellite operation, "rather than getting lost trying to get to Lockerbie and losing continuity."

About 4 o'clock in the morning, the ringing of the phones became less insistent. During the lull, Kennedy managed an hour's rest, then boarded the first Chinook helicopter to Lockerbie, arriving about 7 a.m. The superintendent brought 12 staff members with him, leaving a skeleton crew behind.

For the next three months, and as needed thereafter, Kennedy assisted the Dumfries and Galloway Chief Constable John Boyd on the Lockerbie case.

Under Scots law, the responsibility for the investigation of sudden or unexplained deaths lies with the Lord Advocate and the Procurators Fiscal. It is the Chief Constable of the region, acting as the Procurator Fiscal's investigative agent and responsible for the handling and resolution of a disaster, who becomes the lead figure at the scene, becoming the apex of a triangle with all other agencies and support elements reporting to him. Acting now as Boyd's chief press officer, Kennedy served as the lead agency in the dissemination of information to the public through the media.

The Scottish Information Office press officials had already taken over the Masonic Hall as a media center, and Kennedy saw no reason to move it: "That became the point of contact for press conferences and control with the media in ensuing days." The local academy was becoming the control center for police operations, and the decision was made to keep the two centers apart: "That is just normal good police tactics, because there will be occasions when you have a center that you do not want the media to instantly observe and report on specific operations."

With the media center agreed upon, British Telecommunications personnel very quickly moved in and established priorities for telephones. With the town's communications system in chaos, there was a desperate need to establish linkages with the outside world. The media were, of course, clamoring for telephones. That's when a stranger walked in with a van filled with cellnet telephones. "I wouldn't know him today if he walked in the door," Kennedy smiled, "but it was a gift from heaven."

Another communications problem stemmed from the sheer fact that this was an international story, attracting crews from media outlets worldwide, some of whom spoke no English. The police force has official translators, but those officers were needed for the recovery effort, searching for bodies, luggage, and evidence. "So," Kennedy said, "we got high school teachers, who fortunately were on their Christmas holidays by this time." The German and French teachers helped the European journalists. Fortunately, when the Japanese crew arrived, they brought an interpreter with them.

In day-to-day relationships between government or corporate officials and reporters, there is often a "we-they" mentality. Angus Kennedy sees it differently, and for him, Lockerbie exemplified that difference dramatically.

"Unless you were there, you have absolutely no concept, and never could have, of what it was actually like," he said. "I describe it with one word, 'surreal.' That's exactly the way it was. And what you *must* understand, the media were *players* in that surreal scene"(author's emphasis). When reporters become actors in this scenario, Kennedy said, the relationship moves away from "we-they" and a special kind of relationship quickly develops between the media and the officials.

Kennedy illustrated how this happened in Lockerbie, when reporters began asking what anyone on the inside of the investigation might call "silly" questions. "But they weren't silly, because they were asking legitimate questions that the members of the public would ask. People are attuned to air disasters where there is a neat heap of wreckage and some skid marks at the end of a runway, or there's a 100-yard swath of trees down and there's a pile of aircraft parts on the side of a mountain. What they're not attuned to is 845 square miles of tiny little fragments...There was debris ranging from major parts of the aircraft to places where the whole thing had been vaporized, to papers being blown into the North Sea." So reporters were asking questions in the early hours of December 22 such as "Can I have a full name of (so and so passenger)?" or, "Can you give us a list of the dead?" or "Have you recovered the flight recorder?"

In those early hours, police were in no position to answer a great many of the questions being posed by reporters, Kennedy said. But he understood that these were legitimate questions for reporters to ask; these are the questions the editors were asking back at New York, Glasgow or London, or Hong Kong.

On the other hand, the police were having trouble dealing with the sheer size and scope of the disaster. "Now, you try and explain that and maintain credibility," said Kennedy, "and it's very difficult."

So Kennedy decided to show rather than tell them. "By this time the disaster area had been divided up into sectors and these sectors were controlled by police as far west as possible." He waited until emergency personnel had most of the horror covered, if not recovered, making at least a "semblance of 'sanitizing' the thing, so that people's senses were able to take it in." Then with the permission of the Chief Constable, the police spokesman took a convoy of 60 vehicles around the most immediate sectors. Reporters and photographers were able to see for themselves the rolling countryside where, he said, "pieces of aircraft were lying like confetti at a wedding."

Kennedy said "I didn't get any more silly questions after that, because it was so apparent to everyone exactly where they and we were at in this situation. And then we settled into what I think was a productive, constructive and sympathetic liaison with the media."

Despite this forged understanding with the first wave of reporters, Kennedy recognized a need to create some order in the media coverage, to prevent a circus atmosphere from developing. He faced several problems. One was the enormity of the story, with personal and political implications on many levels. Another was the voracious appetite of news crews, not only from the 21 countries represented by the Pan Am passengers and crew, but from all around the world. Then there were the special constraints of Scottish law on information dissemination, since the fact that this was a criminal inquiry, and not just a recovery mission, became clear very early on. Finally, there were issues of privacy, both for the residents of Lockerbie and for the families of the victims.

One way Kennedy assumed some control was to establish a system of press briefings every two hours. The amount of developing news was enormous, particularly in the first week, so press briefings gave Kennedy the opportunity to keep the flow of information going systematically. "Now, that didn't mean to say that I controlled the media in the sense that they did nothing else. It's a free country. We don't operate an accreditation system. We couldn't accredit 500 or 600 people. There's no way, (but) at least I knew where they were. They didn't stray too far, and they turned up on time for the two-hour briefings. I suppose in a way they just didn't gallop heedlessly around the place, completely uncontrolled. They had deadlines to meet with me, never mind their own deadlines."

After a while, the every-two-hour press briefings were replaced by a system of 9 a.m. press conferences, which set the scene for the day, and then at 4 o'clock or 4:30 p.m., a press conference rounding up whatever had happened that day.

Kennedy's scheduled news conferences were effective, but they could not totally solve the problem of continuity caused by turnover of media crews. "It was fine for four or five days, and then media people were going for their days off, or they went home for Christmas and came back the next day. They broke continuity and it's impossible for an information officer to be able to go back over old ground. There's too much happening, too many new developments. That fact causes confusion and difficulties when they fall behind in their knowledge and continuity in covering the story. Equally, crews who come late to the scene cause difficulties because they're starting to ask questions quite legitimately on the story as it stands with them, but forgetting that the whole body of the press corps are on to other things, and facts being asked are two or three days old. That's a bit difficult to handle at times, because you don't have the time to do what you would normally do, and that is to say to the person, 'Sure, just wait two minutes till I finish this, and then I'll come and I'll bring you up to scratch with what's been happening.' You don't have the time and resources for that. So they have to depend on each other, and you've got this kind of mutual support and sharing and pooling of information amongst the media. That was quite apparent."

Certainly news conferences alone could not totally feed the media's need for different kinds of information nor the voracious appetite for exclusive angles. According to Kennedy, "Somewhere there's an editor pulling the strings and telling them the kind of story they want for their papers because their job is to sell newspapers ...and they're looking for fresh stuff. The other point is: different countries, different organizations, different newspapers, have different levels of interest, stretching right across the whole gamut, from very erudite technical reports of the disaster to human interest. It wasn't easy because there are only 24 hours in the day. We were working 20-hour days."

Kennedy offered a piece of advice to those handling media relations in a disaster: "Never, ever, underestimate the resources you will need to deal with the media."

Kennedy's innate sensitivity to the media's wants and needs and his years of experience paid dividends at Lockerbie. He understood that major news stories have up and down periods and that in each major story are "milestones" that need the undivided attention of the public information staff; each milestone has the potential for a controlled flow of information or for disaster. He ticks off the Lockerbie milestones, starting with the bombing itself, followed by the quick realization that there were no survivors; the arrival of the VIPs (Prime Minister Margaret Thatcher, Prince Andrew, U.S. Ambassador to Great Britain Charles Price); confirmation that the cause was a bomb; the formal memorial service and the return of the first body to America; the establishment of the memorial stone and the garden of remembrance; the criminal investigation; and lastly, the anniversaries of the bombing. Reporters' interest will ebb and flow with each milestone, drawing them to Lockerbie for extended periods, or for occasional trips of intense activity.

Another standard technique used by Kennedy is the "media opportunity," both to maintain control and to give reporters access to stories they would normally be unable to get on their own. Kennedy reports examples of these media opportunities: "a conducted tour of the Police Incident Centre; shots of the 1,000 policemen being briefed in the morning before they started their hill searches; trips to strategic points in the search where there was something happening that was an important element in the story. These could be quite mundane things, like the 'Queen Elizabeths,' which is the name for the huge recovery vehicles used by the RAF to recover aircraft wreckage."

The traditional pull and tug between control and access got a complete workout during the Lockerbie disaster. One Scottish reporter remembers vividly the day American relatives arrived in town: "During the terrible days, of the 22nd, 23rd, 24th of December — when the world's media were going quite happily 'bananas' — when we knew relatives of the victims were coming in, the tabloids in particular were going totally batshit, trying to work out who the relatives were and get to them, and Angus at that morning's press conference said, 'Relatives are arriving this morning. They are *off limits*; if I catch any of you pestering relatives, action *will* be taken.' Just the way he said it, it was eloquent. There was no room for maneuver, no grounds for negotiation, nothing."

But Kennedy could compromise, too. According to the reporter, a few journalists approached Kennedy and during the discussion, "it was agreed that a relative would be approached, one that the police felt was strong enough to cope with the full circus." As the relative who was contacted by Kennedy recalls it, the police superintendent asked for the American's help. The proposal was low key, and when he hesitated Kennedy left him alone. The man, a brother-in-law of a businessman who died in the disaster, describes the experience in an earlier chapter. First he checked with the man's widow and then met with Kennedy again and stated his conditions. He would do the press conference in return for information and access to areas that would be off limits to most people. Kennedy agreed. The man's description of Kennedy as "the consummate professional" squared with what journalists said about him.

David Leppard of the *Sunday Times* still remembers his first encounter with Kennedy. "It was about two days after, and I'd been pestering him for an interview," he recalled. "And I walked into his office, and they had the names of the first five passengers on the blackboard and the names had not been released,[4] and I started, while he was answering the phone, copying them down. And when he put the phone down, he looked me straight in the eye and said, 'You give me that piece of paper right now. If you do that again, I'm never going to talk to you and you can get out of here.' So I gave him the piece of paper, he ripped it up and threw it in the bin. And I said, 'I'm awfully sorry.' He said, 'Okay,' and then proceeded not to tell me anything, but he was very professional about it and he understood the situation that I'm in."

Jim Freeman of the *Glasgow Herald* appreciated the fine line that Kennedy had to walk in dealing with the media. "You've got to remember that in Scotland, more so than any other European country, than practically any other Western country, there's a predisposition on the part of the authorities toward secrecy," Freeman said. "This is one of the strongest forces that we, in Scottish newspapers, have to combat all the time. Official secrecy is total in Scotland. We get information from the Strathclyde Police or from the Scottish Office as a matter of privilege. They dole out information to us as — and when — they feel like it." Then Freeman added, "Naming Angus Kennedy (as spokesman for the investigation) was a masterstroke."

Scots law puts constraints on reporters and public information officers quite unknown to practitioners in America, and Kennedy faced these constraints at Lockerbie once it was determined that it would be a criminal investigation. Reporters may not broadcast or print anything of an evidentiary nature; offenders can be charged with "conspiracy to pervert the court of justice."

Scots law placed upon Kennedy as the police spokesman a responsibility to protect the interests of potential defendants, so that any trial they have, or any plea they enter, is not impaired. Otherwise, he runs the risk of contempt of court. Kennedy explained that "it's called 'The Lord Advocate's Guidelines' and it's quite different to England, never mind America. So I had to be very careful in what I handled and what I gave to the media, so the idea and the criterion I work to is *withhold* only what you must, rather than *give* only what you must."

Faced with a multitude of constraints and pressures, Kennedy said, "Really, the only thing you can do is try and be an honest broker and respond." His ground rules: "You're always truthful, you don't make promises you can't come up with, and so on...By working these rules, I found, you got the desired effect; you got the reaction of trust and so you were building up a trust and understanding, and that is what I got, the understanding of the media at Lockerbie."

Kennedy offered this example. Before an early requiem mass for the dead, he received word that the relatives of the passengers refused to come if the media were covering it. Kennedy went to the media and explained the situation. A compromise was struck involving Kennedy, the parish priest, and the media. The priest agreed to one microphone and acoustic lead, no cameras in the church. The microphone was rigged unobtrusively in the church, just like an ordinary public address system and the cable was run outside to a soundbox provided by ITN in London. Everyone fed off the soundbox, placed around the corner out of sight of the relatives. The relatives felt comfortable enough to come to the service, and the media stood on the other side of the road.

While some relatives hid from the media, others did want to talk. Kennedy set aside a room in the police station where anyone — relative or Lockerbie citizen — could voluntarily come to be interviewed. Kennedy said that this arrangement also helped with the media's need for exclusivity, since they could meet one-to-one with a relative and not be forced to have everything as a "media opportunity" open to all.

An important technique for managing coverage was pooling, in which journalists volunteer to represent the rest of the media and then share what they obtain. Pooling worked well, according to Kennedy, because reporters and photographers understood the difficult situation and cooperated. "I found if I said to cameramen...'We're going in...but there's only room for a certain number of cameras,' very quickly there was no problem in them agreeing for the night who was to be the American camera, who was to be the British camera, because of the two different technological systems for television. And we really then developed a system of a duty press corps on behalf of the other press members, so that if something was happening, I could just say, 'Get the pool team here in five minutes, and we're going off in a police car to film whatever, and that included a reporter or a stills cameraman. And I think this was built on trust and understanding. If I was calling them — and I'm not being egotistical about it — they obviously had decided that they could trust me and trust my judgment."

Kennedy says that he has heard many complaints about the media's performance in Lockerbie, but for him, "I can say, hand on my heart, when I put it to them, I got support and I got understanding and I got cooperation. And I assume a reason I got that was because, in turn, I was providing a service which was allowing them to do their job. The person who benefited at the end of the day I would hope would be a relative, or the community, or the investigation, or the reporter doing his job, or the public. And we could make the best of a terrible situation."

Early on Kennedy said he realized that he had several different audiences. "Material that I was putting out I was able to package in different ways, because what the U.K. market (needed) was not the same as (what) the American market (needed)."

He explains the situation this way: "On Day One of the situation, I put myself in the position...if it was a relative of mine or a countryman of mine who had died in an air disaster over Arizona, I wouldn't have the foggiest notion where it was, (or what is) a 'sheriff' as in John Wayne westerns. Or (who is) Highway Patrol, FBI, State Department, or anyone else who was handling bodies, property, enquiries — 'And who is this guy, the DA? And where does he fit in?' And equally, I'm standing there talking about Chief Constables, Deputy Chief Constables, Lord Advocates, Solicitor Generals, Procurators Fiscal, the law of Scotland, and this is for consumption by people in America and throughout the world. So, you have to adapt your materials."

In the 20-hour days of meeting the information needs of the media, Kennedy said that he tried but failed to monitor the actual end-product. "We weren't able to devote resources to looking in depth at media coverage, interpreting the media coverage, and taking steps to counter, or put a balance on it...We weren't able to research and interpret what was actually appearing and what the level and content of information actually was reaching the consumer, the public. We had a vague idea, but you couldn't have the luxury of time to actually read and analyze (the clips) or TV broadcasts, here in the U.K., never mind the States or anywhere else."

By January and February 1989, Kennedy and his staff were becoming aware of a great deal of negative reaction from the victims' families in the U.S., coming in the form of letters to government officials complaining bitterly about the handling and return of personal effects. The rumors circulating revolved around misinformation that property would not be returned, or that it was going to be destroyed. The Lord Advocate and the Chief Constable were appalled: "Nothing could be farther from the truth," said Kennedy, "and nothing could be more calculated to upset someone who has suffered a loss. We were conscious of this and we couldn't understand it, because we kept making it clear what was happening, regularly putting out information. This misinformation was reaching very, very alarming proportions, particularly in the United States. Now, where it was coming from I don't know — I suspect it was rumor and misinterpretation and the lack of official information in the States."

With the unprecedented backing of the Lord Advocate and the Chief Constable, Kennedy's solution was to arrange a day-long media tour February 16, 1989. Two coaches were hired, taking over 100 international journalists, mostly Americans, to the property store, giving them a 90-minute, detailed explanation of how the property was being handled, logged, and stored for eventual return to the families. Kennedy hoped the media would relay the Scottish government's sensitive handling of this delicate matter, and reinforce the fact that all property would be returned, not destroyed, as had been rumored among the families.

Then the tour moved from Lockerbie to Longton, some 16 miles away, to a Ministry of Defence establishment where, in an enormous shed with three acres of floor space, the "Maid of the Seas" was laid out, still in pieces, but all charted on an elaborate grid system. Eighty percent of the plane had been recovered at that point; to move around the enormous shed, the equivalent of three football fields, police traveled on bicycles. At Longton, Kennedy made sure that reporters got an exclusive, behind-the-scenes look at the elaborate police effort to reconstruct the explosion, to document its devastating effects, and to piece together clues that might lead to the terrorists.

Finally, the tour returned to Lockerbie where Scottish officials held a news conference to answer the visiting journalists' questions. As expected, the question on the status of the criminal investigation was raised. One of the senior officials reported that the bomb had been hidden in a radio cassette player. A follow-up question-and-answer led to the announcement that the airport where the cassette player had been put aboard in a suitcase was Frankfurt.

Kennedy was pleased by the tour, but "very disappointed to find that the misinformation continued" in the United States. "The story ran throughout the world as 'Bomb in radio; balance of probability Frankfurt,' and all the other stuff (about the return of property and the investigation) fell off the edge of the page, and was never used by the media."

Kennedy knew that the cassette player and revelations about Frankfurt would be big news, but he hoped that the many hours of touring the property room and the Longton reconstruction effort would also translate into stories.

"We gave them unprecedented insights; we gave them footage not available before or after, but it did not matter one hoot. Editorial decisions were made on what sells newspapers, and the information on the return of property and the investigation were of interest to a relatively small audience — the relatives and other police investigators — not the general public." Kennedy tempered his frustration with the reality of editorial decision-making: "The story lines the editors chose to run were about bombs and Frankfurt and terrorists. Fine, that's up to them. But what can I do then? You can't recycle old stuff, so what do we do?"

The answer was an age-old communications device: again, with the approval of the Lord Advocate and the Chief Constable, he went directly to the victims' relatives, bypassing media channels altogether. He gathered up his charts and his slides and his handouts and his crew: Deputy Chief Constable Paul Newell; Douglas Roxborough, the officer in charge of the property room; and David MacMillan, the inspector who had spoken to many of the next of kin in the registration of deaths. At the invitation of the American relatives, they travelled to New York, Boston, Washington, Detroit and Canton, Ohio. Kennedy finally was pleased. "That was a very moving, very harrowing experience, but very worthwhile and satisfying in the strict sense of helping another human being with a very real problem, and I think we did that. I'll never forget one minute of that trip to the United States. I think we were able to fulfill for them, at that time, *a very deep need* for information, a very deep need. In some instances we had no choice but to be brutally frank. We didn't try to euphemize the situation. People wanted information and we told them, and we found that they seemed to be able to gather strength from that and the people who came into the room — they were different people going out...That's the wrong way to put it, but they seemed to perhaps be lighter of step or easier in mind, or something, because there was here a connection, and here was information."

To this day, Police Superintendent Kennedy is in frequent communication with the families of the victims of Pan Am Flight 103.

Pan American World Airways

In the 1960s, Pan American Airways boasted a worldwide corporate communications department of 120 staff members. But for Pan Am the 1980s were — as they were for many other major corporations — a time for downsizing and retrenchment. Even many of the Fortune 500, the top 500 industrial corporations in America in terms of sales, had cut back on public relations, merged the function with human resources and, in far too many cases, had eliminated formal public relations units altogether (McCauley, 1990).[5]

In 1988, Pan Am still maintained a communications office, but years of corporate cutbacks had reduced the public relations staff to a Vice President, four managers and two clerical staff, all in New York City. In London, there was a public relations practitioner, but he reported to the marketing department. The budget was approximately $1.3 million; no outside public relations counsel was kept on retainer.

Those changes reflected adjustments that had been made throughout the airline that Charles Lindbergh helped build. In a 1991 article entitled "Pan Am: The Fall of a Legend," Peter Wilkinson described the international carrier in its heyday:

> A national treasure, Pan Am also became part of popular culture. In the fifties, Norman Rockwell illustrated Pan Am ads. Ernest Hemingway told *Look* magazine readers: "Pan Am and I are old friends...I feel as safe with Pan American as I do any morning I wake up to a good working day." Greer Garson was aboard when Pan Am made the first jet run from Idlewild (JFK) to Paris in 1958 — $490 in first class, $272 in economy. Passengers tasted Caspian caviar and truffled Strasbourg goose-liver pate. Gentlemen freshened up with Remington electric shavers before landing. A "bridal suite" was available to newlyweds. Pan Am hotels offered the same Sealy mattress everywhere in the world. Pan Am called itself "The World's Most Experienced Airline," and nobody could argue the point (p. 21).

By 1988, Pan Am had come under unfavorable scrutiny from the financial community. For five consecutive years, a *Fortune* magazine survey had shown Pan Am among the ten least admired corporations in America, according to corporate executives, outside directors, and financial analysts (Baig, 1987). It was no time for a "crisis," defined by Curtis G. Linke of United Technologies' Pratt and Whitney as "any abnormality of negative consequences intruding into the daily course of operations. It is usually a surprise. A crisis can kill, degrade the quality of the living, reduce wealth or diminish reputation"(Carter, 1989, p.166).

For Pan American Airways, the terrorist bombing of Flight 103 fits the definition of "crisis" on all counts. The bombing meant dishonor for the airline, and a step toward its eventual dissolution.

In 1988, the Vice President of Corporate Communications was Jeffrey Kriendler, who had joined Pan Am one month after his 1968 graduation from Cornell University with a degree in hotel administration. He never worked anywhere else. Kriendler knew Pan American World Airways like the back of his hand. He began his 23-year career with Inflight Services, worked in the Operations Division, Dining Services, Public Affairs, Investor Relations,

Financial Relations, and Public Relations. At one point, he headed up Inflight Services, but, in May 1982, he returned to Corporate Communications as its vice president, responsible for media relations, publicity, promotion, internal relations, and investor relations. He served as Pan Am's senior spokesperson.

For Kriendler, the bombing of Flight 103 represented a professional and highly personal tragedy. In May 1991, Kriendler, just 44, suffered a stroke, attributed to job-related stress, and returned to work just in time to witness the final months of his once-superior company. While the bombing of Pan Am Flight 103 did not cause the airline to go out of business, he notes, "it sped the breakup of the company, and thus its demise."

On December 21, 1988, shortly before 2:30 p.m. EST, Pan Am's Chairman and Chief Executive Officer, Thomas G. Plaskett, ran down the hall and interrupted Kriendler's telephone conversation with a *Wall Street Journal* reporter. Plaskett's curt message chilled Kriendler. The words he remembers are: "Jeff, we have an emergency. We believe 103 is down."

Less than a half-hour had elapsed as air control at Prestwick reported to Heathrow that the plane had disappeared, Heathrow relayed the information to Pan Am Operations at the London airport, and Operations notified New York at JFK. Kriendler estimates that by 2:45 p.m., the media calls had begun. By 3:15, it is his recollection that CNN was showing scenes of Lockerbie's burning petrol station.[6]

Kriendler briefed his staff on the scant details available, and while they returned to the telephones, geared up for what he knew would be a long night. First, Kriendler prepared his initial statement for the media: the flight number, its route, the number of passengers, and the point of last contact. It was simple, but it was all the information he had. Then he developed an emergency work schedule that would send home some employees to rest in the wee hours of December 22 so that they could return at 5 a.m. The group who worked through the night would go home for a short time at 5 a.m., returning around noon.

Kriendler's first encounter with large numbers of reporters came at a news conference held sometime between 5 and 6 p.m. EST at Pan American's midtown Manhattan headquarters. Kriendler says that "we felt obligated to respond to the media...We certainly didn't know what caused the tragedy, but we knew we had a disaster of monumental proportions." Kriendler's audience at this point was approximately 70 local and network reporters, and CNN. At that news conference Kriendler promised another briefing later in the evening at Pan Am's terminal at JFK on Long Island. "I went to the airport and did it there, too," he says. "I did it as an accommodation to the media...It was the last thing I wanted to do...It was the worst trip (driving from headquarters to the airport) of my life."

To make Kriendler's distress even more acute, he got stuck in traffic, delaying his arrival at the airport. Kriendler's recollection is that, despite the delay, he still arrived in time to conduct the news conference at the announced time of 8 p.m. Reporters who were on the scene said in separate interviews that, when the promised news conference did not materialize at the appointed hour, many of them started roaming the airport corridors in search of a story. Instead of Pan Am's official spokesperson, they turned their attention to arriving families and friends of the victims.

Kriendler rushed to the appointed place, a room then known as Pan Am's California Lounge (now operated by Delta), which had been set up in typical news conference style: a podium and microphone, a mult box for reporters to plug in their recording devices, rows of chairs, and refreshments. He had no prepared statement, but repeated the information given at the earlier news conference and then tried to answer reporters' questions.

Kriendler remembers the media crowd during the news conference as being not overly aggressive or adversarial: "I thought they were rather well behaved...They were not accusatory; they were respectful and appreciative of Pan Am's loss." The questions dealt predominately with the aircraft itself (its age, dates of its last structural upgrade) and the passengers. The kind of media present were different from the business and travel press with whom Kriendler normally worked. He described that as "part of the problem." He explained, "The people who cover this (kind of story) are the general reporters. And there are a lot of 'hangers-on,' stringers...They're the worst, even in New York."

Even though Kriendler answered questions for nearly 40 minutes, the reporters followed him out of the room. Surrounded by Pan Am security officers, and with reporters swarming about them, Kriendler left the California Lounge and headed for the First Class Lounge, which by that time had become a sanctuary for the grieving families. "I had media surrounding me on all sides, aggressively. The BBC was memorable because they asked about one of their guys (whom they feared was aboard Pan Am Flight 103)."

Kriendler has the highest praise for the security guards who faced the media onslaught that night. "Our immediate objective was to shield the families and to protect them from the media...Airport staff did a wonderful job under tremendously tense circumstances...We knew the media would be intrusive beyond belief."

Kriendler, of course, is well aware of how intrusive some reporters became as they intercepted family members. But since airports have become the equivalent of small cities, since departure lounges are considered public spaces with unlimited access, and since the physical layout of the Pan Am departure area formed a U-shape around the first-class lounge, Kriendler feels that security faced a most difficult situation: "How to protect everyone from the media? That would be impossible."

Pan Am swung quickly into action at the airport, he said. Access to the glass-enclosed First Class and Clipper Class Lounge was cut off both from the outside arrival driveway and from the airport corridors. To control the media, Kriendler said, barriers were set up at least 20 feet away from the double metal doors leading from the inside corridors into the lounge, but the crush of reporters, lights and microphones that confronted family members who tried to reach the lounge remains for relatives an enduring memory of the night. Inside, the collection of luxurious couches, small tables and exotic greenery that usually soothe weary, well-heeled travelers became a refuge for stunned and weeping relatives and friends. Technicians from New York Telephone moved quietly among them, setting up a telephone line for each family. Clergy, Red Cross volunteers, Pan Am staff and airport medical personnel approached the distraught families with words of sympathy and offers of food and beverages. Kriendler himself visited each family group.

In 20 years, Kriendler had seen his share of airline disasters. He remembers two in particular before Flight 103. In 1973 PLO terrorists lobbed grenades onto a Pan Am airplane at Rome's airport, killing 30 people. In 1977, he served as the lead Pan Am spokesperson for the collision at Tenerife in the Canary Islands, involving a Pan Am 747, a KLM 747 and the loss of lives of 577 passengers. Seventy survived, including 15 who were physically unharmed.

Comparing Tenerife and Lockerbie, Kriendler cited important differences, beginning with the fact that the Canary Islands tragedy was clearly a case of pilot error. "As hard as it was that you were involved in such a disaster, the story came out almost immediately that KLM had taken off without permission," he said, adding, "So you had no feeling of responsibility for the disaster; you were absolved of that almost immediately — it's very unusual, but the Dutch investigating team revealed this almost the second day...(Tenerife) was uplifting in that you had survivors and you saw the human spirit of those people who assisted other people in evacuating the aircraft."

More than a decade elapsed before the Lockerbie disaster, which meant ten years of advancement in technology and communications, Kriendler explained. That made communications more instantaneous, and the Scottish site was also closer to London, a world media capital. Tenerife, he said, was rather remote. As is often the case in disasters in outlying areas, (it) "would be a much larger story had (it) occurred nearer a media center." Finally, Kriendler notes that with the other disasters he faced as a corporate communicator, the duration of the story was several days. Lockerbie and its aftermath have stretched on for years.

Kriendler contends that no public relations staff and no crisis communications plan could have met the monumental demands of the Lockerbie disaster: "I think this was a tragedy of proportions that were out of control." He cited his reasons: "One, this was an act of sabotage, this was not an act of God. This was not a human error, but there is the intent here to destroy human life. It was a festive time of year when people were returning home to be with their loved ones. That's true, understand, of the crew members, too — don't separate the crew members who were lost from the passengers. It happened near a media capital; there was no other hard news. It was an act of terrorism. There was a young population on the aircraft. There were so many Americans. And it happened to Pan Am — Pan Am, *the* flag carrier."

The red folder that held Pan Am's emergency plan sat on the desk of every senior officer and key operating manager. Every major discipline that might be involved in a crisis had its own section: Operations, Engineering, Communications (telecommunications), Security, Medical, Legal, Insurance, Marketing, Corporate Communications, Field Services, Cargo, Flight Services, and Flight Operations. Each section contained a checklist of steps to follow. In charge of the overall plan was the head of Operations, the person responsible for the day-to-day activity of the airline.

Kriendler said he does not know the exact origin of the plan, but added, "I'm sure it was the outgrowth of problems the company had experienced, drawing upon the...review of how the event was handled, and trying to establish procedures for the future." After each case, he said, the airline would conduct a post-incident review to go over the emergency plan and update it. Prior to Lockerbie, Kriendler said, the most recent incident would have been the Boeing 727-200 crash in 1982. In that case the airliner was taking off from New Orleans International Airport during a thunderstorm and crashed into a residential section of Kenner, a suburb. All 145 on board the plane perished, eight lives on the ground were lost and 14 houses demolished or heavily damaged. Investigators eventually blamed that disaster on "wind shear," dangerous shifts in wind speed and direction that can throw a jet to the ground. In addition to the post-incident reviews, Pan Am periodically would conduct mock accidents as a test of its emergency preparedness, Kriendler said.

Of this 30-40 page manual, Kriendler estimated that the Corporate Communications plan comprised two pages. The checklist included such activities as coordinating with Operations; distributing advisories to the field, mostly the internal dissemination of information about the incident; dealing with the marketing department on the notification of next of kin; and working with the media in the dissemination of information.

In two separate interviews, Kriendler looked back at the strengths and weaknesses of his department's efforts in the face of Pan Am's greatest crisis.

When he took over the corporate communications department in 1982, it employed approximately 14 people. Shortly thereafter, his staff was reduced to nine. More cutbacks occurred in 1985 and in 1987, bringing the corporate communications staff to a bare-bones crew of four, two managers and two clerical staff. In August of 1988, Kriendler felt fortunate to be able to add two more managers, for a total staff of six. Five months later, these new hires would face a most grueling baptism. Kriendler is proud of the performance of his staff: "In no way would I question the professionalism or the loyalty of my people; they were wonderful."

Despite the company's financial travails in the decade preceding Lockerbie, Kriendler felt that he had the support of CEO Tom Plaskett, and "resources were never a problem during the Lockerbie crisis. But," he continued, "the resource that we desperately needed to do our job properly would be to have a sufficient staff to respond to the media inquiries and to be of assistance. This unfortunately we did not have."

Plaskett, who had been CEO of Pan Am just 11 months at the time of the attack on Flight 103, was "very cognizant of the need to bring in help," said Kriendler, and Plaskett personally contacted Burson-Marsteller, a prestigious international public relations counseling firm with which he had worked in another company's time of crisis. A full working relationship did not materialize during the Lockerbie incident; Kriendler did not feel that outside counsel was the answer at that point because it would take too long to bring the outside counselors up to speed.

Being shorthanded was not the only problem Kriendler faced. Matters were made worse by glitches in the system. First, according to Kriendler, the phone lines were "lit up all night." Although in his estimation they had sufficient lines, global interest in the story caused problems. "What we realized was that we were doing the media a disservice to allow a small Australian radio station to get through, blocking a line, when we should be talking to AP (Associated Press)." In the post-Lockerbie debriefing, Kriendler recommended that his department designate lines for the wire services alone to avoid this problem in the future. Because the wires serve thousands of media outlets, insuring that they are quickly informed expedites the flow of information to everyone.

Compounding the problem of already jammed incoming lines was the fact that television media inadvertently flashed across the viewers' screens the telephone number of the corporate communications office in addition to the pre-established numbers designated by Pan Am for relatives seeking information on the downed flight. Kriendler and his staff found themselves "getting general public calls. This continued all night, into the next day...This takes up time, it takes up a line." Of course, this added to a complaint the authors heard many times from family members: they couldn't get through to Pan Am at all. This would certainly be the case if they were trying the corporate communications number instead of Pan Am's emergency information lines designated for families.

Pan Am's emergency check list for the Marketing Department included such practical actions as the immediate cessation of all advertising. It also reminded personnel not to distribute newspapers on flights the next day, as was customary. Kriendler remembered one thoughtful employee who contacted him for advice at 12:30 a.m. on December 22. She suggested that the scheduled inflight movie be changed and sought Kriendler's approval even though this activity did not fall within his normal span of responsibilities. The current selection was "Die Hard."

Kriendler argued that the employee's sensitive question was a common sense approach and "you can't put that in the manual...A lot of people used excellent judgment that night." But he added, "Some people were shocked and stunned (by the tragedy)...and their judgment was impaired."

One lapse of judgment caused great pain to many family members seeking information by telephone. Since the emergency plan called for reservations lines to be used for family inquiries, many families report being "greeted" by the piped-in Christmas carols normally in place at that season. One relative, when put on hold, had to endure the cruel irony of the instrumental version of "I'll Be Home for Christmas."

According to Pan Am's crisis plan, responsibility for notification of next of kin fell to the Marketing Department. During the evening of December 21, while the Marketing Department was dealing with frantic relatives, Kriendler's group concentrated on the media calls coming in from all over the world. Perhaps the greatest controversy around Pan Am's handling of the media during the crisis relates to the release of the passenger list. Even four years later, Kriendler said he was certain that Pan Am's policy of withholding release of any names until the notification of the next of kin was not violated. Yet television reporters at two different stations in Syracuse, New York, who broadcast a list of student names early in the evening of December 21, cite Pan Am as their source.[7] Robert Hill, Syracuse University's vice president for public relations, said his own call to a Pan Am employee resulted in his obtaining the list, but his office did not officially release student names until the next day (see next section).

Kriendler's conviction is reinforced by his recollection that he was aware "very early on that a large group of Syracuse students was on board. What was disturbing (was) that I thought Syracuse (University) had released the names before we did." He explained that "our procedure is not to release the official list until we had a feeling that most...of the notification of next of kin had taken place."

Kriendler feels such a list is not important to anyone except the media because the relatives have either been notified directly by the airline or have seen news reports and have contacted the airline themselves. "The media, in their quest, which may be overzealous, wants that list to do the local story...They're going to try to get that list. The guy in Phoenix is not so much interested in the story, but he wants the local angle: Did someone from Arizona perish?"

The intense interest from "local" reporters worldwide seeking to know if any of their citizens were on board led to another post-Lockerbie procedure at Pan Am: passengers' nationalities were from that point on entered into the computer, so that the manifest would show names and countries, making it easier to alert families and media.

Whenever there is an aviation accident, the airline involved immediately sends a "go team" of investigators to the site, while other officials remain behind in one or more control centers. By midnight of December 21, a "go team" from London had arrived in Carlisle, on the England side of the border with Scotland. Flying through the night from New York City, another "go team" from corporate headquarters was led by the Vice President for Operations; it included the medical director, flight service staff, maintenance experts and representatives from the union, legal staff, and insurance carrier.

In the memories of many family members who went to Lockerbie in the days immediately after the disaster, there was a distinct difference between the treatment they received from the London staff versus the New York City staff. They contend that relatives who arrived in the first few days after the bombing were treated with great sympathy and empathy by the London staff; they attribute this to the fact that the Flight 103 crew had been London-based and their loss affected their London colleagues personally. They compare this with what they consider the brusque treatment by the corporate staff, and contend that Pan Am was already fearful of monumental lawsuits and translated that fear into a curt and pro forma treatment of the families.

Kriendler said he finds this criticism difficult to understand, and that very little time would have elapsed between the arrival of the two "go teams," and, he added, there would have been no difference in treatment. He said that "things were very homogeneous in Lockerbie...They were one, the corporate team was the London team; they were the same team." His explanation for the relatives' perceptions: "I think longer into it, they (the families) got more frustrated by the red tape of the Scottish authorities in getting the remains out, but I think that the relationship between (our) people they met early on maintained (a) strong bond."

Pan Am's efforts to shield the relatives from the horrors of Lockerbie were also misconstrued, according to Kriendler. Upon the advice of Scottish police and the Pan Am staff in London, the corporate staff tried to discourage relatives from making the trip to Lockerbie. When at least two dozen relatives refused this advice, Pan Am flew them from New York to London. The airline tried to get the relatives to stop at this point, and tried again when the group reached Glasgow. Each time, the relatives would not consider stopping; finally buses were provided, and the group travelled the remaining miles to Lockerbie. Pan Am was also criticized for its handling of the arrival. As the relatives in one group stepped down from the bus, they were forced to walk between rows of reporters who shouted questions to them. The relatives said Pan Am should have planned a route that avoided this encounter.[8]

Another nightmare originated in the airline's "buddy system." The term "buddy system" in itself stirs controversy because of ongoing disagreements in the American airline industry and in legal circles on the role of "buddies." In the eyes of airline officials, "buddies" are caring individuals assigned by the airline to each family who loses a loved one in an airline accident. Their purpose is to serve as a liaison between the company and the family, providing sympathy, information, and human connection to a large corporate entity. To attorneys who represent families in lawsuits against airlines, "buddies" are little more than corporate spies, sent by their superiors at the time of the family's greatest vulnerability, to gather information that can be used by the airline to keep down the cost of lawsuits. Often, plaintiffs' attorneys will counsel their clients to refuse any such overtures.

In the case of Pan Am, the criticism of the "buddies" began almost immediately, even before attorneys entered the picture, because the Pan Am employees had little or no training in this very difficult job. Kriendler admitted this criticism is legitimate.

At Pan Am, responsibility for the development of a "buddy system" fell to the Marketing Department. The network of "buddies" was developed at the time of an accident from the ranks of reservation and sales representatives. "Understand this," Kriendler said. "One moment you're a technician who's involved in creating programs for the reservations system. The next moment you're thrust into this terrible, terrible job (of assisting grieving relatives). No one is prepared for it mentally. Many had never done it before. Many of the people never even realized that they would be called upon to act in this role. Since then — it's all moot now — we did set up a program to train people in advance who might have to deal with these families."

Kriendler added that in such situations, "you're damned if you do, and damned if you don't...Understand that the plaintiffs' lawyers[9] want to finger the airline as the bad guy. They want to criticize this buddy system as a phony system. (The lawyers say) 'They don't really care about you. It's all just PR.'"

Many public relations practitioners are fond of saying that "perception is reality," meaning that how an individual or action is viewed is often more real, and carries more significance, than the actual situation. In the case of Pan Am 103, the airline became — in the eyes of the families of the victims — an irresponsible, uncaring, insensitive company that had sacrificed 270 innocent lives on the altar of corporate greed and incompetence. The early clues that the plane had been brought down by a bomb smuggled aboard the "Maid of the Seas," and that airlines and diplomats had been warned of a bomb threat, changed grief to rage for many relatives. This was no longer "just" a crash; this was pre-meditated mass murder.

Even as the disaster neared its fifth anniversary, key questions about the bombing — especially why it was ordered and by whom — still remained unanswered. In the early days after the disaster, Kriendler said, the family members sought answers to many such questions and they sought a target for their deep and bitter anger. "Not having the enemy...they attacked that which they could put their arms around...Pan Am, the government, security in general, the State Department."

Throughout our interviews with family members, the research team heard complaints about the unceremonial return of bodies from Scotland. One military man's family felt that the coffin was treated like so much air cargo, without the proper respect paid when the coffin was the last item off the plane, and not the first. The fact that the transfers often took place in cargo hangars, infiltrated with the smells of other cargo, was troubling to many. Some told how hurt and angry they were to see the bodies of their loved ones forklifted off the back of the plane in "cardboard boxes."

When Kriendler was asked about this criticism, he became visibly angry for the first and only time during the many hours of interviews. "All of the coffins came in this protective box...I can tell you how much the very nice wooden coffin cost, and where we got them, and how we sent them to Scotland, and I can tell you further that this is a *protective* box that wraps around the outside. It's standard in how you ship coffins by air." The coffins themselves were not cardboard.[10]

Kriendler and his staff had animated discussions on how to handle the mounting criticisms. One staffer in particular felt that Pan Am should be more aggressive in getting its story out through the media. There were two problems with this approach, according to Kriendler: First, in the case of the families, "you don't want to attack their credibility...you want to tread very lightly. In no way did you want to suggest that what they were saying was not correct. You wanted to get your point across, but you...certainly did not want to kick them when they were already down."

Second, unlike many of the families who could vent their frustrations in the media with what they regarded as an irresponsible airline, Kriendler's hands were tied by legal constraints when it came to communicating to newspeople. Kriendler reported many discussions took place between Pan Am's legal and communications departments. "The lawyers' interests are very parochial... Their interests are the trials which will occur three to seven years later. Our concern is immediate image and...marketing, that is — it's going to hurt your business and we want to shore up that confidence with the public as quickly as possible. Legal was concerned that some things you say are going to be drawn into the lawsuits against you."

Kriendler said that "Legal immediately descended on the process. Their *raison d'être*...is to protect the corporation from future liability, and they're going to be over your shoulder as you produce copy and as you speak."

While Kriendler was advised by the legal experts to speak as little as possible, family members were under no such restraints: "The family members were unrelenting, *unrelenting*," he said. "No matter how many times you presented facts...no matter how many times we explained...to the media, the family members continued with their allegations. Even though they weren't true, they permeated the public through constant barrage," he said, "...and it was sort of the popular feeling that Pan Am had been negligent." To this day, Kriendler is "frustrated and tired and angry" that the media would accept the distraught family members' charges that "we were insensitive when we weren't. Did we do a good job in getting (our side) out? Yes. Did they (the media) report it well? No."

Eventually, after about two months, according to Kriendler, "as these myths (about Pan Am's responsibility) perpetuated, and as they over ran the line to becoming a perception because the family members just persisted, Legal allowed us to be a little more aggressive." Was this new tactic too late? "I don't know," he replied.

Experts in crisis communications planning frequently discuss the "right" approach to be taken by the chief executive officer of a company undergoing a crisis. Some see it as imperative that the CEO step forward immediately and assume a very visible role as a communicator, including visiting the site of the crisis. Others are less insistent about having the CEO on site, as long as the public perception is that the CEO is in charge from the headquarters.

Kriendler has the highest regard for Tom Plaskett, describing him as "Excellent. Very cool. Well spoken. Credible. Smart." Yet Plaskett did not appear in public until eight days after the tragedy when he traveled to Lockerbie for the January memorial service. In looking back, Kriendler admits that Plaskett was "probably misguided," and was not aggressive enough in trying to go forward to the front himself. "Some people would criticize him for not being public enough right away, expressing his great sympathy, and being more forward, rather than leave it to a spokesman...This was such a major story that he should have been out front."

Kriendler speculated that the reason Plaskett did not go public right away was the unknown nature of the tragedy. "Usually you know what happened, but in this case it was unknown whether it was an act of sabotage or whether it was a mechanical malfunction, so I think that inhibited his going forward."

Kriendler reported that he did not really push Plaskett to go forward. "I guess I thought it was my job to be the bearer of bad news. Maybe I could protect him; that's what I was there for. That's what 'flacks' are there for — to take the flack." On the other hand, he debated aloud, "if it weren't Plaskett, then I would have thought that the Senior Vice President of Operations should go forward." Kriendler implied that legal and insurance issues played a role here, too: "The way the story was developing, we just had to back off, step back for a while."

Kriendler's comments about taking the flack are revealing of his thoughts on the role of the CEO in a crisis, and of his personal approach to his job. "In 23 years, I never missed a day. I was 'Iron Man' who could manage it all. But the last decade was tough (at Pan Am), and certainly the time since Lockerbie has been devastating."

Kriendler's workday was not really extended by the Lockerbie disaster, but it did change. His pre-Lockerbie routine was to get to the office by 6:30 a.m. each morning and work until 8:30 every night. After Lockerbie, Kriendler had to handle many more calls at home, calls at all hours of the night from reporters around the world, particularly those in the United Kingdom, who with a five-hour advantage would hear about developments in the case, and call him for Pan Am's official response. "As PR people, we understand that we don't leave the job at the door, but these calls were particularly taxing."

Kriendler, too, in a way, became a Lockerbie victim, although the toll it was taking on him became recognizable only after his stroke. "I pushed myself very hard. Interestingly, I thought I had it under control. I had no symptoms — no manifestation medically that a possible stroke victim might have, although I did think that I had taxed my system beyond the point of what one system could take — I was hoping to get to the point where the company either would be taken over or there would be some resolution to the corporate status. But I didn't make it."

Neither did Pan Am. Almost immediately after Lockerbie, the airline's bookings dropped off sharply, through August 1989. All American carriers were affected in their international sales. In March, following a hijack threat against American airliners, IBM had advised its 390,000 employees to avoid U.S. carriers in flying from Europe and the Middle East. News of that advisory exacerbated the trend for business travelers to avoid American airlines, and

British carriers picked up much of the business (Harlow, 1989). According to Kriendler, the bombing "hurt everyone; it hurt TWA; it hurt the U.S. flag. We (Pan Am) were hurt the most."

By September 1989, Pan Am officials could see that sales were coming around a bit, but it was too little too late. On November 14, 1990, Pan Am sold off important trans-Atlantic routes to its larger rival UAL Corporation in an effort to raise money to stay alive. It also announced cutbacks in its work force and passenger capacity in an attempt to shrink in size and become profitable. In early 1991, losing $2 million a day, Pan Am filed for Chapter 11 bankruptcy, which allowed it to keep flying under supervision of the courts. In mid-1991, it sought a white knight to come to its rescue, but it didn't happen. On December 4, 1991, just 17 days short of the third anniversary of the bombing, the company ceased to exist. Once again, reporters roamed the corridors of JFK, this time interviewing tearful employees who mourned the death of their beloved airline.

Kriendler reflects on those three years: "I don't think despite Lockerbie the company would have survived on its own. I think it sped the breakup of the company, and thus ultimately its demise. I don't think the company would have stayed independent, but I think it obviously would have been more attractive as a takeover candidate...I think the company would have been absorbed into another airline."

Syracuse University

Robert Hill, vice president for public relations at Syracuse University, recalls vividly the afternoon and evening of December 21, 1988, and the hordes of reporters it brought to his office: "It resembled a scene out of Alfred Hitchcock's *The Birds*, if you saw that movie. There's a kind of telephone line outside the schoolhouse...They show the scene and there's a bird sitting up there, perched, and they show the kids in the school house, learning and singing, and so forth, and then back to the telephone line, and there's three more birds, and then back to the school house, and then you look again and there's 500 birds sitting up there."

A few hours after he first heard of the tragedy, Hill stuck his head out of his office to see how his staff was coping. "It was the largest collection of reporters that I had seen." What followed is a classic example of the tug and pull between source and reporter and a revealing look at an organization caught by surprise.

Hill's career in higher education spans more than 20 years, but he had been named to the University's top public relations position only six months before the bombing. In addition to building the University's reputation for academic excellence, Hill had to deal with media interest in the school's sports stars, especially its basketball and football teams, which are regularly ranked among the top teams in the nation.[11]

While students bent over their final exams and professors calculated grades, Hill was at his desk developing a strategy for announcing a sensitive piece of news: the University's disciplinary action against a star basketball player and a freshman football player following an altercation with brothers of a campus fraternity. The incident "had popped about a week before, and that really was the big issue on campus: whether or not these guys (the athletes) were going to be allowed to 'get away with murder' or whether the University was going to be firm with them, be good disciplinarians. And...the big skeptics were the local media," Hill recalled.

About mid-afternoon, a secretary slipped Hill a note. It said a plane had crashed, and Syracuse University students and faculty travelling back from London might be aboard. Hill immediately phoned Chancellor Melvin Eggers. The university's top administrator had already heard the same report from Vice President for Undergraduate Studies Ronald Cavanagh, who is responsible for the University's Division of International Programs Abroad (DIPA).

A reporter stopped by Hill's office, seeking information, but the university's top public relations officer had none to give. "When I talked with the Chancellor his position was clear...'We will not make a public announcement until we have all the facts.'" Hill concurred. "He would get that kind of advice from me anyway, if he had not come to it on his own. And I said, 'Okay, that all makes sense,' so we will set about the business of getting the facts."

The decision against making a statement before receiving official confirmation, however, formed the basis of a controversy between the University and local media outlets that night and smoldered for months and, in some cases, years thereafter. "This (policy) is an important point for the local media," Hill acknowledged. "The national media understood it, the local media did not." In fact, Hill would be criticized harshly for his handling of the story by local reporters, editors and broadcasters.[12] Many complained that the problem stemmed from a lack of public relations experience, especially in media relations. Hill, however, does not feel lack of experience held him back during the Lockerbie crisis. "I'm an old hand at higher education," he said.

Robert Hill came to Syracuse University in 1977 as a vice president and special assistant to the chancellor for affirmative action. He held degrees and certificates in marketing and in management from New York University, Manhattan College, and Harvard, and had held a series of positions in college and university administration, the most recent of which was Fairleigh Dickinson University's director of affirmative action. During the turmoil of the late '60s and the '70s, Hill was an administrator for Manhattan Community College's Lincoln Center Campus and had to deal with the takeover of the president's office by faculty and students who were part of the Black Muslim movement.

Looking back over his career, Hill is most proud of his groundwork in reaching out to African-American and Latino alumni of Syracuse University who had never really felt a part of the campus community or who had drifted away from their *alma mater* after graduation. "That was the hardest I have ever worked in my life...These people were essentially lost to the University. As alumni, they were not taking advantage of their University and the University was not using them to great advantage; they were a hidden treasure."[13]

In essence, Hill explains, he has two bosses. As head of public relations, he reports directly to Senior Vice President for University Relations Lansing G. Baker. Today the public relations staff is divided into News Services, National Media Relations, Community Relations,[14] Program Development and Video Communications. They seek, in Hill's words, "to present news and information about the people, the programs, policies and practices to our many constituencies by use of the mass media...Our work really consists of presenting SU in its most favorable light, and when it's not favorable, controlling the damage, minimizing the harm. Everything else," says Hill, "is a detail on those things."

Hill's other "boss" is the University Chancellor, who at the time of the tragedy was Melvin Eggers, an economist who earned his Ph.D. at Yale in 1950 and spent the rest of his academic career at Syracuse University. Eggers had risen through the academic ranks, and had served as chancellor since 1971. In 1988, he was 72 and was expected to step down in the near future; three years later, he did. Hill's role is to serve as the chancellor's press secretary, preparing him for media appearances and handling his media relations. In that capacity, Hill serves as the University's primary spokesperson, issuing oral and written statements on behalf of the chancellor and the institution. Finally, because of his special expertise, Hill advises the chancellor on issues of diversity and affirmative action.

Hill reflected on both his career and the Pan Am 103 tragedy during two lengthy interviews in February and March 1992. The bombing of Pan Am Flight 103 was not his greatest career challenge, he said. To his mind, that was the 14-month-long investigation of Syracuse athletics by the governing body of collegiate sports, the National Collegiate Athletic Association, prompted by a Syracuse *Post-Standard* story in December 1990.[15]

"It is almost unfair, and really almost unthinkable to compare in the same breath something so trivial, like playing basketball, with the life and death issues of Pan Am and international terrorism," Hill said. But he added that in terms of "strategy, use of resources, the intense time put into the issue," the basketball investigation was more difficult. "Pan Am was more concentrated. There were two big 'bumps' — once, of course, when it first occurred, and then...when we planned for the (January 18, 1989) memorial service. And ever since then...it's cropped up...(when) for whatever reason, some piece of it becomes national news."

Speaking of the memorial service, Hill said that "for the public relations practitioner, this is not difficult work...It's much easier to do a memorial service, working with parents, getting information out to the media...Now, you have to worry about sensitivities and appropriate decorum...(but) except for the sadness of it all, all of those features (in a memorial service) are resonant in a Commencement, which is much bigger."For Hill, handling the fast-breaking news story of global proportions was much harder. "Yet," said Hill, "even this aspect is only about 48 hours' worth of work. After that it's routine."

In those first 48 hours, Hill turned his energies to getting the facts. After his telephone conversation with the Chancellor, he called the DIPA offices, across a set of tennis courts and a playing field from the Women's Building where Hill and all of his staff, except the Video Communications specialists, are headquartered. Both offices are about a ten-minute walk from the chancellor's office in the Administration Building.

Initially, there was some confusion: "Apparently, (the DIPA staff) were giving reporters some information, but they didn't have enough to give them all the information. And it appeared as though they were telling reporters more than they were telling us, so that it became a little bit awkward, because a reporter would say, 'Well, we talked to DIPA and they have told us A, B, and C.' When *we*'d call DIPA, (they would say) 'We don't know anything.' I remember cussing and fussing a little bit around here, and I'd say, 'Well, why is (DIPA's director) telling reporters that when we can't get anything out of her?'" To put an end to the confusion, Hill reminded the DIPA staff to refer all calls to the public relations office, as was the University's policy.

Meanwhile, Hill moved the staff of his News Services Department — a director, four writers and secretaries — up from their offices one floor below to handle the flood of telephone inquiries coming into his office. Hill instructed them to tell reporters, "When we have the facts, we'll make a statement. All we have now is some rumor that a plane crashed and that some SU people *may* be on it." Hill remembered, "As the afternoon unfolded, and we began to go into evening, we learned by some means that a Pan American plane was in question. And I said 'Finally, I've got something I can work with — I'll call my counterpart at Pan Am.'"

Surprisingly, despite the flood of incoming calls to Pan Am, Hill had no trouble getting through by telephone to the airline's public relations office, but he did have problems getting information. "If we placed one, we placed 50 calls to Pan Am's PR office. They would not return my calls...I left many messages...I was really worked up about that because I felt that they should be my best source, because it was their plane...We didn't get anywhere with that, and then it occurred to me that we had to be really resourceful and use any means we could employ to get reliable information."

One staff person had a small television set on, and occasionally would come out with updates, but the staff had little time to stop and listen; the phone lines occupied their full attention. Furthermore, Hill did not consider broadcast news bulletins as totally "reliable." He felt he needed more: "...I knew I could go turn on the television or turn on the radio..." but he was seeking official confirmation from a primary source.

Stymied in his attempts to get a response from the public relations staff at Pan Am, Hill drew upon two years of experience as a sales agent for United Airlines in late 1960s and called Pan Am's operations facility at Kennedy Airport. From DIPA staff he had learned that a travel agency had handled the bookings for the students; he knew that would mean the airline would have a roster. He reached an agent at Kennedy and said, "I want to know whether this plane crashed and whether there were any SU people on it, insofar as you can identify." Hill recalled, "I don't know why (the agent) was so cooperative, but (the agent) said, 'You may not quote me. You may not attribute this to me, but here are the names.'" The agent gave him all the names that could be identified as being part of the SU party booked on the flight. "It did not represent those who actually *boarded*...It was without attribution, but hell, I had *something*, and I was glad to get it. And I took that, and I compared it against (DIPA's) names, and it accounted for a good many."

Meanwhile, restless reporters gathered in the small reception area and the narrow hallway of the Alumni Relations offices, leading to the public relations office. Reporters took over the desks in a complex of small offices, cubicles and workstations. "And I said 'Okay, you go up to the lounge and relax and when I have something I will give it to you." Hill said he thought they would be more comfortable in the Alumnae Lounge on the floor above his offices. "I just moved them out of here because they were taking over people's desks, and fortunately, this was Alumni Relations, not the Development Office where you could see how much (money) people had given...(but) these were people's offices and they were entitled not to have reporters all over their desks."

When Hill sent the reporters outside, they did not go upstairs. "They were afraid they'd miss something, so they stayed out here (in the main corridor). Then they'd come in and say 'Can I use your phone?' and we'd have to let them use the phone at the receptionist's desk. In the meantime, we kept making our calls (to Pan Am)."

For Hill, the crush of reporters posed more than just a physical problem. In addition to wishing to present useful information to the public only after insuring its reliability, the university administration had what it regarded as an even larger goal. "That is to make sure that parental and familial notification had been effected. I needed to know who from SU was on that plane, who from SU had perished, and make sure that the families had been notified, and only after those three (criteria were met), would we make a public statement...So those criteria just had primacy."

As late as 1992 Hill was unaware that two Syracuse television stations had obtained lists of students very similar to the one he got from the agent at Kennedy Airport and broadcast them on the early evening news. Their lists apparently were passed on to the networks[16] and these became a point of contention between Hill's staff and the local media.

"What made that difficult for the local media to comprehend was that by as early as 5 o'clock, no later than 6 o'clock, Dan Rather had it (the list of SU students), Peter Jennings had it, Tom Brokaw had it, all the radio stations and the AP (Associated Press) had it...okay, and that put tremendous pressure on me to verify. People (reporters) were coming in here and saying 'What's taking you so long? Rather has already said it, why don't you confirm it? You *know* SU people were on there!' Well, I didn't know that officially. I didn't know it even unofficially until 5 or 6 o'clock. What is the responsible response of an institution, of a university, of a public information officer in that institution? Do you come out and say, 'We think...' or, 'We have it on unconfirmed reports...' while everything you know about this business tells you that you don't do that. While, on the one hand, you have a salivating press corps that's like *The Birds* outside your door, that just want *something*,...you're balancing all of these needs, the needs of the families, the needs of the next of kin, the University, the DIPA people, the local media...and you've got to make judgments about all of that. And that's what formed my next two to three hours."

Hill reports that eventually he held three news conferences during the evening of December 21. At approximately 6:30 or 7 p.m., Hill recalled that he read a prepared statement outside his office, announcing that the University had confirmation that a plane had crashed, and that it was likely that Syracuse University students were aboard. Hill and his staff continued their telephone inquiries, and the DIPA staff tracked down information from the travel agency, but soon it occurred to those directing the public relations operation that "we had better make the Chancellor available so he could say that he was aware that it had happened, and what his feelings were about it, so (reporters) would know that we weren't trying to hide anything, we weren't sitting on anything, we were being open with them, giving them what we had." So Melvin Eggers arrived at the Women's Building, and Hill escorted him down a back staircase into his office. "I prepped him for his news conference, and then we sent him back out the front to meet with them. And he was very good...He said, 'This is the saddest day of my life,' and that just captured the moment — a soundbite, big time."[17]

Hill recalls another news conference he held at approximately 9:30 p.m., but he says "there really wasn't anything new and after that the media went away." Hill himself left the office for home sometime after 11 p.m., and forwarded his calls to his home telephone, answering media inquiries from around the world throughout the night and early morning.

Despite these news conferences, the media continued to call DIPA, which referred calls to the public relations office, and public relations would not give any information beyond the basics. But, according to Hill: "Reporters complained to DIPA that 'public relations won't tell us anything, so you tell us' and the calling went back and forth. So DIPA was feeling put upon during that period, and because the calls kept coming back, DIPA thought — see, reporters, as you know, they lie; they tell little, not big lies; well, some of them tell big lies, but most responsible reporters lie a little to get the story — so they would tell DIPA that we weren't answering the phone...so DIPA had the impression that they were being mistreated...by public relations."[18]

Across the Atlantic, Syracuse University's London Centre was also besieged by reporters, primarily those based in London. Those inside the shuttered building were so busy answering phone calls and trying to locate students who might or might not be on the plane that they were not even aware initially that television lights were trained on the Centre. They worked through the night, under instructions from the Syracuse campus to make no statement to the media. Reporters who arrived later found a sheet of paper taped to the door referring all inquiries to Robert Hill at Syracuse University. Hill contends that the Centre's director "behaved properly. He couldn't have handled the media converging...even on a routine basis, much less on a crisis."

No Syracuse University administrator slept well that night, least of all Chancellor Melvin Eggers. He arrived alone at NBC's Syracuse affiliate, WSTM, shortly after 6:30 a.m. to appear live by satellite on the "Today Show." A few minutes later, Robert Hill arrived and so did Syracuse Mayor Thomas Young, who was to join Eggers in the interview with Jane Pauley. Waiting for the show to begin, the group learned for the first time that the crash might have been deliberately caused by a bomb.

Pauley's interview style was gentle and sympathetic, but she did ask one question that seemed to take the Chancellor by surprise: did the University, upon hearing about the crash, consider postponing its basketball game against Western Michigan? The chancellor paused, seemed uncertain of his answer, and said "I can't say that it was seriously considered, but it was a scheduled activity, and there was a recognition of the tragedy (a moment of silence right before the tip-off), but I just felt that it was not necessary" (Kane and Garew, 1988).

Playing basketball on the heels of the tragedy caused great debate on a campus that can easily attract 20,000 to 25,000 or more fans into the domed stadium even on a frigid weekday evening. The crowd that night had been no exception; even with most of the students already away for the semester break, the stands were filled with area residents and with fans from as far away as Rochester, Binghamton and Utica. Many in attendance, especially those travelling to Syracuse, had not heard about the crash before arriving at the Carrier Dome and gasped in surprise when the Reverend Michael Schultz-Rothermel, a Hendricks Chapel chaplain, stepped to the microphone and asked the crowd to join him in silent meditation and prayer.

Coach Jim Boeheim had learned of the tragedy by watching the 6 p.m. local news at home. Some of his players learned about it during the pre-game prayer in the team locker room, just before 8 p.m. "When Father Charles (Borgognoni, the Catholic chaplain) asked us to remember the students who died in the crash, I said 'What crash?'" then-freshman player David Johnson told the *Herald-Journal*'s executive sports editor (Poliquin, 1988). Another player, Matt Roe, was quoted by the sports editor as saying: "I sat in here thinking about the crash, and it sent chills up and down my spine. It made me wonder what we were doing here at all."

Why wasn't the game canceled? Two camps seemed to emerge around that question: One was angry that the University would appear to be so insensitive at such a time. Sportswriter Phil Mushnick of the *New York Post* called playing the game "a disgrace" and theorized that "big-time collegiate athletic programs are virtually divorced from mainstream student activity. The ballplayers are there to play ball. As the bits and pieces of 38 Syracuse students lie scattered across a countryside in Scotland three days before the celebration of Christ's birth[19]...the school's basketball team tipped off against Western Michigan. And perhaps the saddest part is we know better than to be surprised" (Dec. 27, 1988, Sports). The other point of view was that in the face of tragedy, each person grieves in his or her own way, and life must go on. So residents of Lockerbie began playing bingo within minutes of the disaster, and the widow of a passenger told two of the authors in an informal conversation that she had taken strength from the fact that the basketball game had gone ahead as scheduled. She personally had attended a Christmas pageant with her children that night, believing that is what her husband would have wanted.

Robert Hill, who did not take part in any decisions about playing the game, recalled that it became clear that students were on the flight literally minutes before the game was scheduled to tip-off.[20] "And, people were already there — some people get there two hours before, when the doors open. They paid their money, the start of the game (was) imminent, so they (the athletic department) decided to go ahead."

Hill was not part of those discussions, "because, frankly, there was not much discussion. When you're in the realm of rumor, and the heat of the moment, you've got the big press of the game with a schedule that isn't easily altered, millions of dollars in commitments, fans coming from miles around...and the one thing you don't have, which might be the determinative factor, is (that) you still don't know that SU has had students killed in a plane crash. Apparently their judgment was 'We'll go.'"

Hill also appeared to be unaware that the initiative for the moment of silence came from the campus chaplains, and that there had been some resistance initially to the proposal. Although the public relations chief was notified by a chaplain about the hastily organized prayer vigil scheduled for 9 p.m. Hill said he did not realize on the night of the tragedy that reporters were at Hendricks Chapel. "I thought all of the reporters were here, because we were dealing with them here. We stayed at our stations as the service went on. And, we have a small staff."

In retrospect, knowing that many of those in attendance at the prayer vigil were appalled by what they considered intrusive behavior of the media, Hill mused aloud about what would have happened if he had sent a couple of his staff members to the chapel. "Two people would not have been able to handle the media," he said, explaining his decision.

That the event would draw a crowd that filled the chapel's main floor and spilled over into the balcony was not anticipated, he said. In that respect, Hill was correct. As the Reverend Michael Schultz-Rothermel wrote later in an article directed to the staff of campus chapels across the country, the event was organized by chaplains who agreed "it's important to do even if it is just us who are there" (1991, p. 16).

In Hill's view, the open nature of American universities creates problems in times of crises. "When you have something like the Bhopal disaster...you assume the world press is going to converge upon Bhopal, as well as on Dow Chemical," he said, "but when you go to Dow, you can't get in, there's security checkpoints." He contrasted that situation with universities. "For all of the complaints, it is pretty easy to drive on campus. These buildings are open, students are coming in all the time. And, the most aggressive reporters who are trying to make a name, and get a Pulitzer, and who work the streets are young people, so they look like students...they dress like students...so therefore it's pretty easy for them to get access." One alternative, he said, would be to become more restrictive, but he finds that unacceptable. "I mean, I know how to have a reporter thrown out, but we don't do that."

In the case of the Hendricks Chapel evening prayer service, Hill said that he had neither time nor staff to control the reporters, and he resisted the notion of using the University's security force:[21] "They (the chaplains) could have had an orderly service," he said. "We could have kept the media out altogether, but that requires security, and I didn't want uniformed officers dealing with journalists at the Syracuse University chapel."

University events of all sorts, both sacred and secular, are regularly held at the chapel. "We have a system for where the broadcast media may array themselves, covering an event in the chapel, and our flexibility on that is dependent upon the solemnity of the event," Hill said. "If I had more staff, I would have dispatched staff over — maybe — to deal with the news media who wanted to cover the chapel service. But that would have required a very rapid turnaround, because — I don't know when we learned it, but it wasn't much more than a half hour or 45 minutes before (the event)...that we were aware that they (the chaplains) wanted to do that."[22]

At 10 a.m. on December 22, key University officials met in the Chancellor's conference room to assess what had already been done, and what steps were needed next. Heading the agenda was the finalizing of the list of DIPA-enrolled students lost aboard Pan Am Flight 103. Using DIPA records, the handwritten notes taken by Hill the night before during his call to Kennedy Airport, and information gained from contacts in New York, the office of U.S. Senator Alfonse D'Amato (an alumnus), and at Hancock International Airport, the staff developed a final list. Also addressed were questions about handling the media at a second prayer service scheduled for noon.

The media, while constrained to a balcony, again disturbed the service with what a television professor called "inexcusable noise." In a letter to the Dean Richard Phillips, who heads the chaplaincy staff, he wrote:

> We have become too accepting of the news gatherers. We are too willing to allow their noise, their clutter and their questions to intrude upon the most private moments of our lives. We have come to believe that we have an obligation to help these people do their jobs. But we should insist that these intrusions are not appropriate, have nothing to do with journalism, and will not be allowed.[23]

On December 22, Hill conducted two news conferences: the first at approximately 9:30 a.m. to complete the unfinished business of announcing the University's resolution to the athletes' disciplinary action. Hill decided to get this unpleasant piece of news out at this point "because (in light of the previous night's tragedy) nobody will care." At approximately 2:30 p.m., after two earlier postponements to allow more time to complete the list, Syracuse University held a news conference to release the names of the 35 students killed aboard Pan Am Flight 103.[24]

Within days of the bombing, faculty at the Newhouse School of Public Communications, on the other side of the campus, began hearing from local media about what they perceived as problems with the way the university had dealt with them. But Hill reports he was not aware of the smoldering animosity among local reporters and editors until early in the new year when he was invited to speak before the members of the Syracuse Press Club to give his opinions of the local media's performance in covering the disaster. Hill took the opportunity to criticize the media for contacting family members before they had been officially notified, and told them parents had been upset by the media's insensitive posing of such questions as "How did you feel when you heard the news?" He called the way reporters had contacted families of students not aboard the plane as sloppy reporting techniques. Hill argued that the media should not shrug off such practices as "the price of doing business."

Members of the Press Club listened in silence until the question-and-answer period. "Then," said Hill, "they pounced." One TV news director yelled, "You don't know what you're doing," and angrily chastised the University for taking 24 hours to verify the names when the national media was comfortable in broadcasting them early in the evening. Hill shot back: "That (type of verification) may not be the standard of news organizations but that must be the standard of a responsible university."

The criticism went public in late January, when Assistant Managing Editor Stan Linhorst's frustrations were voiced when he wrote a rare "View from the Newsroom" opinion piece entitled "Why Does SU Seem to Hold the Community in Such Low Regard?"

> Syracuse University's vice president of public relations spoke Monday night before the Syracuse Press Club. Judging by the view of the assembled journalists, the university isn't building good relations with this segment of the public... Hill's visit was an interesting glimpse at town-gown relations. In effect, Hill told the town to take a hike. His message from the university during the two-hour meeting was simple: We'll tell the town what we think it ought to know when we want it to know. . .The week before Christmas, Pan Am Flight 103 crashed, killing 35 students . . .But it was more than 24 hours after the crash before SU was able to hand out a list of the students. The world already knew what SU was unable to say. What was the University's explanation? Don't be in such a rush, Hill said.
>
> The university was quick to call its employees in London and elsewhere. Don't talk to anyone, was the order minutes after the crash. Make everyone go through the public relations office.

> Reporters trooped to the PR office to ask their questions. Shoo. Go away, they were told. Can't you see we're busy?
>
> Nobody much cares about whining from the press corps. But it seems the real message is that SU is carrying on its tradition of thumbing its nose at the community. A tradition of throwing its weight around (Linhorst, 1989).

Hill recalls those early stormy days in his new position philosophically. "The news media have a role, a job to do; the University has a job to do, and by definition, their ultimate ends are not one and, in some cases, are incompatible, and there is this inherent tension between news sources and the news media." Hill said that if both sides understand that tension, "I think we will both do our best to achieve our goals, and if, in the process, we behave according to the standards of our profession and the standards of civility and appropriate ethics and the like, that if one or the other doesn't fully achieve his goal, then we understand why, we live with that, and we go on to the next one. I believe that some in the local press feel that way and operate that way, and some don't. I treat them all the same, whether they're friendly or whether they're hostile. Now, in that manner, I believe that I've been able to develop good relationships with the media."

Looking back to the tragedy, Hill is generally pleased with the University's performance during those dark days. He is highly complimentary to his staff, and would make changes only in a few areas. The experience did not turn him into an advocate of written crisis communications plans. "I have not written an elaborate plan, but I *have* a plan...I established it with the Chancellor (at the time, Melvin Eggers)...and it is known to everyone who needs to be aware of it."

Hill described a crisis management process that begins with a meeting of his senior people — he has added two senior staff to his inner circle since 1988, a community relations director and a national media director. The discussion starts with a determination of the interest groups and audiences involved. "We then suggest a course of action," Hill said, including suggestions on who should serve as spokesperson. "I then have a conference with the Chancellor and the key senior officers whose area of responsibility is affected."

Once the Chancellor signs off on the course of action, each university administrator with responsibilities carries out his or her portion. "In my case (media relations), the Chancellor and I, or the key senior officer and I, make the determination as to the spokesperson. I then determine with my team...the strategies for getting the various messages out to the various...audiences."

After that the public relations staff determines any other audiences that are not being reached through the broadcast or print media, such as alumni and parents, and suggests a strategy for communicating with them, and a timetable.

Then an officer in that area (for example, the head of alumni relations) makes sure that communication gets out.

Since 1988, Hill has developed a written policy indicating that people contacted by the media on breaking news should refer those calls to him. He now issues that statement annually.

Because Hill's plan calls for only senior officers of the University to speak on major issues, he does not believe that spokesperson training is practical or necessary for mid-level and junior officers. At the time of the Pan Am Flight 103 tragedy, only Chancellor Eggers had had outside training by a professional firm specializing in that skills area. Since that time, one other official who faced prolonged exposure to the media on a critical issue has been trained. "If you've got finite dollars, as we do, I wouldn't invest them in training (junior officers)," he said. An alumnus has agreed to help the public relations staff with training in this area, so that it, in turn, can train more university officers.

"It has not been our practice to place people inexperienced in dealing with these issues in a position overnight to have to be expert at handling them," Hill said. "The other thing is that universities are complex, and the Fourth Estate in this town has ready access to various aspects of the University community...Because the University is so dominant in this community there are many spins and aspects that one could place on a story, and you can have pretty ready access to people who don't need permission to talk, like students and professors. We never attempt to restrict the access of the media to students or professors."

Hill feels that working with the media during the Pan Am crisis would have been easier if he had had a crisis management center. "I need one now," he said. "Pan Am wasn't the first time I've had a news conference in a hallway. I don't have a place for reporters to prepare their stories, to call them in on the phone, to even call their offices. (That night) we locked them out of here and said, 'Go upstairs.' They didn't want to go up there. They were afraid that someone would sneak by and scoop them, get in to me."

He rejected using an existing facility — the University's telemarketing center with its phone bank and workstations — because of the sensitive nature of the fundraising work that goes on there. "I couldn't get it turned around fast enough. There needs to be a dedicated space."

A final change Hill would make would be to have better coordination between the public relations office and the university unit most affected. In the case of the Pan Am bombing, Hill feels that reporters deceived the DIPA staff into believing that the public relations staff had gone home at 5 p.m., leaving them alone to respond to the media. Hill believes that the lesson he learned in this situation helped make subsequent situations, including the NCAA basketball investigation, easier.

On January 18, 1989, Syracuse University held an interfaith memorial service in the Carrier Dome for the 35 students killed in the bombing of Pan Am Flight 103. This time, the Public Relations Department took a proactive approach in helping the media cover the event. An elaborate media pool system was set up, but it angered some reporters and photographers by its restrictions on placement and angles. Robert Hill told the weekly *Syracuse New Times*:

> We respect the need for accuracy and we respect the rights of the media. And throughout all of this there has been, and will continue to be on the part of the University, an effort to balance interests. And our primary responsibility is to respect, and be sensitive to the rights and needs of the faculty, staff and students of Syracuse University (Leahy, 1989).

Contrasting responses

Pan Am Flight 103 offers a sobering but unique opportunity to examine the role of public relations practitioners in organizational crises. The plane that exploded at 31,000 feet over Lockerbie was a single stimulus that produced reactions from at least four major organizations: The Scottish Office, the Scottish police, Pan American World Airways, and Syracuse University. How well did each of their public information specialists and public relations managers serve both organizational needs and the demands of the international media? What lessons can be learned for future improvements?

The authors purposely used lengthy direct quotes from each of the professionals interviewed so that readers could judge these performances for themselves. With the luxury of hindsight, anyone can become an expert, seeing the failures, the glitches in the systems, the should-have-beens and the needed-to-be-dones. But anyone not in the shoes of a professional communicator that night or the terrible days that ensued cannot fully understand what it was like, or know how he or she would behave when faced with scores of reporters, each demanding answers to questions, or the emotional trauma of walking through a devastated neighborhood or into a room of weeping relatives.

If this were traditional research, the authors might state a formal hypothesis predicting that the "best" performance under the pressures of the Lockerbie bombing would come from Pan American World Airways and Syracuse University. Certainly, an airline, by the very nature of its business, must be prepared at all times to deal with the eventuality of a crash, whether from human error, mechanical failure, adverse weather, or sabotage. And certainly, the hypothesis might presume a university, the equivalent of a small city, with all of a small city's complexities and potential dangers, would be prepared to deal with crises. Conversely, it might predict that a small market town in the southern hills of peace-loving Scotland, suddenly the scene of devastation and chaos, with the rescue workers, police and government authorities rushing to its aid, would be ill-prepared to deal with an invasion of international media.

These hypotheses would be proven wrong. An examination of the performance of each of these organizations during the Lockerbie disaster shows that size, sophistication, and complexity of organization had little to do with performance. What made a difference were such factors as the existence of a formal crisis communications plan; regular role-playing by key officials of crisis scenarios, including information dissemination; the backgrounds and past experiences of the principal communicators; the communicators' level of understanding of journalistic practices in covering disasters; a coordinated effort, with the ability to marshal forces and resources quickly and efficiently; and the presence, both real and symbolic, of the CEO.

Just as human beings set up defense mechanisms to fend off unpleasant or threatening news and events, it is not unusual for organizations to put off dealing with the possibility of a crisis. Few managers want to think about adversity. American Motors' former chairman Gerald Meyers believes the reason behind this organizational problem is that "leaders in any field find failure distasteful. . . Every aggressive, successful person is conditioned to think success; plan for success; allow no negative thinking; associate with positive people; and emphasize accomplishment and cast off losers" (Meyers, 1986, p.3).

Meyers' theory seems borne out in numbers: A recent study by *pr reporter* (1989) found that two-thirds of the American corporations surveyed had experienced a crisis of some kind in the past five years, yet only one third of them have a crisis communications plan in place and a task force that meets regularly to discuss potential crises. Despite the long list of corporate disasters, both natural and man-made — Hooker Chemical Company at Love Canal, Metropolitan Edison at Three Mile Island, Union Carbide at Bhopal, Procter and Gamble with its Rely tampon, Johnson and Johnson with Tylenol, Exxon and the Valdez, and Dow-Corning with its silicon-gel breast implant materials — corporate executives seem to believe that crises happen to *other* companies.

While some executives may scoff at the need to create a crisis plan and its accompanying communications plan, the careful development of such strategies seems to have made a significant difference in Scotland. A key role for the professional communicator of any organization is to serve as an "early warning system," detecting any potential threats (and opportunities) awaiting the organization. A series of disasters, some in their own country, and others on the international scene, had convinced the Scots to create and implement a crisis plan. Even with all of the horror of Lockerbie, David Beveridge and his SIO colleagues were able to swing into action and feel confident that "we were just doing our job."

Beveridge differs from Pan Am's Jeff Kriendler and Syracuse University's Robert Hill who both believe that the enormity of the Lockerbie disaster diminished, even erased, any potential effectiveness of a crisis communications plan. Indeed, Beveridge's experience shows just the opposite. While it is certainly true that no one (except perhaps intelligence agents) might suspect the possibility of such a horror, and while it can be argued that each disaster is unique, certain practices can automatically be put into place, regardless of the type or scope of the disaster. As the SIO team raced down the highway from Edinburgh, they still did not know *what* they would find, but they *knew* for certain that the media would descend upon Lockerbie and they would need a central source of information. Within minutes of their arrival, the team created a media center. The well-rehearsed disaster plan had kicked into high gear.

Even with a plan in place, some organizations let it gather dust, retrieving it only in times of crisis. Such a plan needs frequent review, rehearsal and adjustment with key leaders involved. Prior to Lockerbie in 1988, the most recent run-through of the entire Pan Am plan was 1982, although exactly one week before the bombing of Flight 103, Pan Am had been the participating airline in an emergency exercise at London's Heathrow Airport.[25] It was Pan Am's practice to do an evaluation *after* a crash, which is helpful and necessary, but less frequently in *anticipation* of a disaster. Like so many corporate efforts in crisis communications, the emphasis in mock scenarios at Pan Am tended to be on the operational response (i.e., rehearsals of putting out fires, evacuating passengers, caring for the injured, routes to the nearest hospitals), while ignoring a critical element of disaster management: communication of information to key audiences in the outside world.

Contrast, for example, the SIO's insistence on getting the outward flow of information started quickly with Pan Am's emphasis on communicating primarily with *internal* units. The SIO knew taking control of the flow of information was critical; for Pan Am, the airport news conference was "an accommodation" to the media. At Syracuse University, the crisis communications approach seemed on the surface to be a reasonable process developed by the public relations vice president and the chancellor. Yet it would be more suited to what Reinhardt (1987) classifies as the "emerging crisis," an event that may be a surprise, but which gives some time for analysis and reaction (e.g., new government regulations), but too slow for what Reinhardt calls the "immediate crisis," one that allows no time for research or developing a detailed action plan.[26]

At Pan Am, CEO Thomas Plaskett's idea to bring in outside public relations counsel to assist was good, but too late. December 21, 1988 was not the time to start and build a working relationship between in-house staff and outside public relations counsel. That relationship should have been created in calmer times, so when disaster struck, outside counsel could have joined in, with the invaluable assets of objectivity, experience, vast media contacts and capable extra hands.

Kriendler's situation was made far worse than that of the other practitioners in this study because of the intervention of lawyers. While their fears for the corporate welfare are certainly legitimate in this type of situation, the need for public relations practitioners and lawyers to work together *before* a crisis is illuminated by the Lockerbie disaster.

Lawyers defend their clients in a court of law; public relations professionals represent their clients in the court of public opinion. Kriendler rightfully observed that the concerns of the lawyers are long-term, focusing on potential actions many years into the future. But the perceptions formulated by various audiences of an organization in the hours and days immediately after a crisis may well affect future litigation, and certainly affect public opinion. By restricting the words and actions of the corporate communications staff, Pan Am's legal team created the exact opposite of what the SIO was so successful in doing: creating and maintaining a steady flow of information that put the SIO in a proactive position, able to manage information.[27] In content analyses of national and international newspapers after the bombing, the very small number of official statements by Pan Am contrasted with those of other organizations, giving the appearance early on that the company had gone into official hiding. This was compounded by the fact that Pan Am's CEO made no public comments until eight days after the tragedy.

Kriendler's attempts to humanize the organization through corporate letters of condolence to the families were thwarted; the letters never found their way out of the corporate maze of approvals demanded by the insurance and legal departments. Family members took this as an insult and some interpreted the failure to send even a simple letter of condolence as a cold, inhuman response and further evidence of guilt. This clash of legal and public relations needs discussion at the time the crisis communications plan is being developed, not in the heat of the crisis itself. By the time Pan Am's legal counselors yielded to the insistence of the public relations staff, attempts to balance information against the criticisms of the victims' families were probably too late and too weak to be effective. The media vacuum left by Kriendler's inability to distribute Pan Am's information was quickly filled with angry accusations by the victims' relatives.

Summing up the need for active rather than reactive communication, Donald Stephenson, director of public issues for Dow Canada, observes: "When a company assumes a defensive position, that is taken by the media and the public as an indication of guilt...When a company is completely open, it can be credited with statesmanship" (Reinhardt, 1987, p. 44).

Virtually every book, article and manual dealing with crisis communications stresses the importance of conducting rehearsals and mock crisis drills. The tragedy at Lockerbie brings the textbook wisdom to life.

Contrast the situations in Scotland, New York City, and Syracuse. Despite the horror all around them and their own personal anguish, the public information specialists from the SIO and the Scottish Police were able to function as if they were "in the middle of a big exercise." Their rehearsals of disaster situations allowed them to perform almost routinely; the element of surprise was there, but controllable. In New York, Kriendler's informal in-house training for his public relations staff could not carry the day, especially since half of his staff had only been on the job for less than six months, and they had limited experience working together as a team.

In Syracuse, the University's public relations staff and its Division of Programs Abroad knew one another and had worked together on "good news" dissemination. The behavior of both staffs in the first hours after the crash seemed as if no worst-case scenario of a tragedy affecting students or faculty had ever been discussed. The lack of coordination between the two offices created frustrations among the staff and projected an appearance of disorganization and ineptitude to reporters. Syracuse journalists became distrustful when two departments of the university responded differently to the same questions in a halting and sporadic manner.

The approaches taken by the individual professional communicators in responding to the pressures of the international media clearly reflect their professional backgrounds, levels of and amounts of experience, and personal attitudes toward the media. Certainly, the backgrounds of Beveridge and Kennedy seemed to serve them well. Beveridge had spent years as a reporter before becoming a public information specialist, and Kennedy had dealt with reporters at many crime scenes. Kriendler's experience was extensive, but primarily with business and travel writers, only occasionally with the "wolf pack" journalists who cover breaking stories. Hill had the least prior experience; his office was experienced in developing and placing positive stories with relatively friendly reporters and editors on the education beat instead of crisis responses.

Again, in terms of staff, Beveridge and Kennedy were leading teams of experienced personnel; only two of Kriendler's four managers had strong media backgrounds, the other two had none. At Syracuse University, one of Hill's team had been a radio reporter in the Syracuse market; the others had been trained in a school of journalism and mass communications, but were fairly inexperienced. For most of the staff at Pan Am and Syracuse University, this was their introduction to crisis communications.

The first rule for any professional joining a communications department is to get to know the organization inside out, and in this regard, all of the professionals interviewed here rated very high. The differences emerged in relationship to rule number two: know the media inside out. Years of experience gave Beveridge and Kennedy the ability to predict what the media would do, and they planned and acted accordingly. Aware that trying to deny reporters access to information or access to sites would be like trying to push back the ocean, the Scottish officials took control of the situation while working to meet the voracious appetite of the international media.

Kriendler's actions became entangled in the web of legal and insurance issues, so his ability to be effective was greatly hampered. Hill's performance was greatly hurt by his lack of experience: someone more experienced in media relations would know that reporters in search of information will not try *just* the public information office; they will talk to any and all sources. Journalists kept waiting without any information will be furious, and grow even more insistent and suspicious. Newspeople seeking the human interest angle will not go to the public information office; they will search for individuals caught up in the tragedy. On December 21, 1988, that meant converging on the aisles and pews of a house of worship.

This predictable behavior of the media was not lost on the University's chaplains; as they planned the evening prayer vigil they knew that the media would arrive. In fact, with no campus-wide information system available, the chaplains used the local broadcast media, in particular the 6 p.m. newscasts, as a way to announce the plans for a 9 p.m. prayer vigil. According to Michael Schultz-Rothermel, the Lutheran pastor on campus, "We told them (Hill and other administrators) that (the chapel) was going to be really where the action was because this was going to be the first opportunity for the students to gather together. That's just a natural draw for the media."

Kennedy's performance at Lockerbie may well be a model. While refusing to compromise Scottish law or the privacy of the victims' families and of the Lockerbie residents, he knew and respected the need to share the story throughout the global village. Kennedy recognized the multiple needs created by the wide range of nationalities, types of publications and broadcast outlets, international time zones, and experience levels of reporters, and he took all of this into account in his dealings.

Personal attitudes toward the media are revealing. The SIO and Kennedy demonstrated a keen appreciation that all — reporters and sources alike — were in this disaster zone together, and a spirit of cooperation, though strained at times, was created. Kennedy's straightforward manner and willingness to help the media, within legal limitations, earned him trust and understanding from reporters, even when he restricted them.

Across the Atlantic, both Pan Am and Syracuse University seemed to regard the media as adversaries. The result for Pan Am, which staged its news conference at Kennedy Airport only after the story had been developing for several hours, was that news media concentrated not on the limited information made available during that meeting, but on the unfiltered reaction of grieving relatives. Later the media became the unwelcome messengers of the families' vengeful accusations. To Syracuse University's public relations office, the media seemed intrusive and demanding, keeping the staff, including the vice president for public relations, from what they saw as the single most important task: verifying facts.

Development of a working relationship with the media in the face of a disaster is central to any crisis communications plan. The actions of the Scottish professionals could serve as a mini crisis management manual:

- Know the media, their needs, and their procedures.
- Know and respect media deadlines; help reporters meet them.
- Remember that the public is a key audience that needs and deserves information.
- Use multiple channels to reach key audiences; don't just depend on mass media outlets.
- Tell it all, and tell it fast. Give only completely accurate facts, but give what is known in a timely fashion, and as quickly as new facts develop. The *complete* picture may not be known for years, so waiting until all the facts are known is not reasonable in a crisis.
- Respond quickly to misinformation and negatives.
- In times of crisis, cooperate. Non-cooperation sends reporters and editors to seek other sources, usually less knowledgeable and one-sided.

Interviews with dozens of journalists on both sides of the Atlantic and the professional experience of the authors suggest that what the media need and expect in such circumstances include:

- Access to the scene and/or timely information that helps them describe the scope of the disaster and efforts to cope with it.
- Enough access to the grieving to help convey the human dimensions of the tragedy.

- Timely notification of the next of kin.
- Timely release of names of victims and survivors upon notification of next of kin.
- Timely sharing of emerging facts and developing stories.

Notifying next-of-kin and releasing names of victims is critical in any disaster. In the case of Flight 103, excruciating delays in getting the passenger list caused difficulty for all of the public information officers and public relations practitioners involved. The problem was hardly unique. United Airlines had a similar problem in two serious incidents. In February 1989, Flight 811 bound for Sydney, Australia, was crippled when a 10 by 20-foot section of fuselage was ripped from the aircraft after a cargo door opened suddenly in flight. Nine people were lost at sea, but the captain managed to return the plane to Honolulu with 354 survivors. Five months later, in July, 1989, Flight 232 bound for Chicago from Denver was disabled when an engine failed and disintegrated. The captain circled the Sioux City, Iowa, airport for 45 minutes, then attempted to land. Millions watched television sets in horror as CNN captured the DC-10 cartwheeling through corn fields. One hundred and twelve people perished; 184 survived. Looking back to the handling of these crises, Robert A. Doughty, then manager of external communications for United Airlines, remembers:

> In both accidents, the only criticism I heard was that we did not release the passenger lists soon enough. We faced the criticism head-on by walking the media through the intricacies of how a passenger manifest is created — actually, there are three lists — and how difficult it is to reconcile those three lists against the actual passenger load. The *New York Times* found the information interesting enough to write an article about the process, portraying United as a caring company that was treating all aspects of the aftermath in a sensible and responsible manner: the article effectively blunted the criticism that we were acting too slow (1992-93, p. 41).[28]

Although there was some early confusion about the number of passengers on board Pan Am 103, a bigger problem stemmed from confusion within the airline about how the manifest would be released and to whom. State Department officials could sympathize with Robert Hill of Syracuse; they too were trying desperately to obtain a list of passengers. Consular officials first asked for a manifest sometime after 5 p.m. when it established a "working group" to manage the crisis, then had to wait more than seven hours for the list.[29] That meant that ten hours or more elapsed before Pan Am was ready to work with State Department officials in notifying next of kin. Meanwhile, the undoubtedly well-intentioned act by one or more airline employees had passed an unverified list of 38 Syracuse University students, three of whom were not on the plane, to two Syracuse television stations and sometime later to the university's vice president for public relations.

Contrast that response with the Delta Airlines' crisis plan, revised following its 1985 crash at Dallas-Fort Worth Airport. It recognized, in the words of its vice president for communications, William D. Berry, that "names are a big part of the story," but that it had an obligation to survivors to break the news, either personally or by phone. "That's one area where we're going to control release of the information until we have fulfilled our responsibility as a carrier to the passengers' next of kin," Berry told the Society of Professional Journalists.[30] So when the next crash involving fatalities occurred at the same airport in August 1988, Delta's updated crisis plan allowed it to notify most relatives and then release that information to the media within six hours.

The way Delta went on the offensive to take control of the information flow in that accident was demonstrated by its first announcement to the media, which Berry issued about three minutes after receiving word of the crash. It said a news conference would be held every hour on the hour at the airline's headquarters in Atlanta, and every hour on the half-hour at the Dallas-Fort Worth Airport, until the story was over.[31] The Delta response was so exceptional that Newsday devoted nearly 2,000 words to describing it, including:

> Even while the wreckage was smoldering and details were scant, the company set into motion its response effort, called by some "The Delta Force."
>
> A news release announcing the crash and providing a phone number to call for details was sent immediately to major news organizations. Within an hour, a jet with more than two dozen Delta executives and technical experts was on its way to Dallas, where other company employees were already trying to contact passengers' families.
>
> Neil Monroe, manager of public relations, said the emergency response plan was developed over the years by Delta personnel and was couched "on the theory of providing the highest level of customer service we can at all times."
>
> By early afternoon, the airline had secured scores of hotel rooms for survivors, some of whom received counseling by a Dallas psychiatrist hired that day by Delta. Rooms also were reserved for the families of the 13 who died.
>
> As in 1985, Delta workers trained in crisis response were dispatched to Dallas. Some were assigned to shield survivors from the media. Others were at the disposal of survivors and the families of the dead, company officials said. Airline employees also escorted passengers on shopping trips for everything from toothbrushes to free clothing to replace lost items (Moyers, 1988, p. 6).

Delta clearly treats such efforts as part of its responsibility for being in the airline business. Pan Am's approach may help to explain why it went bankrupt, although its response was more typical of the airline industry than Delta's.

Lobbyists for the industry combined forces in 1992 and persuaded Congress to eliminate a requirement that American carriers on international routes compile and release passenger manifests to help the State Department notify next-of-kin when air disasters occur outside the United States. The requirement that a manifest be prepared in three to five hours after an airline disaster, which had been passed two years earlier at the urging of the Presidential Commission on Aviation Security and Terrorism, never went into force. The aviation industry argued that it would place American carriers at a disadvantage with those of other countries.[32]

The "Delta Force" has sometimes been criticized by attorneys for victims and their families, who see its friendly offers of help as a ploy to reduce lawsuits against the airline, but interviews with families who lost loved ones on Pan Am 103 indicated most of them would have appreciated some real help from the airline. Instead they received phone calls through Pan Am's buddy system, which consisted of the Marketing Department turning to its sales representatives to serve in the delicate art of grief counseling, with no prior training. Many of these people had trouble dealing with their own emotions in the face of this tragedy, yet they had to staff the phones, reaching out to the devastated families of the passengers aboard Pan Am Flight 103. As Kriendler admits, on December 20, these people were selling tickets to adventure; a day later they were expected to perform as grief counselors. One father of a victim angrily recalls his interaction with the assigned buddy: "She was very young, she was sobbing the entire time, and we ended up consoling *her*. She was of no use to us." Another mother remembers the inexperienced and self-conscious buddy ending each telephone conversation with "Have a nice day."

Syracuse University asked individual faculty members to act as hosts for each family of one of the students at the time of the January 18 memorial service. Hosts were briefed on their role and on the grieving process; they were given background on the family they were hosting and were asked to use a "hot line" for questions they could not answer personally. Two faculty were assigned to each family and met them at the airport or at their hotel and served as their personal escorts. They sat with them during the memorial service, and when requested arranged for them to meet faculty who had taught their son or daughter. Families said in interviews that such personal contact helped on this painful visit to campus. A number of families made contact with their faculty hosts when they returned to campus for the dedication of the memorial wall in 1990.

Details matter in a disaster, and most of them require people. All the communications professionals interviewed for this book bemoaned the lack of staff. Kennedy warned never to underestimate the number of staff needed in times of crisis. Others pointed out, rightfully, that it would be impossible to have as many staff in normal times as would be needed in a crisis. Kriendler came up with the right solution — unfortunately, for Pan Am, too late — in recruiting knowledgeable people from throughout the company to be trained in media relations. Once a crisis hits, these auxiliaries to the public relations office can swing into action, answering the phones, dealing with routine inquiries, preparing background kits, thereby relieving the public relations professionals for direct media relations work.

At Syracuse University, Hill had a unique source of help: an internationally recognized school of public communications with a faculty who have many years of experience in print and broadcast journalism, advertising, photography, and public relations. Hill chose not to call upon these former practitioners; he said he would prefer to use departmental secretaries, in-house people familiar with responding to inquiries.

Few organizations have personnel with such media experience in their ranks, so training of staff becomes key. The intense training and role-playing of the Scottish information officers would appear to be the ideal, worth all the time and effort required. Kriendler's training had been done in-house in informal sessions. Hill saw professional media training as affordable and practical for only the very senior administrators. Since Flight 103, Hill has taken advantage of an alumna's offer to conduct in-house training for the public relations staff; they, in turn, can train other junior level administrators throughout the university.

The Scots also demonstrated the extent to which survivors of a disaster and grieving relatives can and cannot be shielded from the media. The affected area was too vast to cordon off, and following the initial impact, authorities were caught up in the critical acts of helping those endangered by the flames, containing the raging flames and trying to determine the nature of the disaster. But by daylight, the neighborhood surrounding the crater was blocked off, in part to protect the evidence and in part to shield those who had been able to return home. Later the other major impact area in the town, where the fuselage had come down between two rows of council houses, was blocked off. Angus Kennedy, acting on behalf of local police, used firm but friendly persuasion to dissuade some journalistic intrusions, and townspeople worked together to shield those they felt should be protected. Kennedy took the responsibility of organizing pools and making other arrangements for religious services, and with a few exceptions, he received the cooperation of the media.

The dramatic scenes at Kennedy Airport and the embarrassing behavior of some media there must also be considered a failure for Pan Am's crisis plan. At Salt Lake City, the destination of the second Delta plane to crash at Dallas-Fort Worth, that airline's personnel, easily identifiable by their red Delta jackets, stood near the doors leading into the airport to intercept family and friends of the passengers and tell them of the accident. A "command post," not unlike the VIP Lounge that Pan Am arranged at Kennedy, was set up for relatives, but according to a United Press International report at the time "about half a dozen security officers and Delta employees formed a human wall in front of the room, faced by about 20 reporters waiting to spot relatives going in or out of the room." When a couple who escaped unharmed from the crash arrived on a later flight, Delta employees helped them elude reporters (Harrie, 1988).

The authors would say to universities, including our own, and to other institutions with special responsibilities for young people that a crisis plan ought to include a degree of protection from unwanted media intrusion. While a campus is essentially open space, students ought to be guaranteed privacy in the area they call home, be it a dormitory, sorority or fraternity house or, in some cases, off-campus housing. Newspeople have uniformly condemned the act of the anonymous reporter who, having been turned away at the front door, climbed up on the window sill of the sorority house which had three sisters on Pan Am 103. Staff responsible for student life need to be trained to call campus security or municipal police in the face of such behavior. A campus security car parked in front of the building would probably dissuade most journalists, even the few who might be tempted to pull such a stunt; the prospect of being arrested for trespassing and missing a big story should be deterrent enough.[33]

Schools should also be prepared to take similar action to protect students in classroom situations. At Concord High School in New Hampshire, reporters, photographers and television crews were recording the reaction of students to the lift-off of the space shuttle Challenger, carrying their teacher Christa McAuliffe, when it exploded into pieces. Although television cameras recorded the shock and sorrow, as soon as school officials realized what was happening, they ordered reporters out of the building (*Los Angeles Times*, 1986).

Some young people may want to speak to the media about their loss, just as some did at Syracuse University. The university rightly respected that desire for students, faculty and staff.

Such individual expressions differ from speaking *for* the organization. Conventional wisdom is to have a single spokesperson, particularly in times of crisis, but media training can and should be given to mid-level managers. While they should not speak on behalf of the organization unless pre-arranged or designated in special circumstances, training can help staff understand how reporters operate, explain the need for coordination and consistent messages, develop working and workable procedures for referral of inquiries, and provide practice in mock scenarios. Again Lockerbie and Syracuse provide a striking contrast: When a mid-level public information specialist was contacted by reporters who said that Angus Kennedy had told them that she would provide them with certain information, she recognized this as a common ploy of reporters who cannot get their facts from a primary source. At Syracuse, some of the DIPA staff were unwittingly led by reporters to give out information. A media relations seminar could have prepared them to be alert to such media tactics.

Another important detail involves arrangements to monitor the media reports. The professionals interviewed here were too involved in the heat of the crisis to track what was being said about their organizations in print and broadcast reports. Organizations can either hire outside professional services or train people in-house to monitor the media. In either case, the professional communicators should know whom they can contact in a moment's notice to begin the print and broadcast clipping processes.

United's Doughty gives an example of the effectiveness of this approach:

> In Sioux City, our monitoring picked up a potential devastating and disruptive news report on one of the major national networks. Combining pieces of unrelated sound bites, the network sensationalized their "breaking story" with the lead-in that "there is shocking new evidence that a mechanic's failure to close an engine cowling in Philadelphia the night before may have led to the crash of Flight 232..." The story was ludicrous. As soon as we heard the report, we joined forces with the NTSB [National Transportation Safety Board] media relations staff and approached the network. They retreated on their story and ceased perpetuating it. Two days later, they issued a retraction (1992-93, p.43).

Telecommunications have become a critical element during any crisis. In Lockerbie, local telephone lines were jammed with area residents trying to determine the safety of their friends and families; reporters were clamoring to call their editors; telephone company servicemen hastily installed courtesy phones for the victims' families huddled at Kennedy Airport; communications professionals were inundated by the flood of incoming calls. Thinking ahead and assessing possible needs might help alleviate these situations.[34]

While few organizations can afford the luxury of a permanent crisis center, or even a dedicated media briefing room, the crisis communications plan should incorporate an assessment of facility and equipment needs, and how they would be mobilized in a moment's notice. What lines would be dedicated to incoming calls from relatives? What lines would be dedicated to media inquiries? Where could key officials gather in a kind of "crisis control center," away from intrusions? Where could the media gather? (Conventional wisdom calls for these areas to be separate, so that sensitive operations are not jeopardized by reporters' inquiries.) What equipment will be needed for each area? What can be purchased and stored? What must be retrieved on a moment's notice?

Again, money is not the issue here — even a Masonic Hall served the purpose at Lockerbie. What does matter is the immediate creation of a central location where the media can gather, a site staffed for regular news updates, and stocked with the equipment and supplies needed for long durations. The possibility of feeding large numbers of staff and reporters working round the clock should also be addressed.

Although money can become an issue, especially in crises of long durations, none of the organizations interviewed for this study seemed to suffer for lack of funding; monies were found to meet the unexpected needs. Part of crisis planning includes anticipation of emergency funds and establishing procedures to bypass normal requisitions.

An institution's crisis response, both in the short-run and over the long-term, takes its cue from top leadership. The Chief Executive Officer or equivalent leader cannot, in the words of the SIO's Brian Reid, "take the disaster to his bosom and exclude everyone." The CEO needs to recognize the public's interest in the disaster and take a visible role early on in the communications process. Knowing the appropriate action in that process is critical.

In the case of Union-Carbide, Warren Anderson's rushing to the scene at Bhopal resulted in his arrest by Indian officials, thus removing him from the managerial helm at a crucial juncture. On the other hand, the take-charge message conveyed by Johnson and Johnson's James Burke in nationally televised ads is credited with helping the company maintain its credibility during the Tylenol crisis (Murray and Shohen, 1992).

In Lockerbie, various approaches were used. The Scottish officials had the luxury of working with a police chief, John Boyd, who not only understood the need to share information with the world, but also had been trained by media experts and who was comfortable under media scrutiny. Beveridge's folksy statement about the media not wanting "the monkey; they want the organ grinder" is echoed by John Klose, the public information officer who handled the media coverage of the Cleveland Elementary School Massacre in Stockton, California. He believes that public relations practitioners are not always the best spokespersons, but that their job is to advise the CEO who acts as spokesperson. "If you do your job well, you're invisible. Your job is to take people with the questions, hook them up with the people with the answers and get out of the way" (Briggs, 1990, p.39).

Pan Am's Plaskett all but disappeared for more than a week. Whether he was warned by lawyers and insurance executives, or whether he was misguided by his public relations counselor, or simply decided by himself not to step forward, the result is the same: By not appearing in public for eight days, Plaskett fueled the angry fires of the families who perceived Pan Am as a cold and calculating corporation, with money, not passenger safety, as its priority.

Plaskett had to look no further than the experience of another CEO to see the repercussions of avoiding the public. During the March 1988 Valdez disaster, Chairman Lawrence Rawls decided to stay in EXXON's corporate headquarters in New York, insisting that he had capable managers on the scene in Alaska. Rawls has since changed his mind, based on the harsh criticism of his decision; if he were to do it again, he says, he would go directly to the site.

At Syracuse University, the appearance by Chancellor Melvin Eggers seemed to assuage the angry reporters. One reporter told the researchers it was probably one of the best statements he had ever heard after a tragedy. A subsequent editorial praised the Chancellor:

> Syracuse University Chancellor Melvin Eggers is an economist, a practitioner of the dreary science, accustomed to hard-edged realities and solid results. After all, one plus one equals two.
>
> Week before last, his head-on encounter with a tragedy of Pan Am Flight 103, a hunk of reality of almost surreal proportions showed Melvin Eggers is also deeply human. His actions after the crash and reflections in a *Herald-American* interview last Sunday, we feel, portray a depth of human spirit that challenges each of us to pause and think about (the) real meaning of humanity and education (January 1, 1989).

Disasters, almost by definition, do not end in a day or even a week. The magnitude of such events means that they will preoccupy the institutions for months and even years. This certainly was the case with Flight 103 and it presented special challenges to public relations practitioners and public information professionals interviewed here. For the Scottish Office public information officers and Angus Kennedy, the years have been filled with new situations and criminal investigations that consume their attention, but a new twist in the Pan Am 103 story will set their phones ringing again with reporters seeking information, confirmation and statements. While Pan Am no longer exists as a corporate entity, the lawsuits against its insurers will last for years to come. Jeffrey Kriendler continues to recuperate from his stroke and has begun a new phase of his public relations career as a consultant.

At Syracuse University, Robert Hill's office still receives the occasional media inquiry, but the primary activity is an outgrowth of the program begun on the night of the bombing: reaching out to the parents and families of the victims and an attempt to make sense of this enormous tragedy.

On the evening of December 21, 1988, when it became clear that Pan Am was not contacting many of the families, the Chancellor's Office, the Vice

President for Student Affairs and his staff, and the Division of International Programs Abroad began calling families of the students lost in the disaster. Many families remember with gratitude the sympathetic and sensitive approach of the University staff. The families' appreciation deepened at the time of the January 18 memorial service. Many returned to the campus on April 23, 1990, as the University dedicated a "place of remembrance," a granite and limestone memorial set off by plantings of Scottish heather, at the main entrance to campus.

Each year since 1990, 35 scholarships honoring the slain students, each valued at $5,000, are awarded to help finance the recipients' senior years at Syracuse University. These, now considered the University's most prestigious scholarships, are awarded on the basis of academic achievement, service and an essay each student writes on the meaning of the Flight 103 tragedy. Members of the photography department at the University's S.I. Newhouse School of Public Communication work with Dr and Mrs Peter Tsairis, parents of Alexia Tsairis, to create a "Photography for World Peace" competition through which students from across the nation compete for scholarships to study overseas in the DIPA program. The University and the Lockerbie Trust, established at the time of the bombing to manage donations that poured in from around the world, collaborate to fund scholarships each year for two young people from Lockerbie to spend a school year studying at Syracuse University.

Part II: The Aftermath

5 *The Changing Role of Survivors: From Victim to Advocate*

By February 6, 1989, frustration and anger of American relatives over the lack of response from the State Department and the administrations of President Ronald Reagan and newly inaugurated George Bush had reached crisis proportions. The families were particularly incensed by the December 5, 1988, warning to the U.S. embassy in Helsinki, which had been shared with the diplomatic community in Moscow but not with those who boarded Pan Am 103. About 100 relatives gathered at the Grand Hyatt Hotel in New York City ready to face media summoned on their behalf by the National Victims Center.[1]

Although many had spoken about their loss to journalists, few had ever attended a news conference, much less the array of cameras, reporters and photographers that such an event can draw in Manhattan. Some relatives wore photographs of their loved ones, a practice many would continue during group functions months and years later. Their sincerity touched many in the press corps. Writing for *Newsday*, Dennis Duggan put aside the neutral voice journalists generally use to report news conferences:

> You can say 270 — the number of people who died in the explosion of that jumbo jet six weeks ago — over and over in your mind, but it isn't until you are confronted with the living wreckage of the survivors and their stories that you begin to grasp the enormity of the tragedy.
>
> At a press conference organized by the National Victims Center...close to 100 relatives came to break what they called a "wall of silence" that has formed since the air tragedy four days before Christmas.
>
> One by one they rose to speak and in their sometimes cracking voices you could feel the nights of unspeakable anguish they have endured since that terrible day. Always there was the still unanswered question: Why were some told of the bomb threat but not others? (1989, p. 8)

Two days after the disaster, a reporter had asked then President Reagan whether the public should have been given the same warning about a bomb threat that had been sent to American diplomats. The warning, posted in the

Moscow embassy December 13 and signed by William Kelly, administrative counselor of the embassy, said the Federal Aviation Authority had notified it that sometime within the next two weeks there would be a bombing attempt against a Pan American aircraft flying from Frankfurt to the United States. The posted note, which said Pan Am had been notified, left to the discretion of "individual travelers any decisions on altering personal travel plans or changing to another American carrier" (Duggan, 1989).

Reagan's reply to the White House press corps was, "I think all the precautions that could be taken were taken with regard to warning the airline and all. But as you stop to think about it, such a public statement with nothing more to go on than an anonymous telephone call, you'd literally have closed down the air traffic in the world."

Paul Hudson, who had begun researching the FAA's warnings after the funeral of his 16-year-old daughter Melina, told the news conference Reagan was wrong. The FAA's own reports showed a small number of threats to the 6 million scheduled flights per year, Hudson said. A "positively tiny number" were classified as "high-level" threats, he said. "The threat to Pan Am Flight 103...was apparently classified as such a high-level threat" (Duggan, 1989, p. 8).[2]

Bert Ammerman, whose businessman brother Tom had been killed in the bombing, told the media that he had asked for a 10-minute meeting with Bush to discuss allegations that Libya, Syria and Iran were harboring terrorists involved in the bombing. He wanted to discuss appropriate action the government might take. "We've asked the State Department what it has to say about this, but it doesn't know what to say. I think the President will have to make the decision," he said (Winship, 1989).

The relatives also issued a statement that complained of the "utter silence" of high government officials who extended no offers of condolence, did not attend memorial services and had not responded to their letters (Abrams and Collins, 1989).

Ammerman remembered being surprised at how many media showed up — between 100 and 150. "It was a massive turnout. It was the first opportunity, which we didn't know at the time, for the New York press to get their dibs on it, because you have to remember that most of the press people who were over in Scotland were sent there from London or from other agencies. So the big-time hitters, the golden boys and girls of the New York media, now had their opportunity to ask questions." Ammerman said that showed him there was interest in their cause, "but the interest was in what we wanted to happen to the country that did this to us. They were looking for us to say, 'Nuke them. Blast them.'"

With the news conference behind them, the families began to form a group.

Already their individual responses to the tragedy had drawn them together. Paul Hudson and Bert Ammerman had met on the trip to Lockerbie. Georgia Nucci, the mother of Syracuse University student Christopher Jones, obtained a list from the university of other parents of victims and wrote them, suggesting they might want to contact each other for support. By the time of the memorial service at the University on January 18, more than two dozen family members had already met informally at the Mendham, New Jersey, home of Tom and Dorothy Coker, who lost twin sons in the disaster (Cox and Foster, 1992). The memorial service itself brought the families of the 35 Syracuse University victims together, and a January 29 mass at St Patrick's Cathedral on New York's Fifth Avenue provided a source of comfort for more than 600 family and friends of those who had died in the bombing. The news conference was the direct result of the meeting Hudson organized following the St Patrick's service.

Hudson, the head of a real estate firm in Albany, New York, was certainly no stranger to activism. An attorney, he had worked with the New York Public Interest Research Group, best known in New York as NYPIRG, and had also served as a victims rights lawyer for the New York State Crime Victims Board. NYPIRG is affiliated with a group headed by consumer activist Ralph Nader, who operates out of a Washington office and has links to a number of advocacy groups, including the Aviation Consumer Action Project. The project works on behalf of air travelers and has also helped relatives of plane crash victims.

An organizational meeting for relatives was scheduled for Sunday, February 19, at a Hasbrouck Heights, New Jersey, restaurant called the Crow's Nest. Before the meeting, about 15 or 20 gathered at the home of Wendy Giebler, whose husband William had been killed in the bombing just nine months after their wedding. The group asked Ammerman, Max Saunders and Georgia and Tony Nucci to come up with a preamble or statement. The four of them came up with four goals that still represent the mission of the organization:

> To provide support, assistance and information for all family members of the victims; to encourage Congressional committees to investigate the events regarding the bombing of Pan Am Flight 103 and the actions and policies of the FAA, Pan American World Airways, the State Department and other involved parties; to identify and provide specific recommendations for near term and long term improvements in airline and airport security; to demand that changes and a more aggressive stance be implemented by our government regarding terrorism, to the end that there be no safe haven anywhere for terrorists.

While the quartet was writing, the rest of the group worked on the organization's structure. Ammerman recalled, "I can still remember coming upstairs and (being told, amid) a little laughter, 'Congratulations, you're political action chairman.'" Then they went to the Crow's Nest and Hudson made a presentation. "At that time, everyone was still in a lot of grief," Ammerman said. It was decided that the work of the organization would be directed by a steering committee, which included Hudson, Ammerman, Rick Hartunian, Betty Capasso, Joe Horgan, and Max Saunders. Hudson came up with a name for the group: Victims of Pan Am Flight 103.

Between 75 and 100 relatives attended the organizational meeting, which also drew a number of media. They did a live interview for a 6 p.m. newscast. "That's when it hit me that (a reporter) could be a very viable source in carrying our story," Ammerman said. "I realized the press could become our advocate or ally instead of being someone you didn't want to talk to."

The group began its quest for answers and action in Washington. One of the first doors they opened led to Senator Frank Lautenberg, a Democrat from New Jersey. As a senator from a state where many victims' relatives lived, he had a vested interest in their complaints, but he also chaired the transportation subcommittee of the Senate Appropriations Committee, which gave him a ready platform to begin investigating their concerns.

On March 14, Lautenberg and his subcommittee questioned the FAA's security director, Raymond Salazar, who testified that the only warning U.S. officials had received was the anonymous call to the Helsinski embassy. Two days later news reports revealed that all American carriers operating overseas had been warned on November 18 about evidence uncovered by German intelligence that terrorists might hide explosive devices in a Toshiba portable radio — the same brand of radio that investigators in Lockerbie had said concealed the bomb that brought down Pan Am 103. Lautenberg called a news conference, demanded an independent commission investigate the Flight 103 bombing and came close to calling Salazar a liar. "It's fair to say I wasn't told the truth. He fudged it. What we saw was word smithery." Salazar had testified there was no specific warning about the event. The senator said, "All airlines and airports were alerted to the fact that this particular device had to be looked for" (Bass, 1989).

Ammerman said that contradiction of Salazar's testimony really got the attention of the press. "When that took place, that's when the press really became like sharks and advocates of what we were doing, because they now realized that there was a rat here; there was something really wrong. And that was the turning point of the entire process — in our relationship with the press, and in our cause. It turned everything in our favor, because now the press overwhelmingly came on our side, and said, 'You people have something going.'"

In Europe, reporters learned the earliest warning had been sent November

10 to all airlines operating in West Germany. The warning included a photograph of the radio-cassette player containing explosives seized following a raid on a Frankfurt apartment used by members of the Popular Front for the Liberation of Palestine General Command (PFLP-GC). German officials said specifically that the warning was sent to Pan Am. British authorities had sent a bulletin by telex to airlines on November 22, describing the radio-cassette bombs and advising security authorities to look for telltale signs: a machine that would not play, one that rattled when shaken, more wiring than a normal radio and tape over the antenna socket. To the government's embarrassment, the *Daily Mirror* also learned that British officials had issued another warning on December 19, but mailed it at the height of the Christmas postal crush. Pan Am claimed it did not receive that warning until January 17 (Marks *et al.*, 1989).

The Victims group testified before Lautenberg's committee on March 16 and held a news conference on Capitol Hill on March 21. But they were also working on a big media event, a vigil across from the White House 103 days after the tragedy.

In early March, Ammerman made a speech for Stan Maslowski, the father of Pan Am victim Diane Maslowski, at his Lions Club in Haddonsfield, New Jersey, and several of the most active members of the group came to provide support. Afterwards, they went to Maslowski's home, and began talking about what they were going to do politically. "Someone said we should have a vigil," Ammerman recalled. "I said, 'Why don't we have it on the 103rd day?'" They immediately saw the symbolism, the potential interest for the media. The idea of staging it as a march on the White House came next. Ammerman took the idea to the Political Action Committee. "Right from the first or second week of March, it took us three weeks to put that all together," he said.

Shortly thereafter a group of 40 gathered at Ammerman's house. Wendy Giebler enlisted friends with a videotaping business who spent the whole day taping family comments regarding the State Department and the tragedy. They edited it into a 12-minute film that the relatives took to Washington, making a copy for President Bush, and one for each senator. "We realized how important video, multi-media presentation was even then," Ammerman said.

They also met in Connecticut to assign responsibilities for the vigil and the march on the Senate. All the senators were to be contacted. Ammerman sent a letter to the President, and on March 29, received word through the Transportation Department that Bush wanted to meet them. "We really boxed the President in," Ammerman said. "If he didn't meet with us, if we walked on the White House, we'd be arrested, and it would have been a sympathy thing. And if he did meet with us, we got our point across. And that's what happened."[3]

Families and friends of victims in Britain had been suffering many of the same frustrations as their American counterparts. On April 1, about 35 relatives and friends of U.K. victims met at the Russell Square Hotel, not far from the British Museum. They formed U.K. Families-Flight 103 and immediately called for an independent inquiry and an explanation from Paul Channon, the Transport Secretary, on the status of airport security in the weeks before the disaster. In what sounded like an echo from their trans-Atlantic counterparts, they criticized "the silence of the Government and the lack of expression of condolence which has added greatly to our dismay and distress" (Langton, 1989, p.1).

The response from the Department of Transport was hardly comforting. It said Channon had "made statements in the House of Commons on January 10 and March 21, making his position quite clear as regards the circumstances of the tragedy, and that he sees no need for a public inquiry" (Harlow, 1989, p. 2).[4]

The atmosphere of the Saturday meeting in Russell Square was very different from the session in a New Jersey restaurant that marked the formal beginning of the American group. For one thing, no media were notified in advance, although Linda Mack, a Cambridge post-graduate student who served as spokesman for the group following the first meeting, was part of an investigative team for the U.S. television network, ABC.

No mention was made in the group's public statement of one of the most dramatic parts of the meeting. In fact, more than a year would pass before Dr Jim Swire, who was to become the leader of the U.K. group, would tell a *Sunday Times* reporter that he had displayed a dummy bomb at the meeting in Russell Square (Grove, 1990). After information was released about the bomb confiscated from a terrorist cell in Germany, the doctor had studied pictures of the bombs confiscated by the West Germans and fashioned a dummy bomb in a cassette recorder using marzipan, a confection made of almonds. Similar to the plastic explosive Semtex, it can be easily molded. The device included a dummy detonator, timer, batteries, and pressure switch. It epitomized the lengths to which Swire would go in trying to understand the catastrophe that had claimed the life of his eldest child, Flora, a medical student (Grove, 1990).

That same weekend, a Pan Am pilot, Bruce Smith, whose British wife Ingrid was killed in the bombing, announced in London that he was launching an appeal to raise a reward of $2.5 million (£1.5 million). The reward, which was for information leading to the apprehension of those responsible for the bombing, was purposively set at the amount offered by Ayatollah Khomeini for the assassination of Salman Rushdie following publication of *The Satanic Verses*; at the time, the Iranians were widely considered the probable sponsors of the Pan Am sabotage. Smith said he would launch the appeal in Washington on April 3 and pledged the $100,000 compensation he was receiving from Pan Am for his wife's death (Langton, 1989).[5]

The American relatives' meeting with Bush on April 3, which Ammerman said was scheduled for 15 minutes, lasted more than an hour. The relatives pressed the President for the appointment of an independent civil commission to investigate, but received no commitment. Across the street, in Lafayette Park, the vigil of the 103rd day dramatized the families' devotion to the memory of their loved ones and to their cause. Their numbers were swelled by friends, and by classmates of the Syracuse University students who had come down by bus. As the media watched, relatives came forward with white carnations, each labeled with the name of a victim, and wove their stems into an evergreen wreath. Then they marched to the White House gate and passed it to a guard. After that they headed for Capitol Hill to lobby senators.

Transportation Secretary Samuel Skinner was ready for the media attention. Within hours of the White House meeting, he announced a series of measures to guard against sabotage and tighten security at airports around the world. The media gave the most attention to a decision to speed up installation of devices to detect explosives at high-risk airports in the United States and abroad. The first of six thermal neutron analysis (TNA) devices was to be installed at Kennedy Airport in June; the other five would be installed at unnamed airports overseas, with 100 more to be installed at the "earliest possible date."

Skinner rejected the relatives' demand for public warnings of terrorist attacks, but did say new regulations would require that the bulletins be shared with pilots-in-command. Skinner also announced that the bulletins, which had been issued on an advisory basis in the past, would now require that airlines acknowledge them within 24 hours and submit action plans on how they intended to counter the threats within 72 hours. While presented as initiatives, the new regulations showed how little attention the FAA had paid in the past to the way airlines responded to security threats.

The *Los Angeles Times* asked people it described as experts within the counterterrorism community and the airline industry for their reaction. They characterized Skinner's initiatives as "moderate" and predicted they would have little immediate practical effect (Jehl, 1989).

The relatives held another news conference before they left Washington, and Hudson reiterated their demand for an independent civil investigation. He vowed to keep working to change the policy that forbids the sharing of terrorist threats with passengers, although he was encouraged by "a strong indication of the President's concern" (Jehl, 1989, p. 1).

For American families, the success of the April 3 assault on Washington had been a prelude. Much bigger achievements lay ahead. But the relatives, many of them still in a highly emotional state, also had to work through a struggle over leadership. Journalists who have tried to reconstruct the split have come up with several different scenarios, but they all boil down to differences between Hudson and Ammerman about the goals of the organization and the methods for achieving them. Many family members told us that it was "personality differences" that finally came to a head April 29 at a highly emotional meeting in Fishkill, New York. Attempts to work out the problems lasted through the summer, but by September 19 Hudson and five other of the 15 directors who had been elected in June quit the organization and formed a new group, Families of Pan Am 103/Lockerbie.

Nevertheless, it had been a productive summer. On August 4, President Bush had finally agreed to name the presidential commission the families had been seeking for months. Anne McLaughlin, former Labor Secretary in the Reagan administration, who was named to chair the commission, had been personally acquainted with three of those killed on the flight. Aphrodite Tsairis, a member of the Victims board of directors whose daughter Alexia had been a photojournalism student at Syracuse University, was named as liaison to the commission.

The campaign for answers and action had already moved into the international arena. On August 19, Ammerman led a delegation of six to London and Scotland. The next day they announced they had joined forces with Jim Swire and U.K. Families-Flight 103.

That same day the *Sunday Telegraph* carried an outline of the overhaul of airport security being prepared by the government of Margaret Thatcher. The newspaper said Transport Minister Michael Portillo would present the measures to the relatives on Monday. The move replayed the scenario of the group's meeting with President Bush, when Transportation Secretary Skinner had suddenly produced new safety measures. The British government's Transport Secretary Cecil Parkinson was planning, the *Telegraph* said, to introduce a new aviation act in the autumn that would create a new team of aviation security inspectors with power to ground flights, withdraw security clearance from cleaning and catering firms and workers, and take passengers to court if they prejudiced security arrangements (Jones, 1989).

Swire joined the Americans as they met with a number of key players in the investigation and government, including Portillo, the police team at Lockerbie and the British Airports Authority. They were pushing for an independent inquiry in Britain that would parallel the one taking place in the States, as well as for closer cooperation between governments and airlines to stop terrorist attacks. On the last day of the Americans' visit, the group had what legal experts called an unprecedented meeting with the Lord Advocate,

Lord Fraser. Normally, because of his overall responsibility for the criminal investigation, the Lord Advocate would not meet with the relatives of crime victims during an investigation or before suspects had been brought to trial.

Ammerman and Swire planned a joint visit to West Germany for November. The American group also talked to Swire about using the media. "We kept harping on him, 'The media can become your friend. You need the media because if what you're doing is not publicized, then no one knows about it, therefore it's not worth it because nothing is ever going to get done,'" Ammerman recalled.

In his search for information about the disaster, Swire had already decided newspeople could be helpful. "We very soon found that the media appeared to know a lot more about the circumstances of the crash than official sources were prepared to tell us," he said. "We came up immediately against a blanket of silence. When we would ring up (officials) and ask if any reason was known why, for instance, someone would blow up this airliner over Scotland, we wouldn't be fed any comment or any support, any help of any kind. We would simply be brushed off and given phrases like, 'No comment,' 'We have no comment to make,' this sort of thing."

The British doctor's subsequent use of the media was often dramatic. Swire had been a person with no knowledge of public relations, Ammerman said. He turned into "one of the whirlwinds." The joint appearances by the two men helped give Swire visibility in Britain, and after Ammerman left, the doctor continued pushing for an independent inquiry that would focus on security issues.

One of the first efforts Swire made on behalf of the cause took place at the Malta summit in December. The relatives had sent an open letter to Bush and Mikhail Gorbachev, appealing for their help to eradicate terrorism, specifically by pressuring Syria and Iran to cease overt and covert support for terrorist groups. The summit was plagued by bad weather, which also complicated the ceremony that Swire had planned with the Rev. John Mosey of Britain, whose daughter Helga had perished aboard Pan Am 103, and American relative William Marek, who lost his sister Elizabeth in the tragedy. The three men, who had arrived late after missing their original flight, wanted to cast a flower into the sea for each of the 270 victims and then release a dove to symbolize their campaign for "peace in the skies." The problem, Swire remarked to one of the American CNN reporters, was that they had no dove. "To my amazement (the reporter) just snapped his fingers and said, 'Joe, white dove!' and, in minutes, a local retainer brought a fertilizer sack containing a white dove which he just handed us." The yellow and white chrysanthemums and red dahlias were cast onto the waves, but the dove was buffeted by the high winds and flew straight back to its dovecote (Grove, 1990).

The emphasis on using the media was a hallmark of the Ammerman faction. One of the first steps it took after the split with Hudson was to hire a public relations firm to help develop media contacts. Hudson's group, by contrast, hired a Washington lawyer as its lobbyist on Capitol Hill.

Soon Ammerman and other members of Victims of Pan Am Flight 103 were making the talk show circuit. They had appeared on the Geraldo Rivera show even before they signed the Kamber Group as their public relations consultants, and soon began a series of appearances: Phil Donahue, Joan Rivers, the breakfast television news shows. "I can say that TV-wise I don't think there's been a show that hasn't been done with good taste," Ammerman said. "And that even goes for Geraldo Rivera, but he was the first talk show that we did. And I have to say that on that day, you could have no complaints about him. The Donahue show maybe was the best Donahue show he's done in about three or four years. You see, Donahue was into it when he did it with us," Ammerman said, echoing other members of the group who still remember the way the talk show host spent time with them before the show, during the commercial breaks and at the end of the programs. "He did a superb job."

Ammerman gained respect for the morning television stars, particularly Jane Pauley, who was still with the "Today" show during the first years of the relatives' campaign. "She took the time to look over the work that her researchers had done the night before," he said, explaining that whenever he goes on one of the morning shows, a researcher calls and tapes an interview, which is passed on to the person who will be doing the on-screen interview. Pauley met with him about 6 a.m. and said, "Look, this is the issue; here are the questions I need to get answers for. What's one question you would like me to ask?" "I'll never forget that," Ammerman said. He added that he has also enjoyed working with Bryant Gumbel, who still hosts "Today" and with Joan Lunden of ABC's "Good Morning, America."

Bruce Kozarsky of the Kamber Group was very clear about why he respected these clients: "I thought they were just wonderful, just terrific people, who took the most horrible thing that could ever happen to them in their lives and made something really positive out of it. You know, despite the depressing nature of the subject matter, there was something really very uplifting about working with them. The other main impression I have is that these are people who are pretty smart and pretty savvy, whose basic instincts on these types of things are good, who may have gone into the media business as amateurs but who certainly had a lot of good natural skills to begin with and built on them very quickly, and I think were largely very effective spokespeople."

Kozarsky saw the role of the public relations firm as "helping channel some of their talents and their energies in the right direction, and in making sure that they came across as a calm and responsible organization. You know, there were times when they might have some ideas about things that we might say, 'Well, that might not play so well, you might try a different way.' That type of thing. But really we were more just kind of coordinators, facilitators, advice givers. It was really to their credit entirely that they were able to do as much as they have."

The presidential commission ended its work in May 1990, and on the 15th, both Ammerman and Hudson met with Bush at the White House to receive folded American flags and a briefing on the commission report. Then each group held a news conference. Ammerman's group scheduled its at the National Press Club, and it was carried live on C-Span, the cable channel that transmits congressional debates and other public affairs events and discussions. Both Ammerman and Aphrodite Tsairis, now respectively president and chairman of the organization, were in great demand for interviews.

The commission document, which chastised the FAA for not enforcing its own regulations, said the disaster "may well have been preventable." News reports tended to focus on its recommendation that the United States should prepare for pre-emptive or retaliatory military strikes to protect airline passengers from terrorists. In Britain, Swire rejected military action while renewing his call for a public inquiry into the British aspects of the disaster. "Lockerbie was a revenge attack paid for by Iran," he said, reflecting reports that the bombing had been in retaliation for the downing of an Iranian airliner by the USS Vincennes. "To kill Iranians and Syrians in return is only going to make the situation worse and produce more grieving families" (Fletcher, 1990, Overseas news).

But the immediate focus of both American groups, although they differed in the specifics, was legislation to improve security for air travelers. Lautenberg and Senator Alfonse D'Amato, a New York Republican, who had both served on the commission, sponsored a bill that incorporated its non-military recommendations.

In Britain, the legislation announced by Transport Secretary Cecil Parkinson the previous August had still not become law, and Swire decided to test the beefed-up security at Heathrow Airport. Supposedly security officers had been trained to spot electronic devices that might contain explosives. On May 18, he flew to Boston to meet with the Victims of Pan Am Flight 103, and deliberately took British Airways because it had begun x-raying all baggage. A dummy bomb, like the one he had carried to the first meeting of the U.K. family group, was in his suitcase.

Once Swire arrived in the States, he had key members of the Victims group verify that he had the "bomb" with him. But he waited until July 1 to reveal what he had done.[6] As the doctor told the story, the test had been better, in one sense, than he had expected. Instead of merely passing through x-ray, all bags on that flight had been subjected to a special security check. A woman security officer had opened his suitcase and lifted out the cassette player. Swire said the marzipan was showing through the grill at the back of the player, and he had purposively used a scarlet-colored primer plug to push in a socket in the back of the machine ("They'd been shown a black one and I wanted to make it easier for them") and the entire object was much heavier than a normal player. He watched the woman's face and saw no expression that showed she was aware the object might be dangerous. "I don't think she'd been properly trained," Swire said in an interview in March 1992. "She picked it up, turned it over where she could see the yellow through the grille; she could see the scarlet plug, and asked if I'd taken the batteries out, to which I replied yes." Then, he said, she put the "bomb" back in the case and sent it off to be packed in the hold. "That indicated to me that the security service was not capable of responding to special threats, because that lady had not had a tutorial on the last successful blast, which had blown 270 people to pieces not long before that."

The experience also demolished any faith Swire had in authorities being able to avert future catastrophes. "It did shake up the security authorities very badly in this country, resulting in certain measures being taken very quickly to improve security. The tragedy is that the real underlying issues, which will decide whether the next atrocity is blocked or not — those have not been addressed. It is clear that it has not generated a sufficient sense of urgency to make sure that they are looked at properly."

Swire told of a letter he had received in December 1991 from regulatory authorities regarding steps to start addressing security issues, which used the phrase, "We thought you'd be interested..." The doctor asked how they could use a phrase like that in speaking to someone like him. "By that date, late '91, they thought I'd be 'interested' that it was just starting. I mean, if they'd used the word 'appalled' that would have shown they were on the same wave length. I'm afraid that what this says is that security is a product designed to placate the public, not protect the public."

The week before Swire revealed his test of airline security, Transport Secretary Parkinson had been chastising John Prescott, the Labour Party's transport spokesman, for exploiting the grief caused by disasters for political purposes. Prescott had claimed that failures by the Department of Transport had contributed to the Lockerbie bombing, the capsizing of the channel ferry off Zeebrugge and the sinking of the Marchioness pleasure boat on the Thames. The night that Swire announced his exploit Parkinson called for a full investigation of the case.

On August 2, Saddam Hussein sent Iraqi troops into Kuwait, and in a matter days, American troops and British naval and air forces were ordered to help neighboring Saudi Arabia protect its oil fields from an Iraqi attack. In the early days of August, the significance of events in the Persian Gulf to those campaigning for better aviation security seemed remote. But the world's first post-Cold War crisis would soon reshape diplomatic alliances in some very unanticipated ways. On August 10, a majority of Arab League nations, including Syria, voted to dispatch troops to the Persian Gulf to stand against Iraq. Only Libya and the Palestine Liberation Organization voted with Iraq in the crucial resolution.

That meant the U.S. and U.K. allies in the Persian Gulf crisis would include Syria, which allowed leaders of the Popular Front for the Liberation of Palestine General Command (PFLP-GC), the group often mentioned in lists of prime suspects in the bombing, to maintain their headquarters in Damascus. Libya, on the other hand, sided with the enemy, Saddam Hussein.

That aroused suspicions among some relatives of the Flight 103 dead, who worried aloud to the media that the criminal investigation of the bombing might be hindered by the new alliances. "They are sweeping the deaths of 270 innocent people under the carpet because it is diplomatically convenient to do so," Swire told *The Independent*. "They are not an inconvenience to be forgotten" (Insight, 1990). The Lord Advocate reacted quickly to such reports, making it clear that he had been given no instruction to wind down the investigation. "Nobody gets in the way of the investigation run by the Chief Constable of Dumfries and Galloway constabulary," he said (Gill, 1990).

With the momentous events in the Gulf occupying the attention of both politicians and the public, relatively small headlines greeted the fact that on September 26, Britain's new Aviation and Maritime Security Act had finally become law. It had been delayed for months over amendments added by the House of Lords after its initial approval in the Commons.

With Congress back in session, lobbying by the American families became intense. "The media did a great deal in helping us get the Aviation Security Act passed," Bert Ammerman said. One tactic the group used was to meet a television crew at certain congressional offices. The team would be there with cameras, "and it sort of intimidated the aides if they didn't go along;" a refusal to see the group's representatives could result in a television report that night that the senator or representative was "anti-family."

The media attention, however, also highlighted the differences between the two American family groups. An article in the Style section of the *Washington Post* described the congressional hearing on the bi-partisan bill after the Bush administration asked that it be tabled while they worked on their own plan. Ammerman, the *Post* reported, rose to speak in favor of the legislation. Hudson described the bill as "weak, flawed and inadequate. We call on this committee to strengthen it or defeat it" (McKenna, 1990).

The article, written for the *Post* by Kate McKenna, a reporter for States News Service, drew an impassioned response from Rosemary Mild, a member of the group led by Hudson, and the mother of Miriam Wolfe, one of the Syracuse students killed in the bombing. In a letter to the editor, Mild chastized the *Post* for what she called the gossipy approach of the coverage, noting that:

> Dissension eventually afflicts many organized groups of survivors (as the reporter noted), because they are diverse human beings brought together solely by tragic events. However, to focus on such dissension was misleading and might even have adversely affected current and future legislation to improve airline security and prevent future acts of airline terrorism...
>
> The bill up for a vote in Congress is the Aviation Security Act of 1990 — the result of many Pan Am Flight 103 families' efforts. Why aren't you analyzing its strengths and weaknesses as critical legislation? (1990)

Mild had a point. The article speculated that the drive for legislation was doomed because of the differences between the two family groups, but paid little attention to either side in terms of policy issues. The crux of the article came about 3,500 words into a story that ran nearly 4,000. It said:

> Had the original lobbying organization still been intact, its members might have resolved their disagreements, worked out a compromise and presented a united front before Congress, exercising the same moral authority that brought them this far. That didn't happen.
>
> Saying the bill didn't go nearly far enough, Hudson and his allies drafted 29 amendments that would, among other things, remove all security functions from what Hudson called "the discredited" FAA. He also proposed creation of a rather dauntingly ambitious Aviation Security Oversight Board, composed of presidential appointees representing airline employees and management, passengers, terrorist victims, the travel industry and the general public (1990, p. D1).

The article did not discuss why Hudson thought security functions should be removed from the FAA, or describe what was "dauntingly ambitious" about the proposed Aviation Security Oversight Board. Neither the thesis of the piece, that the legislation would fail if the two groups did not resolve their differences, nor Mild's concern that it would have an adverse effect on the legislation, were born out. Both houses of Congress passed the bill, and Bush signed it into law in November 1990.

Meanwhile, the Fatal Accident Inquiry, a form of inquest required under Scots law, had begun in Dumfries. A number of relatives attended the proceedings, which opened October 1, including George Williams from Maryland, whose only son Geordie had been among the U.S. servicemen killed in the bombing. He told reporters on the opening day that he recognized the inquiry would be limited because of the continuing criminal investigation, but that he and other relatives were looking for the truth to emerge. "We know we won't get it out of our government, the German government, the British government," Williams said. "My only hope is that the stubborn integrity of the Scots will prevail and that we will ultimately get to the truth" (Senior, 1990).

Over the next four-and-a-half months, the inquiry would sit for 61 days and hear 131witnesses (Ryan, 1991). A small group of relatives attended most of the sessions, including Marina de Larracoechea, a New York designer who was given special permission to join in the cross-examination of witnesses. The designer, originally from Spain, was the sister of Flight 103 stewardess Nieve de Larracoechea (Ryan, 1990). Swire was also present, and eventually elected to join in the questioning. At one point, Swire attempted to call Paul Channon, the Transport Secretary at the time of the disaster, and Margaret Thatcher. Both invoked the speaker's rule, an exemption that operated in this case very like the executive privilege which sitting U.S. presidents have used as a shield.

Although Swire initially had expressed doubt that the inquiry could provide much insight into security problems at British airports, since it could not hear testimony *in camera*, he expressed satisfaction at the conclusions reached by Sheriff Principal John Mowat, who had presided over the inquiry. The report said that while primary cause of death for the 270 killed in the bombing was "a criminal act of murder," a list of "reasonable precautions" could have prevented the sabotage. It criticized Department of Transportation regulations for providing "insufficient protection" against an undetected, unaccompanied bag being transferred to the flight, and said "security was given low priority among Pan Am operational staff" (Mowat, 1991). The methodical inquiry was covered in considerable detail by the British press, but ignored by most American newspapers and periodicals.

The same day the Fatal Accident Inquiry produced this encouraging news a judge in the U.S. 2nd Court of Appeals issued an important ruling against the families. He said they would not be able to claim punitive damages in their civil case against Pan Am and its security service, even if they were able to prove the airliner was guilty of "willful misconduct." That meant that the best they could hope for would be compensatory damages. No matter how lax an airline's security may be, it cannot be assessed damages designed to punish it.[7] A jury decision that Pan Am was innocent of any misconduct would limit compensation to the $75,000 amount set by the Warsaw Convention in 1929.

That was just one of the many jolts that relatives experienced in 1991. The Gulf War brought both ups and downs. Aphrodite Tsairis could tell a Victims of Pan Am 103 meeting in Albany in January that security had been tightened at American airports; and curbside check-in of baggage at airports, long a concern of the group, had been suspended. The group had proclaimed itself ready, in the event of terrorism attacks as a by-product of the Gulf conflict, to provide assistance to victims and their families. But the alliance with Syria exacerbated the suspicions of many that both the Bush and Thatcher governments were too ready to overlook President Assad's tolerance of terrorists. A series of trips to Damascus by Secretary of State Baker, first to shore up the alliance in preparation for the Gulf War, and then as part of his shuttle diplomacy to bring about a Middle East peace conference, troubled the relatives. So did parades in Washington and New York, when families learned of plans to display the flags of all 29 war allies, including Syria.

Turning back the diplomatic tide toward closer ties with Syria may have been beyond the family groups' influence, but deterring the display of its flag in a parade certainly was not. They renewed their media contacts and Senator D'Amato, one of the sponsors of the Aviation Security Improvement Act, introduced a "sense of the Senate" resolution against a Syrian presence in the parades. It passed 92-6.

In November, Ammerman and others from the Victims group went back to England and Scotland. A crew from an NBC affiliate accompanied them the whole week, reporting back every day for five days, and filing a story for the network one night, which went nationwide. Whenever the group traveled, Ammerman said, "We sent our itinerary to the press, so the press knew exactly where we were. We also sent out where we would hold our press statements. So we dictated to the press when we were going to make our major statements. Now if you wanted to do a human interest story, we had a liaison we set up...that arranged all the enterprise interviews."

But Ammerman could not tell NBC or other media about the real news the relatives learned during the visit to Scotland. He and Swire had both been alerted by Scots authorities that indictments would be forthcoming about November 14. Ammerman saw that — and the interaction with the media over news of the indictments — as a demonstration of how far the group had come.

"When we first started out, in our relationship with both the media and the government, we were beggars with tin cups. We had no idea what the hell we were doing. We begged to meet with government officials. We looked for any type of radio show, TV show, anyone we could talk to. Today, we've got the gold cup. So we dictate when we want to speak, how we want to speak and to whom we want to speak."

But the night before the announcements, as rumors of impending action circulated, Ammerman was besieged by media at his house, "the first time and the only time, since the first days in Lockerbie, where I was not in control of the media." Live crews from the networks were set up for the 11 p.m. news, even though there was not much he could say. "We weren't allowed to say anything because we were taken into confidence," Ammerman recalled. "I knew what I could say, and I knew what I couldn't say." One member of the group was phoning Scotland to ask the police whether he could make a certain statement. "We couldn't make contact, so I had to soft shoe it."

While the NBC crew was at his home, Ammerman asked what would be a good time for a news conference the next day. One of them said 5 p.m. and suggested holding it at a hotel. When no hotels were available, one of the NBC crew called real estate tycoon Donald Trump, and Trump gave permission to hold it at the Plaza, a luxurious hotel on the south side of Central Park, free of charge. "We got it at 5 o'clock. Because they said if you go 5 o'clock, it'll be carried live; most of your local newscasts go at 5." It would also be timely for the network news, Ammerman's friends from NBC told him.

The group did a separate news conference for print media at 2 p.m. at the home of Aphrodite Tsairis. They said the indictment of two Libyans, Abdel Bassett Ali Al-Megrahi and Lamen Khalifa Fimah, described as Libyan intelligence agents working for Libyan Arab Airlines, showed the bombing was an act of state-sponsored terrorism.

The statement issued by Hudson described it as "a very important and essential first step, but only that," and called for tough economic and diplomatic sanctions (Sharn, 1991). In Britain, Swire called the indictments "very good news," but said the two Libyans were "likely to be small minnows in a very big pond"(Reuters, 1991). He said he believed Iran and Syria had a number of terrorists still free and called for the investigation to continue.

But the fact that the suspects were Libyans — after months of speculation, news reports and briefings had pointed to Syria, Iran and the Popular Front for the Liberation of Palestine-General Command led by Ahmed Jibril — was too much for some members of the group. That feeling was compounded a few hours after the indictments were announced when President Bush, speaking off the cuff during a photo opportunity with his Commission on Educational Excellence for Hispanic Americans, told his guests, "A lot of people thought it was the Syrians. The Syrians took a bum rap on this."

Ana Puga of the *Houston Chronicle* showed the effect that statement had on the families when she described a briefing in Room 1912 of the State Department a week later:

> A frail 35-year-old widow whose husband was killed in the terrorist bombing of Pam Am Flight 103 shook with anger as she confronted Deputy Secretary of State Lawrence Eagleburger.

> "I don't want to hear George Bush say Syria is getting a 'bum rap.' What about my husband? Didn't he get a bum rap?" Eagleburger's voice quavered as he answered Eleanor Bright.
>
> "I'm not going to back off because I haven't suffered as much as you. I'm not asking you to believe one damn thing. All I can say to you is we don't have the evidence to implicate Syria. That is not to say that Syria is innocent" (Puga, 1991).

In London, a few days after the indictments, *The Times* carried a letter from Swire, who praised the work of Scotland's police force and said "now we know that the warped ideology of Libya's dictator seduced two human beings into callous disregard for the lives of others." Swire said he was still waiting to learn whether the bombing was in revenge for the American raid on Libya or the accidental downing of the Iranian airliner by the USS Vincennes. But he renounced acts of revenge as a means of dealing with those responsible for the bombing of Flight 103 (1991).

One of the readers of that letter was a journalist for the Arabic press. He called and asked Swire for "the conventional sort of interview." But as the two men talked in the Swire living room, the interview took an unexpected turn. "He got excited about the idea of actually arranging for me to meet Qaddafi, because this was clearly the place where (revenge) was going to happen if we weren't very careful."

Originally, the meeting was to take place in Switzerland, but then things changed. "It became clear I was going to Libya with him, this particular media person. He did all the arranging. I was aware before I went that it was a risky thing to do…for all I knew it might be turned around and be used for propaganda purposes." Swire also admitted to being worried about the trip in other ways. "When I went to see Quaddafi, I actually felt very anxious about whether I would be assassinated or incarcerated. I had no idea what sort of reception I'd get. But I didn't think it terribly mattered, because it was more important to use that opportunity to try to find out more of the truth." Swire said his belief that he will see his daughter in an afterlife did help him proceed in spite of his fears.

The doctor arranged with the journalist that nothing would be published about the trip until it was over. So Swire and his media companion set off for what was scheduled as a 48-hour trip to Libya. Once they arrived in Tripoli, Swire had to contend with a major media problem. "A lawyer, called Peter Watson, appeared on BBC radio in Scotland, and said he was speaking for relatives, which wasn't true, and said, 'Wasn't it appalling about how the Libyans were behaving, pretending to put these people under house arrest, pretending this, that and the other.'"

The story reached Libya and, Swire said, "It looked very much for about two days that I would just be flung out." He offered to send faxes to Reuters to explain that the lawyer had no right to speak on behalf of the group, and to make it clear that Swire did not agree with the statements. That difficulty was smoothed over by "help from some people in Scotland who faxed back to Libya saying even Reuters shouldn't be told because if we told Reuters, you see, they'd have known where I was, and all the reporters would have jumped on it."

After a number of interviews with Libyan officials "to see if I was a fit person to meet the colonel," Swire finally sat down with Qaddafi and urged the Libyan leader to allow the two suspects to be tried in Scotland. At one point, he spoke "father-to-father" about the Pan Am 103 bombing. The doctor had already visited a museum commemorating the 1986 bombing of Tripoli in retaliation for Libya's alleged involvement in the attack on a Berlin discotheque that killed a U.S. Army sergeant and a Turkish woman and injured more than 200, many of them members of the American armed forces. There he had seen a photograph of Hanah, Qaddafi's 18-month-old adopted daughter, who had been killed in the bombing raid on Tripoli. He gave Qaddafi a picture of Flora and asked that it be placed in the museum, too.[8]

Swire returned to Britain on December 11, and delivered a sealed envelope that Qaddafi had asked him personally to take to Scotland's Lord Advocate. On the advice of "someone who's an expert in the field," Swire decided on a new strategy to break the news once he returned to Britain. "I spent an evening, about four or five hours, talking to a succession of senior journalists, and I explained from my point of view what had happened." The newspapers published the story the next day, and it was reported in the Arabic papers the day after. "Then all hell broke loose," Swire said. But he suggested the way the story was handled may help explain why "response was so much more favorable here than in the United States." Among those reacting negatively was Ammerman, who called the visit "naive beyond belief."

Swire said that in his personal systems of beliefs, everyone — including Qaddafi — has both good and evil. "I don't think the knowledge that the evil side of him has caused havoc in the world for many years should necessarily deny you going to talk to him." The doctor said he did stress that "this was an individual visit by me as an individual relative, but even so it caused anguish to some members of the U.K. group. I felt that it was something that if we didn't do we could reproach ourselves afterwards, saying that we haven't done everything possible."

Swire and his family were unprepared, however, for the personal repercussions of that trip. The doctor had a premonition of the problem as the planned 48-hour visit stretched into one day after another. "I remember saying when they said the next interview couldn't be until the following day, which was Sunday, 'There goes my job.' I had some feeling then that this would cause tremendous problems. In terms of the Lockerbie campaign, I think it was very useful. But in terms of the personal and professional consequences, it was a disaster."

The partners in his medical practice demanded his resignation, and the partnership contract prevented him from practicing medicine in the area. "I don't look forward to seeing this published anywhere," Swire said, "but the situation put across to me — and this is me trying to tell the truth as well as I can see it — was that my partners felt they had done everything humanly possible to support me during the past few years, and they had consulted together and come to the conclusion the best thing from my point of view was to get me to work half-time for the next six months." After that they would offer him locum work, which involves standing in for other doctors. Swire said he recognized that his capacity to practice medicine had been affected by the disaster, but believed he could carry on with three-quarters time in his practice. His partners did not accept the idea.

The reaction of patients also made the partners' actions hard to accept, Swire said. "I can say unanimously (they) are incensed because they realize that it isn't what I wanted. They are incensed at the idea of me having to leave the practice, and they kept saying, 'Can't we start up a petition?' and so on."

Swire's situation was very different from what an American doctor would face; he or she could move to another practice or even work independently in the same community. In Britain, a general practitioner is classified as self-employed and contracts his or her services through the Family Health Services Authority, which is funded by the government. Doctors are responsible for looking after people who sign on to be patients of a particular practice. The six-partner practice to which Swire belonged had an agreement that defines what they shall and shall not do. It prohibits partners from leaving the practice and taking a large proportion of the patients with them to a rival practice.

At the time of the interview, Swire was considering a number of options, none of them as attractive as staying with the practice. "The great glory of British general practice is that you look after the same people in the same families year in, year out, for all of your professional life." Other jobs, such as government work, assessing whether people are fit for work or not, were among possibilities he was considering. "I shall have to get some work to do, to keep us fed, but it would be much less rewarding work." The physician was also struggling with the issue of whether or not he was suffering from post-traumatic stress syndrome. "And if I'm deemed to be suffering from that, then do I retire on health grounds?" he asked.

Swire was deeply troubled by the consequences for his family. "Suddenly our family income has come to a fraction of what it was. Future prospects are not good. We have a cash flow crisis of major proportions. And when you're affected, as we still are, by disaster and grief of this magnitude, you don't have the resources to cater for this sort of thing. The effect on Jane has been absolutely disastrous." He turned to her, "You said yourself the other day it put you back three years. It's like being back in December '88."

Asked by the interviewer if that was because she had experienced a loss of control, she answered quickly, "That's right. I think you've hit the nail on the head. I'm not in control. I'm a victim of circumstance again. I'm playing a game of consequences over which I have no control. And it's deeply disturbing, psychologically, emotionally, everywhere. Yes, I really am back. And I think with Jim, it really hasn't hit him yet in the way that it probably has me. I'm the one actually buying the food and paying the bills. We're not going to manage to do this unless he rethinks his position very quickly. Because bottom line, we've all got to eat."

Jane Swire recognized how important her husband's campaign was, both in trying to bring about changes in policy and to him personally as a means of coping. She saw the situation as "brutal. It reflects the attitudes of the times, which are quite hard and unforgiving," she said. "Brittle, like glass, really. I wish it weren't like that; fervently I wish it weren't. I wish doctors were compassionate, caring men that society gives them the role to be, but in fact they're not. That is harsh reality. Jim has to come to terms with that. In spite of all the other things that we've suffered, we could suffer even more if he doesn't."

Even some media, which had been uniformly supportive toward the Swires until the dispute with his partners, became critical, the doctor noted. "There have been a number of media people who have taken it upon themselves to say that, 'Of course, Dr Swire should get off his constant carrying on about finding out the truth, and get on with looking out for his family.' This is the first aspect that's provided some opportunity for difference of opinion. But it hasn't been a major problem between me and the media."

At one point, Jane Swire interjected, "We all clap for the achievers from the sidelines, forgetting what it costs. People from the sidelines will watch while somebody self-destructs — with sympathy. That's all. I'm sort of horribly aware that could happen. I say that to Jim, he's got to let go and let somebody else do it."

The campaigning for aviation security, in a sense, has been Swire's way of dealing with the isolation he felt from the British government. "I feel that my personal reaction to this might have been very different if the authorities had been open," Swire said. "If they'd said things like, 'I'm sorry, we didn't do things properly. We didn't check the cases and things. But now we're going to put it right.' I think the fact they didn't do that has kept the anger going.

Underneath it all it must be anger that's driving me on in the campaign. Maybe that's where the anger went."

He counted small victories, such as establishing the right of surviving relatives to see the bodies of loved ones, if they wish. The big ones — achieving an emphasis on airline security instead of just air safety, understanding exactly how the bomb was smuggled aboard, and above all, learning the reasons for the bombing — remained to be won.

Early in 1992, the United Nations took its first steps to try to persuade Libya to hand over the two men indicted in the bombing. Its resolution called for their extradition, along with four other Libyans implicated in the 1989 bombing of UTA (Union des Transports Aeriens) Flight 772 over Niger. Although Libya sought to deflect the UN sanctions by appealing to the World Court in the Hague, the ban on air traffic and arms sales and the sharp reduction of diplomatic ties began as scheduled on April 15.[9] The sanctions, while limited, were subject to review every 120 days, and Chris Hedges, reporting for *The New York Times*, said the sanctions were "turning out to be more than a symbolic gesture." He quoted Western diplomats as saying that the departure of 1,700 Russian and advisers had been devastating to the military infrastructure (1992, p. 3, Section 4).

A few days after the sanctions against Libya went into effect, Jim Swire faxed a proposal to Tripoli. It followed a statement by the lawyer for the two Libyans under indictment, who said they might be willing to give themselves up for trial in Scotland or the United States if they had solid guarantees of a fair hearing and if they would not be handed over to foreign intelligence services. The fax Swire sent to Tripoli said the doctor and a few American families would be willing to escort the two Libyans to the West to stand trial. It suggested this would be a "neutral group," not linked to any government (Reuters, 1992).

The "small group of Americans" making that offer did not include Bert Ammerman, who was critical of the overture as he had been of Swire's visit to Libya. "Dr Swire tries to do in his heart what is right, but I don't know how he can consider himself part of a neutral group," the New Jersey man said. By June 1992, Ammerman was optimistic that the two Libyans would be turned over for trial. "Qaddafi is trying to do everything possible to get a compromise so that he doesn't have to (turn them over). There's no question his government's very worried about the economic sanctions." Ammerman suggested the easy way out for the Libyan leader would be to "turn the two men over in body bags, and announce to his horror that he found out that they indeed did this, and he just wanted to show he'd renounced terrorism. Those two guys are nothing; they're pawns. The real question should be what are we doing to the Libyan government, not to the two individuals."

Beginning in late April, many relatives had to alter their behavior toward the media. Those who were parties to the civil suit charging Pan American Airways with "willful misconduct" were under orders from a U.S. District Court judge not to talk to reporters. That directive was particularly onerous because it meant the families could not speak out against a *Time* magazine cover story that appeared the week before the trial. It alleged the bomb had been planted to murder CIA men on Flight 103, and relied heavily on two shadowy figures who had been working with Pan Am and its insurers to develop a theory absolving the airline of responsibility for permitting the bomb on board.

The trial dragged on in Brooklyn for 11 weeks before finally going to the jury on July 8. The lawsuit, brought by families of 213 of the 259 passengers and crew, contended that Pan Am had not followed a regulation of the FAA requiring it to match every bag on its flight with a passenger on board. Attorneys for Pan Am's insurers, who were not allowed to introduce their controversial theory about CIA involvement into the trial, argued that the airline was being sued because those who had perpetrated the bombing could not be reached.

Tension grew when after 24 hours of deliberation jurors sent notes to District Court Judge Thomas Platt reporting that the panel was deadlocked. But the judge instructed them to continue deliberating and on July 10, the jury filed back into the courtroom to declare its verdict. "One of the jurors turned to me and smiled," said Eleanor Bright, who had spent many days listening to the hearing. "And then I think I knew what the verdict would be" (Porterfield, 1992). She was right. The unanimous verdict cleared the way for a series of hearings to determine compensation for loss of each of the 213 victims. Although it was a foregone conclusion that the decision would be appealed, it was a sweet moment for the families in the courtroom.

Georgia Nucci told reporters for the *Syracuse Post-Standard* it was a victory for the traveling public as well. The real winners, she said, will be anyone who boards a commercial airliner from now on. "We have all kinds of legislation about airline security and nobody follows the rules. But you can bet that if the insurers know that a lack of security will cost them dollars, they will make sure there is adequate security" (Foster and Cox, 1992).

6 *The Media Awareness Group: Lockerbie's Response*

Letters flooded into Lockerbie in the weeks following the disaster. They offered sympathy. They offered prayers. Often, they offered help, even when the writers clearly had very little money themselves. "It was very distressing, some of the letters we got," said one of the women who spent several hours a day at the library, writing thank-you notes on behalf of the community. "For some of the people who sent in donations, you felt it was their last pound." Especially touching were the letters from children. "Some would have sales in the garden — just wee tots doing all this, and their mums or their dads would write the letter and they would sign it."

The letters and other offers of kindness meant a great deal to the people of Lockerbie. Two men who led one of the neighborhood residents committees confessed that they found it difficult to read the letters. "I had tears in my eyes," said one. "I was tremendously touched with it — the hundreds of places letters were coming from...from all over the world, Australia, Canada, America. All over Britain."

But one letter, written in pencil by a 13-year-old boy in New Jersey, set in motion a chain of circumstances that might have overwhelmed a less cohesive community. It was sent not to Lockerbie, but to Pan Am's Chief Executive Officer, Thomas Plaskett. The writer enclosed a small amount of money and asked that Pan Am provide toys for the children of Lockerbie who had been deprived of Christmas. According to Pan Am's Kriendler, Plaskett was greatly moved by the boy's thoughtfulness, and told Kriendler that he wanted Pan Am to get behind this boy's wish. Kriendler contacted Lockerbie officials who were excited by the idea of doing something for the town's children, and the plan developed to create a Scottish/American Friendship Day on June 3. Quickly, the event began to take shape. It became known as "Ed's Party," named after the boy, Ed Blaus. Kriendler worked to line up entertainment, to contact corporate sponsors — Disney World, Marriott, Hebrew International Foods, Coca-Cola Co., and the Domino's pizza chain, among others — and to arrange for the Blaus family to fly to Scotland.

One of the simpler definitions of public relations is "doing good, and getting credit for it" (Wilcox, Ault and Agee, 1992, p.5). Part of the problem that arose from Ed's Party, however, stemmed either from a Pan Am decision to play down its role in the party, or from a lack of communications among the airline's public relations staff. That meant that Pan Am behaved with what it may have regarded as magnanimous modesty, but it looked like duplicity to the families and the media.

So when the party was announced in Lockerbie, and news media called Pan Am, its spokeswoman Elizabeth Manners told them, "It's being run entirely by this 14-year-old boy"(Wilson, 1989). She said he had the idea for the party, raised money for it and wrote Pan Am's chairman asking for help. She said the airline was flying the family over and had put them in touch with Marriott, Disney and Coca-Cola, which had also offered support. But the first time Ed Blaus himself knew about the party was when Pan Am phoned and offered to fly him to it. "I wrote to Pan Am because I thought that everyone should have a Christmas, no matter what. I just wanted them to send presents over, and they said they would help me. But it just got bigger and bigger," he told reporters after he arrived in Lockerbie (*Associated Press*, 1989).

A major challenge of public relations is to recognize that an action or communication may be viewed differently by different audiences. Avoiding misinterpretations begins with a clear understanding of the needs and desires of the various audiences. The controversy over Ed's Party demonstrated the difficulty the airline had in recognizing that one of its publics, family members of those on board, held it responsible for a lapse in security that allowed the bomb into the hold.

It also demonstrated the kind of complicated grief a disaster, particularly a mass murder, can produce. A 13-year-old boy in New Jersey could understand that the children of Lockerbie needed cheering up after the disaster had disrupted their Christmas, but many grieving relatives of passengers on the plane still thought of the town as the site where their loved ones fell to earth, a sacred place. At the time, Bert Ammerman was quoted as saying, "While they might have missed Christmas, we will miss our loved ones forever" (Wilson, 1989).

As time passed, more and more of the relatives would recognize the terror and loss that Lockerbie people had suffered. But, at that moment, while many had been deeply touched by the kindness and compassion shown them by individual townspeople, some relatives of the passengers did not really understand the psychogical damage this horrific event had inflicted on the community, especially to its children. The reaction was not confined to American relatives. In one of the earliest statements Dr Jim Swire made on behalf of the U.K. family group, he alluded to evidence the airline was a major contributor to this disaster, and said, "it is disgraceful that the people of Lockerbie should be junketing with them" (*Reuters*, 1989).

The media, which became a channel through which the pro-party and anti-party sides talked at each other, exacerbated the conflict in some cases by publishing misperceptions about plans for the party itself. "I've got a clipping that reported that the party was being held where the bodies were found!" one Lockerbie resident said. "I mean, what do they think we are in Lockerbie?" That headline and others in the same vein were based on quotes from family members who were working with limited information about the geography of the tragedy. Writers for both Reuters (1989) and Gannett News Service (Kocieniewski, 1989) quoted American relatives as complaining that the picnic was being held on ground where bodies fell. Apparently neither writer checked with Lockerbie officials to determine whether those allegations were correct.

Pan Am and Lockerbie officials faced a dilemma. Many of the corporate sponsors withdrew in light of the public criticism, including Disney, which had promised to send Mickey and Minnie Mouse. Yet the Lockerbie children were excited about the prospects of the American-style party. According to Kriendler, the Lockerbie social service professionals felt that the party could go a long way toward returning the community to a sense of normalcy. The event went on as planned — with international media descending on the community again.

"That was an amazingly ham-handed thing," Robert Barr of the Associated Press remembered. "Pan Am's involvement in it was unfortunate. It was so weird to be there. They sort of organized the media for us that day. We were allowed in, allowed out. Nobody wanted us. It was just an occasion to make you cringe. So we were well glad to be gone after getting our two quotes and a photo. I just wondered afterwards, 'What in the world were they thinking about? What were we thinking about, going and covering this.' I don't know. It's one of those messes you get into."

But for the children of Lockerbie and the surrounding areas, who were also affected by the disaster, it was a great day. The parade, a children's show, a magician, folk and rock music, and an American champion player of the Scottish bagpipes entertained an estimated 5,000. Syracuse University football coach Dick McPherson taught the young Scots about the American game. Gift packets, put together by Lockerbie volunteers, were distributed to the kids. Young Ed Blaus was presented with a kilt. Alec McElroy, head of the Community Support office, who had helped coordinate the event, called it a "tremendous day, better than anyone had hoped for."

In New York, relatives gathered in front of Pan Am's headquarters and expressed their anger. "Having this picnic is cruel," said the mother of a

20-year-old Staten Island resident who died in the bombing. "It's like a symbolic recharring of all those bodies" (Queen, 1989).

Despite the criticism, Pan Am's Kriendler has no regrets: "The day was sunny, warm. It was a wonderful, wonderful day. Ed was like a hero...We were told that that day was the day that Lockerbie moved toward recovery."

But the people in Lockerbie, while feeling they had done the right thing for the children, were concerned about the hurt expressed by the families. Two members of the District Council for Lockerbie flew to the States and met with families in Haddonfield, New Jersey, later that month. "The message that we wanted to put over was that people in Lockerbie suffered as well as the victims here," council member Hugh Young told reporters (Mooar, 1989). Most relatives responded well, acknowledging that a party for the Lockerbie children had been a good idea, although some said they wished Pan Am had not been involved. But a small minority stayed angry.

The party had also helped to show some leaders in Lockerbie that they needed to prepare for a future in which media could be expected to show up much more often. One of the representatives of the Sherwood Park neighborhood remembered how he and a number of other local leaders were paraded out to face the media in a tent at 8 a.m. the morning of Ed's Party. "So I was presented with the standard piece of paper that the chairman said, 'Here, we'll read this.' But what he didn't actually say was that he would invite questions from the audience." So as the local leaders faced the barrage of flashbulbs, they also had to respond to some tough questioning. "Really at that point the media were looking for the story that Pan Am had somehow or other arranged this as a publicity stunt, and they were after that angle, which really was a bit frightening."

Since mid-January, the chief media contact in Lockerbie for information about the community's recovery had been Alec McElroy, who directed the Community Support office on behalf of the Regional Council of Dumfries and Galloway. The office had been set up in mid-January to coordinate efforts by various local community groups, clergy, Social Work, the Health Board and Community Education. Housed upstairs in the same block as the library, but reached via a discreet door down a small side street, Community Support became known locally as the place to go for help with a wide variety of problems. That also made it a logical point of contact for news people, especially those who wanted to find local people who would be willing to talk about their experiences and progress. As McElroy put it, one of his roles was to "soak up media attention," either by answering questions himself or by deflecting them to elected council representatives.

Community Support was to work its way out of business by January 1990. As McElroy explained it, the office had been created as a direct result of the disaster, so it represented a "scar" or reminder. Its functions needed to be reassigned, including the "soaking up of media attention."

Before the disaster, McElroy had been in the Education Department of the Regional Council in Dumfries, so he and others on his staff began exploring the idea of some sort of course to teach local people about the media. In May and June, McElroy began thinking aloud about the problem. One sounding board was a social worker assigned to his office, Mike Combe. Another was David Ben-Aryeah, a freelance radio reporter from Edinburgh who was a regular visitor to the office.

Ben-Aryeah, who won the Overseas Press Club award for spot news reporting for a reflective piece he wrote from Tundergarth, was well remembered by many reporters who came to Lockerbie. A Syracuse reporter recalled that it seemed as if everywhere he went in Lockerbie, Ben-Aryeah was there, too. But the big Scot became a fixture of the Masonic Lodge, the Syracuse reporter said. Because Ben-Aryeah made such a point of having spent time in Israel and being so fascinated with the various theories about how the plane was blown up, the reporter said, some of the press corps speculated that he had Israeli Intelligence contacts. Ben-Aryeah said "relatives and officials have since referred to him as 'the keeper of the secrets'."

But McElroy saw something else: Ben-Aryeah's expansive nature and real concern about the Lockerbie people. He enlisted him as the lead tutor for what they would call the Media Awareness course. As fall arrived, McElroy had Combe and Ben-Ayreah begin working in earnest on the project. When Atholl Duncan of the BBC-TV in Glasgow approached Community Support for help in preparing a special for the first anniversary, McElroy made a counter-proposal: that Duncan help with the television portion of the course in return for help with his special. A similiar offer was made to Keren David, a freelance reporter from *Scotland on Sunday*, the Sunday magazine section of the *Scotsman*. McElroy would help her find people to interview if the training group could make an unpublicized visit to the newspaper to understand its workings. The fourth tutor was to be Angela Baxter, the public relations officer for the Regional Council in Dumfries.

On October 23, the course held its first meeting in one of the larger rooms of the Community Support offices. The initial moments were a bit tense. Angela Baxter, David Ben-Aryeah and Atholl Duncan explained from their perspectives what the media had done in the immediate aftermath of the tragedy, including the efforts of public information officers to focus the work and attention of the journalists. For many of the participants in the course, this was new information, even though the events being described had happened virtually on their doorsteps. The trainees questioned their tutors sharply, especially on the accuracy of initial reports.

Every Monday night after that first meeting, the group took another step toward developing skills and understanding. Their exercises deliberately avoided using topics related to the disaster. For example, when they practiced writing news releases, the topic was a hypothetical old bridge on the River Nith in Dumfries that had been found unsafe and was to be pulled down. One group wrote the release from the standpoint of a Council representative, concerned about the costs of repairs. Another took the role of a group committed to saving the bridge, because of its contribution to the scenic beauty and heritage of the town. The third group represented two people who missed serious injury from masonry that fell from the bridge and wanted it scrapped.

Visits to the newspaper and the television station were set up at other times in the week, and arranged to fit into people's work schedules. The trainees also had homework assignments, but clearly the in-class experiences were very important.

One week they did a radio interview, one woman recalled, "and I was the first. There was myself and three men being interviewed. 'Oh,' they said. 'You did very well.' I didn't agree with them, because I didn't feel I had. But the following week I got the chance to do it again, but with television. One of the men from the radio interview group said he noticed such a tremendous difference. I was much more confident. I don't know quite why. I couldn't work it out. But I definitely felt — and I think we all deep down felt — that we could cope with the media a little bit better. We were more aware."

One of the men in the group said they had learned how to handle reporters. Before the course, he said, "I would never have thought to say to them, show me your press pass." That request, they explained, would help them to know which newspaper or periodical they were dealing with. "To the *Sun* and the *Star* I would say, 'No comment.' Not to one of the more respectable papers; I wouldn't mind making a comment (to them) at all."

His partner in one of the residents' committees said, "You learn as you go along. I would never ever have thought of saying, 'Explain what you want to talk to me about.'"

The participants in the course also learned that it was all right to ask a reporter to come back later, after they had time to collect their thoughts. "And another thing — it was Big Dave's favorite saying — KISS, Keep It Simple and Stupid. Don't elaborate too much," one said. "I know last year, when I was talking to the press, I was getting very complicated and talking a lot of rubbish, but I would not do that now, because I'll always remember, you know, KISS. It really works."

A man from another of the residents committees, who became very angry at the media at the time of the disaster, said, "I was quite surprised how well I enjoyed it. I've got a better understanding now. I've probably still got some anger at some of the media, but not the responsible media anyway." At the time of the disaster, the man had been unwilling to speak with the media, "but I'm prepared to do it now...because there's some of the people in the street that you just wouldn't want involved — some of the elderly people and that — so I'm quite prepared to..."

He recalled that early in the course the tutors tried to explain that while the people of Lockerbie were under pressure, the media were under certain pressures as well. "Maybe I understand now, but at the beginning, I just thought, 'Well, that's your problem.' But I had a go at actually being an interviewer, and that's a lot harder than being interviewed."

The course stressed, however, that the interviewee is in charge, not the reporter. "Whereas, days after the disaster, I would say the majority of people didn't realize that with a microphone stuck in front of their face, you don't have to say anything," the man said. "Everybody seems to think, 'Oh, well, I've got to think of something to say now.' What they said is probably not at all what they meant to say, but they just felt they had to say something. Whereas, they could just have said, 'No, go away. Do not bother me.' We know more about the media now than the general public know...I feel a lot of people made a big mistake in saying something, instead of just walking away."

Another man thought that media guidelines relating to disasters could be laid down, and if that failed, legislation might be the answer. But he suggested it would be a pity if it came to that. "I always think the less laws you can abide with, the better," he said.

About two weeks into the course, the group had something of a setback in its developing respect for the media. They were invited down to the Border Television studios in Carlisle for a network program produced by ITN. It was entitled "Lockerbie," and they understood it was to be about the way the town was coping with the aftermath of the tragedy. "In fact, it wasn't," said one member of the group. "They set up a satellite (feed) for 20 minutes with America with that Senator (James) Traficant. And for 20 minutes we were more or less harangued."

The program came shortly after Traficant, an Ohio Democrat, released five pages of a 27-page report commissioned by Pan Am's insurance underwriters. Traficant claimed it showed CIA operatives in Germany protected a "terrorist drug-running operation" because the CIA wanted to gain access to groups holding U.S. hostages in Lebanon. The report alleged a bag from a "mule" in the operation had been allowed to pass by without checking; it supposedly contained the bomb instead of the expected heroin. Two weeks after Traficant's news conference, the *Syracuse Post-Standard* would reveal that the report was prepared by Juval Aviv, who had represented himself as a counter-terrorism expert; the Canadian magazine *MacLean's* found that at the time

Aviv was supposed to be tracking down terrorists, he was working as a cabin steward and security guard for El Al airlines.

So the 20 minutes of satellite time with Traficant ticked away, while the Media Awareness group and English relatives of those on board perched stiffly on steep benches in the studio. A local doctor timed how long Lockerbie people spoke in the 45-minute program, which included one commercial break. He counted one minute and 20 seconds. "That upset a lot of us because we felt we'd been set up," the woman said.

The experience prompted a lively exchange at the following Monday meeting, because there was a sense that the program's producers had not really wanted to know how Lockerbie was coping. In fact, in many ways, the community was doing very well. People in the town and surrounding area had reached out toward one another. They had rebuilt. They had planned more improvements, such as a play area adjacent to the Rosebank Crescent area so that children would not have to go the half-mile to the soccer field for active fun. But they also acknowledged a level of stress as the first anniversary approached.

"We know we've got to get through the next month, and because of the media attention last year, people are genuinely afraid," one Media Awarness trainee said in late November. "It's going to be very, very difficult." The London *Express* had actually carried the first anniversary piece two days earlier. "It's almost as though they had to get it in first," she said.

"Last night I was talking to a girl who lost her house, and she said last week there was a knock on the door and it was a reporter," the woman recalled. "And she said, 'My husband snapped. He's never done that.'" The reporter had obviously gone to considerable lengths to track down families who were relocated from the burned out section of the town, because local authorities were not giving out such information. The anecdote illustrated the need for the work the Media Awareness Group was preparing to do.

In late November and through the December 21 anniversary, members of the Media Awareness Group responded to some of the world's leading media about their community and the role it had played. "It is the Scottish heritage to be resilient and hospitable, and Lockerbie is no exception," Robert Riddet told the *Washington Post*. "We knew the relatives would feel apprehensive, and we wanted them to understand that we were a united family and that they would always be welcome here" (Frankel, 1989).

Tom Carson quietly told a correspondent for the *Press Association*, a wire service that operates within the United Kingdom, that the people of Lockerbie had just one request from the world at large: "Please leave us alone to get on with our lives. While we don't mind relatives and friends of the victims coming to visit the disaster site, it is distressing to local people to be subject to sightseers parking their cars outside our homes, and even bus parties getting out to look at the scene. We would hope that in the next 12 months this would cease"(Clark, 1989).

Maxwell Kerr explained that the return of the media had created a certain tension in the town. "What underlines the irritation of townspeople is the behavior of cameramen. They aren't really bothering anyone. It's just the fact they are there. It brings back memories. Everyone in Lockerbie on the night was affected in some way. But we are fighting back. The scars are healing, both in the people and in the town"(Clark, 1989).

William Miller of the *Boston Globe*, who returned to Lockerbie in December, wrote about a "feeling of poignancy and sadness" as detectable as the smell of jet fuel that hung in the air after the bombing. But he noticed "there is also a feeling of hope that the community's long year of trauma is coming to an end." He recalled the rubble he had seen in the streets, the search teams, the helicopters ferrying bodies in from fields and hills. Some Lockerbie children still were drawing homes on fire and flowers spurting flames, he wrote.

> Yet through it all, the people of Lockerbie have still found the energy to form friendship groups to take grieving relatives into their homes and escort them to the sites where the bodies of their loved ones were found.
>
> Most of the visiting relatives have been Americans, and by last count, 167 have been taken in.
>
> Stuart Murray, a retired headmaster and a founder member of the first such group, said, "The Americans have suffered the most" (Miller, 1989, p. 26).

On the day before the anniversary, American relatives presented a plaque to the community:

> "The town, which was devastated itself, reached out, held our hand, and guided us. We feel bound to you by a chain of grief and love so strong it can never be broken."

Joe Horgan of the Victims of Pan Am Flight 103, who made the presentation, said: "Lockerbie has shown amazing compassion. There were times when we lost our faith in fellow man, but you only have to come here to have it restored" (Frankel, 1989).

The anniversary itself was overcast. During the afternoon about 500 gathered in the Dryfesdale cemetery to dedicate a granite memorial built into the stone wall along one side of the Garden of Remembrance. It listed all 270 lives claimed by the disaster. The ceremony was quiet, but the image many of those attending remembered best was the huge cross formed overhead by vapor trails of two passing jets — apparently a coincidence but so right for the moment that it could have been pre-arranged.

As darkness fell over the graveyard, 270 candles were lit by the new memorial. Eleanor Hudson of Albany, New York, who lost her 16-year-old daughter Melina, told a reporter, "Lockerbie is wonderful. I thought at first Melina died alone, but now I don't think so"(Elgood, 1989).

Some of the relatives made a pilgrimage to Tundergarth, to worship quietly together in the little church across from fields where the nose cone had landed.

Many had expressed a desire to be by themselves or at the site where a loved one died during anniversary minute of the disaster. Police refused to let reporters into Sherwood Crescent. "The residents have asked us not to allow press and visitors in on this of all days," an officer guarding the street told Giles Elgood of Reuters (1989).

One year and one hour after the plane plunged to earth, the communal service began in the town square. The brightly lit Christmas tree outside the Town Hall helped to remind the 2,000 gathered there that the town of Lockerbie *was* recovering from the horror of geo-political murder. A reporter for the Press Association caught the spirit:

> ...the message that went out to the world yesterday was that the terrorists would never win. Father Patrick Keegans, a local Roman Catholic priest, told townsfolk and around 80 victims' relatives, including about 20 from the United States, of the determination to live on.
>
> "To say that there is no recovery, to say things won't get better, to say that we can never live life joyfully again is to say to the terrorists, 'Here, you can have our lives as well.' That I refuse to give them," he said (Quinn, 1989).

A haunting lament by a Scottish piper ended the service.

Across the Atlantic, other members of the community created by the terrorist bomb marked the day with quiet services and tolling bells. And a group of relatives clutching red tulips marched again from the steps of the New York Public Library to the Pan Am Building. The signs they carried demanded, "When will we take a stand against terrorism?" That political act and others that followed it marked the real distance between the family groups and the Lockerbie townspeople. Visiting relatives would learn that they could always seek solace by visiting the small market town, its surrounding hills and the people who had become neighbors through their nearness to the terrible tragedy. But Lockerbie reached a consensus, very quietly, very informally, that it would not play a role in the various controversies swirling around the tragedy. All that they asked of their guests, the relatives and friends of those who had died on the plane, was that they respect that reticence.

So, on June 29, 1990, the night before the last major event memorializing the victims, the Victims group from the U.S. and representatives from the U.K. group met at the Dryfesdale Hotel, a quietly elegant establishment on the outskirts of Lockerbie. With them was David Ben-Aryeah, who sometimes served as press adviser for the two groups, especially during their travels in Scotland, as well as continuing to serve as a resource for the Media Awareness Group when needed. The closed door meeting settled on the topics to be discussed at a news conference scheduled for Saturday afternoon, following the dedication of the Room of Remembrance in the Tundergarth churchyard. Ben-Aryeah carried the message that Lockerbie people wanted "no politics." After much discussion, they agreed that the story of how Jim Swire had smuggled his "bomb" aboard a British Airways flight to the United States, designed to shock U.K. authorities into improving airport security, would not be on the agenda. He would reveal that at another time and place.

The ceremony of dedication began in a steady rain, with most of those standing among the gravestones shielded by umbrellas. That placed the television cameras at a temporary disadvantage. They were perched in a stand at the rear of the churchyard, specially constructed and covered with greenery so that it blended into the scene. But as the ceremony drew to a close, the sun came out, the umbrellas disappeared and cameramen had a few minutes of unimpeded view to capture the footage they needed.

Members of the Media Awareness Group were present in case reporters wanted to interview local people. This was a role that had become relatively comfortable for them in the months since their training. When reporters sought interviews with local people, they could call one member of the group who would arrange a contact with one or more other members. They had shared their experiences: one told how an Austrian television crew did a complete interview, only to discover it had no videotape in the camera. From time to time, as the years passed, they would be asked to do another interview, but probably their greatest contribution to the community had been in helping "soak up" media attention at the time of the first anniversary.

One question that the experiment raised at the outset was answered affirmatively. That was: would the media be willing to interview volunteers instead of seeking out their own subjects in the community? A number of reporters who returned to Lockerbie said they did speak with members of the Awareness Group and found it useful. Graham Patterson of the *Express* said reporters from his paper spoke to several from the group. "They did fine. They probably would have done fine anyway. Nevertheless, they were prepared for our coming. They drew up a list of people who were willing to be interviewed. So if you wanted an interview one day, you knew you were going to a house. There weren't going to be scenes, and things like that. They'd give you a cup of tea and sit down and talk to you. It was very good, that. I think the idea was a good one."

Robert Barr of the Associated Press also interviewed several members of the Media Awareness Group, and felt it worked in this particular case, but warned against using it as a template for every disaster. "It's a unique situation because of the smallness of the town," he said. "Certainly if there was a case in which there was any hint of possible wrong-doing or malfeasance in the community, the media wouldn't cooperate. But clearly they were just people who had a disaster fall on them. And aircraft disasters are stories that run longer than other kinds of disasters."

McElroy believed that the course should have been conducted earlier, possibly as early as May, certainly in the early fall. By the time the course was underway journalists were starting to report and, in some cases, had written their anniversary stories. But one woman cautioned against trying to do such a course too early. She suggested they might have been able to do it about nine months after the disaster, once they had a few months during the summer when media attention eased off.

But probably the most important lesson that the experiment taught the people of Lockerbie is that they could work *with* the media to tell their story. They did not have to wait with dread for a reporter to come knocking on the door; they could tell the community's story on their own terms, and most media would cooperate.

7 *After the Trauma*

Ten days in Lockerbie and London left Peter Marks of *Newsday* feeling as if he had been in a "hermetically sealed environment. It was just me and this story. It was the most intense experience I'd ever had on a news story." He paused. "Obviously it affected me at levels that I didn't really realize."

After Marks returned home to Long Island, the interview he had done with the man who saw the cockpit float down from the sky, who found the bodies of the flight crew and some passengers, became particularly troubling. "It haunted me," the reporter recalled. "I was very agitated and annoyed. I didn't trace it to this exactly. I think maybe it was that I still wanted to be involved in the story." But the scene of the story had shifted, and most new information was coming out of Washington. Besides, Marks admitted, he was not really that interested in the investigation, which focused on terrorism. That made it a story for investigative reporters, and Marks' specialty is human interest.

"I think at some level you sort of absorb a lot that you don't ever put on paper," the reporter said. Slowly he became conscious of the lives of the people on the plane. "It didn't occur to me until later that it could have been me. I love London. I love theater. My wife and I go every year. We'd taken the Pan Am flight from New York to London."

When he was in Scotland, Marks recalled, he did not think that much about the people on the flight. Back on Long Island, he began reading aspects of the story that others had covered. He was especially struck by the stories of the middle class families who had lost sons and daughters. "I could identify with them," he said. "I really feel like I could have been on this plane. And it really freaked me out."

Seeing television reports of the February 6 news conference by the families heightened his interest. "These people were so angry. It disturbed me at a level that I was not used to feeling. They were so intense, and I sort of knew what they were feeling...because I had been there... I sort of knew what their anger was. Or I thought I did." So he proposed a piece for the newspaper's Sunday magazine about the organization that was forming, which he wanted to use as a vehicle to profile several of the families. "And I'll tell you, I have never been so emotionally affected by a story before," he said during an interview three years later. "I still am. I'm still emotionally involved in this story."

The first meeting he went to was in Haddonfield, New Jersey, on June 24. It struck him like a convention at first; everyone was wearing lapel pins with pictures of their loved ones. Seated in the audience, Marks had an experience as riveting as his interview with the farmer at Tundergarth. A State Department representative was responding to questions about the warning that had been posted in the Moscow embassy. Suddenly, Marks remembered, "this woman stands up in the back of the room and starts shrieking like — I felt it was like the 14th century in some primitive culture where that's how they warred. They keened and screamed...This woman erupted. She was shrieking. I have never heard anything like it." The memory was so vivid for Marks that he recreated the woman's intonation as he recalled her words. "My only daughter was on that plane. How dare you say this? My only daughter was on that plane. I loved her."

The woman's cries struck him as primal. "I felt very ashamed, sitting there and not feeling anything," Marks said. "You know, I was writing like crazy. And no one turned around. Everyone just sat there like it was her turn to erupt.

"And at the end of the day, I sat in my car and I cried. It was the level of loss. I felt like I was in this room full of people; they all had the same loss. It was a very profound thing to me. I felt this tremendous duty to them. I felt they had a different standing in society now. They were all victims. They all came from a world that I knew, so I became more and more involved in the story."

He told of an interview with a Long Island mother, whose son had been a Syracuse University student. "She couldn't focus on anything. This is months after it happened and she had not made any sense of it — had followed everything, but I felt she was just shattered." In the middle of the conversation, she told Marks they had just received her son's belongings and asked if he would like to see them. "This is another one of those moments for me — she took them out very matter-of-factly, took out first a golf club. This had all come off the plane.

"The Scottish police, as you know, were meticulous about preserving these people's things. People would come to the door...and present everything but the person. Everything came off the plane. She holds up a pair of underwear, completely shot through. It looked like a rag, but she had them. They had been laundered and folded." Among the belongings were videotapes from her son's last class in which he was doing a public relations presentation. "She's watching it like she's done it before. And I'm like — the level, it was surreal. It was like going through these fields and seeing these holes in the ground where people landed. I had a lot of dreams about people falling out of the sky, too. I began, over and over again, thinking about what that moment was like, that last moment. Did they know? Were they aware? I guess that's like we all do. But I became sort of morbidly curious about how the families were thinking of it.

"I knew how fragile some of these people were. I wasn't trying to take advantage. And that's the other thing I felt. I felt at some level as I was doing this magazine piece, I was trying to weigh the space between doing a story that was honest about them and taking advantage of, preying upon their grief and making them relive it. They all seemed to have an urge to talk about it. But I didn't know if I was encouraging something healthy or not, if I was making it harder for them."

So Marks consulted with a bereavement counselor who was working with some of the families, and was reassured. The writer was very proud of the story he did. "My lead was: 'They are not like the rest of us.' It's a little dramatic, but to me, that's what they seemed to be. They no longer existed in the same plane. They were all obsessed with this. Why it happened to them, they didn't know. It wasn't like, you know, engine malfunction, where everybody dies. They seemed stuck in the moment they found out. They would always be different, always be changed."

But after doing that story, which appeared about the time of the first anniversary, Marks had a feeling that was strange to him. "I wanted to stay with them. I didn't know if anybody else cared about this story. I felt like I was the only one who cared."

He was pleased when he read the book, *The Fall of Pan Am 103*, by Emerson and Duffy (1990). "I'm convinced they read my article because there was a line that was almost verbatim from a sentence in my story, which made me feel good."[1]

Although most members of the family organization liked the story and told him so, Marks did not get much response from readers. "People aren't going to call you and say, 'Thank you for writing about these people's relatives.'" Some families were not pleased, however, that he had written about the split in the group. "I said that the group had experienced a collective nervous breakdown. And they had. Why are there two groups? What are they fighting each other for? I thought the psychology of the group was so interesting. I found the aftermath more interesting than being in Lockerbie."

Marks' personal struggle with the story — feeling haunted by the farmer's story, dreaming of bodies falling from the sky, having recurring thoughts of what the victims' last moments were like, crying after the woman's emotional outburst at the family meeting — resembled experiences that many others described following the downing of Pan Am 103. Townspeople in Lockerbie recounted them to their family doctors. Police who were called in to help with the recovery of the bodies and search for evidence documented them in the biggest survey ever done of police reaction to disaster work. Students at Syracuse University told counselors about them. Grieving families shared them in support sessions.

Their experiences coincide with some symptoms of Post-Traumatic Stress Disorder, which mental health professionals consider a normal reaction to an abnormal situation. Some of the syndrome's characteristics are still being debated by the psychiatric profession, which first listed diagnostic criteria for the disorder in 1980 and has already revised them (American Psychiatric Association, 1989). But post-traumatic stress clearly emerged as an issue as this study proceeded.

Dr Margaret Mitchell, a lecturer in psychology at Glasgow University whose speciality is post-traumatic stress disorder, came to media attention after she began reporting on her research with police who helped at Lockerbie. Mitchell had been attached to Strathclyde Police as a "sort of resident psychologist" at the time of the disaster. She was doing research for her Ph.D. dissertation by interviewing officers who had been injured in the line of duty. She convinced her colleague, the chief medical officer of the Strathclyde Police, Dr David McLay, that they should measure the effects of the Lockerbie tragedy on police.

Between December 21 and New Year's day, Mitchell put together a questionnaire for the police officers. By January 6, the survey was ready to go. Nearly 1,000 (48 percent) of the officers surveyed responded. By late summer, Mitchell began to get some results. "Interesting stuff started coming out in the open narrative section — about how disorganized the rescue effort had been, how helpless and hopeless they felt. And I'm thinking, 'Isn't it weird for a police officer to say that? That's very strange.'"[2]

So she searched the literature and learned these reactions were very typical of people in disaster-stricken communities, as well as rescue workers. She also interviewed, as part of her original Ph.D. project, officers who had been injured. Her interview protocol included a life evaluation, an inventory about what the officers had accomplished in the last year. "This produced these outpourings of talk. Two hours later I'd find myself still talking about Lockerbie. Police officers crying — obviously the first time they'd talked to anybody about it, very concerned about what I was going to think of them. These officers were feeling totally isolated. They thought they were the only ones that felt like that — no mutual talking amongst the ranks — and so this really hit me like a sledgehammer. Boy, this really was significant."

At the time of the first anniversary, Mitchell made her first visit to the Incident Control Centre in Lockerbie, and was struck by the manifestations of stress that she saw in police. "Round staring eyes, talking a lot, very uptight. Very, very thick atmosphere, terrible atmosphere, as a matter of fact." She was particularly impressed by the section where personal property was being held. "There were three or four police officers there, nervous with their bodies... talking a lot." She looked at the shelves down one side, holding cardboard boxes and photographs: passport photos and snapshots. "You slowly realize what you're looking at. You don't realize straight away. You think it's boxes. These are small boxes holding personal belongings of the passengers on the aircraft." The man working there showed her piles of clothing that had been laundered by Lockerbie women. "A lot of personal property was still there a year later. Now this was quite an amazing thing to me." She also visited an area of the Incident Control Centre where photographs of suitcases and bits of suitcases were studied.

"The striking feature about the whole Lockerbie experience was this juxtaposition of very ordinary stuff in a completely extraordinary context," Mitchell said. "You see something like a Samsonite suitcase, which you see all the time, and you realize, of course, that was the suitcase that held the bomb. It was that kind of jarring feeling all the time. I got the sense that this was the same experience these people working around the stuff had had as a steady diet for a year."

Mitchell made news for the first time when she presented a paper before the British Psychological Society in April 1990, reporting on absenteeism among Strathclyde police in the year after Lockerbie. Although the overall increase in sickness for the police force as a whole had been only five percent from 1988 to 1989, the 190 officers who had worked in the mortuary at Lockerbie showed an increase in absenteeism of more than 70 percent (Mitchell, McLay, Boddy and Cecchi, 1991).

Following that report, which covered only a small part of her study, Mitchell gave an extensive briefing to commanding officers of the Strathclyde Police. She found them very attentive. "They too had had experiences. They too were traumatized." They had also recognized that they had officers working in their ranks who were troubled by their experiences at Lockerbie, and the information Mitchell had gathered helped them understand the extent of the problem.

The study challenged the assumption prevailing in Britain at the time that emergency workers could operate in such an abnormal situation and emerge unscathed. Analysis of the narrative statements showed three aspects of the Lockerbie tragedy were particularly troubling. One was the scale and circumstances — the area involved, the number of victims, the early speculation attributing the bombing to Middle East terrorists — which were beyond the experience of the police. Another was the way in which the victims died. "I thought all the time about how the victims must have suffered and whether they were aware of what was happening to them, and I couldn't get rid of the image of bodies and young children falling out of the sky," one officer wrote in the survey (1991, p. 202). Still another was the physical chaos at the site.

The study grouped the police in three categories — those who spent 80 percent of their time in the mortuary, those who participated in the search for bodies and evidence, and those on patrol and security duty — and demonstrated differences in the quantity of post-traumatic stress symptoms they experienced. The police on mortuary duty, who had to move and prepare bodies for various post-mortem procedures, as well as record the details of the forensic scientists' findings, were most affected. Those who took part in the search were also more affected than those on patrol duty. "Those on search duties suffered a form of anticipatory anxiety because they never knew what they would come across," Mitchell and her research colleagues reported (p. 199). For example, nearly 30 percent of the entire sample suffered from sleep disorders, but 43 percent of the mortuary workers reported this symptom. Officers assigned to the mortuary or the search continued to think about their work at Lockerbie significantly more than those with patrol duties.

Surprisingly, officers who spent a short time on mortuary duty and hence had less exposure to the bodies apparently had *more* trouble assimilating the experience than did those who worked consistently at the mortuary. Those who worked there on a regular basis reported fewer physical symptoms and said they thought less about their duties four-to-six weeks later than those who worked there only part-time. Interviews with those who had worked at the mortuary longer showed this experience "provided an opportunity to understand the process of the forensic examinations and to become intellectually absorbed in the inquiries. There was more of a sense of a contribution to solving the crime and making sense of their own role in the event" (1991, p. 204).

Lockerbie was pivotal in making people aware that emergency services are vulnerable, Mitchell said. "Old war horses (among the police) were shocked at how affected they were by Lockerbie. The babies and young kids seemed to have a profound effect on them."

Later, Mitchell studied the experience of general practitioners in Lockerbie, and learned they were impressed by how pervasive stress reactions had been among their patients. They did not recognize symptoms as signs of post-traumatic stress until they received literature from solicitors, and they did not feel equipped professionally to deal with the nature and frequency of symptoms they were finding. The doctors told the researcher their patients had initially been reluctant to seek help for their symptoms "because they did not want to bother the doctor." The first visits came from mothers bringing in children whose behavior was regressing; they had begun to wet the bed, had trouble sleeping or lost interest in eating. Next came the women themselves, who told the doctors they were not "getting over it." The last to arrive were the men, often brought in by their wives; they might have become argumentative or increased their alcohol consumption or changed in the way they responded to their children. Many patients were also sent by solicitors in the spring and summer of 1989 and the same time period a year later. The doctors noticed that post-traumatic stress affected patients of all types, including those who previously had been good at coping with life experiences (Mitchell, Dec. 14, 1991).

The study gave reporters another reason to call Mitchell about Lockerbie. It raised no questions about media roles, but news coverage did emerge as an issue in Mitchell's study of police. Their various reactions to media left the psychologist questioning what the real impact of disaster coverage is. "I can't truly distinguish in my mind how much of the dislike of the media is that it is one of the cultural things that we do, and how much of it is truly an intrusion," she said.

One officer she interviewed had been particularly troubled by what he saw as his failure to control the media. "I think it was the Christmas Eve service, and he felt extremely inadequate and angry at himself, as if he'd been an entire failure — not just as a police officer, but as a human being — in not being able to control what he saw to be the real intrusion of the media who wanted to get into the service," she recalled. "I think one reason why he felt inadequate is that he didn't feel he had been as aggressive as he should have been. He certainly felt more aggressive after the fact. I think he felt terribly caught in the situation. Here he was in a church. His job was to hold back the media, and he was surprised that the media had been pushy at that time."[3]

The presence of the media also made the officers feel that they could not engage in "black humor," one of the releases commonly used by police in stressful situations. "They couldn't even smile to each other and say, 'Hi, how are you?' in case a cameraman caught them smiling," Mitchell said. "Police were really conscious of the media being around the whole time, and they really felt it intruded on what they thought to be their normal discourse."

Also, she said, after a disaster, people get very angry at authorities of any sort, and just as police were angry at their commanding officers, they were also angry at the media. "Not that they recognized the media as being authorities, but they are an institution, if you like. And they got very angry at the media."

In that sense, she said media bashing becomes very normal in such circumstances. "We tend to think of the media as being intrusive and not being appropriate all the time. So there was a lot of negative feelings about the media, that they shouldn't have been there, and that they should have been more respectful."

In a different vein, Mitchell recalled a police officer who told her he kept playing a video of television news reports of the tragedy. "He reported this to me spontaneously, and he was sort of mystified by this behavior," she said. "What he'd done was he'd just collected all the news clips, and he'd put them all together in a video and played them over and over. He didn't really know why he did it. His wife thought it was because he wanted to see himself. She thought he was being eccentric or something like that." The psychologist and police officer talked about that behavior. "When events seem unjust, when events seem chaotic, when things with the world aren't right, human beings try to attribute meaning and try to explain things away, in order to put it into some existing schema," Mitchell said. "After we talked for a bit, he seemed to acknowledge that one of the things he was trying to do was explain the event to himself. So, in a sense, he found the media exposure to be quite therapeutic, quite useful."

Mitchell thinks a lot of that pro- or anti-media attitude depends on the individual personality. "Certainly, not everybody regards the media as being intrusive," she said, adding that she personally has found the media to be extremely useful. However, she has found the way many journalists cover her research to be one-dimensional and preoccupied with the notion that Lockerbie will never recover. "What journalists up here are interested in hearing is how people have *not* recovered; they're not interested in the way people have recovered." The fact that they wanted to think everybody was still having a difficult time "speaks to a lack of sophistication of some of the journalists" about psychology. "It's this 'victims is victims' and boy, if you ever step out of that role, there's no story there. The whole process is so much more interesting than that. (Reporters) come on the phone and they say, 'I'd like to talk to you about Lockerbie.' 'Well, what do you want to know about Lockerbie?' 'Well, are the people still suffering?' 'I don't know. What people do you mean?' 'Are there any groups that suffered more than others? Men? Women? This kind of thing.'"

Mitchell tells them the psychological effect was, in fact, pervasive, but many in the community have learned to function well and work through their symptoms. "None of that stuff ever gets reported. It's all headlines like, 'Hell on earth for Lockerbie residents.'" She said even the quality newspapers fall into this category.[4]

Peter Marks was not the only media person to report symptoms of distress linked to work on this story. A London-based reporter who went to Lockerbie for only a couple of days experienced "a mild depression." David Sharrock of *The Guardian*, another journalist who was in Lockerbie for a relatively short time, reported dreams about what he had seen. "I wouldn't call them nightmares," he said. Andrew McCallum, now retired from the *Glasgow Herald*, found that if he was driving down the motorway past Lockerbie, he would find an excuse to stop by, not to speak to anyone, but just to be there for a while. His colleague, Jim Freeman, who covered the Fatal Accident Inquiry from start to finish, found some aspects of that experience very stressful, especially watching a videotape of the blip on the radar screen that had been Pan Am 103 break into pieces and listening to the lengthy testimony about the injuries of each victim. Since then he has noticed that he develops sweaty palms whenever he has to fly.

Most of the journalists who visited Lockerbie had vivid memories of their early hours in the stricken town. One had trouble recalling specifics, which he attributed to the passage of time. But the interviewer asked him, as she did all those who were there relatively early in the story, if he had seen the body lowered from the roof. She was trying to find witnesses to corroborate the behavior of photographers and cameramen described by Lockerbie residents. The newsman did not think he had been there. The next day he called her office. Just before he fell asleep that night, he had recalled the scene.

Kerry Gill of *The Times* found that Lockerbie affected him less than some other stories he had covered. "I must say about Lockerbie that I've always felt slightly distant from it," Gill said. "I'm not really sure why." He speculated that it was "because everybody was wiped out in one go. I think the only time I felt slightly distressed was when the American relatives came for the service in the graveyard, and you saw the graves with the picture of the girl or boy. It was only then that you're talking about human beings. Everything else was so much figures."

One of the most interesting reactions to Lockerbie was described by an American newsman who can no longer bring himself to watch television shows about rescue work, like "911," which use film clips and re-enactments to portray responses to calls on the 911 emergency number. Whenever he saw such shows come on, the reporter's throat felt constricted, as if he could not breathe. The reporter did not share his experiences with his editor and found it difficult to explain to his wife. Shortly after returning to his newspaper from Lockerbie, he became an editor. "I wasn't reporting any more," he said. But on the first anniversary, the sense of melancholy returned. "I felt really bad." Then he became conscious of his distress in watching shows like "911."

Looking back at the anniversary, the reporter wished aloud that he had been sent to Lockerbie to do the follow-up stories. "It's unfortunate that I didn't stay on the story, because it would have been good to go back," he said, citing the sources he had developed among the local people. "When I think about it now, it probably would have been therapeutic to go back. They had counselors over there for everybody, the army guys out in the field, for the police. They had counselors for the counselors. They had counselors for the families. They didn't have any counselors for reporters."

The reporter said he believed many newspeople would not want to show editors or colleagues how they were affected by a story, "because you'd be looked at as somebody who couldn't stand the heat. You're unreliable to go on another story. You're going to let your emotions figure into the story. You aren't telling people the facts they want to know. There's an unspoken code of machismo among everybody that's probably a defense mechanism. And I think it's what gives people a bad view of reporters. They see you as somebody who's unaffected by this. What are you doing here? You're laughing at a fire scene. What are you doing? You're joking around with other reporters. They look at you like ghouls. But you're not." Reporting, he said, is a hard job. "I don't think it's any mistake that it leaves a lot of dysfunctional lives."

The newsman speculated that the people who rose through the journalistic ranks to become editors probably did not let their reporting experiences "get to them." But he suggested the industry was going through a maturation process. "Maybe it is about time they look at the psychological toll. Maybe they should give you some kind of support, say 'Look, what you're doing is valuable, and you're doing the right thing by doing this.' Probably people in leadership positions at newspapers should say, 'Look, am I asking somebody to do something that I wouldn't do? Does it really add to our mission? What is it we want in these stories? Is this story going to be helped any more by a person that's got tears in her eyes? Should we examine whether we're placing demands on reporters in their twenties which makes them come to grips with things that hardened police investigators and army guys have a hard time dealing with, and then expect them to cover a zoning meeting or a campaign?'"

Dr Michael Blumenfield, a professor of psychiatry at New York Medical College in Vahalla, New York, became interested in post-traumatic stress reactions in newspeople while working with rescue workers following a plane crash at Dallas-Fort Worth. The Red Cross thought his findings were so interesting they wanted him to describe them for the media. Many of the reporters who showed up for the news conference had also covered the plane crash. As the psychiatrist described the reactions of the rescue workers, the journalists started telling him they had experienced the same things.

In 1990, Blumenfield arranged a focus group of New York City journalists to explore their experiences in covering traumatic situations. The group included print and broadcast reporters and photographers. Blumenfield's videotape of the encounter demonstrates that these people are not "hardened" by covering violence and disasters; they are deeply affected by them.

Reporters and photographers of the Gannett Suburban Newspapers in Westchester County, New York, viewed Blumenfield's tape as part of a workshop on "Trauma and the Media" in April 1992.[5] Many had recently covered a USAir crash at LaGuardia. A number volunteered that they had had dreams about the crash. One, a Syracuse University alumnus, had dreamed that she saw a list of names scrolling up a television screen, just as she had witnessed the names of the SU students on December 21, 1988. Two of the names she saw in her dream were the parents of a woman she had interviewed; at the time she spoke with the woman, she did not know if they were among the survivors. Only after her dream did the reporter learn that they had died.

The way the reporter had incorporated the Flight 103 tragedy into her dream about the USAir disaster is not unusual, Blumenfield said. Events that resemble or symbolize a traumatic event often evoke involuntary recollections of that event. Anniversaries, for example, often have that effect; conscious commemoration of an anniversary may be easier to handle psychologically than intrusive thoughts.

Recognition of the possibility of post-traumatic stress in news people and other communications professionals, such as public information officers and public relations practitioners, is so new that little has been written about it. Some public discussion of the phenomenon was prompted by journalists' reactions to the Loma Prietro earthquake in the San Francisco Bay area, but in that case, media people were survivors equally as much as the people they were covering. That media managers recognized the problem and, in some cases, called in therapists to work with their people is encouraging but does not address the problem that Blumenfield identified and that the Pan Am 103 bombing illustrated.

The phenomenon should not be thought of as new. Evidence of its earlier existence can be found in articles about journalists, such as Thomas B. Morgan's 1984 article for *Esquire* about ten former combat reporters in Vietnam. Blumenfield, reading the article with a trained eye, agreed that some of the experiences the subjects described clearly were evidence of Post-Traumatic Stress Disorder. One had a flashback in mid-town Manhattan of a boy she had seen die on the floor of a helicopter. Another became depressed every springtime, and his wife pointed out that it always happened around the anniversary of the fall of Saigon, the Eastern offensive or the invasion of Laos. Some covered war after war, or wrote extensively about the Vietnam War. Blumenfield found interesting the fact that one had amassed a huge library about the war. "Anybody who collects 2,000 books on a subject has to be working through something," he said.

But some of those who experienced distress from covering Flight 103 or the USAir crash did not have experiences nearly as harrowing as Vietnam war correspondents or even the journalists arriving in the first few hours at Lockerbie. They did not meet the first standard of the American Psychiatric Association diagnostic criteria:

> The person has experienced an event that is outside the range of usual human experience and that would be markedly distressing to almost anyone, e.g., serious threat to one's life or physical integrity; serious threat or harm to one's children, spouse, or other close relatives or friends; sudden destruction of one's home or community; or seeing another person who has recently been, or is being, seriously injured or killed as the result of an accident or physical violence (1989).

In a number of cases, journalists had been exposed to the worst trauma of the disaster through interviews with witnesses, survivors or the grieving. Those dreaming of or visualizing the victims as they met their fate were creating images that no one saw and lived to tell about. The fact that police as well as newspeople who had been to Lockerbie had such intrusive thoughts raised an intriguing question: would conducting interviews or being present at the disaster site, even after it had been sanitized to some extent, be sufficient to cause psychological reactions?

Evidence that tends to support that possibility can be found in the writings of therapists about problems they themselves have experienced after listening to patients' accounts of traumatic experiences. Lindy (1988) provides several examples in his casebook on the treatment of Vietnam veterans. A doctor had a delayed response, a torturous, nauseating headache, when a patient phoned in for medication after a harrowing session in which the veteran had "taken" the therapist on a "horrendous mission" that involved killing women, children and old men. Another doctor found himself walking miles to work before dawn on a frigid January morning; only after he finally hailed a bus could he understand his own strange behavior — a patient who had become very close to him had related how he walked through bad weather to help an isolated radio operator in Vietnam, and the doctor unconsciously had re-enacted it.

One pair of researchers has christened this phenomenon "vicarious traumatization" (McCann and Pearlman, 1990).[6] This term comes closest to describing the unexpected reactions described by journalists with limited direct exposure to the event and its victims. Certainly, if therapists can develop symptoms by listening to patients' accounts of traumatic experience months or even years after the event, reporters hearing vivid testimony from survivors and witnesses within hours of a disaster should be susceptible as well.

One of the reporters who went to Lockerbie suggested the phenomenon may be compounded by the kind of people attracted to the profession. "After all, they're kind of creative people, imaginative. They use their brains. They're the kind of kids who daydream. You create a visual image in your mind of what it is (that happened). Part of what makes you creative is you can add a little life to what most people describe as a lifeless thing."

But journalists should not be surprised if they react to some stories and not to others — or if they react to stories, while some of their colleagues are not affected. As McCann and Pearlman write in *Psychological trauma and the Adult Survivor*: "An experience is traumatic in part because it in some way threatens the psychological core of the individual. Thus one person's trauma may be another person's difficult experience" (1990, p. 12). The way Peter Marks unconsciously identified with the people on the plane could help explain why the Flight 103 story was so difficult for him.

Reflections

The story of Pan Am 103 and Lockerbie was overwhelming in its scope and overpowering in its surrealistic details. Yet it had to be told, as quickly as journalists could relay the first facts via modern technology. It had to be followed up, filling in details and responding to those questions that could be answered: What happened? To whom? Where? When? It will have to be covered as long as it takes to find the answers to the questions left open, even after years of painstaking investigation: Who? How? Why?

Those questions come from the human need to make sense of the world, especially when it is fraught with uncertainty. As psychologist Margaret Mitchell suggested in an earlier chapter, "When events seem unjust, when events seem chaotic, when things with the world aren't right, human beings try to attribute meaning and try to explain things away, try to put it into some existing schema."

But in addition to sharing, spreading and explaining the trauma that follows a catastrophe — whether its cause is natural, accidental or intentional — media and institutions have other critical questions to answer: Is the danger over? Can it happen again? Will there be any warning?

With natural disasters, those answers may come from scientists — seismologists, climatologists, biologists, those probing the mysteries of volcanos. To the extent that such events cannot be predicted and their consequences cannot be controlled, humanity will cope psychologically as it has through the centuries, even though it uses advanced technology in its efforts to rescue and rebuild. But accidental disasters are, to some extent, preventable and that both complicates the search for answers and elevates its importance. Such catastrophes involve, in most cases, both technology and human error, ranging from a momentary lapse to a sustained and willful failure to ensure safety. Blame in a natural disaster becomes a moot point, except where its effects could have been prevented or at least alleviated; in an accidental disaster, responsibility is the essential issue. Understanding both the nature of the error and how it was made becomes critical to averting another Chernobyl, Bhopal, Hillsborough or spill of a substance toxic to humans or the environment.

An intentional disaster is not random. It happens because someone wills it to happen. It causes death and destruction because one or more individuals take action to kill and destroy. The answer to the question, "Is the danger over," depends on whether those causing the tragedy are still able or motivated to cause more destruction. "Can it happen again" can be answered in the negative only if steps have been taken to stop those behind a specific tragedy *and* those who might adopt or adapt their methods. "Will there be any warning?" may become, as it did in the case of Pan Am 103, "If there is a warning, will it be heeded?" and "Will those in greatest danger be alerted?"

How well media and institutions answer those questions and how they involve the public in addressing the issues they raise is critical. Analysis of long-term coverage of Pan Am 103 by news organizations in both the U.K. and the U.S. is, in some ways, more disheartening than any of the reportorial excesses that occurred in the tumultous hours and days immediately following the tragedy. A few media on both sides of the Atlantic invested considerable time and money in trying to identify those who paid for, plotted and produced this epic tragedy. But the curve of attention for most media, even the so-called elite press, appeared to follow government action or inaction on the subject. Attention lagged as forensics experts picked over minute pieces of wreckage, soared as indictments were announced, leapt again as the United Nations took steps to force Qaddafi to hand over the two Libyans, then declined steadily as more dramatic international events took over the headlines.

The real impetus for addressing the tough issues of aviation security came neither from institutions nor the media, but from those who might have seemed the least able to act: the grieving families and friends of those who perished. They learned to use the media — and many media, to their credit, cooperated — to focus public attention on security lapses that might permit would-be bombers to repeat the tragic attack on civilian aircraft.

Those grieving the American victims knew early on that their tragedy was being treated as less than a national priority. Not only were some representatives of the State Department unhelpful — and according to families, at times hostile — but neither President Reagan, winding up eight years in office with an extended vacation in California, nor President-elect Bush, indulging in quail-hunting and fishing in Texas before settling down to his new job, behaved in a way that recognized the hurt being felt by families and friends of the victims or the assault on an American aircraft.

Few journalists commented on this inaction by the outgoing Reagan administration. One who did, Bill Plante of CBS, stood outside the president's new retirement home in California on December 28, the day that authorities announced that a bomb had caused the disaster. Asked by anchor Bob Schieffer what the administration was likely to do in view of that knowledge, Plante replied:

> The answer, I'm afraid, is 'not very much.' The confirmation that this was, indeed, an act of terrorism comes at what is essentially an awkward time for the administration. Officials have absolutely no real idea of who was responsible, so they are not anxious for President Reagan to be involved in the issue because there is simply no positive payoff, no upside to it. The White House wants Ronald Reagan, of course, to go out in a blaze of glory in these final days, even as his effective power fades, day by day, and getting stuck in the terrorism briar patch is not exactly what his staff had in mind.

Reagan himself did not comment that day on the announcement that the tragedy had been caused by a bomb; the only White House statement was issued by a deputy press secretary.

Benign neglect has characterized much of the later coverage of Pan Am 103. In fairness, the main thread of the story — who did it and why — does not lend itself to traditional journalistic methods anymore than it did to conventional police efforts. It took a computer to organize the immense amount of detail that police gathered from the scene and from thousands of interviews in at least forty countries. It required U.K. and U.S. investigators to develop an understanding not only of how international terrorist cells operate, but also to achieve working relationships with each other and authorities in Germany, France, Sweden and Malta.

Journalists' problems with the story reflect those of police in many ways. For them, too, the complexities created by the crime tend to be overwhelming. Using computers to analyze and sift through huge quantities of data is a relatively recent innovation in journalism.[1] Building a data base — or analyzing some existing data base — might or might not have helped to cut through the morass of information on this story. It is one possibility to consider.

But the news media face a problem that police investigators never have to worry about, presenting the mass of detail surrounding this story in a way that can be quickly and easily understood by the public. The criminal investigation gathers evidence and builds a case to set before a judge and jury; it can take days or weeks of direct testimony and cross examination to clarify the issues. Neither print nor broadcast media deal easily with such complexity. The amount of background required to make the story understandable to busy readers and viewers is daunting.

ABC's approach to the problem was interesting: its first lengthy special on the case proceeded chronologically, but cut between the plot to bomb the plane and problems with Pan Am security. In reprising the story a year later, it substituted fresh detail for parts of its initial scenario that had subsequently been disproved. This gave viewers the big picture again — with the new information in an understandable context.

Another problem involves the skills and background needed to operate across international boundaries as an investigative journalist. David Leppard, the *Sunday Times* investigative journalist whose close-up reporting on the Scottish investigation of the Flight 103 bombing became a book, said it would have been hard for a reporter from the other side of the Atlantic to develop his sources. Although Nick Cohen of the *Independent* at one point flew from London to Washington and met with a source developed by trans-Atlantic telephone, media are likely to make such investments only when a story is very "hot" or, as in the case of the Syracuse Newspapers, it is seen as exceptionally important to its regular audience.

For those working across language barriers, the problems increase. A few newspeople in the U.K. and U.S. went to the trouble of translating — or paying for translations of — French[2] and German reports, especially *L'Express*, *Stern* and *Der Spiegel*. Those who did found the effort worthwhile. Journalists from the Middle East also followed this story — one played a role in arranging Dr Swire's meeting with Qaddafi — but very few of the reporters we spoke with in the U.S. or U.K. mentioned that they had looked at work from those newspeople or had been in contact with them.

Although some journalistic links were forged across media and across national boundaries on this story — several newspeople on both sides of the Atlantic mentioned Linda Mack of ABC and Leppard of the *Sunday Times* as valuable contacts — there has been no systematic international effort by investigative reporters to collaborate on the story. That is hardly surprising; there is almost no precedent for such an effort. Few foreign correspondents have investigative reporting experience; most investigative reporters hone their skill on problems or sources close to home.

So most reporters assigned to Pan Am 103 on either side of the Atlantic have never exchanged those bits and pieces of information, tips, hunches and just plain guesses — the not-ready-for-publication pieces — that hard work on such a story produces. Many have concentrated on one small piece of the puzzle or have struggled with a big picture that still has too many details missing to be clear. Sharing might help to clarify the pattern in the jigsaw and the pieces that need to be found.

Such an international effort would, of course, be unprecedented, but so is the challenge this story presents. One approach could be a journalistic team, the international equivalent of the one formed in the U.S. by IRE (Investigative Reporters and Editors, Inc.) following the murder of Arizona investigative reporter, Donald Bolles. Its goal was not to find his murderers; the reporters who volunteered for the IRE team rightly regarded that as the job for law enforcement authorities. What they set out to uncover was the mob influence in Arizona, the story that Bolles had been working on for years and that ultimately cost him his life in a car bombing. The six-month investigation by

IRE produced 23 articles on corruption in Arizona, which were published simultaneously by the papers of reporters who worked on the project and which were then made available to any other papers that wanted them — free of charge.

Alternatively, news media that have already invested considerable time and effort in this story could join forces to share information and costs, much as media now regularly do in sponsoring polls. Such an undertaking would look closely at the role of government in protecting its citizens, its commerce and in concert with other states, the safety of international travel against state-sponsored terrorism. Determining the degree of state involvement and the specific states involved is too pressing an issue to be left to diplomatic historians.

The issue in this particular case is not only what part, if any, the two indicted Libyans played in the bombing. It is the degree to which the bombing was authorized and carried out by agents of the Libyan government. It is the degree to which Qaddafi himself participated and supported the act. But, above all, it is whether Libyans or Libya acted alone or were, in fact, sponsored by other states.

By 1987, Libyans already had a special reputation in international intelligence circles. In his controversial book on the secret wars of the CIA, Bob Woodward noted that the principal leaders of the Reagan administration's national security apparatus recognized that the hijacking of TWA Flight 847 exposed the weaknesses of their anti-terrorist capability. Woodward said William Casey, then head of the CIA, was not certain who was behind the hijacking, but his best intelligence on state-sponsored terrorism related to Qaddafi and Libya. Woodward wrote:

> Qaddafi used less sophisticated cryptographic equipment and codes, so the NSA (National Security Agency) broke them consistently. The sheer numbers of intercepts made Qaddafi appear the most active and dedicated of terrorists. His operatives were sloppy, they left trails. Syria and Iran, in contrast, were more disciplined, they operated in the shadows (1987, pp. 469-470).

Two other journalists, David C. Martin of CBS and John Walcott of *The Wall Street Journal*, made a related point in their 1988 book on America's "war against terrorism" in discussing the December 1985 attacks at Rome and Vienna airports. The victims included an 11-year-old American schoolgirl, Natasha Simpson, who was traveling to spend Christmas with relatives. They wrote:

> The terrorists who killed Natasha Simpson were carrying Tunisian passports that the Tunisian government identified as having been confiscated or stolen from Tunisian citizens working in Libya — a classic case of state-supported terrorism. It was not so simple as that, however. The one terrorist surviving the Rome attack later told Italian authorities he had been trained at a camp in the Bekaa Valley by

> Syrian agents who then accompanied him on the journey from Damascus to Rome. Assad, at least, had the good sense to remain silent. Qaddafi was not the only head of state who supported terrorism, but he was certainly the most galling (1988, p. 268).

Was it possible that the real sponsors of the Pan Am 103 attack also recognized the propensity of the Libyans to make telltale mistakes and decided to involve them in the plot precisely for that reason? That would provide the masterminds with deniability; in the event that evidence was found, it would lead back toward Qaddafi's door. Whether Libya acted alone or in concert with other forces in the Middle East, the tiny bits and pieces gathered in the hills around Lockerbie certainly did that.

How journalists cover crises and disasters — and their aftermath — should be studied as carefully as critics and scholars examine media performance in military confrontations and political campaigns. So should the role institutions play in aiding or impeding the information flow. In a complex and interdependent world, studying the messages and messengers without considering the behavior of sources sets up a "kill-or-honor the messenger" mentality when the blame or glory may belong elsewhere.

This case study, in fact, suggests a symbiotic relationship between news media and institutions caught up in a disaster. Their behavior can be mutually beneficial, as in Lockerbie, where those representing the Scottish Information Office and the Scottish police worked *with* journalists to communicate the tragedy to the world while protecting a crime scene of epic proportions, and during sensitive moments, such as memorial services, respecting the privacy of the bereaved.

Or it can be mutally destructive. Pan Am's failure to develop a process for rapid assembly of a passenger manifest, notification of next of kin and timely dissemination of that information set up conditions under which its own personnel felt obliged to help another institution, Syracuse University. That desire to help, it appears, led to the premature and inadvertent release of a list of unverified names to reporters from two Syracuse television stations. Their news directors, in turn, decided to go on the air with those names without further confirmation, setting off a barrage of phone calls that hampered their own news operations. The desperation with which people sought confirmation belies the assertion by Pan Am's Jeff Kriendler that such a list is of little importance to anyone except media interested in local angle. It also suggests that news media and airlines, as well as other institutions likely at some time to experience a disaster, have a mutual interest in addressing the need for such information and the groundrules for its transmission *before* the worst-case scenario becomes a reality.[3]

Planning for disasters and preparing journalists to cover them ought to be given at least the same priority as war and campaign coverage, but the impression left from interviews for this book is that most news executives have not addressed this issue seriously. Fast reaction to the unexpected is the basis of journalistic legend — and, according to sociologist Gaye Tuchman, represents one of the key categories of journalistic practice. Tuchman (1978) observed newsroom behavior by both print and broadcast journalists and found them reacting stereotypically to such stories by hearkening back to other crisis events. These stories were a call to arms; off-duty reporters and editors would call in or just show up ready for tough duty. Editors rubbed their clasped hands together and exclaimed, "What a story!"[4]

In other words, the newsroom management response to crisis tends to be as much after the fact as that of most major corporations and other institutions, including government. Many of the news organizations involved in this story did re-examine their crisis reporting practices, but there are other ways to prepare for the heat of such journalistic battles than "trial by fire." An individual news organization — or the news profession — will not suffer a lack of challenges by thinking collectively about the way it approaches disasters *before* they happen. Being prepared means being ready to focus on the story itself, not problems that could have been anticipated.

The proactive stance of the Scottish Office and the way it involves Scottish police in its communications plan and practice is truly the exception. If Pan Am had been as well prepared, the way this story developed might have been very different. A plan like that followed by Delta Airlines might have alerted Syracuse University directly and enlisted them in contacting the families of students who could be on board. The University and airline then could have coordinated the release of the verified names because next of kin would have been notified.

Communication in time of crisis also provides a useful lens through which to focus on the role of the free press in modern society. How do news organizations respond to the genuine human interest in tragedy? How do they hold institutions, especially governmental leaders, agencies and major corporations, accountable for the way they deal with such events? How do they help the public take part in debating the issues raised?

A totalitarian state and controlled economy may be able to treat such information as irrelevant to the public. After all, as late as 1982, the press of the Soviet Union reported airline disasters only when Western rather than Soviet aircraft were involved (Morrison, 1982). The public in Western democracies — and those in the new democracies of the former Soviet bloc — would be outraged if news of a disaster were suppressed. But they should also be incensed at being left "out of the loop" when the issues revealed by the tragedy are discussed by their elected leaders — and are *not* reported by the mass media. That is just what happened in Washington in July 1992, when the House of Representatives voted, in effect, to reverse itself and prevent the Federal Aviation Administration from requiring background checks of individuals with clearance to work around parked aircraft.[5] A parent, putting a child on a plane to visit grandparents in another country, or a family, seeing off a business traveler, has as much right to have a say about security precautions, passenger manifests and compensation limits as airlines and their insurers. But they cannot voice their opinion if the media treats such issues as relevant only to special interests and the legislators and bureaucrats they lobby.

Even if members of the audience have no obvious connection to the issues raised by disasters, many will have a psychological link. Robert Jay Lifton, professor of psychology and psychiatry at John Jay College and director of its Center on Violence and Human Survival, has asserted that television — and, to some extent, news photography — has made us "survivors by proxy" by taking us to disaster scenes. He notes:

> Actual survivors of death encounters take on a self-imposed responsibility to bear witness to what they have seen and felt as a way of insisting that the world stop the killing and prevent its recurrence. Survivors by proxy are now capable of doing the same (1992, p. 26).

So as members of distant audiences we can be sensitized by the way, as Lifton says, "certain pictures take hold in our minds" and "condense and symbolize all the pain and suffering." Some pictures become part of the public consciousness: Lifton cites the naked Vietnamese girl running down the road after her clothes were burned by napalm, and the tiny Jewish boy with his hands raised at Nazi gunpoint. Flight 103 added to those images: the giant cockpit wrenched from the fuselage by the bomb blast, the huge crater blasted out of a quiet neighborhood in Lockerbie, the weeping students and cheerleader, and for those who saw it, the mother who collapsed on the floor of Kennedy Airport. As Lifton suggests, such images break through our feelings that these are distant events, unconnected to our lives. We empathize, identify and associate those events with others in our own lives. Again, to quote Lifton:

> The empathy enables us to bring our own minds to the experience of victims, to imagine what they are feeling. Identification carries the process further: at least for moments we become those victims. Both empathy and identification are enhanced by a release of memory, which provides models in the form of previous images...
>
> The pyschological process is energized by our discomfort. It represents a healthy awakening of compassion and fellow feeling, qualities all too readily obliterated

> by 20th-century killing and by the technological distancing often associated with that killing (1992, p. 26).

Although Lifton was making these observations in connection with the violence in Bosnia, they are all too applicable to Pan Am 103. Some individuals, he notes, may be able to fend off these images, but they reach many others, making it much more difficult for perpetrators to deny their atrocities. The challenge is for "survivors by proxy" to join forces with those touched directly by this tragedy, to recognize the opportunities for what Lifton calls "life-enhancing action," the chance to make a difference by preventing future acts of aviation terror and alleviating the effects of aviation disaster .

Unfortunately, the post-Cold War era is providing too many opportunities to become "survivors by proxy" of disasters caused by intentional acts. The world's troubles, be they in Northern Ireland or the former Yugoslavia, are immigrating to great metropolitan cities where they can be guaranteed an audience through the news media and then disappear in the urban throng. So unnerving bombings become an unwelcome feature of London life, and New York is shaken by the car-bomb that turned its towering World Trade Center into a choking, smoke-filled chimney.

The answers to those troubles are not going to come easily, and until they are resolved, media and other institutions must prepare to communicate in a way that neither understates the danger to the populace nor heightens its response to hysteria. Having addressed such "worst-case scenarios," they can apply the lessons learned to unpremeditated and natural disasters.

As part of that preparation, they need to consider carefully the way they treat victims of such tragedies. To the authors, the need for more compassion is clear, but some issues involving the coverage of grief and people in the throes of trauma are still debatable. One of our colleagues, Professor Henry Schulte, is famous among his students for saying that a really interesting story is neither black nor white, but comes in shades of grey. Issues such as whether uncontrolled grief in a public place should be treated as public or private seem to fall in such a grey area.

In the wake of the TWA hijacking, conservative columnist George Will coined the term "pornography of grief" to decry the way television journalists approached families and friends of hostages with microphones open and cameras rolling.[6] But a distinction must be made between exploitation of victims and journalists' willingness to provide a forum to victims and survivors.

Roy Peter Clark of the Poynter Institute for Media suggests that journalists may need sensitivity training to fulfill what he describes as "their traditional role of comforting the afflicted" (1987, p. 1D). Clark suggests that reporters, editors, photographers, student journalists and teachers meet with victims, those who advocate for them and psychologists who work with them.

Again this needs to be done in advance. News media must make sure that they are not rewarding the rude and aggressive. The journalist who returns with a "scoop" at the expense of a victim harassed into expressing emotion deserves "early retirement," not a bonus or promotion. Reporters and editors should take responsibility not only for the news they publish or broadcast, but for the methods they use in the process.

Pan Am 103 demonstrated that disasters have consequences for all those caught up in them. The newspeople who covered and edited this story found it difficult and often emotionally troubling. Even the public information officers in Scotland who had prepared for disasters through careful training and rehearsal were marked by their experience in coping with this tragedy. Most of all, of course, it marked those who lost loved relatives, friends and neighbors. Those who can turn from the despair of such tragedies to the forging of new and positive relationships and to the active pursuit of a safer, more peaceful world deserve to be applauded and abetted. Theirs is the good news, that humanity involves caring for and about one another, even when the bond originally was forged out of tragedy in a small market town in the southern hills of Scotland.

Text notes

Introduction

1 This case will be discussed in Chapter 2 under What Survivors Share.

Chapter 1

1 Determination by Sheriff Principal John Mowat in the Fatal Accident Inquiry relating to the Lockerbie Air Disaster, March 1991.

2 James Cusick, "Radar captures flight 103's last seconds," *The Independent*, Oct. 2, 1990, p. 3.

3 *The Firemaster's report on the Role of Dumfries & Galloway Fire Brigade (and reinforcing brigades) at the Lockerbie Air Disaster: 21st December 1988.* Abbreviated version in *Lockerbie: A local authority response to the Disaster*, Neil McIntosh, Chief Executive, Dumfries and Galloway Regional Council, November 1989.

Chapter 2

1 Videotape of 9 p.m. broadcast, December 21, 1988, on file in the Lockerbie Archives of the Regional Library of Dumfries and Galloway, Dumfries.

2 Ibid

3 Ibid.

4 Ibid.

5 Neil McIntosh, Chief Executive, Dumfries and Galloway Regional Council, *Lockerbie: A local authority response to the Disaster*, November 1989, p. 19.

6 The *Sun*, December 23, 1988, p. 1; *Time*, Jan. 2, 1989, p. 77; *Newsweek*, Jan. 2 1989, p. 19; and *Washington Post*, Dec. 23, 1988, p. 1.

7 McIntosh, p. 3.

8 Families in the United States, for example, were not being told the status of the search for their loved ones. The State Department and Pan Am would later be criticized by the Presidential Commission for ineffective communication with survivors.

9 The University's decision to go ahead with the game will be discussed in subsequent chapters.

Chapter 3

1 Tapes deposited in the Lockerbie archives of the Library of Dumfries and Galloway Region, Dumfries.

2 Many of the relatives and friends who came to Lockerbie would later ask to be taken to the exact location where their loved one fell to earth. The impact sites for those who fell on the hills and fields above Lockerbie often had a tranquil beauty, and some visitors would spend a long time there, explaining that they felt close to their loved one.

3 Press Council Adjudications, Chapter 4, "Difficult Decisions: Pictures of Grief and Tragedy," pp. 232–233. See Reporting Reviewed section of this chapter for *Time*'s rationale for using the picture.

4 This unofficial report was circulated shortly after the searches for bodies ended. It was entitled *Lockerbie: a Worm's Eye View* and described the horrific work of junior officers in searching for and recovering bodies.

5 By this time, it would have been nearly 5 p.m. Some families apparently had come early for one reason or another. For example, one of the mothers we interviewed planned to meet a friend for dinner and then wait with her for the plane, which was scheduled to arrive at Kennedy at 9:19 p.m. Its final destination was Detroit, where it was scheduled to arrive at 12:18 a.m.

6 Other witnesses indicated that the notice said something about seeing a Pan Am ticket agent. Santangelo is speaking here from recall without checking the story that was written from the notes he dictated to the rewrite desk. This represents his memory of the scene more than three years after the event.

7 Again, this is Santangelo's recall of the quote. Stories and the videotape record her saying "not my baby" instead of "not my little girl;" his memory of the event shows that he clearly remembered the meaning of what she was saying, since it was her daughter who died on the plane.

8 The woman is an American. She does not speak Spanish. We have been unable to find an explanation of why Douglas thought she was speaking Spanish, although our investigation of stress reporters experienced on this story may provide a clue. See Chapter 7.

9 Bob Teague, describing his own experiences "on the street" in New York City, also uses the term "gang bang" (1982, p. 77).

10 Another edition gave more information in a headline that proclaimed "DISASTER" and then "258 die in fiery jet crash; Syracuse students on board." Again most of the page was devoted to a picture of the woman on the airport floor.

11 In newspaper parlance, a "stringer" is not on the regular staff or payroll, but he or she is on call and will be paid for coverage of stories that happen in his area.

12 Special correspondent is the term *Newsday* uses to indicate that a writer is a stringer, a reporter on call for covering events in his area.

13 The university official who conducted this meeting with the media viewed it as a separate news conference to deal with an issue that had been troubling the university's Public Relations office for several days, charges against Derrick Coleman arising from a fight. This reporter, at least, did not see the two news conferences as distinct. See Chapter 4, section Syracuse University.

14 Breslin, a particularly colorful writer who won the Pulitzer Prize in 1986 for commentary while he was at the *Daily News*, was writing for *Newsday* at the time of the tragedy and did a column on his own feelings of insecurity as he sent his son off to Europe on a Lufthansa flight and then went over to check out the security operations at the Pan Am terminal.

15 It is still considered an attractive test market, although it is becoming less typical. Marketing

experts who have been studying the 1990 census found, for example, that it has a slightly higher proportion of households with incomes between $25,000 and $75,000, which currently is the operational definition of the U.S. middle class, than the nation has as a whole, and a significantly smaller population of minorities. (Pierce, June 8, 1992, p. 1A.)

16 The Syracuse Newspapers also publish a Sunday paper, the *Syracuse Herald-American*, which sells 226,078, but it uses the staff of the daily papers, especially that of the *Herald-Journal*, so it was not examined separately for the purpose of this study. Circulation figures are certified by the Audit Bureau of Circulation and published in *Editor and Publisher Yearbook 1991*.

17 The Syracuse journalists in this section were offered confidentiality as part of a separate local study that asked them to candidly assess their own performances, that of their colleagues and that of their management.

18 This statement represents the reporter's assessment of the list's accuracy. The next chapter demonstrates that other reporters found that the list contained names of Syracuse students who were not on the plane; the airline apparently had not vetted the list by contacting families of those listed.

19 Broadcasting jargon for natural or ambient sound.

20 A kind of news report.

21 Some journalists at a second station noted that they either spent precious time uplinking reports to other localities, time that could have been spent perfecting their own reports, or that they did encounter some difficulties sharing station facilities with other journalists. But largely these reporters said they understood the need to share. Journalists at a third station noted no problems with the way their station handled the networks and outside stations.

22 Confidentiality was also provided to editors and reporters of the Syracuse newspapers.

23 The photographer said available light inside the chapel was 3200 ASA – F2.8 and 125th of a second, which is minimal for photographic purposes, especially for shooting color. The strobe lights he used were triggered by a radio remote unit.

24 This estimate seems low to others who were there, including one of the authors. It helps, however, to explain the photographer's perception that the media presence was not that intrusive.

25 The number 38 was later corrected as it became clear that some students originally booked on the flight had not taken it for one reason or another.

26 This was at least two months before a reporter for the Greensburg, Pennsylvania, *Tribune-Review* called Mrs McKee and worked with her to obtain his service records.

27 The event was sponsored on February 20, 1989, by the student chapter of the Society of Professional Journalists. Most of the coverage highlights that were discussed at the meeting have been described elsewhere in this book.

28 Journalistic behavior at Kennedy Airport and Syracuse University also reflected, in part, the lack of readiness by communications professionals responsible for media relations at those sites.

29 One complaint against the *Sun* newspaper was investigated by a member of the Serious Crimes Squad in Glasgow. It involved allegations of the *Sun* possessing property from the plane that had been taken away from the site. But police said no evidence was found to substantiate those allegations.

30 News executives at the BBC and Scottish Television discussed their decision-making about this footage with us, and we have the testimony of the brother of one of the victims that he saw this scene on "Good Morning America," the ABC breakfast show.

31 Interestingly enough, the *New York Daily News* also had a rule against using body pictures under most circumstances, according to Gil Spencer.

32 *Time* also carried it in its domestic edition. "Terror in the Night," Jan. 2, 1989, pp. 74-78. Picture appeared on p. 77.

33 A flashover is the point in a fire when it becomes all consuming (McLain, 1990).

34 This portion of the code seems to have changed little in recent years. CBS provided its latest version, which was compared with its earlier ones.

35 Archives of these letters are being maintained at the library in Lockerbie and at the Bird Library at Syracuse University. The principal author read many of them, although no structural analysis was made. Some people did identify with individual cases, as in a touching letter from a woman who sent a contribution and asked that it go to help Rosebank Crescent resident Ella Ramsden, who had escaped from the wreckage of her home with her dog. Most seem to be concerned for the Lockerbie community as a whole and for the loss of so many young lives at the university.

36 This was at the recommendation of the Calcutt Committee, appointed by the government in 1989. It was headed by David Calcutt, a Queen's Counsel who has since been knighted.

37 Item 9 of the Code of Practice, *Press Complaints Commission Briefing* p.7.

38 The example given by Webster's Third New International Dictionary of the English Language is "employing a subterfuge to get her own way."

39 A Delta Airlines representative told a Society of Professional Journalists convention that on the second of two plane crashes at Dallas-Fort Worth the company was able to contact enough next of kin to release a list of most of the passengers within six hours. It had streamlined its process following the first crash (Louisville, Kentucky 1990). The list of Syracuse students was obtained from Pan Am less than four hours after the tragedy.

40 Television journalists from Syracuse tended to show a good deal of variation in the way they perceived their own overall performance. For example, the twelve television reporters who were interviewed rated their performance on the night of the tragedy from "superior" to "mediocre." One, rating the performance as 4 on a 10-point scale, said "I could have done more if given better direction." Ten of the twelve gave responses that showed some pride in their performance, although only five gave themselves high marks.

41 The pamphlet can be obtained by writing to Aviation/Space Writers Association, 17 South High Street, Suite 1200, Columbus, OH 43214. The price is $4. Phone (614)221–1900.

42 Most of continental Europe was still struggling with expensive hand-held phones that would work only in one country (Tully, 1989). The exception to this statement was Scandinavia, which created the world's first international cellular telephone network that reached from Denmark to Finland in 1981 (Tully, 1989). Cellular phones would play a major role again in the Loma Prieto earthquake coverage (Mermigas, 1989).

43 See chapter 7.

44 The Press Council initiated a general inquiry into coverage of the Hillsborough disaster and initially received 349 written complaints signed by a total of 3,651 persons, plus a petition from the Merseyside Area Student Organization signed by some 7,000. The

complaints named 35 newspapers and included 56 general complaints about behavior or content that did not specify any newspaper.

45 This conclusion is supported by the findings of the surveys conducted for the Broadcasting Standards Council . For every group of survivors, from disasters to rape, "newspapers were clearly the worst offenders," and it was certain newspapers, specifically the tabloids, that they complained about. (Shearer, 1991, p. 14)

Chapter 4

1 The interviews were conducted 18 months after the disaster. It was the first time the two men had spoken at any great length to an outsider of their ongoing involvement in the Lockerbie disaster. In November 1992, Beveridge left the SIO to join Scottish Nuclear Ltd as executive manager for public affairs.

2 Since Lockerbie, the Scottish Office Information Directorate has held seminars and workshops that include this coordination strategy. In the January 5, 1993, break-up of the oil tanker Braer off the Shetland Islands, all public information officers gathered in one place, improving the dissemination of information.

3 After Lockerbie, British Telecommunications re-examined its system, and developed a way to instantly add additional lines in areas stricken by an emergency situation. Again, the 1993 oil spill off the Shetland Islands provided a testing ground for the new system. It worked. The Scottish Office Information Directorate vowed never to be caught short again: the staff purchased a large quantity of portable phones for use during emergencies.

4 By the time of Leppard's encounter with Angus Kennedy, Pan Am had released the list of passengers. However, it is Scottish police procedure to withhold names of the deceased until recovery of the body is made and notification of the next of kin is officially confirmed. As the confirmations were made, the names of victims were written on a large blackboard in the media center.

5 McCauley (1990) reported that while in 1982 only 44 of the Fortune 500 had no formal communications department, by 1988 that number had reached 63 and was still climbing. In 1989 it was 71, and Jerry Bryan, head of the Public Relations Society of America's Corporate Section suggested many corporations had shifted such functions to PR agencies.

6 It is likely that CNN was reporting at this point that the petrol station was on fire. From what we have learned of the coverage, it would have been impossible for Kriendler to have seen television images of Lockerbie aflame this early. But it is important that this is his recall since it helps to illustrate the kind of pressure he was feeling at the time. Parts of the petrol station did catch fire, but it is our understanding that it was not spectacular; the pictures used by most television outlets were from the Sherwood Crescent area where the wings hit, claiming 11 lives on the ground.

7 See Chapter 3 section Syracuse television.

8 The arrival described here was actually a second group of relatives... A much smaller group arrived earlier (See Chapter 2, Death in the Family).

9 In an ironic twist, the chief attorney for the families in their case against Pan Am is Lee Kreindler, a distant cousin of Jeffrey Kriendler, who spells his name a bit differently.

10 The Presidential Commission on Aviation Security and Terrorism investigated this issue thoroughly and, in essence, confirmed Kriendler's explanation. The Commission did

recommend, however, that the U.S. government "owes special treatment to those who are killed in terrorist acts against this nation, and their families" (McLaughlin *et al.*, p.105).

11 Hill's role vis-a-vis sports is defensive; generally, he becomes involved only when "damage control" is required. The Athletic Department maintains a Sports Information unit that deals with publicity and the general inquiries of sports writers.

12 See Chapter 3 section The local story: Syracuse.

13 Today, Hill supervises the director of this alumni effort, known as Program Development, and it is housed within his Public Relations Department.

14 At the time of the bombing, neither the National Media Relations Director nor the Community Relations Director, both experienced public relations practitioners, had joined the staff.

15 The university also conducted an internal investigation, and the penalties, when they were handed down on October 1, 1992, were lighter because of the university's cooperation in the investigation. The NCAA banned the team from post-season play for the 1992-93 season and the school's entire athletic program was placed on two years' probation. Syracuse acknowledged at least 14 rules violations involving the men's basketball program.

16 See Chapter 3 section The local story, dealing with Syracuse television.

17 Hill recalled that this news conference took place between 8 and 8:30 p.m.; the Syracuse *Herald-Journal* of December 22 reports that it was held at approximately 9:40 p.m.

18 One explanation of the reporters' behavior may be that lines were so jammed into the Public Relations Department that they perceived that phones had been taken off the hook. Another explanation is that, in routine reporting practice, a reporter blocked from official sources will try all other possible avenues.

19 The first lists obtained from Pan Am contained 38 names.

20 Hill's assessment of timing in this statement again illustrates his difficulty in believing information the media were reporting. By 6 p.m., two hours before the game's scheduled start, Syracuse TV stations were running the list of students believed to be on the plane.

21 Some reporters who were posted at Hill's office might challenge this statement. They told another of the authors that Hill had a security officer or officers stationed there. See Chapter 3 section on Syracuse media: Television: out in the night.

22 With information provided late in the afternoon by the Chaplain's Office, local news media carried an announcement of the 9 p.m. prayer service on its early news, about 6 p.m.

23 Printed with the permission of the letter's author, Peter Moller, a professor in the University's S.I. Newhouse School of Public Communications.

24 See chapter 3 section A Tale by Two Newspapers, for a New York reporter's view of this strategy.

25 In 1982, Pan Am had two experiences that gave them a preview of what was to come at Lockerbie: a Boeing 727 was caught in a wind shear upon takeoff from the New Orleans airport, crashing to the suburban Kenner neighborhood below, killing all 145 aboard and eight on the ground. A few weeks later, another Pan Am flight from Tokyo was crippled when a bomb went off under a passenger seat, killing a 16-year-old Japanese passenger and injuring 16 others. The Heathrow exercise, which also involved two American consular officers from the London embassy, was reported by the Presidential Commission on Aviation Security and Terrorism.

26 Reinhardt's third classification is the "sustained crisis," which takes a long time to build and can last for years, fueled by the rumor mill and media speculation, e.g., periodic reports of a corporate takeover.

27 In fairness to Pan Am, it should be noted that the SIO probably stood little chance of being sued as an outcome of the disaster, although its public information officers did operate in a legal climate designed to protect the rights of anyone who might be accused in the bombing and they also were working with a potentially difficult political situation.

28 Doughty is referring to a *New York Times* article, "Query Trails Flight 232: Just How Many Took It?" July 23, 1989, p. 20.

29 Testimony before the President's Commission on Aviation Security and Terrorism recounted on pp.98–99 of its report.

30 Berry took part in a panel discussion on disaster coverage at Louisville in 1990.

31 The plane crash on August 31, 1988, claimed 13 lives and injured more than 30, although many accounts referred to it as a "miracle" because 98 persons escaped the burning plane unhurt.

32 Mrs Georgia Nucci, whose son Christopher Jones was killed in the bombing, had suggested to the Presidential Commission that this information could easily be collected on a portion of the boarding pass that is collected by the airline. The congressional action voiding the requirement for the manifest, which should have been of interest to journalists in light of the problems created by Pan Am's slowness in providing a verified list of passengers, was virtually ignored by the mass media. The only reports of this action found on Nexis, a data base covering many large American newspapers and wire services and several in Britain, were by trade publications of the aviation industry.

33 In the hometowns of some victims, municipal police offered families the protection of a patrol car.

34 Indeed, their experiences at Lockerbie led both British Telecommunications and the Scottish Office Information Directorate (formerly known as the Scottish Information Office) to make changes: British Telecom has improved its system to avoid repeating the cellnet overloads at Lockerbie; they now have the capability to add extra emergency telephone lines in an area affected by a disaster. The Scottish Office has acquired a large supply of portable phones and these were invaluable in the 1993 Shetland Islands oil spill.

Chapter 5

1 The National Victims Center was founded in 1985 by the children of Sunny von Bulow, the American heiress who has been in an insulin-induced coma since December 21, 1980. Her husband, Claus, acquitted of attempted murder charges following two sensational trials, now lives in London.

2 Cox and Foster (1992) said only 372 flights by American airlines in 1988 had been targeted for bomb threats and fewer than 35, including the December 5 warning at Helsinki, had been treated as serious. Duggan (1988) quoted Hudson as telling the news conference that the FAA reports showed 400 to 500 threats per year were made and that in 1988 the number of high level reports had been variously reported as 22 and 24, including the Helsinki warning.

3 Cox and Foster (1992) report that this meeting was arranged through the efforts of Victoria Cummock of Coral Gables, Florida, who lost her husband John in the bombing. They say she was friends with a member of the Bush family.

4 Although Channon's handling of the issues connected to the disaster led to repeated calls for his resignation, he remained in the post until July 24 when he left the Thatcher government as part of the shake-up that brought John Major into the upper ranks of government as Foreign Secretary.

5 The settlement package Pan Am was offering next of kin was the $75,000 to which they were automatically entitled under the Warsaw Convention plus $25,000 for personal belongings.

6 The delay was partly out of respect for the feelings of people in Lockerbie. As will be discussed in the next chapter, some consideration had been given to announcing the exploit at a news conference following the dedication of a memorial room at Tundergarth, but Swire delayed it and held a news conference at his home the next day out of respect for the occasion.

7 The U.S. Supreme Court declined to hear the relatives' appeal of this ruling in October 1991. It was already considering an appeal by families of 137 passengers killed when Korean Airlines flight 007 was shot down by the Soviet Union in 1983. A trial jury in that case had awarded $50 million or $362,000 per family after determining that the airline had engaged in willful misconduct in straying into Soviet airspace. The U.S. Circuit Court of Appeals in Washington upheld the willful misconduct verdict, but ruled that punitive damages are not available under the Warsaw Convention (CA DC. Mp/ 89-5415, 5/15/91). The Supreme Court upheld that decision without comment.

8 A report by Reuters in 1992 said the picture of Flora is now in the museum, along with that of Hanah (Barrouhi, 1992).

9 The UN resolution had been adopted by a 10-0 vote of the Security Council on March 31. China, which had veto power over the resolution, abstained, as did Morocco, India, Cape Verde and Zimbabwe.

Chapter 7

1 Several reporters at the Syracuse Newspapers were also convinced that Emerson and Duffy had read their work, but they were not pleased about it. *Columbia Journalism Review* gave the two authors a "dart" in its "Darts and Laurels" column, commenting on "their want of professional manners" because it said the book "bears a striking resemblance, in both substance and style" to passages in "The Darkest Day," a special edition of the *Syracuse Post-Standard*, although the authors never acknowledged it as a source (July/August 1990, p. 14).

2 Mitchell's surprise at the officers' reaction was understandable. Most observers of the disaster, including journalists who had covered a number of tragedies, described the recovery as quite orderly, given the number of deaths, the extent of the damage and the range over which debris was scattered.

3 See Chapter 2, section Lockerbie Shattered for more on the Christmas Eve coverage. None of the interview subjects mentioned newspeople shoving at the service, but the coverage in the *Sun* did cause distress in the community.

4 Aphrodite Tsairis, a leader in Victims of Pan Am 103, reports a similar experience. She agreed to be interviewed by a CBS reporter on Thanksgiving 1991, only after he agreed to focus on her work as an advocate for airline security. Once he arrived at her house and did that portion of the interview, he insisted that his producer needed something of her talking about the loss of her daughter. Only that portion portraying her as a grieving mother was used.

5 Faculty for the workshop included Blumenfield, Joan Deppa and Lawrence Beaupre, vice president and executive editor of the newspapers.

6 Others, especially those operating from a psychoanalytic framework, have labeled the phenomenon "counter-transference," which Lindy says is broadly used "to describe any reaction that a therapist might have to a patient" (1988, p. 244). Some therapists, for example, have found themselves unable to listen to the painful stories of patients who survived the Holocaust.

Reflections

1 The S.I. Newhouse School at Syracuse University is home to one such program, TRAC (Transactional Records Access Clearinghouse), which contracts with news organizations to analyze data sets, such as computer tapes obtained through the Freedom of Information Act.

2 In October 1989, a French jetliner disappeared without warning after a stopover in Chad. It was a Lockerbie-style bombing and eventually French investigators would focus on Libyan suspects because of forensic evidence, especially the timing device. The 170 passengers and crew on board had included some 100 Africans, 50 French nationals, a Canadian and seven Americans, including Bonnie Pugh, the wife of the U.S. ambassador to Chad (*Facts on File*, 1989).

3 Some criticism related to the notification of next-of-kin also was laid at the doorstep of the U.S. State Department, which the Presidential Commission on Aviation Security and Terrorism found was "simply unprepared" for the Lockerbie disaster. "It did not recognize, much less have in place, the level of services expected in the case of the mass murder of Americans at the hands of terrorists." (Report, 1990, p. 98)

4 Tuchman christened these as "what-a-story" events in her typology of anticipated and unanticipated news events.

5 Congress had enacted the requirement two years earlier as part of the Aviation Security Improvement Act in response to the Presidential Commission that investigated Pan Am 103. The Senate later restored funding so that the FAA could implement regulations requiring background checks, but only after the agency announced much less stringent regulations. An extensive search of on-line data bases showed that only aviation industry publications covered this congressional action and the lobbying campaign that precipitated it.

6 Will apparently made this reference for the first time on "This Week with David Brinkley" on ABC in 1985.

References

Abrams, A. and Collins, T.J. (Feb. 7, 1989) Anger and tears; Plane-bomb victims protest indifference. *Newsday*, p. 2.

Air Accidents and the News Media Columbus, Ohio:Aviation/Space Writers Association.

American Psychiatric Association (1989) *Diagnostic and statistical manual of mental disorders.* (3rd ed.)Washington, D.C.: American Psychiatric Association.

Associated Press (June 4, 1989) Town hit by jet crash finally has Christmas. *Chicago Tribune*, p. 30.

Atlanta Constitution (May 19, 1992) Time magazine admits error in identifying photo. Section D, p. 2.

Baig (Jan. 19, 1987) America's Most Admired Corporations. *Fortune*, p. 18.

Baker, R.W. (Sept. 27, 1989) Bomb detection devices debated. *Christian Science Monitor*, p. 7.

Ball, J.F. (1977) Widow's grief: The impact of age and mode of death. *Omega*, 9 (4), 307-333.

Barrett, F. (Nov. 7, 1992) It is better to travel and arrive. *The Independent*, p. 45.

Barrouhi, A. (April 15, 1992) Libya Displays Photo of Lockerbie Victim. Reuters.

Bass, J. (March 17, 1989) Senators call for independent commission on Pan Am disaster. United Press International.

Berg, E.N. (July 23, 1989) Query Trails Flight 232: Just How Many Took It? *New York Times*, p. 20.

Blum, A. (Oct. 19, 1992) Sanctions Asked in Pan Am Suits. *The National Law Journal*, p. 3.

Bowlby, J. (1979) *The Making and Breaking of Affectional Bonds.* London: Tavistock Publications.

Briggs, W. (Feb.1990) Intercepting Interlopers *Public Relations Journal*, p. 40, 39.

Broadcasting (Nov. 28, 1988) Local TV journalism; special section. p. 63.

Broadcasting (Oct. 23, 1989) Broadcasting's rush to the west: the San Francisco quake, 1989 version, p. 36.

Bumiller, E. (Oct. 20, 1989) Tokyo's top story: Empathy in quake-prone Japan. *Washington Post*, p. B1.

Business Insurance (Nov. 23, 1993) 10 airlines drop Warsaw limits. p. 2.

Butler, E. (Sept. 27, 1992) Ex-Hartford reporter embroiled in another major controversy. *Waterbury Republican American*, p. D1.

Butler, E. and Adams, J.R. (Sept. 27, 1992) Flight 103's insurers humiliated by shoddy defense. *Waterbury Republican American*, p. D1.

Byron, C. (Aug. 31, 1992) Conning the media: How a journalistic rogue duped *Time*, ABC, and NBC on the story of the Pan Am bombing. *New York*, pp. 28-37.

Byron, C. (Dec. 16, 1991) Arms and the Man: Did convict Arif Durrani help set the stage for Iran/contra. *New York*, pp. 38-40, 42-49.

Carman, J. (Oct. 20, 1989) NBC flap over local blackout. *San Francisco Chronicle*. D1.

Carman, J. and Ross, C. (Oct. 18, 1989) How the media dealt with the quake. *San Francisco Chronicle*, p. A8.

Carter, B. (1989) Crisis — Dealing with the Unexpected, in Burger, C., ed. *Experts in Action: Insider P.R* (2nd ed). New York: Longman.
Chicago Tribune (Dec. 31, 1988) Will Pan Am 103 change anything? Perspective, p. 13.
Chiles, N. (Jan. 30, 1989) Cardinal and kin mourn Lockerbie crash victims. *Newsday*, p. 6.
Clark, J. (Dec. 10, 1989) Now leave us to rebuild our lives. Press Association.
Clark, R.P. (Nov. 22, 1987) The underside of journalism: Some news photos merely pander to a leering public. *St Petersburg Times*, p. 1D.
Coates, J. (Nov. 10, 1991) Airlines still failing on baggage security. *Sunday Telegraph*, p. 6.
Columbia Journalism Review (July/Aug. 1990) Darts and Laurels, p. 14.
Communications Daily (July 20, 1988) News roundup, p. 4.
Communications Daily (Oct. 20, 1989) Coping with scant information; broadcasting performance in quake aftermath, p. 4.
Cox, M. and Foster, T. (May 7, 1992) Time's Flight 103 story is old news. *Syracuse Post-Standard*.
Cox, M. and Foster, T. (1992) *Their Darkest Day: The Tragedy of Pan Am 103 and its Legacy of Hope*. New York: Grove Weidenfeld.
Crelinsten, R. (1992) Victims' Perspectives, in Paletz, D.L., and Schmid, A.P. (ed.) *Terrorism and the Media*. Newbury Park: Sage Publications.
Crouse, T. (1972) *Boys on the Bus*. New York: Ballantine Books.

Daily Telegraph (Dec. 23, 1989) Schoolboys find $547,000 in plane debris, p. 3.
David, Keren (Dec. 17, 1989) The legacy of Flight 103. *Scotland on Sunday*, pp. 32-44.
Doughty, R. A. (1992-93) Prepare for the Worst: A Case in Crisis Communications. *Journal of Corporate Public Relations*, p. 41.
Dudman, G. (Jan. 13, 1989) Exposed: Heathrow Security Shambles. *Daily Express*, p. 1.
Duffy, B. (March 9, 1992) The mystery man in the Lockerbie case. *U.S. News and World Report*, p. 44.
Duggan, Dennis (Feb. 7, 1989) 'Wall of silence' angers kin. *Newsday*, p. 8.

Eldridge, E. (Oct. 22, 1989) Is media's coverage of the quake fair? Gannett News Service.
Elgood, G. (Dec. 21, 1989). Families mark Pan Am crash anniversary with candles, prayer. Reuters.
Elgood, G. (Dec. 21, 1989) One year on, families remember Pan Am disaster victims. Reuters.
Elliott, D. (1988) Family ties: A case study of coverage of families and friends during the hijacking of TWA Flight 847. *Political Communication and Persuasion*, 5, 67-75.
Emerson, S. (Sept. 1992) Pan Am Scam: How two self-styled intelligence agents took the media for a ride. *Washington Journalism Review*, pp. 14-20.
Emerson, S. and Duffy, B. (1990) *The Fall of Pan Am 103: Inside the Lockerbie Investigation*. New York: G.P. Putnam's Sons.

Facts on File (Sept. 22, 1989) French DC-10 crashes in Africa, p. 688, C3.
Fatah, E. A. (1979) Some reflections of the victimology of terrorism. *Terrorism: An International Journal*, 3 (1-2), 81-108.
Federal News Service (Oct. 7, 1992) Special state department briefing: Consular information sheets.
Fink, C.C. (1988) *Media Ethics: In the Newsroom and Beyond*. New York: McGraw-Hill.
Fisher, D. (April 16,1989) 93 killed in soccer game crush; victims trampled at English stadium; 200 reported hurt. *Los Angeles Times*, p.1.
Fisher, D. (Jan. 14, 1989) Airport security lapses exposed by British reporters. *Los Angeles Times*, p. 3.

Fletcher, M. (May 16, 1990) Bush urged to strike at the bombers first. *Times*, Overseas news.
Forbes, G. (Jan. 28, 1990) Thatcher and Bush accused of a cover-up in Lockerbie. *Sunday Times*, Features section.
Foster, T. and Cox, M. (July 11, 1992) Jury blames Pan Am for bombing. *Syracuse Post-Standard*, p. 1, A-7.
Frankel, G. (Dec. 22, 1989) Families drawn to Lockerbie to mourn bombing victims; Scottish town hosts memorial 1 year after crash. *Washington Post*, p. A21.
Fricker, M. and Pizzo, S. (June 14, 1992) Outlaws at Justice. *San Francisco Chronicle*, p. 7/Z1.
Frost, B. (Dec. 19, 1990). Firemen awarded £34,000 for trauma after King's Cross. *The Times*.

Gerard, J. (Oct. 24, 1989) The California quake: NBC News tells of errors and obstacles to early coverage of the quake. *New York Times*. Section B, p. 13.
Gerrits, R. (1992) Terrorists' Perspectives: Memoirs, in Paletz, D.L. and Schmid, A.P.(eds.) *Terrorism and the Media*. Newbury Park: Sage Publications.
Gill, K. (Oct. 1, 1990) Tight guard as Lockerbie enquiry opens today. *The Times*, Home news.
Gitlin, T. (Nov. 12, 1989) TV View: gauging the aftershocks of disaster coverage. *New York Times* Section 2, p. 33.
Godson, D. (Sept. 1, 1992) Terror talk in the cloisters; the battle against terrorism is being fought on many fronts by an army of unknown warriors. *Daily Telegraph*, p. 13.
Goldstein, T. (1985) *The News at Any Cost: How Journalists Compromise their Ethics to Shape the News*. New York: Simon & Schuster.
Grotta, G. (1986) Pilot study probes attitudes in media coverage, in *Crime victims and the news media: Proceedings of national symposium* pp. 26-30. Fort Worth: Texas Christian University, Department of Journalism.
Grove, V. (May 20, 1990) Doctor driven to find the truth about Lockerbie. *Sunday Times*, Features section.
Guttenplan, D.D. (Nov. 3, 1988) Polls, Spins & Sound Bites; The campaign has changed and so has the press corps: The Boys on the Bus have become the People on the Plane. *Newsday* Part II, p. 4.

Harlow, J. (April 3, 1989) Lockerbie group calls for inquiry. *Daily Telegraph*, p. 2.
Harlow, J. (March 27, 1989) Americans turn to BA flights after IBM advice. *Daily Telegraph*, p. 2.
Harrie, D. (Aug. 31, 1988) Planecrash-Family, Salt Lake City. *United Press International*, Domestic News.
Hauser, S. (Aug. 6, 1991) The doctor's doctor: A physician's real-life battle with cancer is at the heart of William Hurt's new movie. *People*, p. 71.
Hedges, Chris (June 28, 1992) Libyan doubts about Qaddafi are growing. *New York Times*, p. 3, Section 4).
Holonen, D. (Oct. 23, 1989) After the quake; disaster tests news operation. *Electronic Media*, p. 1.

Insight (Sept. 30, 1990) Lockerbie bombers likely to escape justice. *The Independent* ,Home news.

Jehl, D. (April 4, 1989) Pressured by families, U.S. acts to tighten air security. *Los Angeles Times*, p. 1.
Johnston, D. (1989) *Lockerbie: The real story*. London: Bloomsbury.
Jones, G. (Aug. 20, 1989) Airline inspectors may ground flights. *Sunday Telegraph*, p. 2.

Kane, D. and Garew, G. (Dec. 22,1988) SU's Eggers: Best and brightest lost on the saddest day of my life. *Herald Journal*, p. 12.

Katz, S. and Florian, V. (1987) A comprehensive theoretical model of psychological reaction to loss. *International Psychiatry in Medicine*, 16 (4), 325-345).

Kaufman, J. (Oct. 22, 1989) 1989; blinded by the television lights. *Boston Globe*, p. A21.

Kelly, D. (Nov. 29, 1989) Traficant. States News Services.

Kelly, W.E. , ed. (1985) *Post-Traumatic Stress Disorder and the War Veteran Patient.* New York: Bruner/Mazel.

Kessler, G. (April 6, 1989). Using Radiation to Screen Bags; NRC report raises concerns on use of machine to detect bombs. *Newsday.*

Kessler, G. and Fessenden, F. (Dec. 16, 1990) Flying at Risk. *Newsday*, pp. 4-5.

Kocieniewski, D. (May 25, 1989) Barbecue. Gannett News Service.

Kraul, C. (Nov. 19, 1991) Science Corp.'s 'Magic Bullet' for bomb detection misfires with FAA. *Los Angeles Times*, Part D, p. 2A.

Lacayo, R. (May 4, 1992) No matter what happens to Roe *v*. Wade, the doctors who perform abortions and their patients face formidable obstacles. *Time*, pp. 27-32.

Langton, J. (April 2, 1989) Lockerbie: $2.5 million offer for killers. *Sunday Telegraph*, p. 1.

Laufer, P. (Oct. 29, 1989) The great quake hype: Why we Californians resented the network circus. *Washington Post*, p. B1.

Lavin, C. (Sept. 12, 1989) New machines can detect terrorists bombs, usually. *New York Times*, Section C, p. 1.

Leahy, A.(Feb. 15-22, 1989) The Fallout from Flight 103: Coverage of SU Memorial Service Makes Media and Newsmakers Assess their Ground Rules. *Syracuse New Times*, p. 1.

Leapman, M. (June 10, 1992) Media: Decency and the Cuckfield Syndrome. *The Independent*, p. 17.

Leppard, D. (1991) *On the Trail of Terror: The inside story of the Lockerbie investigation.* London: Jonathan Cape.

Levine, J.B. (Dec. 5, 1988) Craig McCaw's high-risk empire: He's No. 1 in cellular phones, a business that's starting to sizzle. *Business Week*, p. 140.

Lifton, R.J. (Aug. 23, 1992) Television view: Can images of Bosnia change the world? *New York Times*, Section 2, p. 26.

Lindemann, E. (1944-45) Symptomology and management of acute grief. *American Journal of Psychiatry*, 101, 141-148.

Lindy, J. D. (1988) *Vietnam: A Casebook.* New York: Brunner/Mazel.

Linhorst, S. (Jan. 29, 1989) Why Does SU Seem to Hold the Community in Such Low Regard? *Syracuse Herald-American*, p. F3.

Los Angeles Times (Jan. 28, 1986) 'It's too awful'; McAuliffe's School in Stunned Disbelief, p. 2.

Maneholt, C.S. (June 14, 1992) A grim wasteland; New York by TV: Crime and more crime. *New York Times*, p. 41-42.

Margueles, L. and Goldman, J. (Oct. 18, 1989) Networks scrambled to report disaster. *Los Angeles Times*, Part A, p. 7.

Marks, P. , Harper, T., Shaw, G., Foran, K, Drury, B., and Kessler, G. (March 17, 1989) 3 alerts, with details; warnings were sent before crash in Scotland. *Newsday*, p. 5.

Martin, D.C. and Walcott, J. (1988) *Best Laid Plans: The inside story of America's war against terrorism.* New York: Harper & Row.

Martzke, R. (Oct. 20, 1989) Michaels exits 80s as voice of the quake. *USA Today*, p. 3C.

Matthews, M. (April 4, 1990) Inspector found Pan Am passengers flying 'at great risk.' *Baltimore Sun.*

McCann, I. L., and Pearlman, L.A. (1990) *Psychological Trauma and the Adult Survivor: Theory, Therapy and Transformation.* New York: Brunner/Mazel.

McCann, I.L., and Pearlman, L.A. (Jan. 1990) Vicarious traumatization: A framework for understanding the psychological effects of working with victims. *Journal of Traumatic Stress*, Vol.3, 131-149.

McCauley, K. (July 1990) 71 of "Fortune 500" have no PR departments. *O'Dwyer's Directory of Corporate Communications.*

McConagha, A. (Oct. 20, 1989) For Series reporters, sports ended and news began. *Washington Times*, p. B4.

McKeever, J. (Dec. 23, 1988) A loss shared; counselors help students cope with tragedy. *Syracuse Post-Standard*, p. A-10.

McKenna, K. (Aug. 30, 1990) The two tragedies of Pan Am 103; for the victims' families, a coming together, and a falling apart. *Washington Post*, p. D1.

McKenna, K. (July 24, 1991) FAA must move to prevent future bombings, House panel told. States News Service.

McKibben, G. (April 16, 1989) 93 crushed to death in stadium; soccer fans rush gate in Sheffield, England; more than 200 injured. *Boston Globe*, p. 1.

McLain, L. (March 23, 1990) Extinguish the dangerous risk. *Financial Times*, p. 10.

McLaughlin, A., D'Amato, A., Hammerschmidt, J.P., Hidalgo, E., Lautenberg, F.R., Obserstar, J.L., and Richards, T.C. *Report of the President's Commission on Aviation Security and Terrorism*, May 15, 1990.

Mermigas, D. (Oct. 23, 1989) Quake uncovers sticky affiliate, cable relationship. *Electronic Media*, p. 3.

Meyers, G.C. (1986) *When it hits the fan: managing the nine crises of business.* Boston: Houghton Mifflin Co.

Mild, R. (Sept. 15, 1990) Don't gossip — investigate. *Washington Post*, p. A21.

Miller, W.G. (Dec. 21, 1989) Lockerbie's lot: visions of a disaster that won't go away. *Boston Globe*, p. 26.

Mirabella, A. (Dec. 23, 1988) Airport scene rough for reporters. *Daily News*, New York, p.80.

Mitchell, M. (Dec. 14, 1991) Learning psychology on the job. *New Scientist*, pp. 51-52.

Mitchell, M., McLay, D., Boddy, J., and Cecchi, L. (1991) The police response to the Lockerbie Disaster. *Disaster Management*, Vol. 3, No. 4, pp. 198-205.

Mooar, B. (June 25, 1989) Families of Pan Am bombing meet with Scottish officials. United Press International.

Morgan, T.B. (July 1984) Reporters of the Lost War. *Esquire*, pp. 49-60.

Morrison, J. (Oct. 4, 1982) Twice a night, five nights a week, millions of Soviet television viewers tune in to brief glimpse of the world. Reuters.

Mowat, J. (March 1991) *Determination by Sheriff Principal John Mowat in the Fatal Accident Inquiry relating to the Lockerbie Air Disaster.*

Moyers, C. (Sept. 4, 1988) Delta's Reputation Holds Steady: Moved to safeguard image after crash. *Newsday*, p. 6.

Murphy, S. (1984) After Mount St Helen's Disaster stress research. *Journal of Psychological Nursing and Mental Health Services*, 22 (7), 9-19.

Murray, E. and Shohen, S. (1992) Lessons from the Tylenol tragedy on surviving a corporate crisis. *Medical Marketing & Media.*

Murray, I. (Dec. 23, 1988) Blood on the fairway: Scores of mangled bodies rain down on golf course. *The Sun*, London, pp. 3-4.

Mushnick, P. (Dec. 27, 1988) Equal Time. *New York Post*, Sports section.

Nimmo, Dan, and Combs, James E. (1985) *Nightly Horrors: Crisis Coverage by Television Network News*. Knoxville, Tenn.: University of Tennessee Press.

Palacios, A., Cuell, J., Camacho, J., Cleriga, R, Cueva, P., Ayala, J., and Cossof, L. (1988) The traumatic effect of mass communications in the Mexico City earthquake: Crisis intervention and preventive measures. *International Review of Psychoanalysis*, 13(3), 279-293.

Pascoe-Watson, George (April 10, 1989) I could bomb Pan Am. *The Sun*, p. 1.

Paz, U., Raviv, T, Cheffer, C., Brog, A., and Witztum, E. (May 23, 1992) Israelis in sealed rooms: mental health and the mass media. Panel, International Communications Association Convention, Miami.

Pierce, F. (June 8, 1992) We're not so typical anymore. *Syracuse Post-Standard*, p. 1.

Plude, F. (Aug.1990) *Coping with disaster: How media audiences process grief.* Paper presented at the annual meeting of the American Psychological Association, Boston.

Porterfield, B. (July 11, 1992) Pan Am guilty; Jury cites misconduct by airline in Flight 103. *Newsday*, p. 7.

pr reporter (Nov. 20, 1989) Survey of CEOs' crisis-time behaviour finds some basic PR principles have finally sunk in but PR ranks low in list of "who to call first," p. 4.

Puga, A. (Nov. 21, 1991) Electric moments; Kin of Pan Am victims told of probe, but many remain doubtful and angry. *Houston Chronicle*, p. 1.

Quarantelli, E.L. (1989) The social science study of disasters and mass communications, in Walters, L.M., Wilkins, L., and Walters, T. (eds.) *Bad Tidings: Communication and Catastrophe.* Hillsdale, N.J.: Lawrence Erlbaum.

Queen, J.W. (June 4, 1989) Party in Lockerbie, outrage in New York. *Newsday*, p. 2.

Quinn, J. (Dec. 22, 1989) Lockerbie lives on. Press Association.

Randolph, E. (Oct. 26, 1989) Amid the hunger for numbers, inflated estimates made news. *Washington Post*, p. A26.

Raphael, B. (1983) *The Anatomy of Bereavement.* New York: Basic Books, Inc.

Raphael, B. (1986) *When Disaster Strikes: How Individuals and Communities Cope with Disaster.* New York: Basic Books, Inc.

Raver, Anne (May 15, 1990) Sculpting grief, posing questions. *Newsday*, p. 3.

Reid, R. (Feb. 4, 1989) Lockerbie 'stories' criticized. *Daily Telegraph*, p. 2.

Reinhardt, C.(Nov. 1987) How to handle a crisis. *Public Relations Journal*, pp. 43-44.

Reuters (April 19, 1992) Victims' group makes offer to Lockerbie suspects.

Reuters (June 3, 1989) U.S. teenager gives Lockerbie the Christmas it never had.

Reuters (June 4, 1989) Families of plane crash victims protest against Lockerbie party.

Reuters (Nov. 14, 1991) Lockerbie charges raise doubts that real perpetrators named.

Rhule, P. (Oct. 18, 1989) Covering the quake. Gannett News Service.

Rice, R. (Nov. 19, 1992). An airline decision born of embarrassment. *Financial Times*, p. 5.

Rice, R. (Nov. 19, 1992) Japanese airlines to scrap limit on liability for victims. *Financial Times*, p. 1.

Rosenthal, D.N. (Oct. 22, 1989) Media aftershocks; locals think quake coverage rings too loud on the Richter scale. *Chicago Tribune*, p. 6.

Rowan, R. (April 27, 1992) Pan Am 103: Why did they die? *Time*, p. 24.

Ryan, F. (Feb. 13, 1991) Pan Am inquiry ends in a moment of silence. United Press International.

Ryan, F.(Dec. 16, 1990) Lockerbie families look back in sorrow. *Sunday Times*, Features.

Ryan, M. (Oct. 17,1989) TV sports. Gannett News Service.

Senior, A. (Oct. 1, 1990) Pan Am relatives pin hopes on Scottish Lockerbie inquiry. Reuters.

Shackleton, C.H. (1984) The psychology of grief: A review. *Advances in Behavior Research and Therapy*, 6, 153-205.

Shales, T. (Oct. 18, 1989) Live from San Francisco, a gripping drama; TV scrambles to cover the earthquake. *Washington Post*, p. B1.

Shapiro, S. (Jan. 16, 1989) Pan Am liability insurer sets $ 60 million reserve. *Business Insurance*, p. 2.

Shapiro, S. (July 20, 1992) Families win jury verdict but Pan Am fight not over. *Business Insurance*, p.3.

Sharn, L. (Nov. 15, 1991) Families aren't satisfied. *USA Today*, p. 3A.

Shearer, A. (1991) *Survivors and the Media*. London: John Libbey & Co. Ltd.

Snoddy, R. (1992) *The good, the bad and the unacceptable. The hard news about the British press.* London: Faber & Faber.

Stewart, L. (Oct. 20, 1989) Michaels does it all, including news. *Los Angeles Times*, Part C., p. 3.

Syracuse Herald-American (Jan. 1, 1989) Eggers: Scope of His Humanity is Revealed by Tragedy, p. F2.

Tan, Y.H. (Dec. 7, 1990) Law report: Hillsborough disaster claims lead to wider nervous shock categories. *The Independent*, p. 18.

Tan, Y.H. (Nov. 29, 1991) Law report: Hillsborough claims fail. *The Independent*, p. 15.

Teague, Bob (1982) *Live and Off-Color: News Biz*. New York: A&W Publishers.

Thompson, T. (Nov. 2, 1990) Pan Am suggests U.S. had warnings of bombings. *Washington Post*, p. A50.

Towhidi, J. (Sept. 20, 1989) Airline suspects bomb attack on DC-10, says no survivors. Reuters.

Travel Weekly (Oct. 19, 1992) Bush signs bill freeing frequent flyers of airport facility charges.

Tuchman, G. (1978) *Making News: A Study in the Construction of Reality*. New York: The Free Press.

Tully, S. (Aug. 1989) Europe goes on a telephone binge. *Fortune*, p. 107.

United Press International (Aug. 20, 1989) Group calls for increased vigilance against terrorism.

United Press International (June 21, 1989) Probe reportedly blames Pan Am bombing on Palestinian group.

Wilcox, D.L., Ault, P.H. and Agee, W.K. (1992) *Public Relations Strategies and Tactics*. New York: Harper Collins.

Wilkinson, P. (July, 1991) Pan Am: The fall of a legend. *Conde Nast Traveler*, p. 21-25; 106-110.

Wilson, K. (May 21, 1989) Kin of jet crash victims assail plans for party in Lockerbie. *Newsday*, p. 38

Winship, F.M. (Feb. 7, 1989) Pan Am crash victim families protest. United Press International.

Woodward, Bob (1987) *Veil: The secret wars of the CIA*, 1981-87. New York: Simon & Schuster.

Yin, R.K. (1984) *Case Study Research: Design and Methods*. Beverly Hills, Calif: Sage Publications.

Yoakman, R.D. and Cremer, C.F. (1989) *ENG: Television news and the new technology*. Carbondale: Southern Illinois University Press.

Name Index

Subject Index